UNDERSTANDING THE PENTATEUCH AS A SCRIPTURE

UNDERSTANDING THE PENTATEUCH AS A SCRIPTURE

James W. Watts

WILEY Blackwell

This edition first published 2017

Registered Office(s)
John Wiley & Sons, Inc., 111 River Street, Hoboken, NJ 07030, USA
John Wiley & Sons Ltd, The Atrium, Southern Gate, Chichester, West Sussex, PO19 8SQ, UK

Editorial Office
9600 Garsington Road, Oxford, OX4 2DQ, UK

For details of our global editorial offices, customer services, and more information about Wiley products visit us at www.wiley.com.

Wiley also publishes its books in a variety of electronic formats and by print-on-demand. Some content that appears in standard print versions of this book may not be available in other formats.

Library of Congress Cataloging-in-Publication Data

Name: Watts, James W. (James Washington), 1960– author.
Title: Understanding the Pentateuch as a scripture / James W. Watts, Syracuse University, NY, US.
Description: Hoboken : Wiley, 2017. | Includes index. |
Identifiers: LCCN 2017012536 (print) | LCCN 2017024992 (ebook) | ISBN 9781118786390 (pdf) | ISBN 9781118786383 (epub) | ISBN 9781405196390 (cloth) | ISBN 9781405196383 (pbk.)
Subjects: LCSH: Bible. Pentateuch–Hermeneutics. | Bible. Pentateuch–Criticism, interpretation, etc. | Sacred books–Comparative studies.
Classification: LCC BS1227 (ebook) | LCC BS1227 .W38 2017 (print) | DDC 222/.1066–dc23
LC record available at https://lccn.loc.gov/2017012536

Cover Design: Wiley
Cover Image: Samaritan Torah scroll held high during Passover on Mount Gerizim'; photo Zeev Elitzur 2007; used by permission

Set in 10/12.5pt Meridien by SPi Global, Pondicherry, India
Printed and bound in Malaysia by Vivar Printing Sdn Bhd

10 9 8 7 6 5 4 3 2 1

CONTENTS

LIST OF BOXES

LIST OF TABLES

LIST OF FIGURES

ABBREVIATIONS

Abbreviations of Biblical and Apocryphal Literature

1–2 Chr.	1–2 Chronicles
1–2 Cor.	1–2 Corinthians
1–2 Kgs.	1–2 Kings
1–2–3–4 Macc.	1–2–3–4 Maccabees
1–2 Pet.	1–2 Peter
1–2 Sam.	1–2 Samuel
1–2 Thess.	1–2 Thessalonians
1–2 Tim.	1–2 Timothy
Bar.	Baruch
Col.	Colossians
Dan.	Daniel
Deut.	Deuteronomy
Eccl.	Ecclesiastes
Eph.	Ephesians
Esth.	Esther
Exod.	Exodus
Ezek.	Ezekiel
Gal.	Galatians
Gen.	Genesis
Hab.	Habakkuk
Hag.	Haggai

Heb.	Hebrews
Hos.	Hosea
Isa.	Isaiah
Jas.	James
Jdt.	Judith
Jer.	Jeremiah
Josh.	Joshua
Judg.	Judges
Lam.	Lamentations
Lev.	Leviticus
Mal.	Malachi
Matt.	Matthew
Mic.	Micah
Nah.	Nahum
Neh.	Nehemiah
Num.	Numbers
Obad.	Obadiah
Phil.	Philippians
Phlm.	Philemon
Prov.	Proverbs
Ps./Pss.	Psalm/Psalms
Rev.	Revelation
Rom.	Romans
Sir.	Sirach/Ecclesiasticus
Song	Song of Songs (Song of Solomon)
Sus.	Susanna
Tob.	Tobit
Wis.	Wisdom of Solomon
Zech.	Zechariah
Zeph.	Zephaniah

Abbreviations of Bible Translations

CEB	Common English Bible
NRSV	New Revised Standard Version

Abbreviations in Citations of Rabbinic Literature

b.	Babylonian Talmud
m.	Mishnah
y.	Jerusalem Talmud

PREFACE

The title of this book, *Understanding the Pentateuch as a Scripture*, requires some explanation. Chapter 1 will give attention to defining the nouns, "Pentateuch" and "scripture," and their relationship to another name for this literature, "the Torah." Here I need to explain why I chose this phrase for the title of this book, and particularly why "scripture" is preceded by the indefinite article, "a."

Biblical studies is an ancient and flourishing field. Scholars put great effort into explaining the language, meaning, and history of biblical books down to their tiniest detail. They have done so for more than 2,000 years and continue to do so today. The published literature on the Pentateuch is vast, and keeps growing.

Yet little of this research focuses on how the Bible, much less the Pentateuch, functions as a scripture. Biblical scholars tend to concentrate on the meaning of biblical texts within the literary contexts of individual books and within their original historical settings in ancient Israel, Second Temple Judaism, and early Christianity.

Forty years ago, the historian of religions Wilfred Cantwell Smith criticized biblical scholars for focusing only "on the Bible in its pre-scriptural phase." He wanted to position biblical studies within research on religions generally, rather than just within the study of Judaism and Christianity. Smith called for studying "the Bible as scripture" in comparison with other religious scriptures, such as the Qur'an, the Vedas, the Bhagavad Gita, the Buddhist sutras, and the Sikh's Guru Granth Sahib. He understood that a religious studies context would draw more attention to how people in various times and places have interpreted the Bible. It would also highlight how they have used it in their personal and communal rituals, in their art and theater, in their economic activities, and in their politics.

One of Smith's students, William Graham, took such a religious studies approach to scriptures by comparing their oral performances in various traditions. Noting the importance of oral recitation to Muslims' veneration of the Qur'an and to Hindu Brahmins' use of the Vedas, Graham also observed the prominent role that reading scripture aloud plays in Jewish and Christian worship. He thought that modern publishing had obscured the importance of oral performance of scriptures. He argued that oral performance, more than interpretation, established and maintained a text's status as scripture within a religious community.[1]

Another academic movement that takes seriously the Bible's function as scripture is canonical criticism, which is oriented towards theology rather than religious studies. Brevard Childs wrote a book with a title similar to this one, *Introduction to the Old Testament as Scripture* (1979), in which he advocated a canonical approach to biblical interpretation. Childs argued that reading the Bible "as scripture" should focus on its theological meaning within the context of the Jewish or Christian canons as a whole. While he employed the full range of historical tools to understand the development of biblical texts, Childs emphasized that its final canonical form should be decisive for its religious meaning. Childs has been much more influential than Smith on biblical scholarship. It is fair to say, however, that neither Child's nor Smith's approaches dominate the field.[2]

What has changed in biblical research over the past 30 years is that more attention is being directed at the history of the Bible's interpretation. Such studies often include not only its interpretation by theologians and preachers, but also its use by artists and creative writers of poetry, novels, plays, and films. This trend has spawned several new journals in the field, such as *Biblical Interpretation, Postscripts: The Journal of Sacred Texts and Contemporary Worlds*, and *Biblical Reception*. Prominent book series, such as the Blackwell Bible Commentaries, focus on reception history. Some of this research takes a theological interest in the history of Jewish and Christian religious traditions that resembles Childs' canonical approach. But much of this research abstains from theological commitments, and discusses instead the cultural influence of the Bible in religious and secular contexts.

Nevertheless, biblical scholarship remains focused on *interpretation*, that is, on how people have understood the meaning of the Bible's words and utilized them in various ways. Much less research focuses on how people perform those words in religious and secular contexts, and even less on how they make use of the physical books of Jewish and Christian scriptures: Torah scrolls, tanaks and bibles. Performance Criticism has gained a foothold among biblical scholars, but still tends to reconstruct the original performance settings of particular books more than the history of biblical performances. Outside of biblical scholarship, the rise of book history as an academic discipline has drawn attention to the history of religious publishing and reading since the adoption of mass printing in the fifteenth century. But very little has been done to integrate these strands into a unified account of how the Bible functions in religious and secular cultures as a scripture.

I was a student of Brevard Childs during my PhD studies. I was drawn to his work because he focused on scripture as the defining characteristic of the Bible. Like him, I think biblical scholars should give more attention to the Bible's status as Jewish and Christian scripture, because that is what attracts people's attention in the first place. Were it not for the Bible's contemporary prestige and influence, the field of biblical studies would be a minor part of the study of ancient Middle Eastern literature rather than a subject of popular and scholarly interest around the world.

I have, however, spent my teaching career in departments of religious studies, first at Hastings College and then at Syracuse University. That context has shown me the benefits of comparing the Bible's scriptural status with the scriptures of other religions. Comparison reveals similar strategies for using sacred texts across cultures, even when the literary contents and theological meaning of the books differ dramatically.

For the past 15 years, I have engaged with a growing number of collaborators in a research project on the social uses of books and other written texts. Originally called the Iconic Books Project, it has more recently evolved into a scholarly association, the Society for Comparative Research on Iconic and Performative Texts (SCRIPT). We do research on how physical books get manipulated and depicted as well as on oral performances and their artistic illustration, and the social effects of these activities. The early results of this research were brought together in several journal issues and then in the collection *Iconic Books and Texts* (2013). This collaboration continues to produce innovative research by scholars working on a wide variety of religions, cultures, and time periods.[3]

Understanding the Pentateuch as a Scripture brings this comparative research on textual performances and iconic books into Pentateuchal studies. Applying comparative scripture studies to the Pentateuch is productive because the Pentateuch was the first part of the Bible to function as a scripture and its example has influenced the use of all subsequent scriptures in Western religious traditions. In this book, I bring historical and literary biblical criticism and the history of the Bible's cultural reception into interaction with the comparative study of scriptures. The results integrate what we know about the Pentateuch as an ancient Middle Eastern document with what we know about its material, oral, artistic, ritual, and interpretive uses today.

So I use an indefinite pronoun in the title of this book, "... as *a* Scripture," to indicate a comparative perspective on the Pentateuch's scriptural function. This, then, is not the canonical approach to scripture that I learned from Professor Childs. I am very grateful for his instruction and support, and I do not discount the importance of theological interpretation of the Bible for Jewish and Christian audiences. I simply think that a comparative analysis allows us to understand its influence and function in ways that theological interpretation does not.

This book introduces innovative ways of thinking about biblical literature as well as surveying established conclusions in the field. That combination might seem strange in an introductory textbook. In the field of biblical studies, however, an "introduction" has long served to provide a critical evaluation of the state of the field. It shows how biblical studies should go forward as well as surveys where it has been. This book follows in that tradition by demonstrating how the study of the Pentateuch can be re-envisioned from a religious studies perspective on comparative scriptures. It show that research on the Pentateuch's scriptural function can integrate investigations of its origins with its cultural history. The results illuminate its contemporary interpretation in the academy as well as in synagogues, in churches, and in the wider culture.

I hope this book will be read with interest by people in many different settings. It has, however, been organized with classroom instruction in mind. Instructors might use this book at the beginning of a course on the Hebrew Bible or Christian Bible, or to introduce or conclude a course on the Pentateuch. They could assign its chapters and sections at different times during a course, interlaced with other topics and more detailed analysis of Pentateuchal texts.

Chapter 1 introduces the concepts that are crucial to this book's approach: the idea of scripture, comparative scriptures studies, and the meaning of the words "Pentateuch" and "Torah." It also introduces the time of Ezra, 2,400 years ago, when the Pentateuch first began to function as a scripture. Chapter 2 then surveys the contents of the Pentateuch from literary and rhetorical perspectives, which it introduces and defines. My expectation in writing this chapter is that it will accompany assignments to read large parts, preferably all, of the Pentateuch.

Chapters 3, 4, and 5 analyze how the Pentateuch functions as a scripture in each of the dimensions defined in Chapter 1: the iconic, performative, and semantic dimensions. Each chapter first describes the Pentateuch's ritualization "after Ezra," that is, after the time that it began to function as scripture up to the present day. Only then does attention turn to the time "before Ezra," that is, before the Pentateuch was scripturalized. It is this period that has traditionally received most of the attention of biblical scholars. Presenting the history of the Pentateuch in this sequence allows students to compare cultural history with historical criticism directly. Class discussion will likely include frequent consideration of the relative amounts of evidence for various periods and scripturalizing activities, of the different kinds of historical arguments that various kinds of evidence and periods require, and of the significance of particular developments for shaping the meaning and use of the Pentateuch and Bible in the present day.

Chapter 6 briefly extends this book's analysis to the larger scriptures of Judaism and Christianity. It suggests a historical template for understanding key moments in the scripturalization of other biblical books in the developing Jewish and Christian traditions.

I have included many images and quotations of ancient texts for illustration. Text boxes appear periodically to define key ideas and give examples referred to in the immediate context. The table of Contents therefore provides a detailed list of the chapter subheadings to aid in constructing a course syllabus. A sample syllabus for assigning this book in a Hebrew Bible course can be found at http://jameswwatts.net/Understanding.

The literature on the Pentateuch that this book presupposes is voluminous. I have cited in the "Cited Works and Further Reading" sources of direct quotations. I have also included references to a very small number of English-language publications where instructors can find more detailed discussions of particular issues and fuller bibliographies. Some of these texts could also serve as further reading assignments to supplement the summaries in this book.

ACKNOWLEDGEMENTS

Many people have generously supported my work on this book and the longer research projects that contribute to it. I am very grateful to all those scholars who have joined me in the research of the Iconic Books Project and in SCRIPT. They are too many to mention, but I should especially single out Dorina Miller Parmenter, S. Brent Plate, Yohan Yoo, and Jason Larson. My colleagues in the Department of Religion at Syracuse University have been generous with their time and support for my projects. I especially appreciate the support for SCRIPT and Iconic Books by Joanne Waghorne, Philip Arnold, and Zachary Braiterman, and the valuable feedback from the members of Lemadim Olam. The College of Arts and Sciences of Syracuse University enabled me to write this book by granting a research leave for the 2015–16 academic year, and the Käte Hamburger Kolleg in the Center for Religious Studies at Ruhr University Bochum enabled its rapid progress with a generous visiting fellowship during that year. I am very grateful to Dean Karin Ruhlandt in the College at Syracuse and to Professors Volkhard Krech and Christian Frevel in Bochum, as well as to all the participants in the 2015–16 seminar on the theme of "religion and the senses." I am most grateful to my wife, Maurine, who accompanied me to Germany and has participated gamely in too many conversations about the Pentateuch.

This book culminates and summarizes much of my previous research on scriptures and on the Pentateuch. It therefore includes many ideas and arguments that I have published previously in articles and books.

References to those works appear where appropriate in the lists of "Cited Works and Further Reading." I have occasionally reproduced paragraphs previously published elsewhere. I am grateful to the publishers of the following works for permission to reproduce these selections here:

"Narrative, Lists, Rhetoric, Ritual and the Pentateuch as a Scripture," in *The Formation of the Pentateuch* (ed. Jan C. Gertz et al.; Tübingen: Mohr Siebeck, 2016), 1135–45.
"From Ark of the Covenant to Torah Scroll: Ritualizing Israel's Iconic Texts," in *Ritual Innovation in the Hebrew Bible and Early Judaism* (ed. Nathan MacDonald; BZAW 468; Berlin: De Gruyter, 2016), 21–34.
"Ritual Legitimacy and Scriptural Authority," *Journal of Biblical Literature* 124/3 (2005), 401–417.

English quotations of biblical verses are my translations unless otherwise noted. Photographs are my own except as noted.

1

RITUALIZED TEXT
THE PENTATEUCH AS A SCRIPTURE

The Pentateuch consists of five books: Genesis, Exodus, Leviticus, Numbers, and Deuteronomy. The most obvious fact about these books is that they are scripture. In fact, they are revered as scripture by three different religious traditions.

Jewish tradition names these five books the *Torah*, which in Hebrew means "law" or "instruction." The Torah is the first part of the Jewish Bible, which is often called the *Tanak*, an acronym for its three sections that also include the Prophets (the *Nebi'im*) and the Writings (the *Kethubim*). The Torah has always been the most important of the three parts. Its five books have shaped Jewish thought and life far more than the other books of Jewish scripture.

Christian tradition preserves Jewish scriptures in the first part, the Old Testament, of the Christian Bible. (For a neutral designation of the collection of books that Jews and Christians both regard as scripture, scholars now usually call it the Hebrew Bible.) So the bibles of different churches all start with the Pentateuch just as the Jewish Bible does. However, Christians emphasize the New Testament, which consists of uniquely Christian books, more than the Old Testament. They focus especially on the four Gospels that contain stories about Jesus's life and teachings, and on the letters of Paul.

Understanding the Pentateuch as a Scripture, First Edition. James W. Watts.

There is another religious tradition that reveres the Pentateuch as scripture. The Samaritans now number fewer than 1,000 people, but two millennia ago they were a large and vibrant community. Since antiquity, they have used the Torah as their only scripture.

You could object that the "Pentateuch," by that name, is really nobody's scripture. That name is a scholarly label for the contents of the Jewish and Samaritan Torah. Samaritans venerate the Torah as their only scripture. Jews venerate the Torah as the most important part of scripture, but the Tanak also contains 19 other books. Christians do not usually distinguish the Pentateuch from the rest of the Bible. They venerate it only as the first five books of their Old Testament, which is overshadowed in Christian thought and liturgy by the New Testament and, especially, by the four Gospels. The phrase, "the Pentateuch as a scripture," in this book's title is artificial. All three religious traditions define the scope of their scriptures differently from one another and by different names.

Nevertheless, describing the Pentateuch as a scripture draws attention to the similar ways in which all three religions treat their scriptures, including these five books. Saying the Pentateuch is a scripture means much more than just that it appears among the sacred books of these three religions. Congregations and religious individuals ritualize these books in distinctive ways that distinguish them as scriptures. Describing the Pentateuch as a scripture therefore requires us to consider the nature and function of scriptures in religious communities generally.

First, however, we need to discuss the term that evokes the Pentateuch's scriptural function for Jews and Samaritans most vividly, the name "Torah."

Torah and Pentateuch

The word *torah* appears in the Hebrew Bible frequently to refer to specific instructions (e.g. Lev. 6:9, 14, etc.). It may also refer to sets of instructions (Lev. 7:37) and, together with *mishpatim* and *huqim*, to all the stipulations of God's covenant with Israel (Gen. 26:5; Exod. 24:12; Lev. 26:46). The word *torah*, by itself, often refers specifically to priestly instructions or "teachings" (Deut. 33:10; Mal. 2:4–9). It typifies one of the priests' major responsibilities (Deut. 17:11, 18; Ezek. 22:26).[4]

Torah has traditionally been translated by "law." The first to do so were the ancient translators of the Septuagint who used the Greek word *nomos*. Many interpreters now find this translation too restrictive, because *torah* connotes instruction in the form of advice and direction as much as legal mandate. Furthermore, ancient Middle Eastern law collections do not seem to have functioned as normative legislation. Actually, the Greek word *nomos* described correct performance of temple rituals just as priestly *torah* does in the Hebrew Bible. In fact, written ritual instructions seem to have functioned as normative texts long before written legislation did, and may have been the stimulus for the gradual development of normative written law.

Deuteronomy uses *torah* most often to refer to itself as containing all the stipulations of the covenant (e.g. Deut. 1:5) in the form of a written scroll, *sefer hatorah* "the book of the Torah" (e.g. Deut. 28:61; cf. 2 Kgs. 22:8, 11). Other books of the Hebrew Bible connect this book with Moses, *sefer torat Moshe* "the book of the Torah of Moses" (e.g. Josh. 8:31; 1 Kgs. 2:3; Ezra 7:6; Neh. 8:1). By the early Second Temple period, "the Torah" had come to refer to the Pentateuch in more or less the form we have it today.

Early Christian writers referred to the collection as *ho nomos*, "the Law," often together with "the prophets" to describe all the scriptures. The Greek name *pentateuchos* "Pentateuch" means "five cases" and refers to the five books of the Torah. It appeared first in second- and third-century CE Christian authors such as Origen and Tertullian, and probably reflected Hebrew or Aramaic phrases used by the ancient rabbis, such as "the five books of the Torah" (*y. Sotah* 5:6) or "the five fifths of the Torah" (*b. Meg.* 15a). However, the Torah's division into five books was already reflected in the first century CE by Philo (*De Abrahamo* 1) and Josephus (*Apion* 1.8), and perhaps by a fragment among the Dead Sea Scrolls (*1Q30*).

For Jews and Samaritans, "the Torah" remains the name of the five books of the Pentateuch. It evokes not just the literature but the entire tradition of interpreting and living according to its teachings. Thus "Torah" names how the Pentateuch functions as scripture for these religions. But what does it mean to call the Torah, or any other text, "a scripture"?

Scripture and Ritual

Scholars of religions struggle to define the word "scripture." Religious communities tend to describe their scriptures as holy or sacred, as inspired by God, and as authoritative for their beliefs and practices. They also tend to describe their own scriptures as unique, unlike any other books or texts on earth. Religious communities therefore often resist classifying their sacred texts as belonging to the same category as the scriptures of other religions.[5]

Those who study multiple religions notice, however, that many traditions venerate some texts as sacred and distinguish them from all other texts.

Scholars of religion have therefore filled the category "scripture" with books from many religions. They often distinguish "book religions" from traditions that do not venerate sacred texts. Already in the Middle Ages, Muslim theologians described Judaism, Christianity, and Islam as "religions of the book." In the nineteenth century, Oxford University Press published 50 volumes of English translations of *The Sacred Books of the East*. The editor, Max Müller, wanted to expose Westerners to the scriptures of Hinduism, Buddhism, Islam, Zoroastrianism, Taoism, and Confucianism. Now textbook anthologies, such as Robert Van Voorst's *Anthology of World Scriptures*, make excerpts available from the scriptures of all these religions.

However, reading these various scriptures together shows that their contents have little in common. They contain stories, laws, oracles, moral principles, philosophical speculation, practical advice, prayers, hymns, spells, and much more. No one genre of literature describes them all. "Scripture," then, is not a literary category. Instead, what these texts have in common is that religious communities venerate them.

The nature of scripture

William Graham observed: "A text becomes 'scripture' in living, subjective relationship to persons and to historical tradition. No text, written, oral, or both, is sacred or authoritative in isolation from a community. A text is only 'scripture' insofar as a group of persons perceives it to be sacred or holy, powerful and meaningful, possessed of an exalted authority, and in some fashion transcendent of, and hence distinct from, other speech and writing. ... The 'scriptural' characteristics of a text belong not to the text itself but to its role in a community. 'Scripture' is not a literary genre but a religio-historical one."

Veneration of scriptures takes the form of public and private rituals of various kinds. Rituals draw people's attention to specific practices and ideas. They focus attention on the ritual activity itself in order to make participants more aware of their own relationship to what it represents. Studies of ritual (see Box, "Ritual theories") have revealed the central role that rituals play in human societies at every level.

Rituals, however, have a bad reputation. People associate ritual with unreality, with superstition, and with magic, which they contrast with practical, effective actions. Though this attitude feels modern, it is actually rooted in ancient religious polemics. Christians contrasted "empty rituals" and superstition with knowledge and "true faith" long before rationalists and scientists employed the contrast. Protestants used the term "ritual" to

Ritual theories

Throughout the twentieth century, many anthropologists and scholars of religion have studied rituals and how they work. They have increasingly focused not on distinguishing rituals from non-rituals, which can be hard to do, but rather on the activity of performing rituals or "ritualizing" which can take place at almost any time and place.

> "Ritualization is a way of acting that specifically establishes a privileged contrast, differentiating itself as more important or powerful." (Catherine Bell)

Ritualizing requires participants and audience to pay attention to what is being done, how it is being done, and who is doing it. Ritualizing involves doing ordinary activities, such as eating, entering a room, or reading a book, in a formal and regulated way.

> "Ritual relies for its power on the fact that it is concerned with quite ordinary activities placed within an extraordinary setting, that what it describes and displays is, in principle, possible for every occurrence of these acts." (Jonathan Z. Smith)

By performing rituals and witnessing them, people identify themselves with the values represented in the rituals.

> "By performing a [ritual] the participants accept, and indicate to themselves and to others that they accept whatever is encoded in the canon of that order." (Roy Rappaport)

So rituals identify (index) participants with the institutions and traditions that promote and perform those rituals.[6]

attack Catholic ceremonies during the Reformation, medieval Christians used it to disparage Jews, and ancient Christians used it to criticize and suppress pagan sacrifices.

In contrast to the reputation of rituals, scriptures have been venerated as containers of knowledge and truth. Reading has been cast as the opposite of ritualizing. It can therefore sound very odd to hear reading and writing described as rituals in some circumstances. The concept of ritualized books is so strange that scholars have done little research on this phenomenon, in contrast to the massive amounts of scholarship on the interpretation of books and religions.

Nevertheless, the display, reading, and interpretation of scriptures play obvious roles in the worship services – the rituals – of Jews and Christians, as well as of Muslims, Sikhs, Buddhists, Jains, and many other religious groups. In fact, ritualizing scriptures clearly encourages people to believe that these books are authoritative and inspired texts that establish the truth and legitimacy of the religious tradition. By setting aside the polemical history of debates over ritual, we can better understand how ritualizing books promotes religious ideas and practices, and secular ones too.

Rituals make participants pay attention to people, objects, and actions that they otherwise take for granted. Ritualized meals, for example, draw attention to the food itself, how it is prepared, and what it means: the unleavened bread of a Passover Seder, the bread and wine of Communion, the tea of a tea ceremony. Ritual processions require attention to the manner and order in which people enter and leave a room. Ceremonies that mark life transitions focus attention on particular people: the bride and groom at a wedding, the graduates at a college commencement, or the recently deceased at a funeral.

Ritualizing scriptures therefore draws attention to the books themselves – their verbal contents, and also the sound of their words and their physical form and appearance. Scriptures get ritualized in three distinct ways that correspond to the three dimensions of texts.

The Three Dimensions of Written Texts

Every written text consists of three aspects or dimensions. We usually focus on its meaning, the significance of its words and what they tell us. This interpretive act engages a text's *semantic dimension*.

Before we can understand the meaning of writing, we must turn the visual signs into words. The text must be read aloud or enunciated in our heads. This oral or mental performance engages a text's *performative dimension*.

But before we can even perform a text, we must recognize it as a written text. We have to interpret visual marks as written language (letters or signs), not as art or natural patterns, or we must recognize the shape of an object as likely to contain writing (an envelope, a scroll, or a book, for example). This act of recognition engages a text's *iconic dimension*.

We usually do not pay attention to the three different dimensions of texts. Consider this book that you are now reading. You instantly recognize its shape as a book that probably contains written text. You recognize its Roman letters and (if you are reading this) you turn them into English words

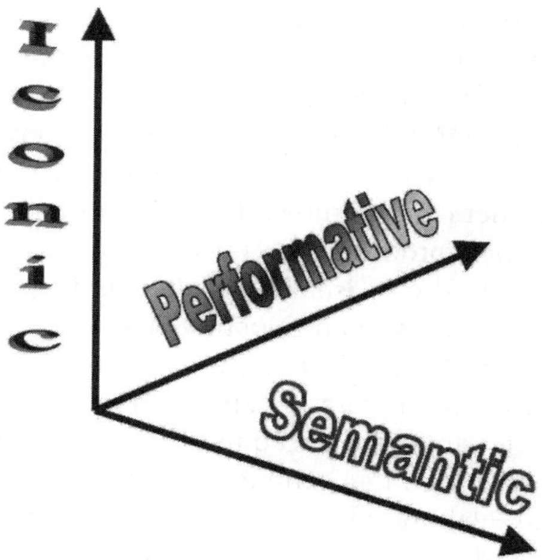

Figure 1.1 The three dimensions of written texts.

without thinking much about what you are doing. I hope that you also understand the meaning of these sentences without too much difficulty.

We pay attention to the individual dimensions of texts only if we have difficulty – if we have trouble figuring out their meaning (the semantic dimension), if we cannot read smudged type or illegible handwriting (the performative dimension), or if we cannot decide whether marks on paper represent written words or art or random patterns (the iconic dimension). Otherwise, the three dimensions of texts are trivial features of the experience of reading and usually ignored.

When texts get ritualized, however, the three dimensions become important, because texts can be ritualized in each of the dimensions.

The semantic dimension of interpretation can be ritualized by delivering lectures and sermons, by staging debates, and by writing interpretive commentaries on texts. For example, laws and national constitutions get ritualized regularly in the semantic dimension by oral and written interpretations that multiply and grow more elaborate over time. They serve the ritual function of drawing attention to the laws and they index the readers' and listeners' responsibilities under those laws.

The performative dimension of texts can be ritualized by private and public readings and recitations. Religious worship services often focus on reading selections of sacred texts. People may memorize the text. Oral performances may be standardized as chants or set to music as songs. Theatrical scripts, for example, are designed for public performance in ritual spaces (theaters). They expect audiences and actors to behave in conventional ways that call attention to the play being performed.

The iconic dimension of texts can be ritualized by changing how a book looks and by handling it in special ways. The text can be written in distinctive scripts or printed in unusual fonts. Its pages can be decorated and illustrated. Its binding or container can be embellished with art and valuable materials. For example, publishers produce collector's editions in leather bindings and gilt edges so buyers can show visually that they find a particular book valuable. Texts can also be displayed prominently on shelves or tables, held up for people to see, and paraded in elaborate processions. Rare books frequently get displayed in museums, in libraries, and even in private homes.

Only written texts can be ritualized in these three dimensions. A visual symbol such as a cross or a flag can be ritualized in the iconic dimension: it can be displayed, elaborated in art, and paraded in processions. Visual symbols can also be ritualized in the semantic dimension: their meanings can be elaborated and debated, sometimes at great length. But crosses and flags cannot be ritualized in the performative dimension: they contain no written words that can be turned into mental or oral language. On the other hand, an oral epic can be ritualized by retelling it or even staging it. Its interpretation can also be elaborated and debated at length. But there is no physical object to display or decorate. Therefore, oral epics and other oral traditions can be ritualized in the performative and semantic dimension, but not in the iconic dimension, while visual symbols can be ritualized in the iconic and semantic dimensions, but not in the performative dimension. Only written texts can be ritualized in all three dimensions.

Ritualizing Scriptures in Three Dimensions

Most texts do not get ritualized much in any dimension, and those that do usually get ritualized in only one or two dimensions. A distinctive feature of religious scriptures is that they get ritualized in all three dimensions.

Religious traditions that emphasize scriptures give prominent attention to their semantic interpretation. They include Muslims, Sikhs, Buddhists, Taoists, Hindus, and Jains, as well as Jews, Samaritans, and Christians. All of them sponsor speakers and literature that interpret their scriptures, and give their best interpreters positions of respect and influence. Most of them encourage lay people to study the scriptures and their interpretations. Ritualizing the semantic dimension tends to increase the authority of scriptures and the authority of people who can interpret them convincingly. These religions therefore give respect and influence to scholars, priests, preachers, rabbis, imams, or sages who are expert in the scriptures and their interpretation.

These traditions also highlight the oral performance of scriptures, to the point that reading or reciting scripture is a key component of their worship services. They often require that scriptures be performed orally in distinctive ways, with particular pronunciations or with prescribed chants. Verses of scriptures frequently get sung to melodies, with or without instrumental accompaniments. Some scriptures that contain vivid stories get performed theatrically. Traditions of enacting scriptural stories are thousands of years old in Europe and India. Now they frequently appear on television and in films. There is even older evidence for artistic traditions of illustrating scriptural stories and calligraphy that elaborates the written texts artistically. All these media can be used to perform the words and contents of scriptures. Ritualizing their performative dimension in these ways draws people's attention to the scriptures and inspires those who hear and see the performances. They often regard inspiration as characteristic of scripture.

Religious traditions that emphasize scripture also ritualize the physical form of their scriptures. The script or typeface may take distinctive forms and be arranged in unusual ways. The pages may be decorated and their contents may be illustrated. The cover or binding of the book may take a stereotypical form so that people easily recognize it as that scripture, or it may be bound in expensive materials. People display scriptures in their congregations, sanctuaries and homes. They carry them in the form of

The effects of ritualizing scriptures

Ritualizing each of a scripture's three dimensions makes the book's message more persuasive to those who venerate it. Theories of rhetoric, that is, of persuasion, help us understand how this works. The ancient Greek philosopher Aristotle (384–322 BCE) described three factors necessary to make a speech persuasive. The words (*logos*) of the speech must, of course, make a convincing argument. The speech, however, must also appeal to the audience's assumptions and feelings (*pathos*). And the speaker must project an attractive and trustworthy character (*ethos*). Scriptures are not speeches, but ritualizing their three dimensions increases their persuasive appeal in these same ways: interpreting them increases the authority (*logos*) of their contents and their interpreters, performing their words and contents inspires audiences (*pathos*), and displaying and decorating them legitimizes (*ethos*) the communities and traditions that venerate them.[7]

complete books or as miniature amulets. They wave them in rituals of worship or preaching, of celebration or protest. In all these ways, the visual appearance of scriptures distinguishes them from other books and emphasizes their importance. Ritualizing their iconic dimensions in these ways draws attention and legitimizes the religious tradition that venerates them and the people who possess and handle them.

Ritualization plays an important role in making some texts seem more authoritative than others. Regular and repeated interpretation of the same book makes its contents seem more important for how to think and act. But the reverse is also true: displaying a book of instructions makes rituals seem more legitimate. The visible presence of authoritative books counters doubts about the competence or honesty of the person leading the rituals.[8]

In fact, people in the ancient Middle East first began regarding some texts as normative, that is, as authoritative for how to behave, when those texts described how to conduct rituals. Kings and priests and magicians from Babylon to Egypt consulted ritual texts to tell them, for example, where to build temples, when to make offerings to the gods, and how to cast curses. But the famous law code of Hammurabi and other royal law codes were not consulted for how to conduct criminal trials, which were based on custom instead. Textual authority developed first around ritual texts.

The same pattern can be observed in the developing authority of biblical books. Many claim inspiration from God, most obviously books like Isaiah and Jeremiah that state that God gave the prophets these messages. The first Jewish scripture did not consist of prophetic books, however, but of the Pentateuch. Genesis 1 does not begin with any explicit claim of inspiration or even of authorship. The Pentateuch does contain laws spoken by God to Moses. But what differentiates it most from other biblical books is that ritual instructions lie at its center in Exodus 25–40, Leviticus, and parts of Numbers. Stories of the Torah's growing authority in the Second Temple period emphasize that it first dictated ritual behavior, especially how to celebrate the annual festivals of Passover and *Sukkot* (Booths). Only centuries later did its laws begin to apply in criminal courts and civil society. (See "The Rhetoric of Law After Ezra" on p. 200.)

The Pentateuch in Three Dimensions

Understanding how a book functions as scripture therefore involves how it gets ritualized in each of three dimensions and the social effects of these rituals. Chapters 3–5 will describe how religious communities have ritualized the Pentateuch. The specifics vary from one tradition to another and from time to time and place to place.

For example, Jews and Samaritans use scrolls of the Torah in synagogue services. The form of the book itself therefore distinguishes it as sacred scripture. Torah scrolls also receive distinctive covers and get housed in cabinets, Torah arks, that emphasize the sanctity of the text. Christians, by contrast, use a different book form for their scriptures, a codex that binds folded pages together on one edge. Because of Christian influence, the codex became the standard shape for almost all books in Western cultures. But Christians continue to distinguish their Bibles, with the Pentateuch included, by decorative bindings and distinctive typography. Jews, Samaritans, and Christians have reproduced quotations from their scriptures in monumental form on walls, plaques, and gravestones. All three religions tend to display their books of scripture prominently and parade them publicly. So they all ritualize the iconic dimension of their scriptures, even though the specific forms and methods vary.

Jews, Samaritans, and Christians also give prominent attention to reading scriptures. Reading selected texts aloud is so common in their worship services that it is a defining characteristic of what makes them worship services. The services of Jewish and Samaritan synagogues highlight the Pentateuch by reading the entire Torah through sequentially over the course of a year. Christian churches focus on other parts of their bibles and usually read only selected parts of the Pentateuch aloud, mostly from Genesis, Exodus, and Deuteronomy. The readings often take musical form as chants. Scriptural texts are also set to music and sung by congregations and choirs. Biblical stories, including the Pentateuch's, are a major source of themes for artistic illustration and theatrical productions, now including television and film. Though the methods and forms vary, all three religions ritualize the Pentateuch's performative dimension to a high degree.

The three religions that venerate the Pentateuch as scripture also give attention to interpreting its meaning. Worship services feature sermons based on scriptural texts. Congregations promote group study of scripture by children and adults. To support these activities, scholars write commentaries explaining the texts. The published literature about the Pentateuch is therefore vast and grows every year. Most scholars would distinguish their activities from the rituals of congregational worship. But their repetitive focus on religious texts bears all the hallmarks of ritualizing activity, and has the same effect: it draws attention to the scriptures and publicly enhances their value. So, again, though the methods vary over time and by tradition, Jews, Samaritans, and Christians have all ritualized the Pentateuch's semantic dimension from antiquity to today.

Deuteronomy commands Torah's ritualization

YHWH spoke these words to your whole congregation on the mountain in a loud voice out of fire, cloud and darkness, and added nothing more. Then God wrote them on two stone tablets and gave them to me. (Deut. 5:22)

Have the words that I am commanding you today in your heart. Repeat them to your children and talk about them when you sit at home and when you walk down the road, when you lie down and when you get up. Tie them as a sign on your hand and make them a symbol between your eyes. Inscribe them on the doorposts of your house and on your gates. (Deut. 6:6–9)

YHWH said to me, "Carve two stone tablets … and make a wooden ark. I will write the words on the tablets … and you must put them in the ark." (Deut. 10:1–2)

Moses wrote down this law and gave it to the levitical priests, who carry the Ark of the Covenant, and to all the Israelite elders. He commanded them, "Every seventh year … you shall read this Torah in the presence of all Israel. Gather the people, men, women, children and immigrants among you, so that they may hear and learn to be in awe of YHWH your God and to be careful to do all the words of this Torah." (Deut. 31:9–12)

Moses commanded the Levites who carry the Ark of the Covenant of YHWH, "Take this Torah scroll and put it beside the Ark of the Covenant of YHWH your God, where it will serve as a witness against you." (Deut. 31:25–26)

The tendency to ritualize the Pentateuch can partly be explained by the fact that the Pentateuch itself commands its ritualization in all three textual dimensions. Deuteronomy 31:10–13 requires that the Torah be read aloud to all the Israelites every seven years (see Box, "Deuteronomy commands Torah's ritualization"). The performative nature of this activity is clearly marked by scheduling the reading every seven years, by its setting during *Sukkot*, the Festival of Booths, and by requiring that everyone participate, including men, women, and children. The ritual aims explicitly for instructional goals, "so that they may hear and learn," thus also ritualizing its semantic dimension. Later, the same chapter commands its iconic ritualization. The physical scroll must be placed beside the ark in the holiest part of Israel's sanctuary as an icon of Israel's covenant with God. The ark itself contains the tablets of the commandments (Deut. 10:1–5) that God spoke aloud to Israel, according to Deut. 5:22 (and also Exod. 20:1–19, 25:16). The ark, then, served as a reliquary, a container for a sacred relic. In this case, that relic is a text, stone tablets of the commandments that were written by God.

Deuteronomy also requires that at least parts of the Torah be ritualized by Israelites at home. It emphasizes meditating regularly on its words "in your hearts," that is, by memorizing them, and teaching them to children. Such performative and semantic ritualization should be joined with iconic ritualization by wearing its words on arm and forehead and writing them on gates (Deut. 6:6–9).

So the writers of Deuteronomy anticipated that Torah would be ritualized as scripture in all three of its textual dimensions. And, in fact, the Torah's three dimensions did get ritualized when it first began to function as a scripture, in the time of the priest and scribe Ezra.

Scripturalizing Torah in the Time of Ezra

The biblical books of Ezra and Nehemiah describe Ezra as a Jewish priest and scribe from Babylon. The Persian emperor commissioned him to appoint judges. Ezra also devoted himself to religious reform based on "the Torah of Moses that YHWH God gave to Israel" (Ezra 7:6). He focused especially on two issues. He led the Jerusalem community to prohibit marriage to foreign women and to dissolve such marriages that had already taken place (Ezra 10). This ban on intermarriage was more comprehensive than what the Pentateuch actually requires. That discrepancy has led some historians to think that Ezra's Torah was not exactly the same as the Pentateuch that we now possess. Others argue that Ezra simply interpreted the Pentateuch more strictly than necessary. At any rate, the story implies that Ezra used the Torah's authority to regulate marriages.

Ezra also led the Jerusalem community in a public reading of the Torah scroll (Neh. 8, see Box, "Ezra's Torah reading"). He was visibly supported by community leaders standing on each side of him. When he displayed the scroll, the people responded with ritual words ("Amen") and bows of reverence. They stood at attention while Ezra read aloud for the whole morning. Levites interpreted or translated the meaning of what Ezra read. Readings and study continued on the following days. They culminated in celebrating the annual festival of *Sukkot* on the basis of the Torah's instructions (Neh. 8:14–17). Later, the whole community renewed the covenant with God and committed themselves to funding the temple in Jerusalem (Neh. 10).

This scripture reading ceremony illustrates a typical feature of rituals (see Box "Ritual theories," above). Simply by participating and being seen to participate in this ritual, the people of Jerusalem accepted the legitimacy of the Torah and of Ezra as its authoritative interpreter. Whatever their private misgivings may have been, they publicly committed themselves to obey the commandments of the Torah. That meant, to begin with, celebrating *Sukkot* correctly.

Ezra's Torah reading

All the people joined as one … and asked Ezra to bring the book of the Torah of Moses which YHWH had commanded Israel. … He read from it … from dawn to noon to the men and women and children old enough to understand, and the people listened closely to the Torah. The scribe Ezra stood on a wooden speaker's platform, and [the priests and elders] stood next to him. Ezra opened the book where all the people could see, because he was standing higher than the people. When he opened it, all the people stood up. Then Ezra blessed YHWH, the great God, and all the people raised their hands and responded, "Amen, amen." Then they bowed down before YHWH with their faces to the ground. … The Levites helped the people in their places understand the Torah. Thus they read from the book of the Torah of God with interpretation to explain the meaning, so they could understand the reading. (Neh. 8:1–8)

To later Jews and by the standards of the Torah itself (Deut. 6:1–9; 31:9–13), the description of Ezra and his actions in Nehemiah 8 exemplifies what a rabbi (a Jewish religious leader) should be and do. He leads the people to read and study the Torah, and to observe the laws of God that it contains. Ezra establishes the model of scholarly religious leadership that has predominated in Judaism for 2,000 years, and in Christianity and Islam as well.

So it is surprising to notice that Ezra is almost the first person in the Bible to be shown acting in these ways. Moses, of course, exemplifies this kind of leadership in the Pentateuch, and his successor, Joshua, also read and inscribed the Torah for Israel (Josh. 8:30–35). However, from the time of Moses and Joshua until the time of Ezra more than 800 years later, there is only one story about Israel's political or religious leaders behaving in this way. In fact, the stories of events during these centuries contain almost no references to the book of Torah, except three times in commentary by characters or narrators (1 Kgs. 2:3; 2 Kgs. 14:5–6; 17:34–40). Only one story features a Torah scroll as a key element. That is the story of the Torah found in the late seventh century and its ritualized reading by King Josiah (2 Kgs. 22–23). But the resulting religious reform seems to have had no lasting impact. The stories of the following kings and of Judah's exile from its land do not feature a book of Torah. In the Bible after the Pentateuch and apart from 2 Kings 22–23, the Torah appears as a prominent feature of the plot only in the books of Ezra and Nehemiah and in the books of Chronicles, which is a history of the kingdoms written after the time of Ezra. The Bible suggests that from the generation of Moses to the post-exilic generation of Ezra, the religious practices of Israel and Judah were not based on a written book of scripture.

It was only in the time of Ezra and afterwards, that is, in the Persian period (539–ca. 330 BCE), that the Torah began to function regularly as scripture for many Jews. Chapters 3, 4, and 5 will detail the evidence for this claim. For now, it is important to notice that, according to Nehemiah 8, Ezra ritualized all three dimensions of scripture. He displayed the physical scroll to the people, who rose to their feet at the sight and then bowed down (iconic dimension 8:5–6). He read it aloud on each day of the festival (performative dimension 8:3, 18). And the Levites interpreted its meaning to the people, while the leaders studied it for guidance (semantic dimension 8:7–8, 13). Here we find the three-dimensional ritualization that distinguishes later scriptures, such as the Torah scroll, the Bible, and the Qur'an, from secular texts.

The Persian Empire and the Pentateuch

The Babylonian Empire conquered the Kingdom of Judah in 587 BCE. Many Judeans, especially upper-class priests, scribes, and royalty, were exiled to Mesopotamia. Less than 50 years later, the Babylonians themselves were conquered by the Persians. The Persian conqueror, Cyrus, issued a decree allowing exiles to return to their native lands and rebuild their homes and temples. Descendants of the Judean exiles began to slowly make their way back to Jerusalem. They rebuilt their villages and their temple (Ezra 2–6), but restoring the city and its economy took hundreds of years.

Sometime in the next century (historians give dates ranging from 450 to 399 BCE), the Persian emperor sent Ezra to the province containing Judea. Some historians argue that Ezra's story shows that the Persian Empire played a role in turning the Pentateuch into official Jewish law. At least the biblical writers claimed there was imperial support for scripturalizing the Torah in the Persian period.

Whatever the historical facts may have been, Nehemiah 8 shows that its authors thought the Torah should be ritualized just as Deuteronomy requires. Chapters 3–5 will demonstrate that from the time of Ezra in the Persian period on, the Pentateuch was in fact increasingly ritualized in all three dimensions as a scripture. So the story of Ezra's Torah illustrates a turning point in the history of the Pentateuch's scripturalization, whatever the role of the Persian Empire may have been.

Ezra in history and tradition

The Persian emperor sent Ezra "to appoint judges," according to Ezra 7:25. He apparently carried with him a Torah scroll (7:14). Ezra, besides being a Persian official, was also a Jewish priest and "a scribe skilled in the law (torah) of Moses" who "had set his heart to study the law of the Lord, and to do it, and to teach the statutes and ordinances in Israel" (Ezra 7:6, 10). The biblical books of Ezra and Nehemiah depict Ezra as entirely concerned with the people's religious faithfulness. Once he reached Jerusalem, Ezra reformed the community's marriage laws (Ezra 10) and ritual calendar (Neh. 8) according to his interpretation of the Torah. He even required Judean men to divorce and send away their foreign wives for fear that the immigrants would introduce their gods to the Judeans.

Many historians suspect that the biblical writers changed Ezra from being a Persian official who oversaw the appointment of judges to being a religious reformer. They think that the biblical writers reinterpreted the commission of Ezra as a Persian bureaucrat (Ezra 7:12–26) and turned him into a Torah scribe and religious reformer. In that case, Nehemiah 8's depiction of Ezra reading the Torah scroll may not be historically accurate. Other historians defend the story as a plausible account of how the Persians sponsored the development of local ethnic laws (see Box, "The Persian Empire and the Pentateuch).

What is clear is that the biblical writers present Ezra as a model of Torah observance. They were not interested in Persian bureaucracy. Instead, they use the story of Ezra to show how Torah *should* be ritualized and what its effects *should* be.

Within a century after the books of Ezra and Nehemiah were written, someone revised them to emphasize this theme even more. The author of the book of *1 Esdras* omitted the governor Nehemiah as well as the criticisms of the priests' marriages. This rearrangement turned Ezra's ritual of Torah reading into the climax and conclusion of the work. *1 Esdras* thus presented Torah observance as the ultimate solution to the problem of sin and divine punishment.[9]

Historical arguments about the accuracy of the biblical depiction of Ezra and his Torah in the context of Persian imperial policies (see boxes, "The Persian Empire and the Pentateuch" and "Ezra in history and tradition") do not affect the claim that the Pentateuch began to be ritualized as scripture, as Torah, during this time. The story of the priest and scribe Ezra who brought the Torah from Babylon and read it to the people of Jerusalem so that they renewed their commitment to God and the temple, that story shows how the writers of Ezra and Nehemiah thought the Pentateuch should be ritualized. From the time of Ezra on, Jews and Samaritans did ritualize the Torah more and more. There is no sign that this was the case before this time. It is only from the time of Ezra on, that is, from the middle or late Persian period or, more broadly, from the early Second Temple period, that the Torah began to function regularly as scripture.

The story of Ezra serves therefore to mark a turning point in religious history and in the history of scripturalization. It provides information about the political, social, and religious reasons Jews began to ritualize the Torah in all three dimensions. It shows us how they imagined doing it properly, and this model of ritual behavior corresponds more or less with how later congregations ritualize their scriptures. The story illustrates the social effects of ritualizing Torah: in the iconic dimension by legitimizing Ezra's leadership, in the performative dimension by inspiring the whole community to devote themselves to following Torah, and in the semantic dimension by empowering the authority of Torah's interpreters, of Ezra and the Levites who assisted him.

This book will therefore organize its discussion of the scripturalization of the Pentateuch around this turning point in the time of Ezra. Since the Torah began to be scripturalized in this period, Chapters 3, 4, and 5 will first describe the Pentateuch's ritualization from this time forward in each of the three textual dimensions respectively. I will survey the history of the Pentateuch's ritualization "after Ezra" right up to the present day. Only then will we consider the Pentateuch's prior history. I will evaluate what we can know about the origins and ritualization of each of the Pentateuch's dimensions "before Ezra," that is, before they began to be ritualized regularly to turn the Torah into the first written scripture of Western religious history.

Reading the Pentateuch as a Scripture

Almost all readers of the Pentateuch know about its status as scripture before they start reading. That is why I have begun by discussing the nature of scriptures and the Pentateuch's ritualization in the three textual dimensions of scriptures. People learn that the Torah or the Bible is scripture because they have been exposed to its ritualization in one or more dimensions. Only then do they begin to read the text for themselves, either on their own or in a congregational study group or in a college class. Almost everybody reads the Pentateuch knowing that it functions as Jewish and Christian scripture.

Many readers find, however, that the contents of the Pentateuch are not what its status as scripture led them to expect. They find stories that depict God differently than do Jewish rabbis and Christian preachers. They find ritual instructions for sacrifices that Jews and Christians do not follow. They find laws that conflict with modern standards of justice and ethics, and they find stories that contradict modern science. The Pentateuch's literary structure also confuses readers because it does not correspond to how modern novels or textbooks are organized.

While understanding the Pentateuch as a scripture helps to explain how it gets used by Jews and Christians, it does not explain its contents. The contents of scriptures in other religious traditions differ too much from the Bible and from each other to provide any guidance for how to read this particular scripture. Therefore the next chapter surveys the contents of the Pentateuch from a different perspective, namely, that of rhetoric. I will summarize the Pentateuch as a work of literature that has persuasive effects on devout readers.

2

TEXTUAL RHETORIC
THE PERSUASIVE SHAPING OF THE PENTATEUCH

The Pentateuch begins with the creation of the universe and ends with the death of Moses. In between, it tells sweeping stories about worldwide catastrophe (Noah's flood in Gen. 6–8) and political conflict (the tower of Babel in Gen. 11, Israel's emigration from Egypt in Exod. 1–15) as well as intimate stories of family life (Abraham and Sarah's struggles with childlessness in Gen. 15–22, Moses and Zipporah's courtship and marriage in Exod. 2:15–22). The later books of the Pentateuch, but not Genesis, increasingly feature religious conflicts (the golden calf in Exod. 32, priestly malpractice in Lev. 10:1–3) and conflicts over religious leadership (Num. 12–17).

More than half of the Pentateuch's contents do not consist of stories at all, but rather contain lists of instructions, laws, donations, and genealogies. The Pentateuch's narrative casts the instructions and laws as speeches by God in Exodus, Leviticus, and Numbers or by Moses in Deuteronomy. The donation lists and genealogies are voiced by the Pentateuch's anonymous, third-person narrator. So the lists are set within a narrative plot that explains their position: God speaks laws and instructions to Moses at Mount Sinai, and Moses repeats and interprets these laws to Israel before he dies. Nevertheless, you notice that lists increasingly dominate the further you read through the five books.

Understanding the Pentateuch as a Scripture, First Edition. James W. Watts.

How should we read such a text? The stories indicate a literary approach, but the instructions and laws suggest other reading strategies. This chapter will survey the contents of the Pentateuch, and also suggest ways to understand their intended effects when read as a scripture.

The Pentateuch as Literature

The Bible consists of literature. It can therefore be studied using the ideas and tools of literary analysis. This has been a fruitful approach for exposing the skill and artistry of the biblical writers. They sketch very memorable and distinctive characters such as Abraham (Gen. 12–25), Sarah and Hagar (Gen. 16, 18, 21), Jacob (Gen. 25–35), Joseph (Gen. 37, 39–50), Deborah (Judg. 4–5), and David (1 and 2 Sam.). They excel at composing pithy stories, such as Adam and Eve in the Garden (Gen. 3) and Abraham's attempt to sacrifice Isaac (Gen. 22). These stories imply more than they say and require readers to think through the issues they raise. The writers insert powerful songs, such as the Song of the Sea (Exod. 15) and Moses's Song (Deut. 32), to bring their stories to a moving climax.[10]

However, together the five books of the Torah make for a very bad story. The Pentateuch's poor literary form is one of the principle reasons that historians of the last 200 years have divided it into different sources and editorial layers (see Chapter 5).

The Pentateuch suffers from at least three kinds of narrative difficulties. First, the story contains many repetitions and contradictions. The repetitions include two creation stories (Gen. 1–2), three wife-sister stories (Gen. 12, 20, 26), and two calls of Moses (Exod. 3, 6). Contradictions in the plot include different sequences for the creation of animals and humans (compare Gen. 1:20–27 with 2:4–25) and different counts for the numbers of each species of animal in Noah's ark and for the length of time they stayed in the ark (compare Gen. 6:19–20; 7:2–4, 8–9, 12, 15, 17, 24; 8:3, 6). Contradictions also appear in characters' motivations, especially God's motivations. For example, YHWH decides to destroy the human race but then saves Noah and his family (Gen. 6), and commissions Moses to free the Israelites from Egypt and then tries to kill him (Exod. 3–4).

Problems of repetition and contradiction affect not only the stories, but also appear in the Pentateuch's lists of instructions. The legal collections duplicate and contradict each other on some issues. For examples, compare the altar laws (Exod. 20:24–26; Lev. 17:3–9; Deut. 12:13–15), the different calculations of reparations for theft (Exod. 22:1–4; Num. 5:7), or the three versions of the Ten Commandments (Exod. 20:2–17; 34:11–26;

Deut. 5:6–21). They omit topics that we might reasonably expect to be included, such as how to kill offering animals and rules for making legal contracts.

Though the problems of repetition and contradiction have drawn the most attention, the Pentateuch deviates from the usual ways of telling stories in two other ways as well. Many lists interrupt the story, especially after Exodus 19. The Ten Commandments (Exod. 20) are followed by successively larger collections of laws and instructions: the Covenant Code (Exod. 21–23), the instructions for building the Tabernacle (Exod. 25–31) followed by a list-like narrative of their fulfillment (Exod. 35–40), the instructions for offerings in the Tabernacle (Lev. 1–7) and for cleansing impurities (Lev. 11–16) followed by the Holiness Code (Lev. 17–27), genealogies (Num. 1–3) and lists of offerings (Num. 7) including and followed in the rest of Numbers by other ritual and legal instructions mixed among the stories of Israel wandering in the wilderness. The Pentateuch concludes finally by repeating the whole exodus and wilderness story including the laws and instructions, this time in the voice of Moses in the book of Deuteronomy. As a result, more than half of the Pentateuch consists of lists of one kind or another. Though narrative genres such as epic and the novel are usually capacious enough to incorporate many lists and other kinds of texts, the preponderance of lists in the latter part of the Pentateuch undermines the narrative flow. At least, that is the experience of many modern readers who abandon their plans to read through the Bible after encountering the lists of Exodus and Leviticus.

A third major deviation from storytelling norms appears in the fact that the Pentateuch's story does not have a proper narrative ending. Moses completes his speech and then dies (Deut. 34), which also ends the Pentateuch. The end of Deuteronomy leaves most of the Pentateuch's plot expectations unresolved. The most obvious loose end is the expectation that the people of Israel will occupy the land of Canaan, an event anticipated already in Genesis (12:1–2; 15:18–20; 17:8; etc.). At the end of Deuteronomy, however, they remain camped on the eastern side of the Jordan river. The conquest of Canaan is narrated only in the book of Joshua. Scholars have therefore tried to provide the Pentateuch with a better ending by recreating an older tetrateuch (the narrative of Genesis through Numbers) or hexateuch (Genesis through Joshua), or by simply accepting the addendum of the Deuteronomistic History to create an enneateuch (Genesis through 2 Kings).

These well-known literary problems have motivated a great many historical reconstructions of the Pentateuch's composition (see Chapter 5). Our modern expectations for narrative genres are not unreasonable. The writers of biblical literature did know how to tell good stories with strong narrative climaxes. Readers usually think the book of Samuel's throne succession narrative (2 Sam. 11–20) is the best prose narrative in the Bible (and among the best in world literature), but the Pentateuch's writers also knew how to write well-plotted stories on a fairly large scale. The Joseph story is certainly one (Gen. 37, 39–50). The exodus story, despite all its multiple layers and intrusions, manages to maintain narrative suspense over 14 chapters (Exod. 1–14), including a double climax in the death of the firstborn and the crossing of the Reed Sea, followed by the cathartic celebration of the Song of the Sea (Exod. 15).

Exodus 1–15 shows that the Pentateuch's editors could conform to narrative plot conventions even when incorporating multiple sources, doublets, contradictions, and lists of instructions. The fame of Exodus 1–15 as "the exodus story" throughout Jewish and Christian cultures shows that these literary problems need not prove fatal to narrative success. The Exodus story, however, provides one thing that the Pentateuch as a whole does not: a satisfying narrative climax and conclusion. We should therefore think carefully about the failure of the Pentateuch overall to abide by a common narrative convention that is evident in its own pages.

The skills that biblical writers can deploy in plotting narratives tell us that their failure to meet narrative expectations in the composite Pentateuch was not the result of authorial or editorial incompetence. The writers and editors chose to deviate from narrative expectations. Their choices were literary and rhetorical choices, but they were not narrative choices. They made no attempt to conform the whole Pentateuch to the standards of how to plot and conclude a story, then or now.

Nevertheless, the choices they made were successful. The fact is that it is *this* form of the text, *this* genre-breaking amalgam of stories with lists of all sorts, *this* Pentateuch, that has survived, rather than the sources that preceded it. And the Pentateuch has done more than survive: it has succeeded to an unprecedented degree compared to all other Jewish literature – or, frankly, all other ancient literature until Christian scripture imitated and incorporated the Pentateuch while simultaneously trying to supersede it. The fact that it was the Pentateuch in this form that was scripturalized as Torah and became the first scripture of Western religious history is the fact that most needs explanation. The pressing question is: Why did ancient Jews and Samaritans scripturalize this text and in this form, rather than any other? Answering this question requires thinking about what the Pentateuch does as religious literature, and how it does it.

Considering the scriptural function of the Pentateuch's contents soon leads to issues that go beyond analyzing the Pentateuch as a "story" or even as "literature," as these words are usually understood. They do not begin to describe its role as scripture. Devout people throughout time and across cultures experience their scripture as normative. That is, they not only study its contents, they try to live by its instructions. They claim to be motivated by the book's exhortations and they change their behavior because of the text's teachings. In other words, they find their scripture *persuasive*.

The Pentateuch as Rhetoric

Rhetoric studies the means of persuasion. Persuasion can use literary techniques such as narrative plot, poetic word plays, characterization, and irony. Rhetorical strategies also include more direct kinds of arguments and appeals. The Pentateuch contains stories shaped with literary artistry, but many speeches by God and Moses directly address the readers and hearers of this text as well as the Israelites in the story.[11]

Rhetoric pays close attention to the relationship between speaker and audience, or between author and reader. The audience/reader must respect the speaker/author enough to take the text seriously. And the speaker/author must appeal to the reader's/audience's values and expectations. If the audience does not share the speaker's or writer's premises, the argument fails to persuade them.

As a result, speeches or texts that persuade one audience may fail to move a different group of people. For example, the book of Leviticus presupposes that its audience will want to avoid personal pollution, a fairly safe assumption in many ancient and traditional societies. Most modern readers, however, do not share its understanding of pollution and purity. As a result, they are bewildered by its exhortations to purify themselves, or they try to stay pure in completely different ways than the writers of Leviticus imagined.

Theories of rhetoric were developed to understand persuasive speech. Rhetorical analysis suits well the oral performance and aural reception of scriptures, but can also illuminate its private study by individual readers. This difference, between reading aloud publicly and private study, was less clear in ancient times than it is now. Ancient scribes usually read aloud, even to themselves. Expert scribes memorized the classic texts that they studied. Written documents served primarily as study and memory aids. These circumstances recommend rhetorical analysis for studying the shaping and use of ancient scriptures, and they indicate the need to pay attention to mnemonics and studies of cultural memory as well.

Rhetoric

Rhetoric is the discipline that studies forms of persuasion. Rhetoric asks: How do people persuade each other to do or believe something? Why are some people more persuasive than others? What kinds of speeches and actions are more persuasive than others?

When applied to written texts, rhetoric studies the literary forms of persuasion: What literary forms are persuasive? Do different kinds of literature have different persuasive effects?

For any given text, rhetorical analysis asks: Who is trying to persuade whom of what

... by writing this text?
... by reading this text?
... by copying or printing or publishing this text?
... by interpreting this text?
... by decorating this text?
... by dramatizing this text?

Rhetoric provides a useful way of studying the Bible because Jews and Christians have found that scriptures can be persuasive for how they conduct themselves individually and as communities. This has been true ever since the Pentateuch first began to function as scripture, even though different people have understood its teachings in very different ways. So rhetorical analysis highlights one of the characteristic features of normative texts.

Rhetoric also provides a methodological framework within which the results of other kinds of analysis (literary, historical, legal, theological, sociological, etc.) can be related to each other. It provides a convenient way to search for the overall effect of a particular passage or book. Rhetoric pays attention both to a text's literary form and to its social function. So it asks why the text is written this way and it also asks what effect the text had on readers from the time it was first written until now.

Of course, we frequently do not know how readers responded to what they read or heard read. Nor do we know exactly whom writers were addressing. We have to try to figure that out inductively from what the text says. So rhetoric combines literary analysis of the biblical text with historical research into its production and use in various situations and cultures from antiquity to the present.

Rhetoric has to be adapted to the culture of ancient Israel that produced the Pentateuch. Rhetorical theories were first developed by ancient Greek and Roman rhetoricians. Aristotle, Cicero, and Quintilian presupposed the legal and political institutions of Greece and Rome. Their influence has led most theorists of rhetoric to think within those parameters ever since. But the religious, legal, and political institutions of other cultures require different kinds of persuasive strategies. The study of rhetoric is therefore beginning to analyze how persuasion differs from one culture to another. Comparative rhetoric provides new and useful resources for understanding Israel's persuasive texts in the context of other ancient Middle Eastern cultures.[12]

Logos: The Story-List-Sanction Rhetorical Strategy

Israel's culture was similar in many ways to the cultures of ancient Egypt, Phoenicia, Syria, and Mesopotamia. Like the Pentateuch, many ancient Middle Eastern texts combine different kinds (genres) of literature to make a more persuasive argument (logos: see Box, p. 10).

One typical combination employed a distinctive story-list-sanction pattern. First, the texts tell stories about the past that establish obligations between different people or groups of people. Then they list a series of rules or instructions to direct their listeners' or readers' behavior. Finally, they promise blessings on those who obey and threaten curses on those who do not.[13]

For example, an eighth-century BCE inscription by Azatiwata, the Phoenician governor of a provincial town, tells of his governmental roles, his building projects, and his military accomplishments. Then it mandates a short schedule of offerings:

> *A yearly sacrifice: an ox; and at the season of plowing: a sheep; and at the season of reaping/harvesting: a sheep.*[14]

The inscription ends with blessings on Azatiwata and the inhabitants of his city and curses on any future ruler who might obliterate this inscription (see Box, "Kurigalzu's inscription" for another example).

Ancient inscriptions of various kinds use the story-list-sanction structure for persuasion. They include the law code of King Hammurabi, which precedes and follows the laws with stories of the king's military victories and gifts to temples and concludes with curses on anyone who might modify or destroy his inscription.

Kurigalzu's inscription

An inscription of Kurigalzu, a king of Babylon in the mid-second millennium BCE, provides a short example of the rhetorical strategy of story-list-sanction that can be quoted in full:

> *Kurigalzu, great king, mighty king, king of the universe, favorite of Anu and Enlil, nominated (for kingship) by the gods am I! King who has no equal among all kings his ancestors, son of [Kadash]man-Harbe, unrivalled king,*
>
> **(Story)** *who completed the fortifications of ... who [fin]ished the Ekur, who [prov]ides for Ur and Uruk, who [guar]antees the rites of Eridu, who constructed the temples of Anu and Ishtar, who [guarantees] the regular offerings of the great gods, I caused Anu, father of the great gods, to dwell in his exalted sanctuary.*
>
> **(List)** *To Ishtar, the most great lady, who goes at my side, who maintains my army, shepherds my people, subdues those disobedient to me:*
>
> *From the town Adatti, on the bank of the Euphrates, as far as the town Mangissi, bordering on the field Duranki, beloved of Enlil. From the town of my lady, Bit-Gashan-ama-kalla, as far as the border of the city Girsu, an area of 216,000 kor using a ratio per surface unit of 30 quarts of seed barley, measured by the large cubit, to Ishtar I granted.*
>
> *3 kor of bread, 3 kor of fine wine, 2 (large measures) of date cakes, 30 quarts of imported dates, 30 quarts of fine(?) oil, 3 sheep per day did I establish as the regular offering for all time.*
>
> *I set up boundary stones in all directions and guaranteed the borders. The towns, fields, watercourses, and unirrigated land, and their rural settlements did I grant to Ishtar, my lady.*
>
> **(Sanctions)** *Whosoever shall arise afterward and shall alter my deeds and change the command which I spoke, shall take out my boundary stones, shift my boundary lines, take away the towns, fields, watercourses, and unirrigated lands, or the rural settlements in the neighborhood of Uruk, or cause (another) to take (them) away, or who shall attempt to convert them to state lands, may Ishtar, the most great lady, not go at his side in battle and combat, but inflict defeat and heavy losses upon his army and scatter his forces!*[15]

The story-list-sanction pattern appears frequently in ancient texts, and modern persuasion also uses it. It is effective because it combines past, present, and future to persuade people to obey its instructions. First it tells a story to explain what led to the present circumstances. Then it lists a series of actions that must or must not be taken. Finally, it promises good results if its instructions are followed or disaster if they are ignored.

The Pentateuch uses this rhetorical strategy too, though on a much larger scale. The book of Deuteronomy divides clearly into the story-list-sanction outline. Moses recounts the story of Israel's journeys in the wilderness (Deut. 1–11) before repeating the lists of laws and instructions given by God on Mount Sinai (Deut. 12–26). He concludes by promising God's blessings if the Israelites obey the covenant and divine punishments if they do not (Deut. 27–30, 32–33).

A more complicated variation on this pattern also structures the entire Pentateuch. Genesis and the first half of Exodus tell the story of Israel's origins by God's actions starting from the creation of the world. The rest of Exodus, all of Leviticus, and much of Numbers present instructions for building the Tabernacle and for worshipping God in it, as well as moral, civil, and criminal rules for conducting Israel's community life. Deuteronomy as a whole can be viewed as delivering, in the voice of God's prophet, exhortations predicting future blessings or punishments depending on Israel's behavior.

Outline of the Pentateuch's rhetoric

At a very general level, the whole Pentateuch takes the shape of the story-list-sanction pattern:

1 Stories (Genesis 1–Exodus 19)
2 Lists (Exodus 20–Numbers)
3 Sanctions (Deuteronomy)

A closer look shows that the rhetoric moves back and forth between stories, lists, and sanctions even as the preponderance of stories at the beginning shifts to lists of laws and instructions and finally to sanctions as the Pentateuch progresses:

1 Stories of origins, including:
   - Where the world and nations came from (Genesis 1–11)
   - Where Israel's ancestors came from (Genesis 12–50)
   - Where Israel came from (Exodus 1–18, parts of Numbers)
   - Where Torah came from (Exodus 19–20, Deuteronomy 1–11, 31, 34)
   - Where Israel's Tabernacle came from (Exodus 32–40)
   - Where Israel's priests and rituals came from (Leviticus 8–10, parts of Numbers)

2 Lists of laws and instructions for the present (Exodus 20–23, 25–31, Leviticus, parts of Numbers, Deuteronomy 12–26)
3 Future sanctions for obedience or disobedience (Leviticus 26, Deuteronomy 27–30, 32–33)

Another way of summarizing the Pentateuch's story-list-sanction rhetoric is to say that it uses the *rhetoric of origins*, the *rhetoric of law*, and *the rhetoric of promise and threat* to persuade its hearers and readers to accept their identity as a people in covenant with God. The Pentateuch uses past, present, and future to urge readers and hearers to accept their identity as Israel.

The Rhetorical Effect of Inset Genres

The Torah's storyline encompasses collections of laws, lists of ritual instructions, collections of Tabernacle building instructions, and genealogies that together amount to more than half of the Pentateuch's total word count. Story-list-sanction rhetoric provided a conventional structure that its editors used to include long lists within a narrative framework.

The history of the Bible's reception shows that narratively inset genres tend to influence how the narratives around them get read. The frame genre of narrative prose does not lend its reading conventions to the inset genres. The inset genres instead lead readers to interpret the frame narrative by the inset genre's conventions. For example, the history of chanting and singing scriptural texts of all genres takes the performance conventions appropriate to songs and extends them to the prose stories contained in scriptures. We do not know when the practice of chanting the Torah's text began, but it is clear that editors of biblical books were already inserting psalms so their themes and performances would influence interpretation of the surrounding narratives. They used hymns to provide thematic emphasis as conclusions or brackets to narrative blocks (Exod. 15; Deut. 32; Judg. 5; 1 Sam. 2; 2 Sam. 22), which shows that singing the text was not just a post-biblical development. Biblical editors placed psalms within narratives in order to bring the pious enthusiasm of victory hymns to the reading of historiographic stories (despite some scholars' assumption that written psalmody diverted and degraded the piety of oral psalmody).[16]

That is also the case for laws and regulations spoken by God to Moses: their presence in the Pentateuch led to the entire five-book collection being read as law and as oracle. The history of the Pentateuch's interpretation in Jewish and Christian traditions shows clearly that the legal and instructional conventions of these inset genres spread to the surrounding narratives, not vice versa. The stories of Genesis, Exodus, and Numbers have been used to establish religious doctrines, ritual practices, and legal rulings throughout Jewish and Christian history. By contrast, narrative concerns for plot, theme, and characterization appear hardly at all in the history of interpretation until modern times. Of course, the two religious traditions differ dramatically in the value they place on Pentateuchal law. While legal interpretation (*halakhah*) based on Torah became fundamental in rabbinic Judaism and was already dominant in various Jewish groups of the late Second Temple period, Christians displaced Torah with Gospel and emphasized the stories of the Pentateuch more than its instructions and laws. The Christian canon subsumes the Pentateuch into a sweeping narrative history that runs all the way through the book of Nehemiah. But even Christians' preferred forms of interpretation for most of their religion's history did not focus on narrative plots in literary context, but instead applied typology and allegory to both stories and laws.

The Pentateuch's lists of ritual instructions generated its growing authority as scripture. The history of scripturalization in the Second Temple period shows clearly that the Pentateuch was scripturalized before the Prophets, despite the oracular nature of most prophetic books. It also shows that written Torah functioned normatively first as the ritual law of the Jerusalem temple. It was only gradually extended to social and criminal matters after the third century BCE. Of the three components of the story-list-sanction rhetorical convention, the rhetoric of lists requires more extensive analysis than it has received so far in order to understand the origins of Jewish and Christian scripture.

Rhetoric provides a useful way to understand the contents of the Pentateuch as a scripture because the Pentateuch has been extremely persuasive to Jews and Christians for 25 centuries. Yet the religious traditions differ in how they have applied its teachings. They have frequently changed how they understand it when their circumstances have changed. Rhetoric asks, "Who is trying to persuade whom of what by writing/reading/publishing the Pentateuch?" The answers change with every change of audience and context.

However, to introduce you to the Pentateuch, we need to start by surveying its contents. Rhetoric can provide an initial framework for understanding and organizing what you read there. Later chapters will complicate this summary by showing how this material has been understood differently by listeners and readers in different times and cultures.

The Rhetoric of Origins

The Pentateuch's stories, the first part of its story-list-sanction rhetorical pattern, take the form of a rhetoric of origins. The stories of Genesis took place in the distant past even for the Israelites led by Moses in the book of Exodus. All the stories of the Pentateuch took place in the distant past for the Judeans and Samaritans who began to use the Torah as scripture in the Persian period, and even more so for every generation of their Jewish and Christian successors. The stories tell of obligations incurred and commitments made by ancestors long ago. They do so to explain why their descendants and followers should obey the commandments and instructions contained in the Torah.

The Pentateuch's stories tell the origins of things in order to explain why its readers and hearers are obliged to do what God says. The stories of world creation and destruction (Gen. 1–11) establish human obligations to God as the provider of life, environment, food, and family. The stories of Israel's ancestors (Gen. 12–50) document a divine plan for Israel long before the people existed. Exodus grounds the origins of Israel as a people when God rescued them from Egypt (Exod. 1–18), before narrating their willing acceptance of a covenant obliging them and their descendants to obey God's rules (Exod. 19–20, 24). This contract between God and people included the plans for constructing Israel's tent sanctuary, the Tabernacle (Exod. 25–40), and for inaugurating its priestly hierarchy (Lev. 8–9). So the Pentateuch's rhetoric of origins credits God with creating Israel as a people and their religious institutions.

Law and narrative

The legal theorist Robert Cover argued that laws necessarily imply their story of origins, even when they do not state it: "No set of legal institutions or prescriptions exists apart from the narratives that locate it and give it meaning. For every constitution there is an epic, for each decalogue a scripture. Once understood in the context of the narratives that give it meaning, law becomes not merely a system of rules to be observed, but a world in which we live. In this normative world, law and narrative are inseparably related. Every prescription is insistent in its demand to be located in discourse – to be supplied with history and destiny, beginning and end, explanation and purpose. And every narrative is insistent in its demand for its prescriptive point, its moral."[17]

As good stories always do, the Pentateuch's stories establish convincing main characters. Besides all the individual characters, such as Abraham, Sarah, Jacob, Joseph, Moses, and Miriam, the Pentateuch's plot depends on the interaction of two main characters, God and Israel. God's creation of Israel and Israel's relationship with God form the fundamental theme and plot of the Pentateuch, and of the rest of the Hebrew Bible. In the following pages, I will summarize the plots and themes of the Pentateuch's stories, and I will also point out how they characterize God and Israel.

World origins: Genesis 1–11

The most famous stories in Genesis, about world creation and destruction by flood, emphasize a theme that is not so famous, about the world's moral decline from its good origins into widespread violence. God recognizes the world as good at its creation (Gen. 1:12, 18, 21, 25, 31). Subsequent chapters narrate stories of disobedience and punishment (Gen. 3), murder and exile (Gen. 4), widespread corruption and bloodshed leading to cataclysm (Gen. 6–8), and drunkenness leading to sexual depravity (9:20–28). Along the way, the stories attribute the development of civilization to the growth of evil. They credit the invention of cities, domestic animals, instrumental music, and metallurgy to the descendants of the murderous Cain (4:17–22). They culminate in the story of the tower of Babel, in which God frustrates the political ambitions of people who want to build grand cities famous for high towers (11:1–9). So Genesis begins by showing the growth of civilization not as progress or advance, but rather as corrupting a good creation. These stories set the scene for the rest of the Pentateuch, which shows how God addressed these problems by creating a new people, Israel.

The opening chapters of Genesis depict the main character, God, in diverse ways that have stimulated many theories about the book's composition (see Chapter 5). The creation stories show God first as transcendent, systematically commanding the universe into existence without conflicts or problems of any kind (Gen. 1), and then as anthropomorphic, molding the human male out of mud and the human female from the male's rib, and taking evening walks in the cool garden (Gen. 2–3). God also seems moody: the spirit of God broods over the chaos before creation (1:2) and God worries about human evil and violence (6:5–7, 11–13). God even expresses anxiety about humans' desire for knowledge and eternal life (3:22) and about their political ambitions (11:6).

In these chapters, God can be experimental, creating animals to see if the human male will find a companion among them (Gen. 2:18–20) and planting a prohibited tree in the garden to see if the humans will avoid its fruit, as they are commanded to do (2:9, 17). In the face of human evil, God can be alternately patient (by exiling and protecting Cain rather than killing him in 4:14–15) and punitive (by flooding the earth in 6:7 and by confusing human languages in 11:7–9), and sometimes both simultaneously (by exiling humans from the garden while clothing them in skins in 3:21–24 and by destroying human and animal life while saving Noah's family and animals in the ark in chapters 6–8). The rest of the Pentateuch's stories develop and organize these elements of the divine character at greater length. It is the Pentateuch's lists of laws that finally present

YHWH as a God of justice and mercy (Exod. 34:6–7) – the classical characterization of God that echoes in later Jewish and Christian liturgies.

Ancestral origins: Genesis 12–50

The contents of Genesis 12–50 are united and structured by a concern with ancestry and descent. God's promises to Israel's ancestors punctuate the stories about them. The stories about Abraham begin with the three-part promise of a land, of descendants ("a great nation"), and that "you will be a blessing" (Gen. 12:1–3). Genesis does not define this blessing much beyond its initial description (similarly, 22:17–18). It specifies the land grant as stretching "from the river of Egypt to the Euphrates" (15:18) or simply as "Canaan" (17:8). Most of its stories focus on the promise of descendants to Abraham.

Family sets the common theme for Genesis 12–50 and also its literary structure. Genealogies, Hebrew *toledot* "descendants" or "generations," introduce the stories by listing the families that do not inherit God's promises before listing those who do. The stories of three generations follow these genealogical introductions (see Box, "Genealogies in Genesis"). The stories therefore fall into collections focused on Abraham (Gen. 12–25), his grandson Jacob (Gen. 25–35), and his great-grandson Joseph (Gen. 36–50).

Genealogies in Genesis

Other descendants	Divinely favored descendants
Cain's 4:17–24	Seth's 5:1–32
Ham's and Japhet's 10:1–32	Shem's 10:21–31; 11:10–30
Ishmael's 25:12–18	Isaac's 25:19–26
Esau's 36:1–43	Jacob's 37:2; also 35:22–26

Outlining Genesis by the names of major male characters accurately reflects the patriarchal emphasis of these stories. Genealogical structure reinforces patriarchy by emphasizing descent from fathers to sons. But it obscures the fact that many of these stories, especially in the Abraham and Jacob cycles, give significant roles to female characters (as do Gen. 3, Exod. 1–2, and Num. 12). Genesis tells more stories about women than most other biblical books. Nevertheless, the stories of Sarah (Gen. 16–18, 20–21), Hagar (Gen. 16, 21), Rebekah (Gen. 24–27), and Tamar (Gen. 38) revolve around children or their lack of children, specifically male heirs. Feminist critics have rightly seen the need to imaginatively "counter-read" these women's stories as women might have told them themselves, rather than as they are told to meet the patriarchal needs of patrilineal descent.

Almost unique in this regard is the story of the first woman, Eve. Her words and actions drive the plot of Genesis 3 and do not involve motherhood or children (see further discussion in Chapter 5). Her future role as mother is mentioned only once, near the end as part of her punishment (Gen. 3:16), and only then does the man name her Eve, "the mother of all living" (3:20). The next chapter begins with the birth of her sons, Cain and Abel (4:1–2) and concludes with genealogies of the descendants of Cain and of Eve's third son, Seth (4:17–5:32), but mentions no daughters of Eve.

The Pentateuch depicts the ancestral period as a golden age marked by close, even intimate, relationships between God and some humans. The ancestral stories take place in a world without religious conflicts. Abraham can invite YHWH (or YHWH's angels – the difference is not very clear) to dinner and argue with God over how to punish those who offend God (Gen. 18:23–33). Jacob can literally wrestle with God and limp as a result (32:22–32). Both Abraham's family and neighboring peoples interact with the same God, who even speaks to Egyptian and Philistine kings in dreams (20:6–7; 41:16). Occasional notices of polytheistic practices (31:34–35; 35:2–4) pass with little comment and no controversy. This religious setting stands in sharp contrast to the other books of the Pentateuch in which conflicts over the status of gods and over rituals feature heavily in the plot.

Many cultures around the eastern Mediterranean and Middle East in the first millennium BCE remembered the preceding (second) millennium as a golden age better than their own. Their stories featured larger-than-life Bronze Age heroes – Gilgamesh in Babylon, Ptahhotep in Egypt, and Achilles, Odysseus, and Theseus in Greece. Their kings sometimes chose the names of legendary second-millennium kings as their own throne names, such as Sargon and Nebuchadnezzar. In Egypt and Mesopotamia, they sometimes tried to revive and preserve ancient patterns of architecture and literature – as exemplified by Kings Nebuchadnezzar and Nabonidus in Babylon and by the kings of the Egyptian twenty-sixth dynasty.

Genesis similarly portrays a time that it marks off as religiously different from the time of the exodus as well as of the Pentateuch's readers. It is a time when Israel's ancestors enjoyed special relationships with God. These relationships characterize YHWH as "the God of Abraham, Isaac and Jacob" (Exod. 3:6, 15–16; 6:3). Their memory can persuade YHWH to act on behalf of their descendants (Exod. 2:24; 6:8; 32:13; Lev. 26:42; Deut. 1:8; 34:4).[18]

Figure 2.1 Barrel cylinder with a cuneiform inscription of Nebuchadnezzar II, King of Babylon from 605 to 562 BCE, to celebrate the discovery of a temple foundation inscription of Naram-Sin, King of Akkad, 1,700 years earlier. In the Israel Museum, Jerusalem.

Apart from this religious setting and periodic mention of the divine promises, the cycles of stories in Genesis differ from one another (and sometimes even within cycles) in theme, in narrative style, and in their portrayal of the major characters, including God.

The Abraham stories (Gen. 12–25) are a loosely connected cycle of independent episodes. Many of them revolve around the issue of Abraham's heir, or rather his lack of one. Despite YHWH's promise right at the start of the cycle (12:2) that Abraham will have many descendants, Abraham and Sarah grow old and still have no son. They attempt to arrange for other heirs, such as Abraham's slave Eliezer (15:2–3) or Ishmael, the son of their slave, Hagar (16:1–16; 17:18). But God insists that only a son of Sarah will inherit the divine promises to Abraham (15:4; 17:19). After Genesis finally narrates the birth of that son, Isaac (21:1–8), God commands Abraham to sacrifice Isaac, and Abraham tries to do so (22:1–19). The theme of Abraham's missing or endangered heir provides these varied stories with a narrative trajectory.

The Abraham stories present an anthropomorphic characterization of God. Whether called by the divine designation "God" (Hebrew *'Elohim*) or the personal name, *YHWH* (replaced by "the LORD" in Jewish reading tradition and in English Bibles), the deity is an active character in these stories. God intervenes in the plot to punish misbehaving kings (Gen. 12:17; 20:3–18) and cities (19:24–29). God talks directly and frequently with Abraham, visits him for dinner, and tolerates Abraham's negotiations on behalf of the cities of Sodom and Gomorrah (18:1–33). Other texts remark on this extraordinary relationship by calling Abraham God's "friend" (Isa. 41:8; 2 Chr. 20:7). The Abraham stories portray God with many human qualities, though of course also possessing superhuman knowledge and power. The other cycles of ancestral stories portray God rather differently.

Abraham's son, Isaac, does not feature in many stories of his own, but rather in stories about his father or his son. Even the story of how his marriage was arranged (Gen. 24) features Abraham's slave and Rebekah, Isaac's future wife, as main characters rather than Isaac himself.

The cycle of stories that revolve around Jacob (Gen. 25–35) form a more cohesive plot. Now there are too many heirs claiming the divine promises. The story begins with several conflicts between the twin brothers, Esau and Jacob (Gen. 25–28), then continues with Jacob's life story as he competes also with his uncle, Laban (Gen. 29–31), and finally with a man who turns out to be God (32:24–32). This last episode results in Jacob's name being changed to "Israel," which is interpreted as meaning "one who fights with God and humans, and wins" (32:28). These stories characterize Jacob as a competitive trickster. Their rhetoric of ancestral origins does not necessarily recommend the ancestors as models of morality. Nevertheless, the Hebrew Bible uses Jacob's new name for all of his descendants, "the children of Israel."

The stories about Jacob characterize God more mysteriously than did the Abraham stories. God appears in dreams (Gen. 28:11–17) and night visions (32:24–32) rather than speaking directly to Jacob. These experiences cast God in the role of Jacob's protector and also his adversary. In return, Jacob places conditions on his loyalty to God (28:20–22). Though Jacob received the honor of being the eponymous ancestor of Israel, his relationship with God is not as friendly as Abraham's.

The stories about Joseph (Gen. 36–37, 39–50) form a single narrative with a tight plot – a marked contrast in style and composition with earlier parts of Genesis. With the single exception of Genesis 38's focus on Judah, these chapters follow Joseph from his boyhood as Jacob's favorite and pampered son through his brothers' betrayal of him to slave traders and his up-and-down career in Egypt until he rises to the very top of the Egyptian bureaucracy. His wisdom in managing Egypt's agricultural economy leads to a reunion with his brothers and, eventually, with his father when a famine drives them to Egypt in search of grain. The issue of who will inherit the divine promises that provided the theme to the Abraham and Jacob stories does not reappear in the Joseph cycle: these stories presuppose that all 12 brothers will inherit equally. The position of the Joseph stories at the end of Genesis seems to be motivated by the need to explain Israel's residence in Egypt as the setting for the exodus story that follows.

Eponymous ancestry in Genesis

Eponymous ancestry describes the practice of naming a group of people by the name of a common ancestor. Jacob is not the only character in Genesis to lend his name to his descendants. Moab and Ben-Ammi, the sons of Lot, become eponymous ancestors to Israel's eastern neighbors, the Moabites and the Ammonites (Gen. 19:37–38). And, of course, the sons of Jacob and two of his grandsons lend their names to the tribes of Israelites: Reuben, Simeon, Levi, Judah, Issachar, Zebulun, Dan, Naphtali, Gad, Asher, Benjamin, and the two tribes descended from Joseph's sons, Ephraim and Manasseh.

Apart from this contribution to the geographic route of the Pentateuch's plot from Mesopotamia to Canaan, then to Egypt and back again to Canaan, the Joseph story is driven by its own internal logic and themes. Central among them is the theme of God's control over the course of events. Unlike other parts of Genesis, the Joseph stories do not show God talking with Joseph or intervening personally in events. All the action seems motivated by human behavior and intentions. Joseph, however, interprets dreams and his own life story as governed by divine intention. He tells his brothers that "it was not you who sent me here, but God" (Gen 45:8). So rather than the anthropomorphic supernatural friend of Abraham, Joseph's God is transcendent, like a director who controls the action behind the scenes without ever stepping on stage.

The rhetoric of ancestral origins in Genesis provides the background for understanding the following books. It justifies Israel's claim to a "promised land" on the basis of a divine grant to Israel's ancestors (Gen. 12, 15, 35), but it qualifies that grant by requiring obedience to divine commandments (Gen. 15, 17, 22). Though it defines the Israelites as descendants of Jacob/Israel, it broadens Israel's ethnic identity by including in Abraham's family tree the Arameans (Gen. 28:5), the Moabites (19:37), the Ammonites (19:38), the Edomites (36:1), and desert tribes later identified as Arabs (17:20; 25:12–18), and by marriage to the Canaanites (38:2) and Egyptians (41:45, 50–52; 46:20).

Nevertheless, Genesis depicts Israel as something new, an ethnic identity defined by loyalty to covenants with God. This covenant identity must be accepted anew by future generations (Exod. 24; Deuteronomy). So Genesis maintains that both possession of the land and ethnic identity depend on the people's relationship with God. And it shows God interacting with them in a wide variety of ways, ranging from Abraham's friendly relationship through Jacob's struggles to Joseph's intellectual interpretation of God's control over his life. It foreshadows the stories of tumultuous divine–human relationships in the following books by telling stories about Jacob/Israel, the eponymous ancestor of the Israelites.

Israel's origins: Exodus 1–18

The story of the Israelites' departure ("exodus") from Egypt is *the* defining story for the identity of Israel and for Judaism. It tells how God established Israel as a people by rescuing their ancestors from oppression. That rescue gives their descendants reason to accept the obligations of the covenant with God. It also establishes a major new aspect of God's character.

Exodus begins in the same place that Genesis ends, the land of Egypt. For ancient readers and listeners just as for moderns, the name "Egypt" evoked images of great wealth, god-like kings, and great antiquity. The pyramids at Giza were already 1,000 years old by the time this story takes place.

However, the golden age of Genesis is over. Exodus portrays religious conflicts between Israel and the Egyptians and within the Israelite community. Moses presents demands from a new god, or at least God using a new name, YHWH. The Egyptian king, Pharaoh, does not recognize this god and refuses Moses's demands (Exod. 5:2). The Israelites question whether Moses speaks for God (5:21; 6:9) and whether either God or Moses can take care of them (14:11–12; chapters 16–17). The story of God's plagues on the Egyptians that enable Israel to escape into the wilderness establish YHWH's ability and willingness to fight for the Israelites against their wealthy and powerful enemies.[19]

Knowledge of YHWH and of YHWH's power is a central theme in the exodus story. God reveals a new name to Moses: YHWH (Exod. 3:14–15; 6:3). The cryptic explanation of its meaning, "I am who I am," does not diminish Moses's concern that the Israelites will doubt that he brings messages from God. He is right: they do not believe him and neither does Pharaoh. Establishing the reputation of YHWH as the God who rescued Israel from Egypt then becomes a major motive for God bringing 10 plagues on the Egyptians.

The story begins with Egypt subjecting the Israelites to forced labor (Exod. 1). Their dramatic change of circumstances since the end of Genesis is explained by the rise of "a new king" and the Israelites' rapidly growing population (1:7–10). The story of Moses's amazing rescue as a baby (2:1–10) uses ancient literary conventions to emphasize his future importance (see Box, "The birth legend of King Sargon," on p. 247). Exodus raises expectations for Moses's future further by narrating his encounter with

YHWH's reputation in Exodus

"I will take you as my people and I will be your God. You will know that I am YHWH your God who rescued you from forced labor in Egypt" (6:7).

"The Egyptians will know that I am YHWH when I stretch out my hand against Egypt and rescue the Israelites from among them" (7:5).

"... so that you (Pharaoh) will know that I, YHWH, am in the land" (8:22).

"... so that you (Pharaoh) will see my power and so that my fame will echo through the whole land" (9:16).

"I have hardened Pharaoh's heart and his officials' hearts so that I can do these signs among them, in order that you can tell your children and grandchildren how I tricked the Egyptians and what signs I did among them so that you will know that I am YHWH" (10:1–2).

"You shall tell your children (when you eat unleavened bread at Passover) 'It is because of what YHWH did for me when I came out of Egypt' ... for with a strong hand YHWH rescued you from Egypt" (13:8–9; see also 13:14–16).

"I will harden Pharaoh's heart so he will pursue them. Then I will magnify myself at the expense of Pharaoh and his entire army, so the Egyptians will know that I am YHWH" (14:4; see also 14:17–18).

Then Israel saw the mighty hand that YHWH used against the Egyptians. They were in awe of YHWH and they believed in YHWH and his servant Moses (14:31).

God in the burning bush (Exod. 3–4). The dialogue uses the conventions of prophetic call narratives (cf. Jer. 1 and Isa. 6) to establish Moses's identity as a true prophet.

The story of God's plagues on the Egyptians in Exodus 7–12 takes an unusual amount of space. Hebrew stories tend to be short and cryptic. For example, Exodus 2 narrates the stories of Moses's birth, rescue from the river, adoption by an Egyptian princess, growing to manhood, murder of a slave driver, and flight into the wilderness all in 22 verses or sentences. By contrast, the narrator lingers over the 10 plagues, describing the negotiations before and after each one and detailing the enormous suffering of the Egyptians. So it is not just the Egyptians and Israelites who need to recognize the power of YHWH: this repetitive story wants readers and listeners to feel God's overwhelming power and control. As the story progresses, even the king of Egypt is changed from a dangerous opponent into a puppet in God's hands: YHWH makes Pharaoh stubborn ("hardens Pharaoh's heart") to make sure that all 10 plagues occur (Exod. 9:12; 10:20; 14:4, 8). The land, the people, and the king of Egypt are under the control of the God of Israel.

The purpose of this demonstration of divine power becomes clear once the Israelites reach Mount Sinai. God tells them through Moses:

> *You yourselves have seen what I did to the Egyptians and how I carried you on eagles' wings and brought you to myself. Now, if you listen to my voice and keep my covenant, you will be my treasured possession out of all the peoples. The whole world is mine, but you will be a kingdom of priests for me and a holy nation* (Exod. 19:4–6).

God claims "possession" of Israel by right of conquest. Though the whole world and all its inhabitants belong to God from creation (Gen. 1), YHWH takes Israel away from Egypt like a king claiming territory by military force. And like a conquering king, YHWH now offers Israel a covenant of continuing protection in return for their loyalty.

The covenant at Mount Sinai is modeled on ancient political treaties between emperors and the rulers of cities or small territories. The local rulers became vassals of the emperor and promised to remain loyal to him and his successors, to pay taxes, and to supply the imperial army with troops. The emperor promised protection to the vassal from other enemies, and from himself: these treaties were usually negotiated when the imperial army had either already conquered or was threatening to conquer the city (see Chapter 5).

In the exodus story, it is not territory but a people that God takes away from Egypt by force. Now that the Israelites have witnessed YHWH's power over a foreign enemy, God asks them to become YHWH's vassals. They must remain loyal ("no other gods before me" Exod. 20:3) and they must obey God's commandments, including making regular offerings at the sanctuary. In return, YHWH promises economic prosperity and protection from their enemies. Through the covenant, God becomes Israel's king.

The story of Israel's exodus from Egypt mixes together characterizations of God that are distinct in different parts of Genesis. In the plague stories, Exodus depicts YHWH as miraculous and mysterious, both transcendent and immediately responsive to Moses and the other human actors. YHWH speaks directly and intimately with Moses, as with Abraham. At Moses's death, Deut. 34:10 celebrates Moses's relationship to God as uniquely close: "Never again was there a prophet in Israel like Moses, whom YHWH knew face to face." But the Israelites fight with God like Jacob did, to the point that the generation who participated in the Exodus fails to believe that YHWH can conquer Canaan for them. They die in the wilderness as punishment for their lack of loyalty to their divine king. God in this story, as in the Joseph story, completely controls the course of events, including the Egyptian king. But unlike the Joseph story, here God acts directly and decisively. As in earlier parts of Genesis, God is the protagonist who propels the exodus story's plot.

The Pentateuch's unstated premise and enthymeme

If Exodus portrays God as a conquering king, why does it never call YHWH a "king"? Aristotle pointed out that rhetorical arguments usually presuppose common beliefs which they leave unstated. In such an *enthymeme*, the unstated premise unites speaker and audience in an implicit understanding. It makes the speech more persuasive without drawing attention to any problems with the premise.

The Torah's most general enthymemic argument presupposes the imperial ideology of ancient Middle Eastern kingship:

Stated premises: YHWH saved Israel from Egypt and Israel accepted the covenant with YHWH at Sinai.

Unstated premise: Military rescue and subsequent covenant/treaty establish royal authority over vassals and their descendants.

Conclusion: Israel owes YHWH loyalty (stated), because YHWH is Israel's king (unstated except in poetry).

That explains why Pentateuchal stories and instructions do not call God "king." Only some inset poems do (Num. 23:21; Deut. 33:5; cf. Exod. 15:18) just as the psalms often do (Pss. 44:4, 93:1–4, 95:3, etc.). 1 Samuel 8 shows Israelites later arguing over whether God's kingship allows for a human king or not. This story illustrates the conflicts that can arise from exposing the premise of God's kingship to explicit discussion. The Pentateuch leaves God's kingship unstated while showing God performing royal duties by defending Israel against enemy armies, giving laws, and establishing the Tabernacle and its rituals. This unstated premise motivates the Pentateuch's argument that Israel owes God obedience without engaging the political consequences of having a divine ruler.[20]

The Torah's origins: Exodus 19–24 and 32–34

The ceremony of covenant making at Mount Sinai involves elaborate preparations (Exod. 19) to protect the Israelites from God's immediate presence on the mountain. Then God speaks directly to the Israelites (20:1).[21] God self-identifies as "YHWH your God who brought you from Egypt, out of slavery" before speaking the Ten Commandments (20:2–17). But it is not clear whether the Israelites hear God's words or only loud sounds when they witness the lightening and smoke on the mountain (20:18). This experience overwhelms them so much that, from this point on, they ask Moses to listen to YHWH and then repeat the divine messages to them second hand (20:19–21).

Moses listens to the details of the covenant, a collection of instructions and laws which is usually called "the Covenant Code" (Exod. 20:22–23:33). The covenant between YHWH and Israel is then ratified in Exodus 24. Moses repeats to the Israelites everything YHWH said and they agree to follow God's laws (24:3). Moses then writes down the laws (24:4). He conducts a ritual of covenant ratification that includes making animal offerings and reading the law book aloud (24:5–7). After the Israelites again proclaim their willingness to obey the covenant, Moses sprays them with blood from the offerings (24:7–8). Then the elders climb the mountain with Moses where they "see God" and eat a ritual meal (24:9–11). That concludes the ritual of covenant making on that day. But then YHWH calls Moses to climb the mountain again, promising to give Moses stone tablets upon which God has written the laws (24:12).

This time, Moses spends 40 days on the mountain (Exod. 24:18) listening to YHWH's instructions for how to build a tent sanctuary, the Tabernacle (Exod. 25–31). When he finally comes down carrying "the two tablets of the covenant, stone tablets written by the finger of God" (31:18, also 32:15–16), Moses finds the camp in disarray. Because of his long absence, the Israelites think he is dead. They ask Aaron, Moses's brother and priest, to make a statue of a golden calf to represent "your gods who brought you out of Egypt" and they celebrate a festival around it (32:1–7). YHWH is furious and threatens to destroy the Israelites and replace them with Moses's descendants (32:10). Moses intercedes for the Israelites by arguing that their obliteration will ruin YHWH's reputation and by appealing to the memory of Abraham, Isaac, and Jacob (32:12–13). God relents, so Moses himself deals with the disloyal Israelites and, in his anger, breaks the tablets of the commandments (32:19). He burns and grinds up the golden calf and then makes the Israelites drink it (32:20). He then leads loyal

Levites in killing thousands of Israelites, and YHWH also sends a plague on them (32:28, 35).

The golden calf story became the paradigmatic example of idol worship in later Jewish and Christian interpretation. But Exodus itself emphasizes the sin of idolatry less (explicitly only in 34:17) than it does conflicting claims about who gets credit for freeing Israel from Egypt (32:1, 7, 8, 11, 12, 23; 33:1). As a result of this incident, YHWH refuses to accompany Israel further on the journey, saying that only an angel will lead the people (32:34; 33:2–3). The separation between God and Israel is represented in 33:7–11 by the fact that Moses must meet God in a tent pitched outside the camp. That position contrasts dramatically with the preceding instructions for making a tent in which God can live "among" the Israelites (25:8). Moses, however, succeeds in changing YHWH's mind about going with Israel (33:12–17). His persistence is rewarded by being shown YHWH's "glory" or "magnificence" on Mount Sinai (33:19–23). YHWH now agrees to go with Israel (33:14, 17) and to fight Israel's battles personally (34:10–11). God presents a new summary of the commandments (34:12–26), and rewrites the commandments on a new set of stone tablets (34:1, 27–28).

The story of the golden calf creates narrative suspense and intrigue between the giving of the Tabernacle instructions (Exod. 25–31) and their fulfillment (Exod. 35–40). By placing a story of betrayal and punishment in the middle of this account of successful sanctuary building, it enhances the sense of closure when God inhabits the completed Tabernacle (Exod. 40), when Moses ordains Aaron and his sons as priests (Lev. 8), and when they inaugurate the Tabernacle service (Lev. 9). By including the golden calf story, the Tabernacle account has a creation/fall/restoration plot that echoes themes elsewhere in the Pentateuch, such as the creation and flood stories in Genesis 1–9.

The sanctuary's origins: Exodus 25–40

The dominance of narratives in the first third of the Pentateuch gives way to more and more lists in the latter half of Exodus. The Ten Commandments and Covenant Code are discussed under "the Rhetoric of Law," below. But the material having to do with building the Tabernacle contains a unique combination of story and list. It begins with a very detailed list of instructions for constructing the tent, its furnishings, and the priests' clothing (Exod. 25–31). After the golden calf story comes an equally detailed list-like narrative telling how Moses and the Israelites completed that work (Exod. 35–40). Though the latter books of the Pentateuch are full of ritual instructions, this meticulous account of their fulfillment is almost unique. Only Leviticus 8–9 comes close.

Such attention is warranted by the importance of temples in ancient Israel, and in the religious practices of ancient Middle Eastern and Mediterranean cultures generally. Unlike the buildings housing a synagogue, a church, or a mosque, which basically serve as assembly halls to gather a congregation for worship and prayer, ancient temples were more like shrines. They were built on religiously significant locations, holy places, that were associated with particular miracles or revelations believed to have occurred there. They were regarded as the residences of the gods. Temples on such holy places were regarded as places of power, even as the center of the world. People came there, often from great distances, to make offerings to those particular gods and to pray for their protection and aid. In the context of Israel's covenant with YHWH, temple offerings also demonstrated loyalty, just as paying taxes demonstrated a vassal's loyalty to a political overlord.

Michael Hundley observed that the Pentateuch's explanations for ritual behavior become fewer and more ambiguous the closer they get to YHWH in the inner sanctum of the Tabernacle. Exodus presents a more transcendent and mysterious alternative to the cults of other ancient cultures. For example, where other cultures identify and celebrate the arrival of deities into their temples with ritual processions of the gods' statues, Exodus depicts YHWH arriving and acting in a cloud (Exod. 40:34–38) that leads the movements of the Ark of the Covenant and the Tabernacle rather than following them (Num. 9:15–23). Exodus and Leviticus therefore offer few symbolic explanations for the rituals. Their mystery enhances their persuasive power for ancient Jews and Samaritans worshipping in the temples of YHWH. The text's rhetoric aims to ensure that listeners and readers will agree that the rituals are necessary even if they disagree about what they mean.

Modern readers usually find the Tabernacle texts repetitive and boring, but ancient readers and hearers probably found them exciting and inspirational. It was typical for ancient myths and creation stories to conclude with the building of a temple. By doing so, they connected stories about gods in heaven or in the distant past with the existing sanctuary that people could see for themselves. The book of Exodus, or Genesis-Exodus together, reproduces this pattern. Mark Smith observed that the book takes the reader on a virtual pilgrimage from Egypt to Sinai and then on a double tour around the Tabernacle, as if the pilgrim circled the sanctuary twice at the end of the journey.[22]

Exodus's description of the Tabernacle, however, did not match later Israelite temples very well. In the time of Ezra in the Second Temple period, or even in the time of the kingdoms of Israel and Judah, Israelites worshipped in stone temples. The tent Tabernacle, then, did not correspond to the temples known to the first readers and hearers of this story. The instructions and account of building the Tabernacle instead present an idealized prototype for Israel's later temples. Even when these accounts were first written, their writers, readers, and hearers already had to think about how these instructions must be modified to fit the different conditions prevailing in their own time.

Perhaps that is why Exodus 35–40 present Moses's fulfillment of the instructions in such detail. This account assures readers and hearers that the instructions were *once* fulfilled literally. To what degree and in what way they should be fulfilled in their own day was already a matter for interpretation and debate, even before the Torah began to function as a scripture. Unlike the rhetoric of law that clearly intends its instructions to be followed in the present, the Tabernacle texts depict this sanctuary as an institution of Israel's past. Its provisions must be modified to fit present circumstances. That task requires ritual expertise, so the Pentateuch matches the story of the origins of the sanctuary with an account of the origins of Israel's divinely ordained priests.

The origins of religious hierarchy: Leviticus 8–10 and Numbers 11–18

Once the Tabernacle is finished, Moses consecrates Aaron and his sons to serve as its priests. In close compliance with the instructions of Exodus 29, Moses clothes the priests and anoints them with oil and the blood of offerings (Lev. 8) at the same time that he anoints the altar and the Tabernacle. So both priests and Tabernacle are consecrated, that is, made holy for YHWH. Then Aaron proceeds to inaugurate the regular rituals of the Tabernacle (Lev. 9), as they have been mandated in the preceding instructions of Leviticus 1–7 and elsewhere in the Pentateuch. YHWH dramatically validates these rituals by sending a fire bolt out of the Tabernacle to consume the offerings on the courtyard altar (9:24).

Leviticus 8–9 thus concludes a plot arc that began in Genesis 3 with God driving Adam and Eve out of the Garden of Eden because of their disobedience. The Pentateuch narrates the separation of humans from God in Genesis 1–11. It then tells of God's painstaking efforts to establish a new relationship with part of humanity by creating a people from the descendants of Abraham (Gen. 12–50), rescuing them from forced labor in Egypt (Exod. 1–18), establishing a covenant relationship with the Israelites that made YHWH their king (Exod. 19–24), and creating a residence and rituals to enable God to reside among them (Exod. 25–40, Lev. 1–9). With the inauguration of the Tabernacle, its priesthood, and its rituals, the conditions have been established to enable God to live with Israel despite human sin and impurity. The Tabernacle's offering rituals enable sins to be forgiven and impurities to be cleaned, so that humans need not be driven out of God's presence again.

That happy conclusion depends, however, on the rituals being conducted correctly. Leviticus 10 immediately illustrates the consequences if they are not. Nadab and Abihu, Aaron's sons and consecrated priests, do something wrong with an incense offering and are immediately burned to death by YHWH (Lev. 10:1–2). This sudden reversal is emphasized by the fact that they die by the same kind of fire bolt that lit up the altar in celebration in 9:24.

The story does not explain what the priests did wrong, only that they did something "that YHWH did not command them." After narrating Moses's and Aaron's meticulous fulfillment of divine commandments in Leviticus 8–9, that is enough to justify their death sentence. But this story raises the question of how to know whether these vital rituals are being performed correctly. No instructions, no matter how detailed, can anticipate every possible problem and situation that might confront their performance. Laws and instructions always require interpretation to apply them in new circumstances.

The rest of Leviticus 10 resolves this problem by emphasizing the authority of Aaronide priests to decide ambiguous questions of ritual practice. First, YHWH speaks to Aaron directly (not through Moses!) and grants Aaron and his descendants the authority to distinguish two vital ritual categories, holiness and pollution, from their opposites (Lev. 10:10). God also grants them the authority to teach Torah to the Israelites (10:11). So the priests receive a divine commission to arbitrate and teach correct religious practice. Then the chapter shows this authority in action. Moses objects to how Aaron's remaining two sons have dealt with one of the offerings (10:16–18). Aaron, however, defends the priests' interpretation of how to conduct the ritual (10:19). As was the case with the ritual problem in 10:1, the problem is not clear, nor is Aaron's reasoning, but that does not matter. Aaron is now armed with divinely given authority to determine correct ritual practice, and even Moses must concede to his authority (10:20). So Aaron's remaining sons suffer no consequences for their actions.

Priestly (in)competence and priestly authority in Leviticus 10

The sons of Aaron, Nadab and Abihu, each took his pan and put fire in it and put incense on top of it and they presented other fire before YHWH, that YHWH did not command them. Then fire came out from before YHWH and consumed them, and they died before YHWH. Moses spoke to Aaron: "This is what YHWH said: I am sanctified by those present with me so that I am glorified before all the people." Aaron was dumbfounded. (10:1–3) ... *YHWH spoke to Aaron: "... This is a permanent mandate throughout your generations: to separate the holy from the secular and the polluted from the pure, and to teach the children of Israel all the mandates that YHWH spoke to them through Moses."* (10:8–11) ... *Then Moses made inquiries about the sin offering goat. It had been burned up! He became angry with Eleazar and Ithamar, the remaining sons of Aaron.* (10:16) ... *Aaron spoke to Moses: "See today they presented their sin offering and rising offering before YHWH, yet these things happened to me! If I eat a sin offering today, how can it look good to YHWH?" Moses listened, and now it looked good to him.* (10:19–20)

Leviticus 10 thus raises and assuages concerns over correct ritual conduct by emphasizing the Aaronide priests' authority to determine correct practice. Leviticus 8–10 sits at the center of the Pentateuch's rhetoric of priestly hierarchy that spans Exodus 25 through Leviticus and Numbers, and also echoes more faintly in Deuteronomy. It justifies the male descendants of Aaron in exercising a monopoly over the priesthood on the basis of their divinely granted authority. They have the power to determine correct ritual practice, they control the most important rituals, and they have the authority to teach the Israelites how to practice correctly as well. The Torah's mix of moral, criminal, and civil laws, along with its ritual instructions, means that the priests' teaching extends to these other subjects as well. Village elders, tribal leaders, and even kings, if and when they exist at all (the Pentateuch's laws mention an Israelite king only once, in Deut. 17:14–20), all come under the priests' ritual authority. The Pentateuch places the family of Aaron at the pinnacle of the only hierarchy that it recognizes in Israel. And it names these priests as the official interpreters of Torah – in other words, of itself.

This monopoly over religious leadership could well be resented by other Israelites. That possibility is acknowledged by stories in the book of Numbers that reassert Aaronide prerogatives nonetheless. The people's complaints about their living conditions, which were addressed positively in Exodus 16–18, are now met by brutal punishments (Num. 11). Moses becomes worn out by the burdens of leadership and delegates routine tasks to a group of elders (11:11–17, 24–30). But when his brother and sister, Aaron and Miriam, try to claim the ability to speak for God like Moses, YHWH settles the issue in Moses's favor by punishing Miriam (but not the priest, Aaron). This story makes explicit a claim that structures the entire Pentateuch: God's laws for Israel come only through Moses. The ability of other prophets (represented by Miriam) and priests (Aaron) to interpret these laws does not extend to presenting the laws in the first place, as Moses does.

YHWH suppresses other challenges to the leadership of Moses, or of Moses and Aaron, much more severely. First, the Israelites refuse to invade the land of Canaan out of fear of its inhabitants (Num. 13–14). They propose to "choose a captain" to lead them back to Egypt. Moses must prevent God from killing the Israelites on the spot by appealing to YHWH's reputation. Instead, the entire generation is condemned to die landless in the wilderness. Then, 250 leading men challenge Moses's and Aaron's leadership (Num. 16–17). They point out that "the whole congregation is holy and YHWH is living among them" (16:3), which quotes YHWH correctly (Exod. 19:4) and refers to God's residence in the Tabernacle. They challenge both Moses's leadership of Israel as a whole (Num. 16:13–14) and also the Aaronides' elevation above the rest of the Levites (16:11). The ground opens up and swallows many of the rebels and the rest die from fire bolts from the Tabernacle (16:31–35). Only Aaron's intercession by incense offering saves the whole camp from dying of plague (16:47–49). As a final demonstration of Aaron's divine right to the priesthood, YHWH causes his walking staff to flower (Num. 17). The staff gets stored with the Ark of the Covenant as a permanent "warning to rebels."

Adriane Leveen pointed out that cultural memory fuels both sides of the leadership conflicts in Numbers. The memory of Egypt instigates rebellions against Moses and Aaron that dominate the narratives of Numbers 11–17. This counter-memory of rich and plentiful Egyptian food contradicts the exodus story of freedom from forced labor and leads to political challenges against Moses's and Aaron's leadership. The priestly writers admit in these stories that their claims to an Aaronide monopoly over priesthood are contentious. But they use that admission to create cautionary tales to discourage rebellion. They use the theme of memory to construct a polemical object lesson. The rebellion stories reinforce this lesson with reminders in the form of ritual objects: the tassels worn by every Israelite (Num. 15:37–41), the plates visible on the sanctuary altar (16:36–40), and Aaron's rod enshrined before the Ark of the Covenant (17:10).

Numbers, then, does not just depend on the narration of these stories to teach its lessons of priestly authority. It mandates that they be ritualized in everyday clothing and the sanctuary's furnishings as constant reminders of the fate of the generation that rebelled against Mosaic and priestly authority in the wilderness. That fate is also underlined by the way Numbers treats the deaths of the wilderness generation: the people bury and mourn earlier fatalities and Miriam and Aaron (Num. 11:34; 20:1, 22–27), but Numbers mentions no burials for those who rebel against Moses and Aaron (16:49–50).[23]

The rhetoric of origins usually requires readers and hearers to translate it for present circumstances. The application of ancient stories to contemporary people requires comparing ancestors with descendants, the exodus generation in the wilderness with the current generation in the land or in exile, the tent Tabernacle with later stone temples. The Pentateuch's rhetoric of hierarchy, however, required no translation in the Second Temple period when the Torah first began to function as scripture. Priests claiming descent from Aaron governed the temples both in Jerusalem and in Samaria. As the period wore on, their high priests gained political power as well until, under the Hasmonean priestly dynasty in the second and first centuries BCE, they ruled independently as kings of Judea. In stories about the origins of priestly hierarchy, the Pentateuch's rhetoric of past obligations applied directly to present circumstances. This fact not only reinforced the priests' legitimacy, it also bolstered the authority of the Torah as scripture for Samaritans and Jews.

Because priestly authority was a present reality as well as grounded in a story about the distant past, the Pentateuch expresses it not just in stories about the past but also in laws that govern present behavior. In Leviticus 1–16, the instructions for conducting rituals in Israel's sanctuaries emphasize the centrality of Aaronide priests at almost every turn. The topic of hierarchy therefore brings us to the rhetoric of law.

The rhetoric of lists

Writing seems to have been invented around 5,000 years ago for recording lists in the form of accounts and receipts. The writing and interpretation of lists was the most basic and also the most prestigious scribal activity in Mesopotamian cultures for more than 2,000 years. Comprehensive lists of omens represented the pinnacle of scribal expertise.

The power of lists has not waned since. Lists govern modern bureaucracies in the form of regulations, procedural instructions, and filing systems. Lists play a determinative role in human behavior. J. D. O'Banion, a theorist of rhetoric, remarked that

> Rendered as tallies, recordings of the movements of the stars, word lists, dictionaries, or codified laws, the list is a powerful tool for arranging and disseminating isolated pieces of information. It also comes to arrange and, to a considerable degree, dictate the nature of the lives of those who are affected by lists.

As tools for economic and legal control, lists dictate modes of exchange and social standing. The historian of law Cornelia Vismann observed that "Lists do not communicate; they control transfer operations." The original and continuing dominance of lists in literate cultures justifies Jonathan Z. Smith's description of them as "the most archaic and pervasive of genres."

Readers use lists differently from how they use stories or poems. Lists invite readers and listeners to choose items relevant to themselves and ignore the rest. Whether the list contains omens, ritual instructions, or recipes, readers act only on those parts they regard as appropriate to their situation. When a list appears in a scripture, people often assume that all of it must be relevant somehow, but they still pick and choose as their own wishes, time, and circumstances require or allow, leaving the rest for another occasion.[24]

Jewish and Christian interpreters have extended the pick-and-choose characteristic of lists to every verse of the Torah and the Bible. The common belief that somewhere in the Torah or the Bible, some verse of scripture must be relevant to me, now – that belief extends and develops an inherent feature of lists of laws and instructions. This characteristic way of reading lists has become a distinguishing feature of how many religious individuals and communities read scriptures. James Kugel showed that this search for relevance became typical of Jewish and Christian use of the Pentateuch.[25]

Figure 2.2 Stone administrative tablet from Mesopotamia recording a land grant, ca. 3100–2900 BCE. In the Metropolitan Museum of Art, New York.

The Rhetoric of Law: Exodus 20–23, Leviticus, Numbers, Deuteronomy

In the instructional lists that dominate much of the Pentateuch, narrative recedes into the background. The rhetoric of origins in the past is eclipsed by the obligations of readers and hearers in their own present circumstances, that is, by the rhetoric of law.

The story of the exodus and wilderness still surrounds the lists of laws. The laws and instructions are all spoken by YHWH to Moses to repeat to the Israelites at Mount Sinai or during their travels through the wilderness. Yet the contents of the laws make little attempt to preserve this narrative setting. Instead, they address the Israelites' circumstances after they have settled in the land.

The setting shifts already in the instructions for the celebration of Passover in Exodus 12–13. These rules appear at the point in the story when the Israelites are about to leave Egypt suddenly. They have half a day to prepare to flee the country. They must immediately slaughter lambs to paint their door frames red with blood to save their firstborn children from death (Exod. 12:21–23), and they must take unleavened bread with them because there is no time for the dough to rise (12:34). But God's instructions for Passover require selecting a lamb four days before slaughtering it (12:3–6) and then celebrating the festival of Unleavened Bread for seven days (12:15–20). Readers and hearers of the book of Exodus learn how they should respond to the story of their ancestors' rescue from Egypt, to the point of what they should tell their children (12:26–27; 13:8, 14–15). The narrator's comment at the end of the instructions, that "the Israelites did just as YHWH had commanded Moses and Aaron" (12:28), merges readers and hearers in the present with the Israelites of the exodus. The implication is that both groups are obliged to obey God's commands because God saved all of them from Egypt. This rhetorical strategy of identifying the present audience with past Israelites shapes the presentation of most of the Pentateuch's instructions and laws.

Law collections in the Pentateuch

Interpreters typically identify three separate collections of laws in the Pentateuch. These collections cover many of the same subjects but often differ in how they treat them. They are:

- the Covenant Code (Exodus 20:22–23:33)
- the Holiness Code (Leviticus 17–27)
- the Deuteronomic Code (Deuteronomy 12–26).

Another collection of instructions containing rules for offerings and impurities appears in:

- Leviticus 1–7, 11–16 with parallels and additions scattered through Numbers.

The Ten Commandments appear separately from these collections and twice in nearly identical form:

- Exodus 20:2–17
- Deuteronomy 5:6–21

and once with very different contents that have earned it the name "the Ritual Decalogue," which is followed by one of only two explicit references to "the ten words" in the Pentateuch, in:

- Exodus 34:14–28.

Other laws and instructions on specific topics appear in various stories, such as:

- the rule against eating blood in Genesis 9:2–6
- instructions for circumcising male descendants of Abraham in Genesis 17:9–14
- instructions for celebrating Passover in Exodus 12–13.

Instructions in ancient Middle Eastern literature typically took *casuistic* form. They were stated in the third person as "if/when …, then …" clauses. Casuistic style sounds systematic and dispassionate. Ancient scribes used it to write ritual instructions, omen lists, medical manuals, and laws. Pentateuchal laws and instructions frequently take casuistic form too. For example,

> *When an ox gores a man or woman to death, the ox must be stoned and its meat may not be eaten.* (Exod. 21:28)
> *If their offering is a rising offering from the herd, they must present a perfect male.* (Lev. 1:3)
> *When someone sins … by stealing or withholding from their associate, … they must make it good as it was to begin with by adding one-fifth and giving it back to the one it belongs to … and by bringing a perfect ram from the flock as their guilt offering to YHWH.* (Lev. 6:2–6)

Casuistic style conveys a sense of academic expertise and bureaucratic regulation that makes it seem trustworthy and authoritative. Therefore, despite its dispassionate form or, rather, because of it, casuistic rhetoric makes texts more persuasive.

Pentateuchal law collections also use a more urgent rhetoric of direct address. God and Moses often speak to "you," sometimes singular and sometimes plural. Within the framework story, "you" indicates the Israelites in the wilderness, but direct address is easily understood by later readers and listeners as addressing themselves. Some Pentateuchal laws use second-person address in otherwise casuistic formulations.

> *When you find your enemy's lost ox or donkey, you must bring it back.* (Exod. 23:4)
> *If your present is a fried commodity offering, you must make it of semolina with oil.* (Lev. 2:7)

Many other laws take *apodictic* form as direct commands.

> *You must not kill, you must not commit adultery, you must not steal.* (Exod. 20:13–15)
> *Love your neighbor as yourself.* (Lev 19:18)

Of course, instructions intended for individuals such as Moses take second-person form (e.g. Exod. 25–30), but so do many laws and instructions directed explicitly to all Israelites in every generation (e.g. Lev. 3:17).

It is not always clear why some laws use second-person address while others are stated in the third person, or why the writers alternate between casuistic and apodictic forms. In many texts, however, direct address and apodictic commands are clearly used for emphasis. For example, the Covenant Code (Exod. 21–23) surrounds its casuistic lists with direct address at the beginning (20:22–21:2) and the end (23:1–33). The effect is to emphasize to readers and hearers that these laws apply to them. The ritual instructions of Leviticus use second-person address for baking bread offerings (Lev. 2) and for much of the list of unclean meats (Lev. 11), which lay people must observe at home without priestly supervision. It also uses direct address intermittently for urgent commands, such as prohibitions on eating or drinking blood (7:27; 17:12–14). Second-person direct address shapes Moses's final speech to Israel, which takes up almost the entire book of Deuteronomy.

> *Hear, Israel, YHWH our God, YHWH is one. You must love YHWH your God with all your heart and with all your life and with all your strength.* (Deut. 6:4–5)

Most famously, all three versions of the Ten Commandments take the form of apodictic commands.

> *I am YHWH your God, who brought you out of slavery in Egypt: You must not have any other gods before me.* (Exod. 20:2–3; Deut. 5:6–7)

As a result, the Decalogues and Deuteronomy sound more urgent than do the casuistic collections of Exodus and Leviticus. The Pentateuch uses both a "hot" rhetoric of direct commands and a "cool" rhetoric of dispassionate instructions to persuade its readers and hearers to accept its authority and to do what it says.

Very few of the Pentateuch's laws provide any reasons for their requirements. Those that do are frequently so cryptic that they are hard to understand.

> *You may eat any animal that has a split hoof and regurgitates cud.* (Lev. 11:3)
> *You must not eat the blood of any meat, for the life of all meat is its blood.* (Lev. 17:14)

The laws of the Holiness Code (Lev. 17–27) distinguish themselves by frequent appeals to the holy nature of God to explain their provisions.

> *You must be holy, because I, YHWH your God, am holy.* (Lev. 19:2)

The command to observe the Sabbath day of rest in Exodus 20's version of the Ten Commandments explains it with a rare reference to the creation of the world.

> *The seventh day is a Sabbath to YHWH your God. You must not do any work – neither you nor your son or daughter nor your male or female slave nor your livestock nor the immigrant who lives in your towns. For YHWH made the heavens and the earth and the sea and all that is in them in six days, but rested on the seventh day. Therefore YHWH blessed the seventh day and sanctified it.* (Exod. 20:10–11)

Motivations for following the law appear more frequently than explanations, though still with only some laws. They appear more often in Leviticus and Deuteronomy than they do in the Covenant Code of Exodus. Most motive clauses simply promise benefits for following the law or threaten punishment for disobedience.

> *Honor your father and your mother so that you will have many days on the land that YHWH your God is giving you.* (Exod. 20:12; Deut. 5:16)
> *Anyone who eats blood will be cut off from their people.* (Lev. 7:27)

Some laws refer to the frame story of the exodus and wilderness wandering to motivate obedience.

> *Love the immigrant as yourself, for you were immigrants in the land of Egypt.* (Lev. 19:34)

> *When you free a slave, do not send him away empty handed. ... Remember that you were a slave in the land of Egypt and YHWH your God redeemed you. That is why I command you this today.* (Deut. 15:13–15)
> *Watch out for skin contamination; watch carefully! ... Remember what YHWH your God did to Miriam on the way out of Egypt.* (Deut. 24:8–9)

Such references to the story remind readers and hearers of their obligations under the covenant made at Mount Sinai. The only significant difference between Deuteronomy's rendition of the Ten Commandments and what appears in Exodus 20 is the motivation for the Sabbath commandment. Where Exodus refers to the creation of the world, Deuteronomy recalls the exodus from Egypt.

> *The seventh day is a Sabbath to YHWH your God. You must not do any work ... so that your male and female slave may rest as well as you. Remember that you were a slave in the land of Egypt. YHWH your God brought you out with a strong hand and outstretched arm. Therefore, YHWH your God commanded you to keep the Sabbath.* (Deut. 5:14–15)

Such references to the story within the laws illustrate on the small scale the persuasive rhetoric of story-list-sanction that shapes the entire Pentateuch: the stories describe the debt that Israel incurred and the commitment that Israel made to YHWH in the past to explain Israel's obligation in the present to observe the laws, which are the stipulations of the covenant with YHWH. The promises and threats project the consequences of obedience or disobedience into the readers' and hearers' future.[26]

The Pentateuch's laws and instructions include a remarkably wide range of topics. Readers find here rules for cooking and eating, for punishing thieves and murderers, for making ritual offerings, and for sexual relationships. In ancient Middle Eastern cultures, such material was usually divided between the genres of wisdom teachings, ritual instructions, law codes, and international treaties. Each of the Pentateuch's three major law collections mixes them together. Even the tighter focus on ritual in Leviticus 1–16 occasionally involves criminal and civil law (e.g. Lev. 5:1, 4; 6:2–5).

This unusual combination of topics is best explained by the frame story in which Israel agrees to a covenant that accepts YHWH as king. The idea of the covenant comes from international treaties, so it naturally requires Israel's unwavering loyalty ("you must not have any other gods before me" Exod. 20:3) and provision of supplies to the divine overlord. The inscriptions of ancient kings often mandate offerings in support of temples, so mandatory offerings during festivals also fit the characterization of YHWH as a royal lawgiver. The instructions on how to conduct rituals fall more naturally into temple ritual texts, but the identification of Israel's king as YHWH brings them under the same covenant. The advice of wisdom teachers, such as in Proverbs and Ecclesiastes, is also associated with kings (Prov. 1:1; Eccl. 1:1) and often claims to transmit the wisdom of God (Prov. 8:22–36). Maybe this explains why the Pentateuch's laws sometimes regulate even thoughts and feelings (Exod. 20:17; Lev. 19:18; Deut. 6:5). Though peoples' minds lie beyond the reach of criminal courts and ritual regulations, a divine king's rule can extend there as well.

The fact that the Pentateuch contains multiple collections of laws and instructions produces a great deal of repetition. Many topics get addressed several times, and some many times. The command to observe the Sabbath as a day of rest appears 12 times in the Pentateuch, and there are seven different regulations for punishing murderers. Repetition serves rhetorically to ensure that the audience hears and remembers at least the most basic ideas. Repetition emphasizes the importance of certain issues and also establishes thematic consistency across the Pentateuch.

In the Pentateuch, however, provisions dealing with the same topic do not always agree with each other. For example, the penalties for theft range from 200–500% in Exod. 22:1–4, but are set at 120% in Num. 5:7. Exodus 20:24–25 requires that altars be made of earth or unfinished stones, while Exod. 27:1–8 requires a wooden altar covered in bronze. And Exod. 20:24 allows offerings to be made to YHWH in many places, while Deut. 12:13–15 allows offerings only in the sanctuary but permits slaughter for food elsewhere, whereas Lev. 17:1–8 restricts all slaughter of edible domestic animals to the Tabernacle courtyard alone.

The Pentateuch's laws, then, have not been codified, that is, they have not been organized to eliminate duplication and inconsistencies. These problems have been left for later interpreters to resolve. The Pentateuch does provide some models for how to settle such issues. It depicts both YHWH and Moses responding to questions of legal interpretation by elaborating or revising laws they have previously issued. The best example of this occurs in Numbers, when the daughters of Zelophad claim inheritance rights because their father died without a male heir. YHWH grants their request (Num. 27:1–11). Then when the tribal elders complain that the daughters' marriages to outsiders could lead to the tribe loosing part of its land, Moses modifies the previous ruling. Zelophad's daughters may now inherit from their father only if they marry within the tribe (Num. 36:1–12). The entire book of Deuteronomy models how to reinterpret Pentateuchal law in new circumstances, since here Moses retells the story of exodus and restates the laws given at Mount Sinai to a new generation. The Pentateuch, however, grants interpretive authority to only one group of people: "the sons of Aaron" as Leviticus describes them, or "the levitical priests" in Deuteronomy's language. The Pentateuch's literary form thus requires legal interpretation, but Israel must follow the interpretive decisions of a class of hereditary priests.

The Rhetoric of Promise and Threat (especially Leviticus 26 and Deuteronomy 27–33)

Promises and threats make up the third element in the rhetorical strategy of story-list-sanction. Sanctions lead readers and hearers to imagine their own futures as the consequences of their obedience or disobedience to the requirements in the lists. The rhetoric of sanctions forecasts two possible futures. It gives a sense of urgency to the implications of the stories and lists.[27]

The Pentateuch leaves no doubt that Israel's future depends on observing Torah. Promises structure its plot. God promises Abraham land, descendants, and blessing and repeats these promises to his son and grandson (Gen. 12:1–3; 15:1–21). But the promises are conditional on obedience, as is made clear by the story of circumcision as the sign of God's covenant with Abraham (17:14) as well as the unusual story of Abraham's near-sacrifice of Isaac (22:16–18). The exodus story is driven by YHWH's promise to rescue Israel from Egypt and settle the people in Canaan (Exod. 3:7–8). Israel only watches while YHWH plagues the Egyptians, but taking possession of Canaan requires their willing obedience. When they prove unwilling (Num. 13–14), an entire generation is doomed to live and die in the wilderness. It is their children who will finally settle the land (26:63–65).

The Pentateuch's stories demonstrate YHWH's power and willingness to destroy those who act contrary to the divine will. This point appears early in Genesis in the stories of Noah's flood (Gen. 6), the tower of Babel (Gen. 11), and Sodom and Gomorrah (18:16–19:29). The story of the plagues on the Egyptians to punish Pharaoh (Exod. 7–12) provides the most thorough illustration of YHWH's power and willingness to use it against wrong-doers. Moses recalls this story as a warning to the Israelites of what YHWH can do (Deut. 28:27, 60).

In ancient cultures, divine promises and threats frequently took the verbal form of blessings and curses. People invoked the name of a god to promise good or threaten evil to others. Thus Noah cursed his grandson Canaan while blessing two of his sons (Gen. 9:25–27) and Jacob blessed his grandson Ephraim over his older grandson Manasseh (48:8–20). The Pentateuch's ritual instructions incorporate curses and blessings as well.

The trial by ordeal of a suspected adulteress employs a written curse that must be drunk in water (Num. 5:23–24). On the other hand, the priests must pronounce blessings on the people after concluding their offerings (Lev. 9:22–23). The Pentateuch mandates what words the priests must say.

> *You must bless the people of Israel in this way, by saying:*
> *May YHWH bless you and keep you,*
> *May YHWH's face shine on you and favor you,*
> *May YHWH smile on you and give you peace.* (Num. 6:23–26)

The words of this priestly blessing continue to be repeated by priests, rabbis, and ministers in Jewish and Christian congregations to this day (see further in Chapter 4).

The story of Balaam provides an extended narrative illustration of how blessings and curses should work (Num. 22). Balaam is a foreign prophet hired by an enemy king to curse the Israelites. An angel intervenes and forces Balaam to proclaim God's blessings on Israel instead. Balaam himself explains the power of his words as coming from God: "Do I have the power to say just anything? I must say what God puts in my mouth" (22:38). His blessings take the form of extended poems that anticipate Israel's military victories over its neighbors (Num. 23–24).

The Pentateuch's rhetoric of sanctions reaches its fullest expression in the long lists of blessings and curses that conclude the major law collections. This pattern reflects the ancient convention of concluding treaties by invoking all the gods' blessings on those who fulfill the treaty and cursing those who do not. Lists of sanctions in the names of many gods also appear in the conclusions of royal inscriptions of many types, including Hammurabi's Law Code.

The Covenant Code concludes with positive promises of good for Israel if they obey YHWH's laws. They will be victorious in war, have plenty of food, and suffer no disease or difficulties in bearing children (Exod. 23:20–31). The only negative sanction appears in the vague threat, "Do not rebel against (my angel), for he will not take away your guilt" (23: 21).

The Holiness Code concludes with an entire chapter of promises and threats (Lev. 26; chapter 27 seems to be an appendix to the main collection of laws). First comes the condition, "if you follow my mandates and keep my commandments" (26:3), then the blessings: agricultural abundance, peace, victory in war, and large families. They culminate in the promise of God's continuing presence with Israel: "I will walk among you and be your God" (26:12). But if the people disobey (26:14), punishments will follow. God threatens famine, plague, war, and defeat. If they continue to be disobedient to the covenant, they will be conquered by foreign armies that will devastate their cities and exile the survivors away from the land. The language is vivid and horrifying: "You will eat the bodies of your sons and your daughters. ... I will pile your carcasses on the carcasses of your idols" (26:29–30). Leviticus describes the coming exile as a "sabbath for the land," a vivid image of the land as suffering while inhabited by the rebellious Israelites (26:34–35). In exile, Israel will continue to be punished by oppression. In the end, however, Leviticus offers a glimpse of hope: if the exiled people confess their sins, YHWH will remember Abraham, Isaac, Jacob, and the covenant (26:45).

Eternal sanctions

Readers often expect the Pentateuch, like many later Jewish and Christian texts, to include eternal sanctions in the afterlife, such as a blessed life in heaven and eternal punishment in hell. However, the Pentateuch contains no trace of such ideas. At most, it grants the possibility of some lingering pollution of people and land due to violent deaths (Gen. 4:10; Num. 35:33).

Instead, the Pentateuch projects future blessings and punishments only in the course of normal human life. Peace, long life, and prosperous circumstances are all signs of divine blessing. The Pentateuch distinguishes its heroes by these attributes. Abraham gathered wealth throughout his life and lived to be 175 years old, according to Gen. 25:7–8. Moses lived 120 years and was strong and keen-eyed to the end, according to Deut. 34:7. But God promised neither of them a heavenly afterlife.

Afterlife beliefs varied in other ancient Middle Eastern cultures. Egyptian religion and ritual aimed at achieving a good afterlife, as shown by its elaborate tombs and the Egyptian *Book of the Dead*. Mesopotamian religions, on the other hand, nurtured more skepticism of that possibility, as in the *Epic of Gilgamesh*. The Hebrew Bible resembled the latter (see Eccl. 3:1–21; 9:5–6), until the growing popularity of apocalyptic ideas in the later Second Temple period raised expectations of reward or punishment in the afterlife (Dan. 12:1–4).

Deuteronomy deploys the rhetoric of blessing and curse most fully and elaborately. Already by chapter 4, Moses anticipates Israel rebelling and suffering exile as punishment.

> *I call on heaven and earth to witness today that you will soon die out from the land ... YHWH will scatter you among the peoples.* (Deut. 4:26–27)

Near the end of the book, he summarizes all his speeches in the form of sanctions.

> *I have set before you life and death, blessing and curse. Choose life, so that you and your descendants may live.* (Deut. 30:19)

At a very generalized level, then, the whole book of Deuteronomy can be viewed as the sanctions that complete the Pentateuch's rhetoric of stories (roughly Genesis through Exodus 19) and lists (Exodus 20 through Numbers). But as we have seen, sanctions and even long lists of sanctions show up within the stories and laws throughout the Pentateuch. Deuteronomy mixes them together as well, though the book has clearly been organized by the rhetoric of story (Deut. 1–11), followed by lists (Deut. 12–26), and concluding with sanctions (Deut. 27–30, 32–33). The book's narrative setting provides only a very short framework at the beginning and end (1:1–5; 34:1–12) and a somewhat longer account of how Moses transmitted the Torah and leadership to his successors (Deut. 31).

Lists of sanctions bring the Pentateuch to a climactic finale in Deuteronomy 27–33. Chapter 27 actually takes the form of instructions for performing blessings and curses after the people enter the land. The Levites must recite the curses and the people accept them by responding "Amen." In Deuteronomy 28, Moses recites promises and threats himself. Deuteronomy 29–30 take the form of a ritual renewal of the covenant with the new generation of Israelites who are about to enter the land. After some brief references to events in Egypt and the wilderness, Moses warns the Israelites of future catastrophe and exile for abandoning the covenant. But then he promises that, if the people repent, God will restore them to the land. Moses then recites two poems whose evocative language intensifies the rhetoric of threat (Deut. 32) and promise (Deut. 33) even more.

Both Leviticus and Deuteronomy anticipate Israel's future history. Not only will Israel conquer the land, Israel will then be exiled from the land. Both also promise, however, that God will continue to remember the covenant and remain Israel's God in exile (Lev. 26:45) or restore the people to the land once again (Deut. 30:3–5).

Ethos and *Pathos* in Pentateuchal Rhetoric

Aristotle pointed out that effective persuasion depends not only on making rational arguments (*logos*), but also on exhibiting a trustworthy character (*ethos*) and appealing to the audience's feelings and values (*pathos*).

The speaker and audience often bring a certain ethos and pathos to the situation. We have already observed that a book of scripture's physical appearance and oral performance invoke ethos and pathos to establish its legitimacy and inspiration (see Chapter 1). But Aristotle also observed that the contents of a speech establish or reinforce ethos and pathos. On the one hand, a speech can characterize the speaker explicitly by describing her or his education or experience and implicitly by using language skillfully to elicit the audience's admiration and respect. On the other hand, a speech can lead the audience to think of itself and its values in certain ways and not in others.

So, in addition to paying attention to the persuasive argument advanced by a text, rhetoric makes us consider how it characterizes its speaker/author and audience/readers. In the case of the Pentateuch, the relationship between author and audience works at several levels. Three voices reinforce each other's messages. God and Moses both speak major portions of the text, and are themselves characters within the story voiced by an anonymous third-person narrator. God gives commands but never tells stories, and the narrator tells stories but does not command, while Moses does both in Deuteronomy by repeating, and modifying, the stories and laws of Exodus, Leviticus, and Numbers. The resulting Pentateuch combines divine, prophetic, and storytelling voices into one authoritative, and so very persuasive, discourse.

The multiple speakers create multiple audiences. God and Moses address the Israelites in the wilderness. More accurately, God mostly addresses Moses, who is expected to repeat the speeches to the Israelites. The narrator addresses the readers and hearers of the Pentateuch. Much of the Pentateuch's rhetoric works to identify readers with the wilderness Israelites. Moses says so explicitly to the new generation 40 years after the revelation of the Torah at Mount Sinai/Horeb.

> *YHWH our God made a covenant with us at Mount Horeb. YHWH did not make this covenant only with our ancestors but with us who are alive today. YHWH spoke with you face to face out of the fire on the mountain.* (Deut. 5:2–4)

But the Pentateuch also blames the people of the exodus generation for their lack of faith in God's promises and their disobedience to Moses's commands. They are punished by dying in the wilderness. This persuasive lesson wishes readers and hearers to distinguish themselves as obedient to the Torah's teachings in contrast to the generations of Israelites who were not. In this way, the speeches of God and Moses break out of story time and address readers and hearers in their own time. The Pentateuch tries to convince its readers and hearers to understand themselves as directly addressed by God's commandments and Moses's interpretation of them.

The Rhetoric of Authority and Narration

Prophetic books often name and describe prophets to legitimize their claim to present revelations from God. For example, the book of Jeremiah begins,

> *The words of Jeremiah, son of Hilkiah, of the priests of Anathoth in Benjamin, to whom the word of YHWH came in the days of King Josiah of Judah, from the thirteenth year of his reign ... until the captivity of Jerusalem in the fifth month.* (Jer. 1:1–3)

The Pentateuch never introduces its narrator. The narrative books of the Hebrew Bible make no attempt to identify and legitimize their authors. Genesis begins without introducing either its author or its sources.

> *When God started to create the heavens and the earth ...* (Gen. 1:1)

Despite the lack of claims to prophetic inspiration, the Pentateuch's narrator knows everything necessary to tell stories of world creation and a thousand years of human history. The narrator can even tell us what God is thinking.

> *God said, "Let us make humans in our image."* (Gen. 1:26)
> *YHWH regretted making humans on the earth, and it disturbed God's heart.* (Gen. 6:6)
> *The Israelites groaned under their forced labor and their cry rose up to God. God remembered the covenant with Abraham, Isaac and Jacob, so God looked at the Israelites and paid attention to them.* (Exod. 2:23–25)

The Pentateuch's narrator is a typical third-person omniscient narrator. Such anonymous, all-knowing narrators appear frequently in both ancient and modern literature. Calling the narrator "omniscient" does not make a theological claim in the same way as calling God "omniscient" does. The narrator should not be confused with the writer who composed the story. Omniscient narrators are simply a literary device for telling stories. Authors create narrators who know everything about the story. Omniscient narrators appear so commonly that few writers find it necessary to explain how the narrator knows all the details of this story.

The Pentateuch nevertheless restricts its narrator to relating only the story. This narrator does not comment very much about the characters in the story and their behavior. The narrator never voices laws or instructions, and does not pronounce blessings or curses. The narrator is restricted to telling stories about the past and introducing the speeches of characters. It is the characters, YHWH and Moses, who pronounce normative teachings and make predictions about the future.

The divine character, alternately called "God" or "YHWH" or sometimes both together (e.g. Gen. 2–3), dominates the Pentateuch from beginning to end. God can therefore be considered the Pentateuch's protagonist, the character who drives the plot both with narrated actions and by quoted direct speech. God's character as revealed in actions shows considerable variation in Genesis, as we have seen. In Exodus, Leviticus, and Numbers, the divine character is both miraculous and mysterious, transcendently in control of nature and history, even of foreign kings like Pharaoh, yet immediately responsive to Moses and the people. God is notably unable or unwilling, however, to control the minds of the people of Israel. More than Abraham or Moses or Pharaoh, therefore, it is Israel who emerges as the true antagonist to the divine protagonist. It is the interaction between YHWH and Israel that drives the plot of the later books of the Pentateuch, and also of the future that the Pentateuch's sanctions anticipate.

The Pentateuch's depiction of God's character, however, does not depend entirely or even primarily on narrated action. Readers also gain an impression of a character by what that character says. The narrator quotes God speaking throughout the Pentateuch, from the very first chapter to the very last. From Exodus 19 through the book of Numbers, God's speeches take up most of the text, and Moses spends much of Deuteronomy paraphrasing what God said. The laws, instructions, and sanctions characterize God as much as the stories do.[28]

Laws try to characterize their authors as just, fair and merciful. This may have been the original function of written law codes. Ancient law collections did not govern the legal practices of their law courts, so far as we can tell. Instead, they depicted the kings who promulgated them, such as Hammurabi, as just kings. That characterization helped legitimize their rule, especially if they came to power violently. Hammurabi, for example, usurped the throne from his predecessor.

The Pentateuch differs from most other ancient legal collections by placing the laws in the mouth of a deity, rather than a king. By doing so, it reinforces the impression that YHWH is Israel's king. The contents of the laws and instructions then reveal this character's interests. Cataloguing their topics provides a summary of God's main concerns. YHWH is obviously very interested in gaining and preserving Israel's loyalty. That is expressed by banning the worship of other gods and the use of images in worship (Exod. 20:3–5; Deut. 5:7–9), and by restricting ritual worship to the Tabernacle or centralized sanctuary (Lev. 17:1–8; Deut. 12:2–7), among other things. The detailed ritual instructions in Exodus 25 through Leviticus 16 express a concern that holiness and purity be preserved so that YHWH can live in Israel's midst. God is also concerned about how the

Figure 2.3 (a) Diorite stela of Hammurabi's Laws, from Babylon, ca. 1700 BCE. Relief at top shows King Hammurabi standing before the god Shamash. (b) The cuneiform text of the laws covers the front, back, and sides of the stela. In the Louvre, Paris.

Israelites behave towards each other. This concern is expressed through moral instructions regarding right behavior and attitudes (Exod. 20:12–17; Deut. 5:16–21), criminal legislation for the punishment of murderers and thieves (Exod. 21:12–14; Lev. 6:1–7; 24:17–22), and exhortations against sexual relations regarded as immoral or impure (Lev. 18). God's concern for human relationships extends to immigrants who live in Israelite territory and to slaves: while the Pentateuch does not ban slavery, it does require slave owners to allow slaves to rest on the Sabbath (Exod. 20:10; Deut. 5:14) and to release Israelite slaves after six years of service (Deut. 15:12–18). God's concerns include many more issues, as the detailed stipulations of the Pentateuch make very clear.

God does not just ask Israel to obey the covenant. YHWH promises rewards for obedience and threatens dire punishments for disobedience. In this way, God assumes the role of judge and enforcer, traditional roles of ancient kings. In fact, the Pentateuch emphasizes this role as the epitome of divine self-expression. When Moses sees God on Mount Sinai, he hears YHWH proclaim:

> *YHWH, YHWH, a merciful and gracious God, slow to anger and great in steadfast love and faithfulness, who keeps steadfast love to the thousandth generation, who forgives guilt and transgression and sin, but who certainly does not acquit but rather punishes children for the parent's guilt and the children's children to the third and fourth generation.* (Exod. 34:6–7)

This self-description appears also in the introduction to the Ten Commandments in Exod. 20:5–6. Moses quotes it in Num. 14:18 and Deut. 7:9–10. The promises and threats of the Pentateuch's sanctions therefore express a fundamental aspect of its characterization of God.

Just as Mesopotamian law codes served to establish the justice and legitimacy of the kings who issued them, the Pentateuch's lists of laws and sanctions characterize the king of Israel, YHWH. The rhetoric makes it clear that God wants the Israelites to do as the laws say. But the laws and sanctions also aim to get the Israelites, and later readers and hearers, to recognize the justice of these laws and, therefore, that their promulgator, YHWH, is a just and merciful king. The laws' reputation should be a credit to Israel.

> *See, I have taught you mandates and regulations … You must keep them and do them, because this is your wisdom and your understanding in the sight of the nations who will say when they hear of all these mandates, "This great nation is surely a wise and understanding people." For what nation is so great that God comes near to them like YHWH our God whenever we call on him? For what nation is so great that it has such righteous mandates and regulations as all this Torah that I have set before you today?* (Deut. 4:5–8)

The effect of these stories on readers' impressions of the divine character can be judged from the history of liturgy. Jewish and Christian prayers and hymns emphasize God's character as ruler and judge and the qualities that go with these roles: justice, mercy, and steadfast love (*hesed*). Despite modern readers' tendency to focus on the stories and ignore the laws, liturgical characterizations of God show that Pentateuchal law has exerted greater power in shaping later estimations of God's character.

Another major character in Exodus, Leviticus, Numbers, and Deuteronomy is Moses. He plays a central role in every story. He hears all of God's laws and instructions, and carries many of them out, such as building the Tabernacle and consecrating the priests. He repeats and interprets the laws to Israel. John Van Seters therefore described the literary form of the Pentateuch, or actually one of its major sources, as a biography of Moses, with Genesis as prologue.[29]

Moses, however, rarely instigates the action. That role falls to YHWH or, occasionally, to the Israelites, who therefore function as the protagonist and antagonist of the story. Moses stands in between them as messenger and mediator, a position to which both God and Israel commission him (God's commission appears first in Exod. 3–4 and 6, and gets repeated throughout; Israel's commission of Moses to act as intermediary appears in Exod. 20:18–20). Most of what he does is at the command or request of YHWH or Israel. Moses shows the most independence when he argues with one or the other. That happens frequently, and Moses wields great influence with YHWH as well as with the people. For example, his arguments limit divine punishment of the Israelites after they worship the golden calf (Exod. 32:11–14; 33:12–17), though he then punishes them himself. It is, of course, his words that sum up and conclude the Pentateuch in Deuteronomy.

In all these ways, the Pentateuch presents Moses as the model mediator between God and humans. He sets an example for later mediators, who in biblical traditions appear usually as priests and prophets, and later as scribes. The job of the priests is to make offerings according to Moses's instructions to intercede with YHWH on behalf of the Israelites (Lev. 4, 16). The Pentateuch presents true prophets as those who urge Israel to learn and obey Torah, and who announce God's judgment on those who do not keep the covenant. Deuteronomy compares their role explicitly with that of Moses (Deut. 18:15). However, by repeating and interpreting the laws of God, Moses also models the behavior of scribes, who read and copy the Torah's text and explain it to the people. The Pentateuch's Moses therefore sets the pattern that the priest and scribe Ezra emulates in scripturalizing the Pentateuch as Torah (see Chapter 1).

In fact, the Pentateuch's depiction of Moses models how to ritualize the three dimensions of Torah and of later scriptures. He both copies the Torah and he ritualizes its semantic dimension by interpreting and applying Torah to the lives of hearers and readers. Moses thus models the authority of scribes/rabbis/scholars. He also ritualizes the performative dimension by reading the text aloud and requiring the people to do so. Moses therefore models the devotional performance of scriptures. And he commands veneration of the text in the form of tablets and scroll along with its reliquary, the Ark of the Covenant. Moses's story provides Torah with a foundation myth: he meets God "face to face" (Exod. 34; Deut. 34:10), he brings heavenly tablets to earth, and he installs both tablets and written Torah scroll in a holy sanctuary. Moses thereby models the legitimizing power of iconic texts.

The Pentateuch thus uses a complicated strategy of authority. It deploys three authoritative voices – those of an omniscient narrator, an omniscient

God, and a divinely inspired prophet – to legitimize its message. The voices play distinct roles and reinforce each other's authority and messages. The narrator's voice encompasses those of God and Moses, since they speak only as direct quotation within the narrative. Yet the narrator restricts its voice to stories of the past, while the voices of YHWH and Moses address readers and hearers directly. Readers who accept this direct address will feel the force of the deity's and prophet's commands in the present moment and worry about their predictions of the readers' possible futures. The authority of the divine and prophetic voices therefore tends to dominate the Pentateuch's rhetoric.

The Rhetoric of Identity

The Pentateuch's rhetorical force depends, however, on hearers and readers accepting it as addressed to themselves. To this end, the Pentateuch works very hard to construct a particular vision of who Israel is, in hopes that hearers and readers will claim that identity for themselves.

The origin stories of ancestors and of divine covenants provide the essential elements for understanding Israel's identity and obligations to God. Israel does not appear among the peoples of the earth listed in Genesis 10. The Pentateuch describes Israel as a late-comer on the stage of history, a new creation by God. Unlike the boundless optimism that calls the creation of the world unequivocally good (Gen. 1), the much longer story of the creation of Israel consists of struggles. Conflicts between God and the people of Israel, individually and corporately, dominate the plot of Genesis 12 through Deuteronomy, and beyond. Jacob's tortuous life journey and conflicts with humans and with God typify the history of his namesake descendants, the Israelites, as told in the Pentateuch and in the larger Bible.

The Pentateuch wants readers and hearers to see their own experience in the trials of Jacob and of exodus Israel. But more than that, it wants readers to adopt the identity of Israel, of this new people created by God in the wilderness. According to the Pentateuch's story-list-sanction argument, this identity requires hearers and readers to take Israel's covenant obligations as their own. That means, first of all, understanding what those obligations are. Like ancient vassals bound to their imperial overlord by suzerainty treaties, Israel owes God loyalty, taxes (offerings and tithes), and nonaggression against other Israelites. The overall quality of the Israelites' relationship to God and to each other is marked by steadfast love, which was a conventional ideal in ancient treaties. The laws and instructions play the dominant role in shaping the behaviors that the Torah exhorts its hearers and readers to adopt.

However, readers and hearers must also feel dependent on God, just as the Israelites of the exodus were dependent on YHWH. To do that, the Pentateuch works to get readers and hearers to place themselves inside the story of the exodus. Celebrating Passover by eating unleavened bread while standing in traveling clothes (Exod. 12:11) lets later generations take their place among those whom YHWH rescued from Egypt. They will accept Moses's claim that God made the covenant at Sinai "not with our ancestors but with us" (Deut. 5:3). Then they will accept for themselves the obligation to observe Torah.

The Pentateuch's rhetoric also distinguishes readers and hearers from the exodus and wilderness generation. First of all, the narrator speaks only to them. Readers and hearers are therefore in a *better* position to understand God's covenant with Israel than was the exodus generation, because they hear the entire story as well as the laws and sanctions. Furthermore, many of these stories present the Israelites behaving badly and suffering the consequences. The Pentateuch asks readers and hearers to learn from their example. Therefore, this rhetoric aims to turn its audience into a better Israel than the people described in the text. The Pentateuch's rhetoric tries to convince communities of readers and listeners that the true Israel lies not in its pages but in themselves.

3

SCROLL, TABLET, AND CODEX

RITUALIZING THE PENTATEUCH'S ICONIC DIMENSION

Written texts are physical artifacts. Books are most commonly constructed of paper and ink and bound in cardboard covers. In the 5,000-year history of writing, books have also been made of parchment, papyrus, palm leaves, and bark. They have taken the form of a continuous scroll as well as a codex, which is made of folded pages bound together between wooden or cardboard covers – what we think of as a book today. Written texts may also be inscribed on stone or pressed into clay. They may be wrapped in envelopes. Texts and books may be displayed publicly for all to see, stored in libraries, or buried in the ground. Texts have frequently been written for all these purposes. Now, many written texts take digital form, but e-books are also material objects made of computer processors, internet servers, memory chips, and screens.

The material form and visual appearance of a book or other written text allows it to be manipulated and displayed like any other physical object. Most texts appear in a form that we instantly recognize as a text by its script or typeface, and by its shape as a scroll or codex or screen. These forms allow their appearance to function symbolically. Carrying or displaying a book can represent the owner's education or wealth. If the book's contents are well known, it may also show that the owner ascribes to the

Understanding the Pentateuch as a Scripture, First Edition. James W. Watts.

ideas contained in the book. The material form and visual appearance of a book make up its iconic dimension.

The Iconic Dimension of Scriptures

Ritualizing a book's iconic dimension pays careful and repeated attention to the form and material of a book. It may involve manipulating the physical book or displaying it or portraying it in art.

Sacred texts often take the first or central position in religious processions during worship services or on holy days. This is the position in a procession that, in other traditions or on other occasions, might be occupied by an image of a god or a saint. Scriptures also get touched and handled during oath ceremonies, especially at inaugurations to religious or government offices. People display scripture verses in their homes and carry them with them as protective amulets. Some copies of scriptures are richly decorated and covered in expensive materials to distinguish them from ordinary books.

Ritualizing the iconic dimension of texts has the effect of legitimizing the tradition, institutions, communities, and individuals to whom the

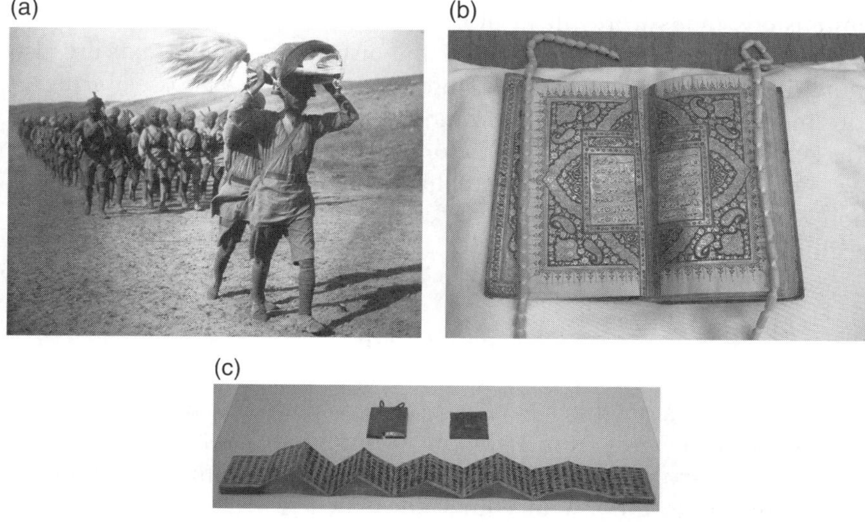

Figure 3.1 Iconic scriptures: (a) Sikh carrying Guru Granth Sahib, image from Imperial War Museum Q24777 Open Government Licence v1.0 via Wikimedia Commons, (b) Qur'an from India, ca. 1851, in the library of the University of Saint Andrews, Scotland, (c) miniature sutra, in the Korean National Museum, Seoul.

texts belong. Clergy and theologians pose for portraits holding a book of scripture to show their scholarship, piety, and orthodoxy. Museums and libraries display the oldest copies of treasured books for the prestige of owning such rarities and to establish the reliability of more recent copies.

Anyone who possesses a scripture can manipulate and display it. People without any expert training or position of authority can ritualize a scripture's iconic dimension more easily than its other dimensions. Pious lay people are therefore especially likely to take offense when someone desecrates a copy of their scripture. Attacks on a tradition try to undermine it by mutilating or destroying its books. Book burnings aim to wound and outrage the sensibilities of opponents. So ritualizing the iconic dimension of scriptures includes scripture desecration as well as scripture veneration.[30]

The Pentateuch's Iconic Dimension After Ezra

The Pentateuch first began to be ritualized regularly as a scripture in the time of Ezra, during the fifth or fourth centuries BCE when the Persian Empire ruled Judea. Scripturalizing a book by ritualizing it in all three dimensions tends to result in more historical evidence for that book's use because more copies get created and distributed. Other texts are also more likely to refer to scriptures. Information about a book's use therefore increases after its scripturalization. There is much less evidence for the Pentateuch's form and uses before it began to function as scripture. We therefore start our study of ritualizing the Pentateuch's iconic dimension with the periods for which we have increasing amounts of evidence, beginning with the time of Ezra.

Ezra's Scroll

The Book of Ezra describes Ezra as a scribe and a priest who led a group of priests and Levites from Babylon to immigrate to Jerusalem in the late fifth century BCE (Ezra 7–8). The Persian king commissioned him to act "according to the law of your God, which is in your hand" (7:14). Ezra's Torah seems to have been the Pentateuch more or less as we have it today.

Ezra ritualized the Torah's iconic dimension deliberately and effectively by gathering the people in Jerusalem's main plaza and carrying the scroll to a raised platform where prominent members of the community stood alongside him (Neh. 8:1–8). This arrangement visually associated the book with its reader, Ezra, and with his supporters. Before one word of the Torah was read, the act of physically unrolling the scroll prompted a ritual response from the audience. They stood up and then, after Ezra blessed them, they bowed down to the ground.

The sight of the physical scroll validated Ezra's claim to be reading the words that God spoke to Moses. Reading the Torah publicly legitimized Ezra's leadership and everything that he proposed to do. It also legitimized the people's identity as Israel. One outcome of the Torah reading was that they celebrated the annual festival of *Sukkot* (Booths) out of obedience to Torah (Neh. 8:13–20). Another outcome was that the people committed themselves to obeying Torah generally and to paying for the temple services (9:38–10:39). They also agreed to "separate from the people of the land for the sake of God's Torah" (10:28). In Ezra and Nehemiah, then, the Pentateuch defines and legitimizes the people as God's people. The Torah has become a fundamental element in defining Jewish identity.

Modern commentators have questioned whether a Persian official would really act in the way that Ezra does. The books of Ezra and Nehemiah have been modified by many editors, as is clear from the many irregularities in the narrative. The most obvious irregularity is the change in languages from Hebrew to Aramaic and back again (Ezra 4:8–6:18 and 7:12–26 are written in Aramaic). Nevertheless, it is clear that the writers and editors of the books of Ezra and Nehemiah portray Ezra as a model of how they thought a scribe and priest should behave with a Torah scroll. This narrative also shows how people should respond to seeing it and hearing it read. Nehemiah 8–10 therefore present a model for ritualizing Torah's iconic dimension. It is a pattern of behavior that became increasingly common as the Second Temple period progressed.

Torah Scrolls in the Late Second Temple Period

In the middle of the Pentateuch in Leviticus 1–17 lie instructions for conducting temple rituals. Temples therefore seem like the Torah's natural home. Torah scrolls were probably kept in the temples of Judea and Samaria in the Persian period. Yet the stories of religious apostasy in Israel's earlier history suggest that the Torah did not govern temple rituals in the monarchic period (so, explicitly, 2 Kgs. 23:21–23). The books of Ezra and Nehemiah indicate much more concern for following the teachings of Torah in the Persian period, even before Ezra's reform (see Ezra 3:4). Presumably, priests stored Torah scrolls in the post-exilic temples and read them regularly in public ceremonies. However, there is no evidence for Torah scrolls and public Torah readings outside the books of Ezra and Nehemiah until after the Persian period. Historians therefore debate exactly when the Pentateuch began functioning as the law book of the Jerusalem and Samaritan temples.

The Letter of Aristeas 177

So they arrived with the gifts which had been sent at their hands and with the fine skins on which the Law had been written in letters of gold in Jewish characters; the parchment had been excellently worked, and the joining together of the letters was imperceptible. When the king saw the delegates, he proceeded to ask questions about the books, and when they had shown what had been covered and unrolled the parchments, he paused for a long time, did obeisance about seven times, and said, "I offer to you my thanks, gentlemen, and to him who sent you even more, and most of all to the God whose oracles these are."[31]

The next clear reference to the Pentateuch being ritualized in all three dimensions appears in the *Letter of Aristeas*, written in the second century BCE. This document tells of the translation of the Torah into Greek in the third century. It lavishes attention on its iconic dimension. It describes beautiful Hebrew Torah scrolls written in gold ink being sent by the high priest in Jerusalem to Egypt for the translators. There, the Greek king bowed down at their sight (see Box, "*The Letter of Aristeas* 177"). Once the work was complete, the Jewish community in Egypt received the Greek translation with more bows (*Aristeas* 317). The Greek Torah probably symbolized the Egyptian Jews' status as upper-class Greek speakers within the Hellenistic culture of Ptolemaic Egypt. Historians think that *Aristeas* exaggerated both the expense of the scrolls and their reception by the non-Jewish king. (We have no examples of ancient manuscripts written in gold ink, though Jewish, Christian, and Muslim scriptures written in gold have survived from the Middle Ages.) Nevertheless, the letter provides evidence for how Jews in the second century BCE thought temple scrolls *should* look and how they *should* be treated ritually.

The only surviving Torah scrolls from the Second Temple period were found among the Dead Sea Scrolls. These fragments of more than 800 ancient Jewish manuscripts were discovered in caves near the north end of the Dead Sea in the middle of the twentieth century. The scrolls were written between the third century BCE and the first century CE. They seem to have been brought to the caves for safekeeping from a local settlement, Qumran, when Roman armies invaded Judea in 68 CE. Around one-quarter of these scrolls contain biblical texts. They are the oldest surviving biblical manuscripts and provide valuable evidence about the state of biblical literature at the end of the Second Temple period in the last two centuries BCE.

The manuscripts show how Qumran scribes ritualized the iconic dimension of the Torah by distinguishing the books of the Pentateuch. Each of the Pentateuch's books appears among the Dead Sea Scrolls in more than a dozen copies (see Table, "Books with more than 10 copies found among the Dead Sea Scrolls," on p. 191). Only the book of Psalms appears more often. Qumran scribes produced especially deluxe manuscripts of Pentateuchal books in a large format with wide margins (though they were not as large as later Torah scrolls – in the first century, it was not yet possible to produce a scroll containing all five books of the Pentateuch). And they sometimes used old-fashioned paleo-Hebrew letters for the books of Moses, instead of the standard Aramaic square letters that they used for almost all other books. These practices all show greater reverence for the books of Torah than for other books.[32]

Several sources tell us that by the second and first centuries BCE, Torah scrolls had become emblems of Jewish identity not only to Jews, but to Greeks and Romans as well. When Roman armies destroyed Jerusalem and its temple, they took a Torah scroll from the temple and paraded it in Titus's victory procession with the golden table and lamp stand (*menorah*). Josephus (*War* 7.121–157, 162), who witnessed many of these events himself, wrote:

> *Last of all the spoils was carried the Law of the Jews.*

Josephus thought it was kept in the imperial palace in Rome. But no Torah scroll appears among the loot from the Jerusalem temple depicted on Titus's arch in Rome. We are left to wonder if the Jewish historian Josephus placed more value on the temple's Torah scrolls than did the Romans or, at least, the Roman artists who designed the reliefs for the victory arch.

More than a century later, the Mishnah remembered that a Torah scroll was brought forward for the high priest to read on the Day of Atonement (*Yom Kippur*).

> *The official of the congregation took the book of the Torah and gave it to the head of the congregation, and the head of the congregation gave it to the assistant [high priest], and the assistant [gave it] to the high priest. The high priest stood and received it and read* (*m. Yoma* 7:1; *m. Sotah* 7:7).[33]

The scrolls were handled by these same officials when a king read Torah in the temple. The Talmud understood the requirement to stand when reading Torah as more than a sign of respect. Ruth Langer pointed out that:

> As the Talmud recognizes (*BYoma* 69a; *BSotah* 40b, 41b), there is a symbolic message encoded in this movement. … Rabbinic law required that every reader stand. In the hierarchy of symbols, Torah reigns supreme over all human beings, including kings. … By standing, the reader emulates, not Moses who stood to receive the Torah, but God who revealed it. The ritual reading of the Torah, then, is not simply an act of study, but a reenactment of Sinai itself.[34]

The Mishnah reflected the synagogue practices of its own time when describing these older temple rituals. Standing to read the Torah aloud and to hear it read reenacts God giving the law to Israel. By revering the Pentateuch in this way, readers and congregations identify themselves with the Israelites who agreed to the divine covenant at Mount Sinai.

Textual Amulets

People often ritualize the iconic dimension of a scripture by manipulating or carrying small parts of it as an amulet. Amulets may depict books of scripture or contain scripture verses. People in many cultures and religious traditions wear them constantly or hold them while praying. They often keep them in their homes to bless their families and protect them from danger. Amulets easily cross religious boundaries. People frequently use scripture amulets because they believe in their power even though they do not identify themselves with the religion that venerates that particular scripture. For example, amulets containing Quranic verses are valued from Africa to South Asia by many people who are not Muslims. Amulets also stir controversy between advocates of traditional practices and critics of "superstition." Many people take a mediating position: they deny that amulets exert any physical effects, yet defend their symbolic value.

The use of certain kinds of amulets has been widespread in Jewish practice since antiquity. It is grounded in the commands of the Torah itself. Jewish families typically install small boxes (mezuzahs) containing texts from the Pentateuch on the doorposts of their homes. People traditionally touch the mezuzah when entering or leaving the room or house.

When praying, Jewish men have traditionally tied small boxes (tefillin) on arm and forehead. Both practices fulfill the commandment to

> *Tie [these words] as a sign on your hand, make them a symbol between your eyes. Write them on the door jambs of your house and on your gates.* (Deut. 6:8–9)

Mezuzahs and tefillin contain parchments on which Exod. 13:1–10, 11–16 and Deut. 6:4–9, 11:13–21 is written in tiny script.

Archeologists found tefillin boxes and their slips of parchment at Qumran, near where the Dead Sea Scrolls were discovered. So amulets incorporating Pentateuchal texts were already in common use by the second or at least the first century BCE. Some of the slips seem to have actually come from mezuzahs and so are evidence that Jews were already putting them on doorposts as well. These discoveries provide our earliest physical evidence for the iconic manipulation of Torah texts.[35]

The Karaites, a Jewish sect that rejects the rabbinic lore of the Talmuds, do not use mezuzahs and tefillin. They understand the commandments of Deut. 6:8–9 as metaphors that require people to internalize the commands of Torah and let them direct their actions. The Samaritans, a religious

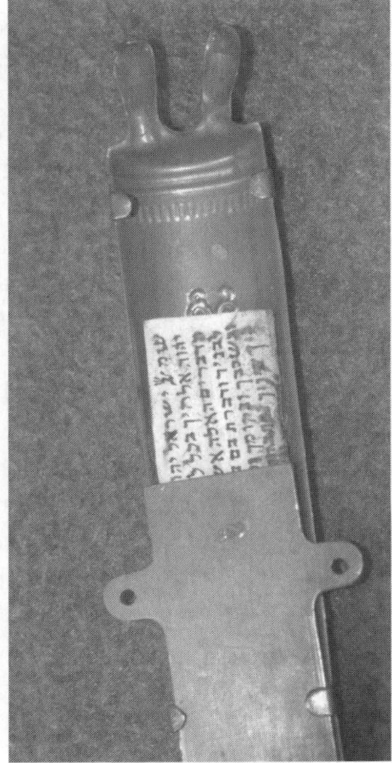

Figure 3.2 A modern mezuzah.

community that traces its origins to the northern tribes of Israel, also interpret the commands metaphorically and do not use tefillin. Samaritan mezuzahs consist of scriptural blessings written in archaic Hebrew script and displayed on parchment or stone tablets.

These differences show that controversies over the proper use of scriptural amulets extend back in time to the ancient divisions between these groups. Even more controversial has been the use of amulets to bring about particular results, such as personal protection or healing. Archeologists have discovered many Samaritan amulets from the middle ages. They often arrange scripture texts in numerological sequences. Modern Samaritans deny that they wear amulets, so these medieval amulets may have been produced for sale to other people.

Belief in the power of textual amulets often grows from belief in the power of the names of God. The Hebrew name of God is written with the letters *yod-heh-vav-heh*, יהוה YHWH, and appears very often in the Hebrew Bible. During the Second Temple period, the tradition developed that only the Jewish high priest should pronounce that name, and only on Yom Kippur. Otherwise, Jews should not pronounce the divine name. This tradition continues today: when reading biblical texts aloud, readers substitute other Hebrews words, such as *Adonai* "Lord" or *haShem* "the Name." The Septuagint, the translation of the Pentateuch into Greek in the third century BCE, already rendered God's name with the Greek title "Lord" rather than transliterating the name YHWH. Many Dead Sea Scrolls written in standard Aramaic letters wrote the divine name in paleo-Hebrew letters to distinguish it and, perhaps, to warn readers not to pronounce it. Rabbinic traditions insisted that any text containing the divine name in Hebrew is, by virtue of this fact alone, a sacred text. Medieval Jewish mystics insisted that all the letters of the Torah are really code for the name of God, written over and over again.

These traditions stimulated the belief that the Hebrew name of God is very powerful. Its use in prayer and incantations became popular across the Mediterranean world in Late Antiquity. Amulets reproduced ΙΑΩ, the Greek equivalent of Hebrew יהוה YHWH, in combination with the names of Greek gods. Greek magical papyri utilized ΙΑΩ more than any other divine name. Far from avoiding its pronunciation, they encouraged chants of its vowels or of all the vowels of the alphabet.

> *I call thy name that is hidden within me: a o ee o ee o eee ooo iii oooo ooooo ooooo uuuuuuu ooooooooooooo.*

Christian amulet scrolls also combined biblical verses and the names of God with the name and titles of Jesus and esoteric symbols.[36]

Ancient Christian biblical manuscripts followed the practice of the Septuagint by rendering the divine name with the Greek word κύριος "Lord." That word appears frequently in the New Testament to refer to Christ. Christian scribes distinguished this and other holy names, such as "Jesus" and "Christ," by abbreviating them. Such *nomina sacra* marked Christian scripture as sacred. In the Middle Ages, they became frequent subjects for artistic illumination.

The Pentateuch then functioned as scripture in cultures that saw divine power in its graphic symbols, especially those that represent the name of God. Of course, the sound of the words and the meaning of the text were also sacred. But in writing, the divine text and name took physical forms that could be manipulated in amulets by Jews, Samaritans, and Christians, and by people of many other religious traditions as well.

Torah Arks

Jewish synagogues keep Torah scrolls and other scrolls of scripture in a cabinet called *Aron ha-Qodesh* "the holy ark." Arks have been used to protect and enshrine Torah scrolls in synagogues for almost 2,000 years. Already at the end of the second century CE, the Mishnah required that scripture scrolls be treated as more holy than any other objects or the synagogue itself (*m. Meg.* 3.1). Some second- and third-century synagogues excavated by archeologists contain niches for scrolls or platforms for placing portable Torah arks. The ark could be carried into the synagogue in procession, or wheeled on a cart.

By the fourth to sixth centuries CE, many synagogues had permanently installed arks. Art from the period shows their typical form. The doors were flanked by two columns, like those that stood in Jerusalem's temple (1 Kgs. 7:15–22). Inside, the scrolls were laid horizontally on shelves. A curtain hung in front. The gable of the peaked roof contained a sculpted conch shell, often flanked by lions. The ark itself was flanked by lamp stands (*menorahs*) like the one in the Tabernacle (Exod. 25:31–38). No ancient Torah arks have survived, but archeologists found the burned remains of a Torah ark in the seventh-century synagogue at Ein Gedi that contained pieces of a Leviticus scroll.[37]

Jewish architecture and art from the Middle Ages has been poorly preserved, due to persecution that frequently expelled Jewish communities from one place to another. But prayer books dating from the tenth century and later show the emergence of a standard liturgy for taking

Figure 3.3 Relief of wheeled ark, ca. third century CE, in the synagogue at Kefer-Nahum/Capernaum, Israel.

Figure 3.4 Gold glass bowl from Rome, ca. 300–350 CE, showing an open Torah ark with scrolls on its shelves. In the Metropolitan Museum of Art, New York.

Torah scrolls from the ark, reading them, and then returning them to the ark (see below).

Synagogue architecture of the last five hundred years is better preserved. Most modern synagogues have wooden arks permanently installed on the wall facing Jerusalem. The ark serves as the focal point of the room. In front of the ark or in the middle of the room is a platform (*bimah*) and table where the scrolls are unrolled and read. When they are not being used, the scrolls get placed in the ark behind closed doors. A curtain (*paroket*) hangs in front of the ark like the curtain that hung in front of the Tabernacle's Ark of the Covenant that contained the tablets of the Ten Commandments (Exod. 26:31–33). Images of those tablets usually appear above the ark's doors. The name, *aron* "ark," the curtain, and the image of the tablets all associate Torah scrolls with the tablets that Moses received from God at Sinai. They also link synagogue arks with the Ark of the Covenant that represented God in the holiest part of the Tabernacle.

Figure 3.5 Torah scrolls in the ark in the Vilna Shul (synagogue) in Boston, Massachusetts, built in 1919.

Many Jews consider synagogues holy because they contain Torah scrolls. The place becomes sacred because of the sacred books housed there. This attitude marks a dramatic shift in how people think about sacred space. Temples in ancient Mediterranean and Middle Eastern cultures, including ancient Israel, occupied specific locations sanctified by stories of divine activity or revelation in those places. Synagogues, by contrast, can be located wherever Jews gather to pray together. They are sacred spaces whenever they house a Torah scroll. Jewish religious architecture has featured such assembly halls for praying and listening to scripture read aloud since antiquity. This assembly-hall model has been imitated by Christian churches and Muslim mosques. These worship places sanctified by sacred books or relics function very differently from ancient temples.

Christians have little that is comparable to a synagogue ark. Their belief that temple worship was superseded by Christ's death gave them no reason to reproduce something like Israel's ark in church architecture. Some Christians instead allegorized the ark as Mary, the mother of Jesus, who carried the "Word of God" in her womb. The equivalent in church furnishings appears in chests called "tabernacles" that contain the Eucharistic bread and wine, that is, the body of Christ. There are also examples of Gospel books and other scriptures being enshrined in boxes and venerated as relics. Medieval Irish monks placed elaborate illuminated manuscripts such as the Lindisfarne Gospels and the Book of Durrow in locked book shrines where they could not be seen, much less read. These books functioned purely as relics of the saints who copied and illuminated them, and as symbols of Christ's presence. These copies of scripture were much less accessible than synagogue Torah scrolls that get taken out of their arks and read publicly at least every week. Most Christian churches also display scriptures openly and make copies readily available for reading.

Synagogue Scrolls

Rules for creating, handling, and storing Torah scrolls emphasize their sanctity and value. The Talmud records precise rules for creating a Torah scroll (*b. Meg.* 18b–19a, 29b; *b. Men.* 29b). The scroll must be made from the skin of a pure animal (Lev. 11). The parchment must be ruled with lines and must be written in a consistent square Aramaic script with large margins on all sides. The scribe cannot add vowels to the consonantal Hebrew text, but seven letters must always be decorated with small crowns (*tagin*) wherever they occur. Up to three copying mistakes can be corrected on a page, but four or more require that the page be buried and recopied on new parchment. The scroll must have two staves, one at each

Figure 3.6 A scribe copying a new Torah scroll. *Source*: Image "Writing a Torah" from Wikimedia Commons under a Creative Commons Attribution-Share Alike 3.0 Unported license.

end. Scrolls of scriptures copied by heretics must be burned. Later legal codes add that scribes must purify themselves before copying a Torah. They must pray before and after their work, and every time they write the divine name.

Talmudic references show that Torah scrolls were already being wrapped in covers in antiquity. Later Jewish cultures developed distinctive traditions of "clothing" the Torah when it is not being read. Ashkenazi Jews from central and Eastern Europe usually wrap the scroll in a mantle. Crowns with bells get placed on its staves and a metal shield hangs over the front of the mantle. Modern synagogues associate these clothes with the ceremonial clothes of Israel's high priest, who wore a mantle, bells, crown, and breastplate (Exod. 28). Art historians doubt, however, that these customs developed in conscious imitation of the high priest's clothing. Sephardic Jews from Mediterranean countries instead keep Torah scrolls in cylindrical cases that open in two halves. Samaritans place their Torah scrolls in three-part cylinders.

A synagogue congregation interacts with Torah scrolls through a sequence of ritual actions and oral responses. They have become a standardized liturgy since the Middle Ages. The congregation stands throughout the Torah reading and the rituals that surround it. When a Torah scroll is taken from the ark, it is processed around the room while the congregation sings a psalm. Then it is laid on a table on a platform (*bimah*) to be unrolled and read. Blessings precede and follow its reading. Any member of the

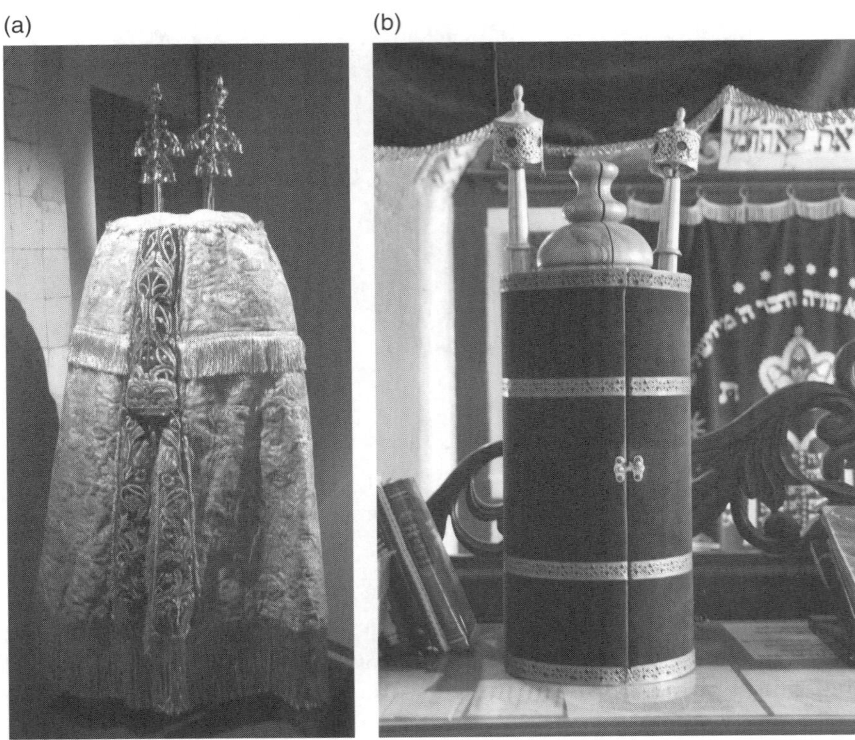

Figure 3.7 (a) Clothed Torah scroll in the Portuguese Synagogue in Amsterdam, the Netherlands. (b) Torah case in the Yosef Caro synagogue in Tzfat/Safed, Israel.

congregation may have the privilege of being "called to the Torah" to recite a blessing. The Torah is rolled up and returned to the ark, or placed on a special stand or chair, when it is not being read. Ruth Langer summarized the ritual effect:

> The emergence of the Torah scroll from its ark, its presence in the midst of the congregation before, during and after its reading, forms the ritual high-point of the service. Far from being a routine reading of the book, these liturgies have emerged as expressions of the deep symbolic significance of the ritual.[38]

More prolonged Torah processions take place on special occasions and particularly on the annual holiday celebrating the Torah (*Simhat Torah*), when Torah scrolls may be paraded through the streets. It is a privilege to carry the Torah. Sometimes, a scroll within its mantle may be handed around the congregation.

Dedicatory Torah plaque

El Shaddai, this takhshit (ornament) was dedicated by the honored Mrs. Esther, wife of Meyuḥas Moses Mazza, to heal her. May God cure her entirely when he enters the Holy Place in the New Holy Congregation on the New Moon of First Adar, in the year 5641 [=31 January 1881], in Ioannina. May the Supreme One Protect her, Amen.

All of this – mantles or cases decorated with ornaments containing two-stave parchment hand-written scrolls that are taken from and returned to synagogue arks in processions accompanied by singing and blessings – all of this serves to mark Torah scrolls as the holiest objects in Judaism. The containers and ornaments mark the Torah visually as different from and superior to all other books. They also mediate materially between the book and the person handling it, so that you never need to touch the Torah's pages with a bare hand. When the Torah is carried through the congregation, people touch it with their prayer shawls or prayer books and then kiss the shawl or book as a form of blessing. In some medieval communities, arks were left open after a service so that women, who otherwise stayed in the gallery, could approach and pray close to the Torah scrolls. Donations of expensive ornaments, clothing, and cases are believed to earn merit. Donors often specify the blessings they seek in dedicatory plaques (see Box, "Dedicatory Torah plaque").

Thus the shape, materials, ornaments, and containers of a Torah scroll all draw attention to its uniquely holy status whenever people see and handle it. William Scott Green observed that

> Whatever else it may have been, the writing we would call "Scripture" was conceived by Rabbinic culture as a holy object, a thing to be venerated. … In the absence of the Temple and its Holy of Holies, the scroll and its writing became for ancient rabbis primary repositories and conveyers of social legitimacy, cultural authenticity, and religious meaning.

These ways of ritualizing the Torah's iconic dimension also make it available to those who do not have the education or status to ritualize its performative or semantic dimensions. The scroll and its accoutrements make its holiness accessible to people who otherwise have little opportunity or ability to read and study Torah.[39]

Desecrated Torah Scrolls

Objects that can be ritually venerated can also be ritually desecrated. Their deliberate mutilation and destruction intends to cause anguish to those who treasure them. Because books represent the values of a culture or religion in condensed form, they have often been targeted by enemies of those traditions. Daniel Sarefield observed that,

> To willfully destroy a text by placing it in a fire is to perform an ancient and persistent action that is in its essence a ritual of purification. Yet a book burning is more than a ceremonial act; it is a spectacle that transmits forceful social and religious messages to victims, witnesses, and participants alike.[40]

The Roman Senate, in periodic attempts to purify Rome's culture that began as early as the third century BCE, ordered books of magic and other unorthodox rituals publicly burned. In the early fourth century CE, persecution of Christianity in the Roman Empire targeted its books. Then Christian emperors rose to power, and the Roman state began to suppress the books of pagans and heretics instead. Burning one's own books became a symbol of conversion (already in the New Testament, Acts 19:18–19). The ancient book religion of Manichaeism died out in the Middle East and Europe by the end of the first millennium due to the destruction of its books and the suppression of its practices by Christian, Muslim, and Zoroastrian rulers. The Samaritans also remember losing many irreplaceable books due to persecutions in this period.

Lost Samaritan books

Samaritan traditions lament the loss of many of their religious books in the early second century CE.

> *In those days the Book of Choice Selections was taken away, which had been in their hands since the days of Divine Favor; and there was also taken away the Songs and Praises, which they were accustomed to utter over the offerings, each offering according to its merits; and also the Hymns, which they used to sing in the days of Divine Favor. Now all these constituted a library which had been preserved with greatest care generation after generation, through the time of the prophets unto that day, by the hands of the chief imams. And there was also taken away the Book of the Imams, which they had, wherein their genealogy was traced back to Phineas; and there was also destroyed the Annals, wherein was recorded their birthdays and the years of their lives, and of these not one ancient book or chronicle was found except the Law and a book containing their lives.*[41]

The Torah also attracted violent attention from enemies of the Jews. When the Seleucid Greek ruler Antiochus Epiphanes tried to suppress Jewish religious practices in the second century BCE, he ordered the destruction of Jewish altars, sanctuaries, and Torah scrolls. This equation of those who obey scripture with those who own a copy is a typical result of ritualizing the iconic dimension of texts, whether to venerate or to desecrate them. Josephus claims that, in the first century BCE, the Roman emperor Augustus decreed that theft of a holy book from a synagogue should be punished as an act of desecration. He reports that, in the following century, a Roman governor beheaded a soldier for desecrating a Torah scroll (*Ant.* 16:164; 20:115–16). These incidents show that before the beginning of the Common Era, Torah scrolls had already become symbols of Jewish identity to Jews and non-Jews alike.

Desecrating Torah scrolls

The books of the law that they found they tore to pieces and burned with fire. Anyone found possessing the book of the covenant, or anyone who adhered to the law, was condemned to death by decree of the king. (1 Macc. 1:56–57 NRSV)

One of the soldiers, who had found a copy of the laws of Moses that was kept in one of the villages, fetched it out where all could see and tore it in two while he uttered blasphemies and railed violently. The Jews, on learning of this, collected in large numbers, went down to Caesarea, where Cumanus happened to be, and besought him to avenge not them but God, whose laws had been subjected to outrage. For, they said, they could not endure to live, since their ancestral code was thus wantonly insulted. Cumanus, alarmed at the thought of a fresh revolution of the masses, after taking counsel with his friends, beheaded the soldier who had outraged the laws. (Josephus, *Antiquities* 20:115–16)[42]

For Jews and Samaritans, preserving Torah scrolls became an important religious ideal. The Mishnah requires that, even on the Sabbath, scrolls of scripture must be rescued from a fire (*m. Shab.* 16). Many stories from antiquity to today tell of Jews risking their lives to rescue torahs from burning buildings.

Relic Torah Scrolls

Some torahs get treated like relics. People value relics for being the specific objects that they are: the bone of a saint's body or a celebrity's personal possession. They are rare, if not one-of-a-kind, and are in theory not reproducible. Relics, as known from Christian and Buddhist traditions and many other religions, are believed to mediate the sacred like icons. But icons are reproducible, while the value of relics lies precisely in the fact that they are unique. Of course, the demand for relics always outstrips the supply, so there are frequent scandals over the (re) production of relics. Relic texts, then, are particular books valued for their individual form or history.

Museums and libraries regularly display relic texts such as rare manuscripts and first editions. In fact, relic texts get ritualized only in their iconic dimension by collecting, preserving, and displaying them like works of art. They are rarely read or interpreted, because non-relic copies of the same texts are usually available for such activities. The iconic display of relic texts enhances the prestige of those who own them and legitimizes other copies of the same text.

Some Torah scrolls have become treasured relics because they survived the disasters of history. Jewish memory has been shaped by catastrophic experiences, from Egyptian servitude and Babylonian exile in the Bible through the Roman destruction of the Jerusalem temple and medieval expulsions, culminating in the twentieth-century Nazi gas chambers of the *Shoah*/Holocaust. Such experiences make survival feel miraculous. Torahs that survived catastrophe represent Jewish survival against history's odds.

The biblical texts among the Dead Sea Scrolls quickly gained the status of relic texts after their discovery in the mid-twentieth century. Because they are 1,000 years older than other manuscripts of the Hebrew Bible, for Jews and Christians they became symbols of the reliability and antiquity of biblical tradition. In 1965, the Israel Museum in Jerusalem built a special structure to house the scrolls and called it "the Shrine of the Book." Its monumental exterior and circular interior, which displays the 24-foot-long Isaiah scroll at its center surrounded by other Qumran manuscripts, emphasizes the manuscripts' uniqueness and importance. Its biblical manuscripts legitimize the antiquity of Jewish and Christian scriptures, and enhance the prestige of the State of Israel that owns them and enshrines them in this way. This exceptional building ritualizes the Dead Sea Scrolls visually and architecturally as relic texts.

Another famous Jewish relic text is the Aleppo Codex. This ninth-century manuscript of the whole Hebrew Bible was celebrated already by Maimonides in the twelfth century. Historians continue to regard it as the best testimony to the text of the Hebrew Bible. So it also serves to legitimize the accuracy of Jewish and Christian scriptures. A fire in the Aleppo synagogue in 1947 damaged the Codex, which lost almost all the pages of its Pentateuch. Israeli spies and politicians worked secretly to bring the rest of the manuscript from Aleppo to Jerusalem, a tale recounted by

Figure 3.8 The Shrine of the Book in the Israel Museum in Jerusalem.

investigative journalist Matti Friedman. But some members of the Aleppo Jewish community kept fragments of the Codex for themselves as amulets (see Box, "Fragment of Aleppo Codex as amulet").[43] Relic texts often create conflicts between the interests of individuals and of communities. Communities ranging from local congregations to nations gain legitimacy from owning and displaying relic texts, while individuals keep them for themselves because they offer prestige or a sense of protection.

Fragment of Aleppo Codex as amulet

The Israeli newspaper *Haaretz* reported on November 6, 2007, that

> Sam Sabbagh salvaged the fragment from a burning synagogue in Aleppo, Syria in 1947. ... Sabbagh believed the small piece of parchment was his good luck charm for six decades. He was convinced that thanks to the parchment, which he kept with him always in a transparent plastic container, he had been saved from riots in his hometown of Aleppo during Israel's War of Independence, and he had managed to immigrate from Syria to the United States in 1968 and start a new life in Brooklyn and make a living.

Only after Sabbagh's death was the fragment donated to an Israeli museum to be reunited with the Aleppo Codex.

The Samaritans of Nablus possess a Torah scroll with a colophon asserting very great antiquity: it claims to have been copied by Abisha, a grandson of Aaron, in the thirteenth year after Israel's conquest of Canaan. In Samaritan cultural memory, this relic from the time of the Pentateuch's wilderness generation provides some compensation for having lost so many books in antiquity (see Box, "Lost Samaritan books" on p. 84). Many historians, however, date the Abisha Scroll on the basis of its handwriting to the Middle Ages instead.

Some Jewish communities have revered particular Torah scrolls as relics. Shalom Sabar tells of

> *La Ghriba*, or the marvelous Torah scroll of Bône (now Annaba) in Algeria, and the *Seghir*, or the small Torah scroll of Darnah in Libya ... they were believed to possess special protective powers or even perform miracles. ... about the latter it is even told it was produced in the time of Ezra. Moreover these miraculous scrolls "traveled" by sea to Alexandria and from there, with no damage caused to them by the water, to the respective communities in North Africa. Many other stories are told about the miracles they performed, and that even Muslims recognized their sanctity.

Stories circulate in many Jewish, Samaritan, and Christian communities about books of scripture that survived miraculously. When thrown into fire by enemies, they jumped out unscathed. Others were found intact in the ruins of burned buildings or vehicles. Such stories use the surviving copies to demonstrate the holiness of scripture.[44]

Fraudulent sales of Holocaust scrolls

The Washington Post reported on October 11, 2012, that Rabbi Menachem Youlus pleaded guilty and was convicted of selling fake Holocaust scrolls and defrauding investors.

> Youlus, the self-proclaimed "Jewish Indiana Jones"... spun cloak-and-dagger tales of "rescuing" sacred Torah scrolls lost during the Holocaust, but those tales were lies.... Despite Youlus's claims that he found holy relics at concentration camps, in monasteries and in mass graves, passport records show he never traveled to Europe.... More than 50 of his purported Holocaust Torahs made their way to congregations in the Washington area and beyond. Synagogues held emotional ceremonies to rededicate the scrolls for worship – a symbolic show of Jewish triumph over Hitler.

Youlus was sentenced to 51 months in prison and ordered to pay almost one million dollars in restitution.

Since the mid-twentieth century, Torah scrolls that survived destruction by the Nazis have gained relic status as "Holocaust scrolls." Congregations are eager to buy them and preserve them in their synagogues. Many such scrolls did indeed survive in hiding during World War II, but the relic trade is famous for deceit, and the sale of relic texts is no different. An American dealer in Holocaust scrolls was convicted of fraud and imprisoned in 2012 (see Box, "Fraudulent sales of Holocaust scrolls"). This scandal has drawn greater attention to trying to authenticate the twentieth-century history of holocaust Torah scrolls.

Relic texts are the exception that proves the rule about ritualizing scriptures in three dimensions. When copies of scriptures are readily available for semantic, performative, and iconic ritualization, a few special copies can be set aside to serve purely iconic purposes as relic texts. Relic texts legitimize a story about a community's identity. People ritualize the possession and display of relic texts to identify with and place themselves in that story.

Torah Myths

Many people believe that the most important relic texts are in heaven. Books in heaven were a common motif already in ancient literature. Sumerian texts from the third millennium BCE describe the scribal goddess, Nisaba, writing down the decisions of the gods in the stars of the sky. Mesopotamian traditions conceived of this book of fate as written on supernatural tablets that gave the king of the gods power to rule on heaven and on earth. These "Tablets of Destiny" remained in heaven, but humans could learn to read their contents in omens and in the entrails of butchered animals. In Egyptian traditions, the scribal deities Seshat and Thoth wrote the decrees and judgments of the gods, including ritual instructions for the living and the dead. Over time, ritual texts originally credited to human "reading priests" were credited to Thoth instead. By the first millennium BCE, the restricted libraries of Egyptian temples were the subject of legends about their divine texts that convey magical powers. Stories of the revelation of divine texts became a common feature of mystical traditions in the Hellenistic and Roman periods.

The Pentateuch's story of Moses receiving tablets written by God fits this broader cultural context well. In fact, it seems modest in comparison with the claims about heavenly texts in other traditions. So by the third century BCE, Jews began to assert that the Torah too has existed in heaven since before the creation of the world. Writers adapted a wisdom hymn

Figure 3.9 An Egyptian Book of the Dead showing, at right, the ibis-headed scribal god, Thoth, recording human worship of the gods. In the Louvre, Paris.

from Proverbs 8 to apply it to the Torah (see Box, "The heavenly Torah"). The idea of an eternal Torah in heaven soon prompted speculation that it could have been revealed to others before Moses. So Enoch sees heavenly tablets according to *1 Enoch* 106:19. The book of *Jubilees* claims that the heavenly Torah was revealed to Enoch, Noah, Abraham, Jacob, Levi, and Amram, as well as to Moses.[45]

The heavenly Torah

Wisdom praises herself, and tells of her glory in the midst of her people. … "My Creator chose the place for my tent. He said, 'Make your dwelling in Jacob, and in Israel receive your inheritance.' Before the ages, in the beginning, he created me, and for all the ages I shall not cease to be." … All this is the book of the covenant of the Most High God, the law that Moses commanded us as an inheritance for the congregations of Jacob. (Sir. 24:1, 8–9, 23 NRSV)

God found the whole way to knowledge, and gave her to his servant Jacob and to Israel, whom he loved. Afterward she appeared on earth and lived with humankind. She is the book of the commandments of God, the law that endures forever. All who hold her fast will live, and those who forsake her will die. (Baruch 3:35–4:1 NRSV; cf. Acts 7:53)

Belief in an eternal heavenly Torah had become widespread by the end of the first century BCE when Christians drew an analogy between the heavenly scripture and the pre-existent Christ. John's Gospel adapted the heavenly book motif to apply it to a living person, Jesus (John 1:1–17). A century or two later, a Valentinian Gnostic writer made the connection even more explicit by speaking of a "living book" and of Jesus as "putting on the book" (*Gospel of Truth* 19–20).

When rabbinic literature began to emerge at the end of the second century CE, it reflected the belief that God wrote the Torah on the evening of the first Sabbath after creation (*m. 'Avot* 5:6), or even before. Rabbi Akiba is quoted as saying that God consulted the Torah while creating the world (*m. 'Avot* 3:14). John Sawyer summarized later rabbinic elaborations of this theme.

> There is in fact a whole series of traditions to the effect that the Torah was written in heaven by God before creation. According to one, when Moses went up to heaven to receive the Torah, he found God sitting weaving crowns for the letters (BT Men. 29b; RA: 168). The pre-existent Torah was written with black fire on white fire (Midrash Psalm 90, para. 12). … When God was about to give the Torah to Moses, the angels at first complained: 'The beautiful Torah which you have hidden away since creation … do you now propose to give to a mere mortal?' (BT Shab. 88b). When God gave the Torah to Israel, the earth rejoiced and the heavens wept (Pes.R. 95a).

Mystical traditions in Hellenistic culture also celebrated this theme. They adapted Jewish as well as Egyptian and Mesopotamian legends about heavenly tablets, as Stephanie Dalley observed.

> The emerald tablet of Hermes Trismegistos contained the secrets of the gods, and was sometimes said to have been sealed with the seal of Hermes. Hermes was called Trismegistos 'thrice great' because he was thought to embody the wisdom of three ancient sages: the Greek Hermes, the Mesopotamian-Jewish Enoch, and the Egyptian god of wisdom and writing Thoth.

In the seventh century, the Qur'an picked up the theme of heavenly tablets. Sura 85:21–22 refers to the Qur'an as a "guarded tablet" and Suras 43:4 and 13:39 envision scripture as a heavenly "Mother Book." Dalley noted that a collection of tenth-century Muslim stories described the guarded tablet as "made of pearl and the pen made of a gigantic gemstone as the first things created by God."

Belief in a heavenly scripture ritualizes the iconic dimension of earthly scriptures by basing their legitimacy on a heavenly original. Books regularly fall victim to human incompetence and neglect, as well as to natural disaster and violent persecution. Scriptures suffer these problems as well, though now their millions of copies protect their contents more than most books. Promises in scriptures that their message is eternal reinforce beliefs that God must preserve the scripture in heaven. That supernatural book then becomes the eternal relic text that legitimizes all its earthly copies.[46]

The eternal word of God in Jewish, Christian, and Muslim scriptures

The word of our God will remain forever (Isaiah 40:8)
Heaven and earth will pass away, but my word will not pass away (Mark 15:31 NRSV)
We have, without doubt, sent down the Message; and We will assuredly guard it (Qur'an 15:9 Yusufali)

Scroll and Codex

The Torah is visually distinctive because it takes the form of a manuscript scroll. Pages of parchment containing three or four columns of hand-written text are stitched together edge to edge. Synagogues today commission new scrolls from highly trained Torah scribes at a cost of $20,000 or more.

Almost all other modern books take the form of a codex. A codex ties folded pages together on only one edge. This allows scribes and printers to put writing on both sides of the page and allows readers to skip quickly back and forth in the book.

The ancient Greeks and Romans used codices as notebooks. They preferred to keep literary and religious works in scrolls. Christians, however, quickly adopted the codex for their religious books. By the early Middle Ages, the codex had become the most common form of book due to Christian influence. Jews, perhaps in deliberate contrast to Christians, have preserved the scroll form for the Torah up to the present day. The physical forms of the scriptures – scroll or codex – therefore function as symbols that distinguish the religions from each other.

Ritualizing the iconic dimension of a scripture can interfere with reading it. Torah scrolls must be unrolled carefully. Their lack of vowel marks makes their pronunciation difficult. They should be kept only in synagogue arks. The rules for making and using Torah scrolls thus restrict access to them and make them hard to read. Jewish culture addresses this problem by also producing scriptures in the form of codices that are less restricted and easier to read.

Jewish scribes began to make torahs and tanaks in codex form starting in the eighth century CE. They supplied vowel points to indicate

Figure 3.10 A Torah scroll open to Exodus 30.

how to vocalize the ancient Hebrew text. They added marginal comments about rare words or variant readings. The Tiberian Masoretes perfected these systems of notation to produce the most authoritative manuscripts of the Jewish Bible to this day: the Aleppo Codex (ninth century) and the Leningrad Codex (tenth century). Since the invention of printing using movable metal type in the fifteenth century, printers have published many codices of Jewish scriptures. The Pentateuch is often printed and bound as a codex (a *chumash*) for individuals to read and study.

As printed and bound codices, the pentateuchs and tanaks do not carry the unique sanctity that Torah scrolls do for Jews. They therefore make the text of the Torah accessible for private study and devotion. Modern advances in printing technology and distribution have made such books inexpensive and readily available. Nevertheless, because the name of God appears in printed pentateuchs, tanaks, and prayer books, many Jews try to avoid desecrating them. They will not leave them open unattended or place other books on top of them. If they drop accidentally, it is customary to pick them up immediately and kiss them.

Unlike Jews, Samaritans use Torah scrolls only for ritual processions and display. They read the Torah from a codex, even when reading aloud to the congregation.

Figure 3.11 Genesis 28–29 in the Leningrad Codex (tenth century CE), in the National Library of Russia in St Petersburg. *Source*: Public domain image from Paul Kahle, *Masoreten des Westens*, vol. 1 (Stuttgart, 1927), plate 23/7 and Wikimedia Commons.

Ritualizing Gospels and Bible instead of Torah

Christians do not ritualize the Pentateuch separately or as a scroll. Since the second century CE, they have used codices for almost all of their books and especially for their scriptures. Now Christian scriptures are usually published together in the form of a single codex bound in distinctive ways to show it is the Bible. Earlier in history, however, Christian iconic ritualization of scripture focused mostly on the Gospels. The four Gospels of the New Testament were commonly bound together and became the focus of attention in church liturgies.[47]

That is still the case in many worship services of Orthodox, Catholic, and Anglican churches. A Gospel book is held high and processed into

Figure 3.12 Processing the Gospel in the Church of the Holy Sepulcher, Jerusalem. *Source*: Photos by Lyn Watts 2014; used by permission.

the sanctuary before being laid on the altar. Some people reach out to touch it for a blessing as it passes them by. The deacon or priest kisses the book before and after reading it. The congregation stands for the reading of the Gospel. The covers of Gospel books display crosses and icons, often in precious materials befitting their prominent role in the worship service.

Ritualizing the Gospels in these ways began early in Christian history. Public reading of the four Gospels was characteristic of proto-Catholic services by the end of the second century. In the third century, Cyprian argued that, after being read, the Gospel book should be placed where it is "conspicuous to the multitude of the Gentiles and be beheld by the brothers" (*Letters* 39, 4). After the Roman Empire adopted Christianity in the fourth century, Gospel books grew larger and more expensive. Their covers became icons of Christ, so that displaying the Gospels simultaneously displayed the icon to the worshipful view of the congregation. The Gospel book represented the presence of Christ in the midst of the congregation. Gospels were enthroned in Church councils and in Roman law courts to represent Christ presiding over the proceedings.

Early Christians ritualized Gospel books in many of the same ways that ancient Jews ritualized the Torah. Where Jews processed and displayed torahs, Christians processed and displayed gospels. By ritualizing the Gospels, Christians distinguished themselves from Jews who ritualize the Torah. Gospel books became a symbol of Christian identity. The persecution of Christians in the early fourth century targeted the owners of Christian books. Many died rather than give up their gospels. The codex of the Gospels or the Bible became a standard feature in Christian art, where it appears in the hands of Jesus, Mary, saints, angels, scholars, priests, and the pious dead. The Christian codex often appears juxtaposed to the tablets of the commandments, which in this context represent Jewish law in contrast to the Christian Gospel.

Since antiquity, the Bible's prestige has led to its reproduction in massive and expensive forms intended for public display. Christian Roman emperors commissioned the production of large bibles by imperial scribes. Medieval monks labored for years on elaborately illuminated manuscripts as acts of devotion. Their products became devotional objects in turn. When Johannes Gutenberg invented printing with movable type, his first commercial products were Latin bibles. Gutenberg bibles remain among the most prestigious and valuable objects in library and museum collections to this day. Nineteenth-century publishers sold massive bibles for use on church pulpits and home altars, as well as millions of inexpensive bibles for personal use.

Hymn, "O Word of God Incarnate"

by William W. How, 1867

O Word of God Incarnate,
O Wisdom from on high,
O Truth unchanged, unchanging,
O Light of our dark sky:
We praise thee for the radiance
That from the hallowed page,
A Lantern to our footsteps,
Shines on from age to age.
The church from thee, her Master,
Received the gift divine,
And still that light she lifteth
O'er all the earth to shine:
It is the sacred casket,
Where gems of truth are stored;
It is the heav'n-drawn picture
Of thee, the living Word.

Christian descriptions of their scripture's divine origins often draw on the Pentateuch's stories of Moses receiving the tablets and depositing them in the Ark of the Covenant. For example, a nineteenth-century hymn (see Box, "Hymn, 'O Word of God Incarnate'") equates scripture with Christ as the "Word of God" come from heaven. It also compares scripture to Israel's ark ("the sacred casket") that stored the tablets of the Ten Commandments. In modern churches, the Pentateuch continues to be venerated as part of the Christian Bible and also provides the foundational stories for understanding the nature of scripture itself.

Most low-church Protestants spurn elaborate rituals that they associate with Catholicism. They emphasize the meaning of the Bible's contents alone. Yet their rejection of icons and relics left the Bible as their only sacred object. As a result, Protestant rituals tend to focus only on the Bible more than the rituals of other Christian churches. In traditional Scottish Presbyterian worship services, the "beadle" led the procession carrying the pulpit Bible, followed by the minister. The Bible frequently sits on church alters and pulpits where the congregation can see it. Many churches emphasize the value of everybody reading from their own bibles during the service. Preachers often model this behavior by holding a bible while they preach. The image of a group of people each carrying a black leather bible to church has become a stereotype of conservative and evangelical Christians. In modern culture, the black leather-bound codex has become just as recognizable as the cross as a symbol of Christianity.[48]

The practice of displaying a book of scripture in the position of greatest honor reaches beyond synagogues and churches into broader Western culture. For example, a Bible is placed on an altar in Masonic lodges and manipulated during initiation rituals.[49] Much more visible to the public are oath ceremonies using bibles. In the Middle Ages, people touched holy objects – relics, crosses, scriptures – when they swore oaths to guarantee their sincerity. After the Protestant Reformation, only the Bible remained available for such use in many countries. It therefore became conventional to take oaths in law courts and oaths of office on a bible. While secular states have now stopped requiring oaths on bibles in courts of laws, they remain popular with politicians catering to their voters' religious sensibilities. As a result, scriptures of all sorts get manipulated in political oath ceremonies in countries around the world.

The books of the Pentateuch remain the first part of the Christian Bible. In that form, their iconic dimension gets ritualized in Christian churches and in modern culture. The custom of standing in respect for the reading of the scripture has been revived in some churches and applied to every part of the Bible. I witnessed the congregation of a large Baptist church rise to their feet for the scripture reading which, that

Figure 3.13 Lectern Bible, Saint Andrews, Scotland.

Sunday, consisted only of verses from Exodus 17. The modern convention of binding Christian scriptures in one volume makes it possible for parts of the Pentateuch, on any given Sunday, to be the main focus of Protestant ritual attention, something that is never the case in more liturgical Christian churches.

The Bible is the only material object that almost all Christians recognize as holy. Though the Orthodox, Catholic, and Protestant bibles differ somewhat in their contents, they all include the Pentateuch. So, of course, does the Tanak containing all Jewish scriptures, which is therefore frequently called "the Jewish Bible." The differences in contents can be ignored to allow the Bible to function as a unifying symbol of the whole Christian religion, and of its family relationship with Judaism as well.

Publishing Torahs and Bibles

Creating books has always been complicated. Scrolls may look simple, but the labor of tanning animal skins to create the parchment, of mixing inks and cutting reeds for pens, and of manually inscribing the text is time-consuming and expensive. The construction of codex books requires additional steps both before and after copying the text. Ancient books were therefore luxury items. Modern books have become inexpensive due to mass production, yet they still depend on investments in paper mills, printing presses, binderies, and sales networks. Publishing a book requires the labor of editors, designers, and salespersons, as well as authors.

The sanctity of scriptures draws attention to how they get produced. Religious communities can be particularly concerned with the accuracy of copies of scripture. They often take measures to regulate the production of scriptures in order to guarantee their accuracy. For example, King Fuad of Egypt commissioned a standardized edition of the Qur'an in 1923 which has become the authoritative version accepted around the world today. Another example: the Sikh community in India has given one publishing company a monopoly on printing its scripture in order to regulate its accuracy and purity.

Similar concerns have shaped the form and contents of Jewish and Christian scriptures since antiquity. The Dead Sea Scrolls show that manuscripts of the same biblical books varied from one another in the late Second Temple period. The rabbis of the following centuries selected one Hebrew text as the standard for each book, and other text types fell out of use. Around the same time, Christian concern over inaccuracies in Latin translations of the Bible led to the creation of a new translation, the Vulgate, which became the official Bible of the Roman Catholic Church.

In the Middle Ages, a Jewish sect called the Karaites rejected the Talmud and focused their attention on scriptures alone. They developed new scholarly tools to guarantee the accuracy of their biblical manuscripts. They invented vowel points and marginal notes about rare words and possible misspellings. They counted and recorded the number of words and letters in each book. Their "Masoretic" bibles, especially the Aleppo Codex and the Leningrad Codex, still are widely accepted models for the Hebrew biblical text.

Scribes often regard manually copying scriptures as a spiritual act that is important quite apart from how the finished book gets used. Medieval Christian monks reproduced and illuminated biblical manuscripts as ascetic exercises to discipline their minds and bodies and to express their commitment to God. Stunningly beautiful manuscripts from the British Isles, such as the Codex Amiatinus, were produced in monastic scriptoria while others, such as the Lindisfarne Gospels, seem to have been the work of individual hermetic scribes working for years alone.

Fascination with Jewish and Christian scriptures has created a commercial market for them. Scribes and publishers have produced very many copies to meet that demand. They have often created deluxe editions to attract the interest of wealthy buyers. Already in the fourth century CE, John Chrysostom complained about Christians who placed more value on how their books of scripture looked than on studying their contents.

> *All their care is for the fineness of the parchments, and the beauty of the letters, not for reading them.*[50]

Beautifully illuminated manuscripts became symbols of wealth and power in the Middle Ages, and some monasteries catered to this market. For example, in the Ottonian Gospels, the monk Liuthar pictured himself giving this book illuminated in gold leaf to Emperor Otto III, who appears on the facing page enthroned like Christ. Many later emperors of the Holy Roman Empire took their coronation oaths on this book. Here the high value of the scripture is represented by its expensive reproduction which explicitly legitimizes its producer, Liuthar, and its owner, Otto III, and his successors. Now it is displayed in the treasury of Aachen Cathedral, where its beauty supports the religious prestige and tourist attraction of this 1,200-year-old church.

After Johannes Gutenberg invented printing with movable metal type in the mid-fifteenth century, print shops quickly appeared in many European cities. Printing reduced the cost of book production by being able to print many identical pages at once. Early print runs numbered

Figure 3.14 Frontispiece of the Ottonian Gospels, ca. 1000 CE, in the treasury of the Cathedral in Aachen, Germany.

only several hundred copies, but they became larger as the technology improved. The invention of printing raised hopes of eliminating errors by identical reproduction, but it also increased the commercial market for scriptures and the risk that publishers would be motivated more by profit than by concerns for accuracy.

Jewish and Christian denominations therefore developed their own publishing businesses to print scriptures and other religious texts. They continue to sponsor new editions and translations which they recommend to their congregations. They have also attempted to regulate the publication of scriptures. The government of England, for example, licensed publication of the "Authorized" Version, more popularly known as the King James Version, to only three publishers over 300 years. In the nineteenth century, bible societies printed and distributed, often for free, millions of copies of bibles in Europe and America, and missionaries carried them around the world. By the end of the twentieth century, bibles were available to almost anyone who wanted one and in almost every language. The Bible had become the most widely distributed book in human history.

Though many Jewish and Christian denominations continue active publishing programs, commercial and academic publishers now dominate the publication of bibles and bible-related books, which is a profitable part of the publishing business. (That includes the publisher of this book: Wiley is a publicly traded corporation with income of $1.73 billion in 2016; it bought Blackwell Publishing, including its religious studies books, for more than $1 billion in 2006.) Commercial interest in generating sales now drives many bible publishing decisions and has resulted in many different editions for every kind of reader. In addition to the old tradition of producing highly edited and illustrated bibles for children, there are now bibles designed specifically for women, for men, for teen boys, and for teen girls. Usually, these books reproduce a standard translation of the biblical text, but surround it with commentary and illustrations directed at the intended audience. Publishers have appropriated the formats of other popular print genres for bibles, including glossy magazines and comic books. Though some devout people find such commercial marketing offensive, many others find it compatible with a religious mandate to "spread the Word" to as many people as possible. Missionary ideals and profit motives often converge in the religious publishing business.

Printing technology not only increased the number of books for sale, it also grew the market for deluxe editions. Wood cuts and copper plate engravings embellished many printed bibles with illustrations of famous scenes. Printing also made it economically feasible to provide many readers access to commentaries on the same page as the biblical text. Such "glossed bibles" had appeared as manuscripts already by 1200 CE, but printing made them cheaper. For example, a "Rabbinic Bible" (*Mikraot Gedolot*) surrounds the text of all the books of the Tanak with commentary by influential medieval scholars, such as Rashi and Ramban. The scholar Yaakov ben Hayyim and the printer Daniel Bomberg established

Figure 3.15 Contemporary English bibles.

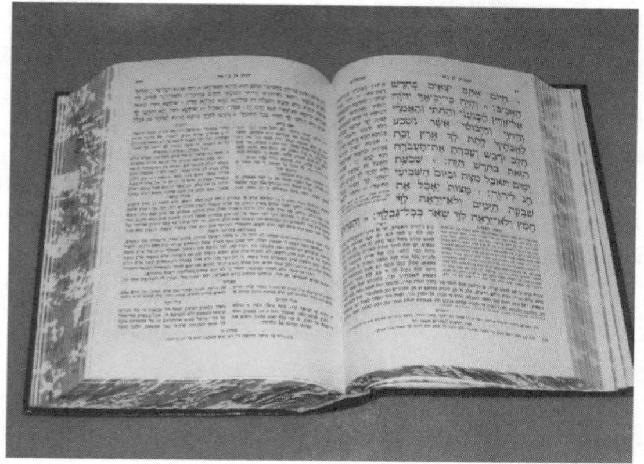

Figure 3.16 *Mikraot Gedolot*, a Rabbinic Bible, open to Exod. 13:4–6 in Hebrew and the Aramaic Targum of Onkelos, and commentaries by Rashi, Rashbam and others. *Source*: Public domain image from Wikimedia Commons.

Figure 3.17 Complutensian Polyglot Bible open to Genesis 1 in Hebrew, Latin, Greek, and Aramaic, with a Latin translation of the Aramaic; in the library of Saint Andrews University.

this form in the early sixteenth century and it has remained popular ever since. Rabbinic bibles shaped the semantic dimension of Jewish scriptures by popularizing the medieval commentators, especially Rashi, as authorities for biblical interpretation. They shaped its iconic dimension by establishing the image of its pages – Hebrew biblical text surrounded by Aramaic targums and commentaries – as a symbol of the Jewish combination of scripture and interpretive tradition. The typographical layout of such bibles encourages readers to always understand the text in relationship to commentary and translation, as David Stern observed.

> The glossed format with the Biblical text and commentaries on the same page was obviously a more convenient text for a student. But more than being convenient, it was transformative. It changed the very nature of Bible-study. ... He (or she) now read it verse by verse with the commentary intervening wherever it existed. The Biblical text was thus atomized into small lexical and semantic units that combined verse and exegesis.

Early printers also produced glossed Christian bibles. The sixteenth-century Geneva Bible was famous for its interpretive notes. Christian scholars seized on the new technology to produce polyglot bibles that placed the ancient sources in their different languages and typefaces side by side.[51]

The marketing of digital texts since the 1990s has provided new ways to gloss biblical texts with multiple translations and commentaries. Indeed, digital "hypertext" seemed ideal for this purpose. While free biblical texts quickly spread on the internet, established publishers and new companies quickly marketed digitized bibles tagged with various kinds of "helps" and commentaries. The arrival of smart phones in the following decade led to their multiplication as downloadable apps. Bible publishers have proven very eager to adopt the newest technology to market their ancient product.

As the printing industry matured, printers refined their typefaces to make reading easier and faster. Their goal has been to make the type practically invisible so that readers absorb the text's meaning without thinking consciously about the forms of the letters. This culminates a process begun already by medieval manuscripts that introduced spaces between words, lower-case lettering, verse divisions, and chapter headings. The goal has always been to make reading visually easier. It has steadily reinforced the efforts of individual readers to understand the meaning of scriptures for themselves. These incremental modifications to the look of a biblical page have joined rising literacy rates, the ever-growing commercial book market, and religious reformations to emphasize individual interpretation and conviction. They encourage individualism and scripture-oriented devotion among Jews and Christians.[52]

A small but notable counter-trend appeared in the work of artists and craft printers who produced art bibles around the turn of the third millennium. For example, the illustrator and printmaker Barry Moser created engravings and modified typefaces to print the limited edition Pennyroyal Caxton Bible, which he finished in 1999. An even more ambitious project was led by the calligrapher Donald Jackson, who assembled a team to hand copy and illuminate the Saint John's Bible. This vellum manuscript, finished in 2011 and bound in seven volumes, combines the qualities of original art, icon, and reproducible book. Images of its hand-written and hand-illuminated parchment pages draw visitors to see the unique original, and also generate interest in buying its reproductions in a variety of formats and at various levels of expense. Unlike most other art bibles, however, the St John's Bible retains a religious context through the monastery, St John's Abbey in Minnesota, that sponsored its production. The monks of St John's ritualize scripture in all three dimensions routinely in their worship services and devotions. The St John's Bible functions as the Abbey's new relic text that reinforces the scriptural identity of the monks that sponsor it, display it, and market its reproductions. They consciously continue the tradition of medieval monks who illuminated books of scripture to bring it fame and glory and, hopefully, to inspire readers as well.

Decalogue Tablets

One part of the Pentateuch is often singled out for separate iconic ritualization. The Ten Commandments, or "Decalogue," appear as two tablets on Torah arks and on the facades of synagogues. The text is usually abbreviated, sometimes represented only by numerals or missing altogether. The image of two tablets is enough to refer to the Ten Commandments or to all the laws of God, and by extension to Judaism as a whole. The image of the two tablets plays the same role in Christian art, where it frequently represents Judaism as "the Old Covenant."

Christians have also used displays of the Decalogue to represent the essence of divine law as a guide to human morality. While Christians reject or ignore most of the ritual and legal instructions of the Pentateuch, they usually revere the Ten Commandments as eternal moral and religious obligations. During the Reformation in the sixteenth century, Protestants often replaced pictorial art with Decalogue boards to emphasize the text of scripture over visual art.

In Christian politics, the tablets of the commandments carry associations with the laws of nations. In England, displays of the Ten Commandments represented the enforcement of national law especially in the churches. Similarly, the pediment of the US Supreme Court building shows Moses holding the tablets as the central and largest figure among three ancient lawgivers. Decalogue boards and plaques that display the full text of the commandments continue to hang in many churches and homes.

In contrast to older Jewish and Christian art that used the tablets to depict Jewish distinctiveness, associating the tablets with national law uses the Ten Commandments to represent common Judeo-Christian values. The popularity of the Hollywood film *The Ten Commandments* led to stone Decalogue monuments being placed in and around US courthouses in the 1950s and later. In recent decades, lawsuits against this government endorsement of religion have removed many of them. Christian Evangelicals, supported by some Jews, have responded by erecting even more. Placing the monuments on government property, especially in courthouses, makes a political claim that the United States is a Judeo-Christian country. Many American Jews complain, however, that Jewish and Christian heritage should not be so easily conflated. Some Christian and Jewish groups believe that government support for this religious icon undermines their religious freedom. They have joined lawsuits to remove the monuments from government properties. Decalogue monuments and plaques have therefore become divisive symbols in American politics and religion.[53]

Figure 3.18 Moses, Solon, and Confucius on the east pediment of the US Supreme Court in Washington, DC. Built in 1935.

Figure 3.19 Ten Commandments on a monument at the Texas State Capitol in Austin.

Summary

The Pentateuch is venerated by Jews and Christians as part of their scriptures, and by Samaritans as their whole scripture. Yet how these traditions ritualize the Pentateuch's iconic dimension shows that their veneration is directed at very different *things*. A Samaritan Torah scroll in paleo-Hebrew script inside a three-part cylindrical case is not the same thing as a Jewish Torah scroll in Aramaic script wrapped in mantle and ornaments. Neither one resembles a Christian Bible much at all. We may well wonder whether the three religions really share a scripture in the iconic dimension or not.

Nevertheless, it is clear that for the last 2,400 years, the iconic dimension of the Torah and of bibles that contain the Pentateuch has been ritualized regularly, often elaborately. Iconic ritualization of torahs and bibles shows no sign of diminishing in the twenty-first century.

The Pentateuch's Iconic Dimension Before Ezra

The story of Ezra displaying the Torah scroll to a crowd of people in a Jerusalem plaza is the earliest example of its ritualization in all three textual dimensions – iconic, performative, and semantic. The first part of this Chapter has documented the gradual increase in evidence for the Torah's iconic ritualization in the Second Temple period until its explicit enshrinement in Late Antique synagogues and rabbinic literature. That might lead you to think that the iconic ritualization of Torah followed from its semantic dimension's growing authority over Jewish worship and conduct. But there is reason to believe that the iconic ritualization of Torah and of parts of the Pentateuch began much earlier in Israel's history. In fact, the text of the Pentateuch models and demands its own iconic ritualization.

The evidence for Ezra's ceremony and for earlier iconic texts in Israel comes only from references within the Hebrew Bible itself. This fact makes it difficult to understand the history of Israel's iconic text rituals because, first, the writing of many biblical texts cannot be dated accurately, especially the contents of the Pentateuch, and second, they were edited many times in antiquity (these issues will be discussed in Chapter 5). Historians do not recognize any Pentateuchal artifacts older than the Dead Sea Scrolls that date from the third to first centuries BCE. The Hebrew Bible provides evidence that ancient Israelites treated Decalogue tablets and Torah scrolls iconically, but we do not know when they did so or how such practices evolved. Nor can we be sure of the contents of these Decalogue tablets and Torah scrolls. However, material and literary evidence from other ancient Middle Eastern cultures provides contexts that can help us understand the Bible's references to iconic texts in ancient Israel.

The Tablets of the Commandments

According to Exodus and Deuteronomy, Moses received stone tablets from God on Mount Sinai. The tablets of the commandments are the most obviously iconic texts mentioned in the Bible.

The stories do not describe the tablets very much, but their stone material indicates their purpose. Stone is the most permanent writing surface. It is difficult to carve, which makes stone inscriptions expensive. Therefore texts inscribed on stone look permanent and extravagant. These qualities have made stone a favorite medium for displaying the propaganda of kings and governments for 5,000 years. Archeologists have found royal inscriptions on stone from most ancient literate cultures, though so far not from the kings of Israel and Judah. Ancient kings also deposited tablets of stone or metal out of sight in the foundations of palaces and temples. Their durable media was intended to remind the gods of the king's architectural accomplishments and worshipful donations forever.

Though the prominent display of Decalogue tablets in Jewish and Christian art resembles ancient displays of royal inscriptions, the Pentateuch's description of the tablets evokes the tradition of deposit texts instead. Moses does not read the tablets aloud or even display them to the Israelites. He deposits them in the Ark of the Covenant. This story also evokes the ancient practice of placing the texts of treaties and laws in temples so that the gods act as witnesses to binding commitments. Stone inscription and temple deposit ratified the contents of the texts and put their legal provisions into force.

The tablets of the commandments

I will give you the stone tablets and the Torah and the commandment that I have written for their instruction. (Exod. 24:12)

God gave Moses two tablets of the covenant, stone tablets written by the finger of God. ... written on both sides, front and back. The tablets were the work of God and the writing was the writing of God engraved on the tablets. (Exod. 31:18; 32:15–16)

YHWH spoke these words in a loud voice out of the deep dark fiery cloud on the mountain to your whole assembly, and added no more, and wrote them on two stone tablets and gave them to me. (Deut. 5:22)

YHWH said to me: Carve two stone tablets like the first ones. Bring them up the mountain to me and make a wooden ark. ... YHWH wrote on the tablets what was written on the first ones, the ten words that YHWH your God spoke out of the fire on the mountain on the day of the assembly. YHWH gave them to me and I put the tablets in the ark that I had made, and there they are, just as YHWH commanded. (Deut. 10:1, 4–5)

The Pentateuch tells a complicated story about the tablets. After Moses repeats God's instructions to Israel and writes them on a scroll (Exod. 24:3–4), YHWH promises to write them down on stone tablets (24:12). Moses receives the tablets 40 days later (31:18) and then immediately smashes them in fury because the Israelites were worshipping the golden calf (32:19). His actions vividly depict the breaking of the covenant. Moses then rewrites the commandments on a second pair of tablets at God's command (34:27). It is not clear, however, whether the mention here of writing the "ten words" refers to the commandments in this chapter (34:12–26, often called "the Ritual Decalogue") or to God's speech to the Israelites in Exod. 20:2–17. Deuteronomy insists, however, that "the ten words" refers to the speech to all the Israelites. It also says that God wrote both sets of tablets personally (Deut. 5:22; 10:1–5).

Exodus and Deuteronomy report that Moses also wrote the whole Torah on a scroll (Exod. 24:4–7; Deut. 31:9). Deuteronomy goes on to say that he gave it for safekeeping to "the levitical priests who carry the Ark of the Covenant of YHWH and to all the Israelite elders." This indicates that the Torah scroll, too, was ritually deposited in the sanctuary (Deut. 31:26). Unlike the tablets of the commandments, however, the Torah scroll circulated publically both orally and in writing (Deut. 31:12–13, 22; cf. 17:18–19).

So the Pentateuch depicts God speaking aloud to the Israelites and writing the words on stone tablets. It also shows Moses writing down God's words on a scroll and reading it aloud to the Israelites. Furthermore, it requires that the tablets and the scroll be preserved in the sanctuary. Later Jewish and Christian ritualization of iconic decalogues, Torah scrolls, gospels, and bibles grew from these precedents in the Pentateuch itself.

These stories and commandments tie writing and oral performance closely together. Writing down the commandments ratifies the covenant between God and Israel. The order to preserve them in the sanctuary and to read them aloud aims to remind the Israelites regularly of their obligations under the covenant. The written texts provide physical evidence to legitimize the claims of priests and prophets who call on Israel to keep the covenant with YHWH.

The Ark of the Covenant as Torah Shrine

Exodus and Deuteronomy say that Moses deposited the Decalogue tablets in the Ark of the Covenant. This ark receives more attention from biblical writers than do the tablets themselves. Joshua describes it being carried into battle during the conquest of Canaan (Josh. 6:4–6; 1 Sam. 4:3–11). Wherever it settled in its tent shrine automatically became the central sanctuary of the Israelite tribes. 1 Samuel narrates how God's anger at the priests of Shiloh led to the Philistines capturing the ark. They installed it in their own temple next to the image of their god. But plague devastated their cities until they sent it back to Israel (1 Sam. 4–6). King David brought the ark to Jerusalem, but even this proved dangerous. On the first attempt, a man who accidentally touched the ark died instantly (2 Sam. 6). The ark then stayed for three months with one family, who miraculously became rich. David was more successful at claiming the ark on his second attempt, and Solomon installed it in the newly built temple in Jerusalem (1 Kgs. 8:4–9; 2 Chr. 35:3). No story tells of the ark emerging from the temple after this time.[54]

Only Exodus 25 and 37 describe the ark in detail. This gilded wooden box measured approximately four feet long, two feet wide, and two feet high (ca. 120 × 60 × 60 cm). Its solid gold lid (called a *kapporet* "mitigation center") was surmounted by two winged sphinxes (*cherubim* in Hebrew) whose wings stretched out towards each other. The ark was carried by two poles attached to its side.

The Ark of the Covenant

YHWH said to Moses: ... Have them also make an ark of acacia wood. ... Cover the ark with pure gold. ... Make poles of acacia wood ... and use them to carry the ark. ... Then make a mitigation center of pure gold. ... Make two winged sphinxes of hammered gold, one at each end of the mitigation center. ... Put the mitigation center on top of the ark. Put the stone tablets of the covenant that I will give you inside the ark. There I will meet with you, there above the mitigation center between the two sphinxes that are on top of the Ark of the Covenant. (Exod. 25:1, 10–11, 13–14, 17–18, 21–22)

The ark was built to contain the tablets of the commandments (Exod. 25:21; 40:20; Deut. 10:5). The Pentateuch portrays it essentially as a book box, and 1 Kings insists that it contained nothing else (1 Kgs. 8:9). But the Pentateuch claims that other objects of great religious significance were also deposited inside or beside it: a jar of manna (Exod. 16:33–34), Aaron's flowering rod (Num. 17:10), and scrolls containing the Torah and Moses's indictment of Israel (Deut. 31:9, 24–26).

The ancient objects that most resemble this description of the Ark of the Covenant are Egyptian Anubis chests. A spectacular example was found in the tomb of King Tutankhamun, who died around 1323 BCE. This gold-plated wooden box with carrying poles is surmounted by a statue of a jackal that represents Anubis, the Egyptian god of burial and embalming. The chest contained several amulets in the form of figurines, a papyrus-shaped scepter, jewels, and embalming chemicals. The chest's gold carvings include speeches by Anubis about embalming. Another tomb contained a less elaborate Anubis chest with papyrus scrolls inside, mostly texts of funeral rituals.[55]

The appearance and contents of Israel's Ark of the Covenant, then, derived from the broader religious culture of the ancient Middle East, or at least Egypt. Its iconography, of course, differs from that of Anubis, who presided over Egyptian graveyards. The Hebrew Bible describes YHWH as a sky god who, like many ancient sky gods, was represented by winged mythological creatures. Phoenician iconography frequently depicted gods sitting on sphinx thrones. But because they believed their gods to be invisible, the Phoenicians installed empty sphinx thrones in their temples, sometimes

Figure 3.20 Anubis chest in the treasury of Tutankhamun's tomb in the Valley of the Kings, Egypt. Photo by Harry Burton, 1926. *Source*: Photo by Harry Burton, 1926. Image distributed under a Creative Commons CC BY-NC-SA 2.0 license.

Figure 3.21 Stone sphinx throne supporting carved stelae; first millennium BCE, Phoenician, in the Louvre, Paris.

with steles on the seat. In the same way in Israel, the ark's cover surmounted by two sphinxes functions as the throne of an invisible god.

> *The Ark of the Covenant of YHWH of hosts who sits enthroned upon the sphinxes.* (1 Sam. 4:4)

Or the ark could be thought of as God's footstool (Lam. 2:1), especially since other ancient cultures frequently deposited important texts "at the feet" of gods in temples.

Exodus says the ark occupied the inner-most room of Israel's tent sanctuary, the Tabernacle, and Kings tells us that it later occupied the inner sanctum of Solomon's temple. The ark took the place of the statue of the god in temples of other ancient cultures.[56] The Ark of the Covenant, then, represented the presence of God in ancient Israel more than any other material object. Its presence inside the Tabernacle and First Temple made these sanctuaries "the house of YHWH." But the Pentateuch portrays the ark itself as the container of even more sacred objects, tablets written personally by YHWH.

It is surprising, therefore, that the priests who rebuilt the temple after the Babylonian Exile apparently did not build another ark for its inner sanctum. Jeremiah predicted that the Ark of the Covenant would not be remade.

> *They will no longer announce, "The Ark of the Covenant of YHWH!" It will not come to mind, they will not remember it or look for it, and they will not make another one. In that time, they will call Jerusalem "The throne of YHWH!"* (Jer. 3:16–17)

Texts from the end of the Second Temple period agree that the "holy of holies" was empty (explicitly Josephus and Tacitus; implicitly 1 Macc. 4:49–51). Perhaps the builders of the Second Temple believed they could follow the instructions in Exodus to rebuild the Tabernacle's other furnishings, but they could not recreate tablets written by God. Since the ark served as a reliquary for the tablets, there was no point in rebuilding the ark for it to stand empty. They apparently could tolerate an empty Holy of Holies, since they believed God is invisible anyway, better than an ark without tablets inside.

The Priestly Blessing Amulets

In 1979, an archeologist found two one-inch-wide silver scrolls in a burial cave above the Hinnom valley in Jerusalem. Once unrolled, they proved to contain words closely resembling the priestly blessing found in Num.

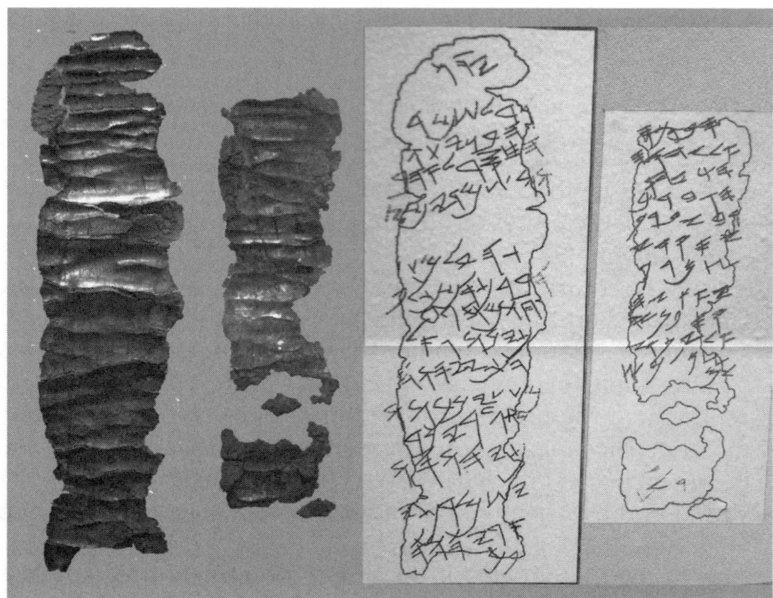

Figure 3.22 Silver amulet scrolls from Ketef Hinnom; seventh to fifth century BCE; in the Israel Museum, Jerusalem.

6:23–26. The writing on the tiny scrolls and other discoveries in the same cave show that they may be as much as 2,600 years old, dating from the last decades of the Kingdom of Judah before the Babylonian Exile or, possibly, shortly after the Exile.

Many have called the Ketef Hinnom amulets the oldest physical evidence for the text of any part of the Pentateuch. It is more likely that both the Pentateuch and the amulets quote the oral blessings pronounced by priests in Jerusalem's temple and circulating in wider Judean society. Many historians do not think the Pentateuch existed yet when the amulets were made. Even if it did, nothing suggests that its priestly texts were widely published at this time. The regular temple liturgy or popular religious practice are more plausible sources for the similar language in the amulets and the Pentateuch. The amulets prove that some Judeans in the seventh to fifth centuries considered the blessing very important, just as its quotation as the only verbal liturgy in the books of Leviticus and Numbers indicates.[57]

The silver scrolls were, of course, never intended to be unrolled. Their silver material and tiny size show that they were created to be carried as an amulet, not to be read, and were probably worn on a string around the neck. Amulets are a common feature of human religious practice worldwide. Textual amulets were common in the ancient Middle East. Tiny papyrus scrolls containing spells for protection have been found in first millennium BCE metal containers in Egypt, and scroll amulets proliferated in Hellenistic and Roman cultures, including among Jews and Christians. That is not surprising, since Deuteronomy seems to require ritualization of the Torah's iconic dimension in the form of amulets and inscriptions.

> *Tie [these words] as a sign on your hand, make them a symbol between your eyes.* (Deut. 6:8)

The priestly blessing invokes YHWH's protection and favor and so is perfectly suited to iconic ritualization in the form of amulets.

The Torah as Monumental Inscription

Deuteronomy 27:8 requires that the Torah be displayed monumentally on Mount Ebal in the land of Israel. Joshua 8 reports that this command was fulfilled immediately after the conquest of the first cities of the land. These texts describing the command and its fulfillment are not exactly the same. Deuteronomy requires the erection of an altar and, nearby, standing stones covered in plaster so they can be inscribed with ink. Joshua seems to have instead plastered the stones of the altar and written the Torah on the altar itself. Two other passages associate the writing down of Torah with setting up stones, but do not indicate writing on the stones themselves (Exod. 24:4; Josh. 24:26).

Torah monuments

On the day you cross the Jordan into the land that YHWH your God is giving you, you must set up large stones and plaster them. You must write on them all the words of this Torah .... You must set up these stones about which I am commanding you today on Mount Ebal and you must plaster them. ... You must write on the stones all the words of this Torah very clearly. (Deut. 27:2–4, 8)

Joshua built an altar to YHWH, the God of Israel, on Mount Ebal. ... And he wrote there on the stones a copy of the Torah of Moses which he wrote before the Israelites. (Josh. 8:30, 32).

No such plastered standing stones or altars have survived from ancient Israel. That is not surprising, since plaster cannot last very long on rocks exposed to the weather. Plaster inscriptions have been discovered on a few interior walls where they have not weathered. Stones, on the other hand, withstand weather rather well and standing stones are a very common feature of cult sites throughout Syria-Palestine. But they do not carry inscriptions and rarely even engravings.

Monumental inscriptions on stone appear frequently among the artefactual remains of other ancient cultures. They usually celebrate the achievements of kings who boast of their victories and temple constructions. They sometimes include instructions and endowments for offerings, though it is rare for an entire legal code to be inscribed monumentally, as Hammurabi did (see Figure 2.3 on p. 63).[58]

Deuteronomy and Joshua propose that monumental inscriptions should consist of Torah. Even a king should occupy himself with writing Torah (Deut. 17:18–19). No royal inscriptions have yet been discovered from the kingdoms of Israel and Judah, nor have any Torah inscriptions as described in Deuteronomy and Joshua survived. We can only speculate, then, whether mandates such as these influenced Israel's culture of monument production or not.

Josiah's Torah Scroll

According to 2 Kings 22–23, a Torah scroll was found in the Jerusalem temple during renovations in the late seventh century BCE. The priests read it to King Josiah, who as a result launched far-reaching reforms of Judah's religious practices.

Stories of lost-and-found ritual books were a staple feature of ancient literate cultures from the Babylonians, Hittites, and Egyptians to the Greeks and the Romans.[59] Already around 2100 BCE, Sumerian king Shulgi boasted about his own scribal and linguistic skills and his zeal in preserving ancient hymns and ritual texts.

> *I am no fool … when I have discovered* tigi *and* zamzam *hymns from past days, old ones from ancient times, I have never declared them to be false, and have never contradicted their contents. I have conserved these antiquities, never abandoning them to oblivion. … So that they should never fall into disuse, I have added them to the singers' repertoire, and thereby I have set the heart of the land on fire and aflame.*[60]

Finding a Torah scroll in the temple

Hilkiah, the high priest, said to Shaphan the scribe: "I have found a Torah scroll in the temple of YHWH." Hilkiah gave the scroll to Shaphan and he read it. ... Shaphan the scribe informed the king: "Hilkiah has given me a scroll." He then read it to the king. When the king heard the words of the Torah scroll, he tore his clothes (2 Kgs. 22:8, 10–11). [The prophet Huldah then authenticates the scroll as representing YHWH's will (22:12–20).] *The king went up to the temple of YHWH and with him all the men of Judah, the inhabitants of Jerusalem, the priests, the prophets, and all the insignificant as well as significant people. He read in their hearing all the words of the covenant scroll that was found in the temple of YHWH. The king stood beside the pillar and made a covenant before YHWH to follow YHWH and to observe all the commandments, the testimonies, and the statutes with all his mind and will and to keep the words of this covenant written in this scroll. All the people joined in this covenant* (23:2–3). [Josiah then removes illegitimate cult objects from the Jerusalem temple and destroys worship sites ("high places") in the villages of Judah as well as in the old northern kingdom around Samaria (23:4–20).] *The king commanded all the people: "Keep the Passover to YHWH your God as it is written in this covenant book." ... Josiah also did away with all the abominations that were found in the land of Judah and in Jerusalem, so that he kept the words of the Torah that were written in the scroll that Hilkiah the priest found in the temple.* (23:21–22)

In the second millennium BCE, an Ugaritic omen text specifies the need to eat the meat offering "in accordance with the documents." Around the same time, Hittite kings cited examining old written documents as proof of their ritual fidelity.

> *And whatever I, My Majesty, discover now in the written records, I will carry out.*

During a long-drawn-out plague, searches of Hittite archives turned up old ritual and treaty texts. When prophets confirmed that failure to follow these texts had brought the plague on Hatti (just like the prophet Huldah confirmed the threats in Josiah's law book, 2 Kgs. 22:13–20), the rituals were reinstated and offerings were made to compensate for the violations.[61]

An example nearly contemporary with 2 Kings can be found in a fragmentary inscription of King Nabonidus of Babylon (539 BCE), which depicts him consulting various kinds of texts about temples and rituals.

> *A stela of Nebuchadnezzar, king of Babylon, son of Ninurta-nādin-šumi, on which appeared the representation of an ēntu-priestess and were described the rites, rules, and ceremonies relating to her office, was brought with other tablets from Ur to Babylon, in ignorance of what Sîn, lord of kings, wished .... He (Nabonidus) took a good look at the tablets and was afraid. He was attentive to Sîn's great commandment.*[62]

Later, during the Roman Empire, the geographer Pausanius (ca. 115–180 CE) described how the Messenian culture survived defeat and banishment by the miraculous preservation of their rituals on a tin scroll in a bronze urn. The Messenians discovered it after returning to their homeland in 369 BCE, which allowed them to revive their traditions. The scroll and urn became venerated relics.[63] So there was much interest in various periods and cultures in the ritual requirements of old texts.

Ancient art and artifacts, especially from Egypt, reinforce this impression. Egyptian art regularly depicts priests holding scrolls aloft in public processions and funerary rituals. Their temple libraries were called "Houses of Life" and were restricted to only some priests. From at least the early second millennium BCE on, Egyptians used portable chests topped by statues or images of the god Anubis to keep ritual texts as well as cultic implements. This artistic evidence combines with literary references to show that, throughout their literate histories, ancient Middle Eastern and Mediterranean cultures manipulated scrolls, tablets, and the boxes that contained them for ritual purposes.

The story of the discovery of Josiah's scroll in 2 Kings uses this widespread motif. Modern historians often doubt that Josiah's scroll was as old as he claimed. They think it may have been a "pious fraud" created by the temple priests. Some scholars argue that the entire scene in 2 Kings is fictional and never happened. There can be no doubt that many ancient stories of lost-and-found ritual books describe forgeries that were created to justify religious and political claims. On the other hand, many ancient kings and priests were really worried about the negative consequences of failing to follow the instructions of ancient rituals. That made them vulnerable to being deceived by forgeries, but it also raised their interest in discovering genuinely old books.

So claiming to have found an ancient ritual book may well be a fictional device used by priests when conducting rituals and by authors when writing about them. The appearance of this theme nevertheless attests to the *existence* of the scroll of Torah at the time that 2 Kings was written in the sixth century BCE, since there would be no point in validating the authority of a non-existent book. The story of the scroll's discovery in the temple was plausible to ancient readers, and King Josiah's reaction

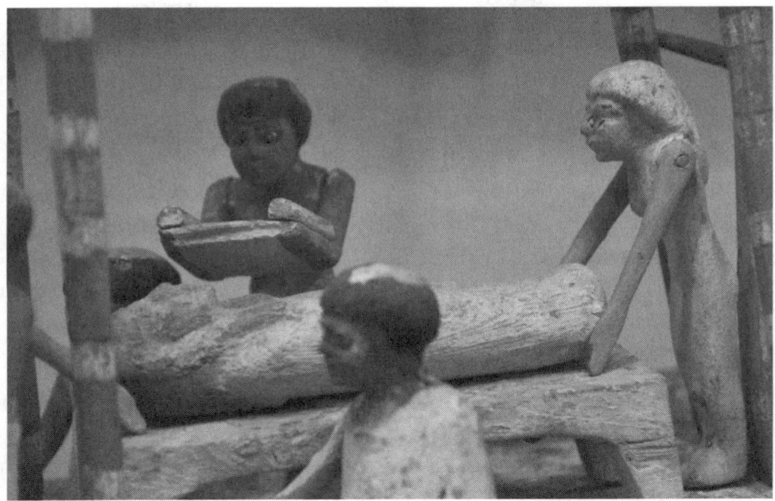

Figure 3.23 Scribe holding scroll over sarcophagus in a model of a funerary boat from the tomb of Djehuty, Egypt ca. 1962–1786 BCE. In the Metropolitan Museum of Art, New York.

resembles stories about pious kings in many literatures of the ancient world. So the story of the book's discovery glorifies Josiah's piety. It also used his good reputation to establish the authority of written Torah.

The contents of Josiah's book are not so obvious. Many historians have associated it with the book of Deuteronomy because of the nature of Josiah's religious reforms. In 1805, Wilhelm de Wette argued that Deuteronomy was written earlier in Josiah's reign to justify the reforms, and that view has dominated biblical studies for two centuries. However, Deuteronomy's restricted view of kingship and its emphasis on legal issues do not fit the Josiah story very well. Some scholars have suggested that the role of the high priest and the emphasis on purifying religious practices resemble the contents of the Holiness Code more than they do Deuteronomy.

Neither 2 Kings nor other biblical texts provide any reason to think that Josiah's reforms had a lasting effect. After he died in battle in 609 BCE, his successors reversed his religious reforms. Twenty-two years later, the Babylonians destroyed Judea and Jerusalem and exiled its king and upper classes. 2 Kings and many other biblical books maintain that this event was divine punishment for failing to keep the covenant with God. There is therefore no reason to think that a Torah scroll was ritualized regularly after Josiah's death, until priests who returned from exile did so to legitimize the rituals of Jerusalem's Second Temple.

The story of Ezra's Torah reading provides our first account of the Torah's ritualization after Josiah, which is our first account of the Torah's ritualization after Joshua. So the Hebrew Bible's story of the written Torah consists of four episodes widely separated in time:

- Moses writes down the Torah in the wilderness.
- Shortly thereafter, Joshua reads and ratifies the Torah in the land.
- Six hundred years later, Josiah discovers and reads the Torah in the temple and renews the covenant.
- Two hundred years after that, Ezra reads and teaches Torah and renews the covenant.

In between these Torah readings, biblical books tell a story of widespread religious infidelity in Israel and Judah which led to the kingdoms' destruction. Their account aims to persuade readers and listeners not to repeat the mistakes of their ancestors. They should instead follow the examples of Moses, Joshua, Josiah, and Ezra by venerating the Torah scroll and obeying its commandments.

The Pentateuch as Replacement for Tablets and Ark

Our discussion of ritualizing tablets and ark before the Exile and ritualizing Torah scrolls in the time of Ezra reveals a major change in ritual focus. Israel's covenant with God was represented by the tablets and ark in Joshua, Judges, and Samuel, but by the Torah scroll in 2 Kings, Ezra, Nehemiah, and later Second Temple literature. The symbol of God's presence in Israel shifted from the ark to the scroll. The Pentateuch uses similar vocabulary for tablets, ark, and Torah scroll to obscure this transition. It persuades readers and hearers that the Torah scroll contains the contents of the divine tablets and can function in many of the same ways as the Ark of the Covenant.

Once Moses deposited the tablets in the ark, no story tells of their reemergence. They are manipulated only within their reliquary, the Ark of the Covenant, just as medieval Christians in Armenia and Ireland displayed and carried sacred texts within book shrines. These reliquaries simultaneously hid and displayed the texts they contained.

The Pentateuch contains the tablets literarily like the ark contained them physically. But both the ark and the Pentateuch contain more than the tablets. Just as the golden ark surmounted by sphinxes is far more elaborate in Exod. 25:10–22 than the wooden box described by Deut. 10:1–3, so the five-book Pentateuch also contains far more than just stories about the tablets, manna, rod, and scroll. Both ark and Pentateuch are baroque elaborations of the original revelation, in iconographic and literary media respectively. Both have repeatedly tempted modern historians to try to reconstruct simpler originals.

The Pentateuch, however, makes the tablets available publicly more than the ark did. The ark was an icon that could be displayed and venerated. A Torah scroll is also an icon that can be displayed and venerated in the same way, but the scroll can also be read. Reading the scrolls aloud made the tablets more directly available to listeners and readers than the ark ever did.

By shifting from iconic text hidden in its ark reliquary to displayed text read regularly to all Israel, Deuteronomy changed Judean religious texts from esoteric to exoteric. This was a ritual innovation with long-lasting implications for Western religions. This was not, however, a shift from ritual to text, contrary to an interpretation that has been repeated since the ancient rabbis. The contents of the ark already provided textual authorization of the ritual (Exod. 34:10–28) and, in any case, the rituals continued unchanged (it is claimed) in Jerusalem's Second Temple. What was new was exoteric textual validation of rituals through the regular iconic display and performative reading of the Torah scroll. As a ritualized public text, the Torah combined the ritual functions of epic and totem in one and the same thing. The ritual change involved a shift from the iconic ark reliquary to iconic scrolls, which eventually gained their own ark reliquaries in Jewish synagogues.

In the form of Torah scrolls, the Pentateuch functions as the physical evidence of YHWH's rescue of Israel (in place of the manna), of the divine origins of the commandments (in place of the tablets), of the rights and responsibilities of the Aaronide priests (in place of Aaron's rod), and of YHWH's promises and threats to Israel (in place of Moses's scroll). The Torah scroll can therefore function as a literary reliquary that replaces the ark's reliquary function of preserving testimony. In the stories of Josiah and Ezra reading a Torah scroll aloud to the people, the scroll functions in precisely this way to convict the people of their sins for failing to observe the festivals it mandates (Passover and *Sukkot* respectively). The Torah scroll functions as a material icon too, ritually displayed as a legitimizing symbol. It legitimized the regulations of Jerusalem's and Samaria's temples and priesthoods. Its authority then gradually spread over Jewish and Samaritan legal institutions and family life. The biblical accounts of Israel's pre-exilic apostasy and post-exilic repentance suggest that Torah scrolls were more effective than the ark and its tablets in keeping the people's attention on the covenant with God.

Thus the Ark of the Covenant evolved into the Torah scroll, displayed and performed for all to see and hear. Both iconography and rhetoric disguise this change as continuity, like most successful ritual innovations. Identification between Decalogue and Torah and between the Ark of the Covenant built at Sinai and holy arks in every synagogue obscured the change from esoteric to exoteric sacred texts that took place at the beginning of the Second Temple period.[64]

The influence of this ritual innovation reached far beyond Judaism. It shaped the veneration of Gospel codices in ancient Christianity and of pandect bibles by modern Christians, and provided precedents for the veneration of books of scripture by Muslims and Sikhs as well. Cherished scriptural texts, displayed for all to see and read for all to hear, became a characteristic feature of Western religious rituals.

4

READING, PERFORMANCE, AND ART

RITUALIZING THE PENTATEUCH'S PERFORMATIVE DIMENSION

The first step in reading written texts is to turn their visual signs into language. The typefaces and layout of most modern texts have been optimized to make this as quick and easy as possible. People who are literate in the text's language usually read silently to themselves – as I assume you, the reader of this book, are doing right now. Ancient texts were not so easy to scan. They lacked many of the visual aids that we now take for granted, such as punctuation, lower case and capital letters, and paragraph divisions. Some writing systems, such as the Hebrew alphabet, omitted most of the vowels. Greek texts contained vowels but usually did not mark word divisions. And, of course, all ancient texts were written by hand.

Readers in ancient times therefore customarily read texts aloud. If they planned to read to other people, they would usually practice in advance, studying the written text and perhaps even memorizing it in order to read fluently. Public readings and recitations were the common way of publishing a text. Traditions of recitation developed that dictated how to vocalize a given text in order to standardize performances. They often included instructions for reading melodically by chanting or singing. Sometimes texts were presented dramatically by multiple actors or accompanied by artistic illustrations to increase audience interest. All these ways

Understanding the Pentateuch as a Scripture, First Edition. James W. Watts.

of transforming written signs into oral language and visual illustration constitute the performative dimension of a text.

The Performative Dimension of Scriptures

Paying careful and repeated attention to oral, dramatic, and artistic presentations of a text ritualizes its performative dimension. Religious communities throughout the world place importance on the oral reading and recitation of their scriptures. That is naturally the case in communities that pass on their tradition primarily in oral form, such as the Brahmins of India who memorize and recite the Vedas and other Hindu sacred texts. But it is also the case in traditions that revere written scriptures. The oral reading or recitation of scriptures is one of the most characteristic features of the worship services of Jews, Zoroastrians, Buddhists, Jains, Christians, and Muslims. Devotional scripture reading by individuals, silently or aloud, is also typical in many traditions.

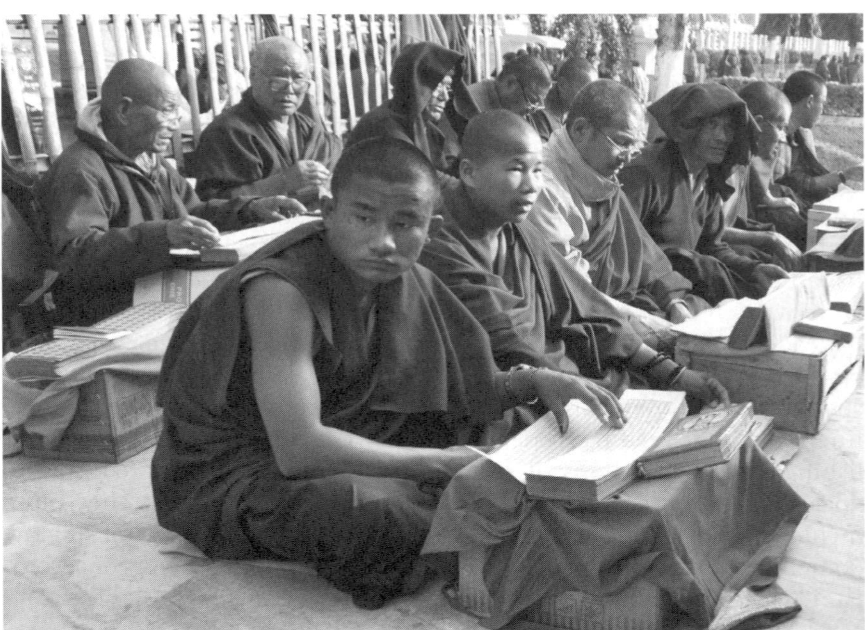

Figure 4.1 Buddhist monks chanting sutras at Bodh Gaya, India. *Source*: Photos by Lyn Watts 2014; used by permission.

Ritualizing the performative dimension of scripture conveys a feeling of inspiration. Of course, religious communities regularly claim that divine inspiration directed the writing of their scriptures. However, it is in their performance that scriptures have inspiring effects on congregations and, often, on the performers themselves.

Communities frequently invite their members to participate in scripture reading and recitation. For example, many Christian services feature lay readers. Jewish coming-of-age ceremonies (*bar* or *bat mitzvahs*) emphasize the child reading a passage from the Hebrew Torah aloud. All Muslims are expected to be able to recite the first *surah* (chapter) of the Arabic Qur'an from memory. In these ways, congregations broaden participation in worship by inviting people to join in ritualizing the performative dimension of their scriptures.

Experts with interpretive authority often perform the texts, too. They may lace their preaching with scriptural quotations and allusions. Thus preaching, though based in semantic interpretation and its authority, becomes inspiring to the degree that it also performs the text. But actors and artists frequently perform the contents of scriptures in ways that inspire audiences quite apart from, or even in conflict with, religiously authorized interpreters.

The inspiring power of oral reading and recitation has not only strengthened belief in the divine inspiration of scriptures. It has also fueled mystical speculation about supernatural words and about sound itself (see Box, "The power of sound, word, and scripture"). Beliefs in a heavenly scripture draw even more attention to the language of that scripture.

The power of sound, word, and scripture

William Graham observed: "In many of the major, literate traditions of history, the idea of the primordial word of power is linked to the power of scripture itself. This is most explicitly evident in theological formulations such as we find in Rabbinic Judaism and medieval Islam concerning the preexistence of the divine word of scripture. Ideas of the eternality of the Buddha-word, the Qur'ān, or the sounds of the Veda also reflect the identification of the preserved scriptural texts with the primal power of the original word of truth."[65]

Most religious traditions that venerate written scriptures employ the original language or, at least, an ancient language of those scriptures for their ritual performances. A few traditions, most notably strands of

Christianity and Mahayana Buddhism, employ translations in most ritual situations. This difference between traditions does not revolve around the decision to translate scripture or not, because almost all translate for purposes of religious education. It instead has to do with what language to use when performing scriptures orally in ritual settings. Rival religious traditions originating in both India (Hinduism and Buddhism) and the Middle East (Christianity and Islam) have developed opposite ritual practices regarding the languages of their scriptures. Hindus and Muslims insist on the importance of performing the Vedas and the Qur'an in the original Sanskrit and Arabic languages. By contrast, Buddhists and Christians have ritualized their scriptures in translations since the origins of their religions.[66]

Theater has frequently been used to perform the stories of scriptures orally and visually. Many paintings and sculptures also depict scenes from scriptural stories. Art in a religious context, such as in a temple or a church, can therefore function as a ritualized performance of scripture. Art, however, usually performs the contents rather than the words of scripture, and mostly focuses on narratives. Like oral performance, religious art has an inspiring effect on devout viewers. Some famous works of art and films on scriptural themes have shaped the religious imaginations of very many people.

The Pentateuch's Performative Dimension After Ezra

By its nature, oral performance does not leave direct evidence behind for historians to examine. We can only look for written references to ritualizing the performative dimension of scripture. This evidence is not as plentiful as it is for the iconic and semantic dimensions in any period of history. Nevertheless, there are indications that the Pentateuch was increasingly being read aloud ritually after it was first ritualized as a scripture in the time of Ezra, during the fifth or early fourth centuries BCE.

Ezra's Torah Reading

Nehemiah 8 tells the story of Ezra's Torah reading. Ezra stood on platform in the open plaza before a main gate of the walled city of Jerusalem. He was flanked on either side by other leaders of the community. The crowd consisted of "men and women and everyone who could listen and understand." Ezra read from dawn until noon. He accompanied the reading with a blessing and the audience responded "Amen, amen" and bowed to the ground. Ezra declared the day of the reading holy. Public readings continued on every day of the seven-day festival of *Sukkot* (Booths). So the story depicts Ezra ritualizing the Pentateuch's performative dimension by the arrangement and posture of the audience, by verbal cues and responses, and by the length and repetition of the readings.

This story appears in a literary context, the books of Ezra and Nehemiah, that describes considerable conflict within the Jerusalem community. The leaders, Ezra the priest and Nehemiah the governor, had both come from Babylon as appointees of the Persian emperor. Ezra required the men of Jerusalem to divorce their foreign wives and send them away in order to keep the religious community pure (Ezra 9–10). Nehemiah excluded neighboring rulers from Jerusalem and feared their military attack (Nehemiah 4, 6). So the social situation was very conflictual both internally and externally.

The immediate consequence of Ezra's Torah reading was that the people learned how to observe *Sukkot*, which they proceeded to celebrate. The story claims that the feast of *Sukkot* had not been celebrated properly since the days of Joshua, some eight centuries earlier (Neh. 8:17, though Ezra 3:4 claims that the returning exiles celebrated *Sukkot*). So public performance of the old book led to the revival and performance of an old pilgrimage festival. Reading the Torah inspired the people's desire to celebrate *Sukkot* in the way required by the old book.

The story of Ezra's Torah reading tells of temple officials, the Levites, standing among the people to interpret the text to them:

> *The Levites helped the people understand the Torah. ... They read from the book of the Torah of God with interpretation to explain the meaning, so they could understand the reading.* (Neh. 8:7–8)

Many commentators think this refers to oral translation into Aramaic. The Pentateuch is written in Hebrew, the vernacular language of people living in the kingdoms of Israel and Judea in the eighth to sixth centuries BCE. Nehemiah 13:23–24 says that, in Ezra's time, many people in Jerusalem could not understand Hebrew. Apparently, Aramaic was already replacing Hebrew as the vernacular by the end of the fifth century. That means, then, that when the Torah was first being ritualized as a scripture, its audience already spoke a vernacular different than the language of the text.[67] The scripture's archaic language distinguished it as an old text and as authoritative for ritual practice.

The book of Nehemiah records a meeting later in the same month when the people gathered wearing sackcloth and ashes and fasted – all symbols of mourning and repentance.

> *They stood and confessed their sins and their ancestors' liabilities. They arose where they stood and read in the Torah scroll of YHWH their God for one quarter of the day, and for another quarter they confessed and bowed down to YHWH their God.* (Neh. 9:2–3)

Again, the Levites play a leading role, this time by voicing the people's prayer of repentance that summarizes the biblical storyline from Genesis through Kings (Neh. 9:4–37). Here reading Torah, as well as a recital of Israel's history, has been incorporated into the people's communal worship. Torah reading now plays an important role in regular religious experience.

Reading Torah in Later Second Temple Judaism

Our next evidence for ritualizing the Torah's performative dimension also involves translation, this time, written translation. The Pentateuch was translated into Greek sometime in the third century BCE. We have a highly embellished account of how this "Septuagint" translation was made in the *Letter of Aristeas*, written one century later. Aristeas credits the translation to the desire of the Ptolemaic (Greek) king of Egypt to include the Torah in his library at Alexandria. It is much more likely that this translation was motivated by the desire of Greek-speaking Jews to hear the Torah read in their vernacular language.

Reading the Greek Torah

Demetrius [the royal librarian] assembled the company of the Jews in the place where the task of translation had been finished and read it to all, in the presence of the translators, who received a great ovation from the crowded audience for being responsible for great blessings. … [The Jewish priests and elders] commanded that a curse should be laid as was their custom, on anyone who should alter the version by any addition or change to any part of the written text, or any deletion either. This was a good step taken to ensure that the words were preserved completely and permanently in perpetuity. (*Letter of Aristeas* 308–312)

Aristeas's account of how the new translation was received (see Box, "Reading the Greek Torah") is probably fictional. It nevertheless tells us how this second-century Jewish writer thought the translated Torah *should* be received: by bowing to the ground and a public reading of the entire document, followed by curses on anyone who would dare change this new text. Three centuries after the Septuagint translation of the Pentateuch, Philo reported that the translators' accomplishment was still celebrated by an annual festival near Alexandria. Rabbinic literature from the second through fifth centuries CE also attests to the practice of reading Torah aloud in synagogue services in vernacular translations. Though the rabbis preferred synagogue readings in Hebrew, or at least interlacing vernacular translations with verses in Hebrew, they admitted that many synagogues were reading the Torah only in Greek.[68]

References to reading Torah or scripture aloud began to proliferate in sources from the first centuries BCE and CE. 2 Maccabees claims that the armies of Judah Maccabee marched into battle to the sound of Torah being read aloud.

> *He appointed Eleazar to read aloud from the holy book, and gave the watchword, 'The help of God'; then, leading the first division himself, he joined battle with Nicanor.* (2 Macc. 8:23 NRSV).

Many first-century CE sources indicate that Torah reading had become institutionalized in synagogues. The Theodotus Inscription summarizes the characteristic activities of such institutions as including public readings and study of the Torah. The New Testament, Philo, and Josephus all portray such synagogues as central institutions in Jewish life. The New Testament book of Acts describes the role of scripture reading in a synagogue service.

> *And on the sabbath day they went into the synagogue and sat down. After the reading of the law and the prophets, the officials of the synagogue sent them a message, saying, 'Brothers, if you have any word of exhortation for the people, give it.'* (Acts 13:14–15 NRSV)

This story already exhibits the standard synagogue ritual sequence of reading a portion of Torah followed by a passage from a prophetic book and then an interpretive sermon.

Multiple references in the Dead Sea Scrolls show that public readings of scripture were routine in the Qumran religious community. In fact, they were required.

> *The assembly shall be assiduous to read the book as a community one-third of each night of the year, and to expound the Torah and recite benedictions as a community.*

Other Qumran texts emphasize readings on the Sabbath and also expect scripture readings to be prominent in the afterlife. The community seems to

Figure 4.2 The Theodotus Inscription, Jerusalem, mid-first century CE; in the Israel Museum, Jerusalem. Translation: *Theodotos, son of Vettenos, priest and head of the synagogue, son of the head of the synagogue, who was also the son of the head of the synagogue, built the synagogue for the reading of the Law and for the study of the precepts, as well as the hospice and the chambers and the bathing-establishment, for lodging those who need them, from abroad; it (the synagogue) was founded by his ancestors and the elders and Simonidas.*[69]

have reenacted every year the blessings and curses of the covenant ceremony in Deuteronomy 27–28.[70] Priests read aloud constantly to the members of the community, and one document prohibits anyone from doing so

> *whose speech is too soft or speaks with a staccato voice not dividing his words so that his voice may be heard, none of these shall read from the book of the Torah, lest he cause error in a capital manner.*

As this sentence from the *Damascus Document* makes clear, the members of the Qumran community dictated how to read aloud because reading scripture publicly carried ultimate stakes. They had exiled themselves from the religious establishment in Jerusalem because of disagreements about ritual practice. They organized their communal life around their ideal of how the Jerusalem temple and community should function. Their rituals of scripture reading probably reflect how scripture was being read in the Jerusalem Temple or, at least, how they thought it should be read there.[71]

Unfortunately, we do not have any direct evidence for how scripture was in fact read in the Temple. Later rabbinic literature described how the rabbis remembered the high priest reading Torah in the Second Temple.

> *The high priest stood and received it and read [the portions] Ahare Mot* [After the death … – Lev. 16:1–34] *and Akh Be-'Asor* [But on the Tenth … – Lev. 23:26–32]. *He rolled up the Torah and placed it on his breast and said, 'More than what I have read before you is written here.' Uve-'Asor* [And on the Tenth …] *in the book of Numbers* [29:7–11] *he recited by heart, and he blessed upon it [the reading] eight benedictions.* (*m. Yoma* 7:1; *m. Sot.* 7:7, 8)[72]

The priest probably recited the Numbers passage from memory because he could not quickly roll a scroll to that passage. The rabbis prohibited reciting Torah from memory in synagogue services and recommended using a second scroll instead. The same Mishnaic passage also reports that King Agrippa read aloud portions of Deuteronomy, including the rule of the king (Deut. 17:14–20), in the Temple during a festival.

Reading Torah in Synagogues

Synagogue rituals of reading scripture began to be reflected in the design of synagogue buildings in the second century CE and later. The ruins of many ancient synagogues built in Late Antiquity show clear evidence of reading platforms (*bemot*) as well as Torah arks (see Chapter 3).

Rabbinic literature from the same centuries reveals how ritual readings were being developed in synagogue liturgies. The Mishnah (ca. 200 CE) shows concern for who may read, the posture of the readers, how often Torah should be read, and what other readings and blessings should accompany the reading. It also recognizes considerable variations between the reading practices of different communities, which suggests that their reading customs were already entrenched from long practice by this time (see Box, "The Mishnah on reading rituals").

The Mishnah on reading rituals

The Megilla (scroll of Esther) *may be read either sitting or standing, by one person only, or by two persons at the same time. They alike fulfil their duty. In places where it is usual to say a blessing (after reading it) it is obligatory to say it, but not when it is not customary. Three men are called to read in the Holy Scrolls on Mondays and Thursdays; and in the afternoon of the Sabbath neither more nor less than that number may be called, nor shall any section from the Prophets then be read. He who commences the reading of the Holy Scrolls shall pronounce the first benediction before reading it, and he who concludes the reading shall pronounce the last benediction after reading it.* (*m. Megilla* 3)[73]

Reading Torah aloud explicitly indexes levels of social prestige and honor within the congregation. The Mishnah lists three Torah readers that reflect the continuing prestige of priestly families in rabbinic Judaism: first, a priest should read if one is present, second, a Levite, and third, another knowledgeable Jewish man. It continues to be regarded as a great honor to "be called to the Torah," that is, to be asked to read the Torah in a synagogue service. Synagogues traditionally grant this honor especially to bridegrooms, to boys celebrating their *bar mitzvahs* (coming of age), to a new father, and to a man mourning his parent or ending his mourning period. Many Reformed and Conservative synagogues call on women as well as men for Torah readings. They also encourage girls to celebrate their coming of age with a *bat mitzvah*. These rituals thus chart disagreements on social issues between Jewish denominations. They also reflect the relative obscurity of Biblical Hebrew for many Jews. Those "called to the Torah" often only recite the blessings before and after a Torah portion which is read by the rabbi or cantor, because it is important that the Hebrew text be read and chanted accurately.[74]

Torah blessings in synagogue liturgy

Blessing before the Torah reading

Bless you, Adonai (the LORD) our God, king of the universe,
who chose us from all the peoples to give us his Torah.
Bless you, Adonai, you give the Torah.

Blessing after the Torah reading

Bless you, Adonai our God, king of the universe,
who gave us a true Torah and planted eternal life within us.
Bless you, Adonai, you give the Torah.[75]

In antiquity, synagogue liturgy settled on reading portions of Torah sequentially over time. That way, the congregation eventually reads the whole Pentateuch aloud. Some ancient and medieval synagogues read it over a period of more than three years. Mesopotamian Jews used a one-year cycle of Torah readings that later became the standard practice in all synagogues. Synagogue liturgies use texts from other parts of the Tanak only piecemeal. Thematically related passages (*haftorah*) from the prophetic books are paired with Torah readings and read after them. Individual psalms are sung at appropriate points in regular and special services. The reading of some other books, such as the five festival scrolls (Ruth, Esther, Lamentations, Ecclesiastes, and Song of Songs), became traditional on special occasions and annual festivals. Some books of the Tanak find no place in the synagogue's services at all. The Torah, then, is ritually elevated above all other books by being read aloud sequentially in its entirety in the course of regular synagogue worship services.

Particular passages in the Pentateuch also get recited separately because of their contents and importance. For example, the *Shema* and the Priestly Blessing feature prominently in Jewish worship. The *Shema* consists of Deut. 6:4–9, 11:13–21, and Num. 15:37–41. Everyone should recite the *Shema* during morning and evening prayers, and before sleeping. The Priestly Blessing, on the other hand, is traditionally recited only by men who claim descent from the first priest, Aaron. It consists of Numbers 6:24–26. The priests (*kohenim*) should recite it over the congregation at the end of a synagogue worship service. This hierarchical restriction has proven controversial in Jewish cultures. The blessing has been modified for congregational recitation in some synagogue services and has also been used privately within families.

Reading the Pentateuch in Churches

The four Gospels replaced the Torah as the scriptural focus of Christian worship services. This change is clearly reflected in how scripture is read aloud in churches. Whereas synagogues read the Torah sequentially and match other scriptural passages to the Torah reading, most Christian orders of scripture readings (called *lectionaries*) read one or more Gospels sequentially. They choose passages from other scriptural books based on thematic links to the Gospel reading or to that day in the Christian calendar. Traditionally, the Gospel is read last, usually by a deacon or the presiding priest who recites blessings before and after the reading. After sitting through the other biblical readings, many congregations stand to hear the Gospel read.[76]

Christian lectionaries have varied over time and between Christian denominations. A recent effort to create more consistency among Protestant and Catholic churches in North America led to a new lectionary for the Catholic Mass and a related "Common Lectionary" for many Protestant denominations. The four suggested scripture readings each day consist of readings from a Gospel and from a Psalm, another from the rest of the Old Testament including the Pentateuch, and one from another New Testament book. This contemporary Christian lectionary includes a larger percentage of the Bible than did many older lectionaries. It also enables semi-continuous readings of some Old Testament narratives over multiple Sundays. Once every three years, this sequence includes Pentateuchal texts that focus especially on the covenant made by Israel at Sinai. Still, only 5% of the Pentateuch, mostly from Genesis and Exodus, is read in Sunday services that follow this lectionary. Its recommendations for daily scripture readings include more, but still only 15%, of the entire Pentateuch.[77]

Many churches do not follow any prescribed lectionary. They leave the selection of scripture readings to the preacher. Some preachers have been known to preach sequentially through the entire Bible, in which case the entire Pentateuch gets read aloud over a period of many Sundays. Apart from this rare exception, however, Christians do not read much of the Pentateuch aloud in Sunday services. The portions that do get read emphasize the stories of creation, of the ancestors, and of the exodus from Egypt. Christians do not ritualize the Pentateuch as a distinct part of Christian scripture, but simply as the beginning of their Old Testament.

Some Pentateuchal passages, however, play a larger role in Christian worship. The Ten Commandments have often been recited from memory by the congregation, especially in some Reformed Protestant churches. And Christian priests and ministers frequently recite the Priestly Blessing (Num. 6:24–26) at the conclusion of a service.

Apart from formal worship services, scripture reading plays a large role in many Christians' devotional experience. Ancient Christian monks made the reading and recitation of scripture the central activity of their spiritual practice. This monastic *lectio divina* "divine reading" has shaped spiritual life for lay people as well. For example, the American Catholic *Manual of Indulgences* promises benefits in the afterlife to "the Christian faithful who read sacred scripture with the veneration due God's word and as a form of spiritual reading."

Reading scripture aloud in ancient Christianity

William Graham observed: "The (ancient) sources reflect the intensity of the preoccupation with the divine word: We find substantial references to memorization of scripture; to recitation/meditation as a major preoccupation in its own right; to liturgical recitation, including both communal worship and funeral rites; to the chanting of psalms and other scriptural passages while walking, weaving, baking, gathering rushes, and welcoming special visitors; and to scripture reading and recitation during the communal meals and as the basis of all teaching and preaching in the community."[78]

Denominations that reject the monastic ideal have nevertheless emphasized spiritual reading as an ideal. The Protestant Reformers encouraged all Christians to read the Bible for themselves. Contemporary Evangelical Christians distinguish themselves by individual and group "Bible study" more than by any other religious practice.

In Christian devotional reading, the Gospels receive the most attention, followed by the rest of the New Testament, just as they do in Christian worship services. Of the Christian Old Testament, Christians read the Psalms and some parts of the Prophets more than most of the Pentateuch, except for many stories in Genesis and Exodus.

The Languages of Jewish Public Readings

Language is a prominent feature of any oral performance. Listeners' responses will be determined by whether they recognize and understand the language they hear. However, recognition and understanding are not the same thing. Many people recognize the sound and cadence of familiar recitations even if they do not understand the language. For example, experienced travelers recognize the sound of the call to prayer echoing through cities and villages of Muslim countries even if they do not understand Arabic.

A synagogue service can be recognized by the sound of the Hebrew Torah and of Hebrew and Aramaic prayers as much as by any visual symbol or architecture. The sound of scripture being read aloud in a synagogue service distinguishes itself in two ways: by its ancient Hebrew language and by its prescribed melodic chant (cantillation). For more than 2,000 years, Jews spoke vernacular languages other than Hebrew, from Aramaic and Greek in antiquity to German, Polish, Spanish, Arabic, English, and many other languages in modern times. The Hebrew language of the scriptures and the prayer book, which also includes Aramaic, distinguishes the sound of worship services from the sound of everyday life.

Now that Hebrew has been revived as the national language of the State of Israel, Israeli Jews may not find the sound of biblical Hebrew as distinctive as do Jews living in other countries. Nevertheless, chanting still distinguishes prayer and public readings of Torah and other books of scripture. The sound of the Hebrew Torah being chanted provides Jews a common experience of worship across different denominations, cultures, and time periods.

Jewish scholars have also translated their scriptures into other languages for more than 2,000 years. Translation may have already been part of Ezra's Torah reading, as we have seen. Oral Aramaic translation was probably the rule rather than the exception from the time of Ezra on.

The ancient rabbis argued that if synagogues use translations, they should always precede an oral translation with reading the Hebrew text. Free translation in Aramaic was interspersed between readings of Hebrew verses. Written Aramaic translations appeared after the end of the Second Temple period. These Aramaic "targums" crystalized into three traditions of manuscripts: the Palestinian targums, Targum Onqelos, and Targum Pseudo-Jonathan.[79]

Centuries earlier, the Septuagint Greek translation of the Pentateuch had been extended to the rest of Jewish scriptures. Greek-speaking Jews read them in that language. That is most obvious in the pages of the New Testament, whose Greek-speaking Jewish authors quoted the scriptures from the Septuagint translation in the first century CE. Aquila, Symmachus, and Theodotion created more literal Greek translations in the following centuries.

Attempts to restrict Jewish scripture to only Hebrew texts gained strength in two periods of ancient Jewish history. In the second and early first centuries BCE, the Hasmonean dynasty of high priests and kings sponsored a collection of Hebrew literature consisting of historical and prophetic books as well as the Pentateuch. The textual evidence for this development is very limited: one sentence in a dynastic history from the second century refers to Judah Maccabee collecting books in Jerusalem just like Nehemiah who collected

> *books about the kings and prophets, and the writings of David, and letters of kings about votive offerings.* (2 Macc. 2:13–14)

This verse seems to describe the historical and prophetic books of the Hebrew Bible and the Psalms ("the writings of David"). Some first century CE texts refer to Jewish scriptures as "the Torah and the Prophets," and sometimes also the Psalms, indicating that this innovation dates to the

A Hasmonean curriculum

David Carr has argued that the Hasmoneans broadened the Jerusalem temple's scribal traditions in an effort to enculturate a wider elite through Hebrew literature. "The Jewish Hebrew Scriptures were defined and functioned within the regional empire of the Hasmoneans as part of a project of specifically Hebrew (and non-Greek) education-enculturation to create a 'Jewish' identity. This identity was analogous yet opposed to the emergent, transnational 'Hellenistic' identity of the Hellenistic educational system."[80]

Hasmonean period. The fleeting reference to Judah Maccabee's library may therefore hint at a broader cultural transformation (see Chapter 6). By the turn of the era, the vernacular languages spoken by Jews were mostly Aramaic and Greek. Yet the Torah, Prophets, and Psalms consist of texts originally written in Hebrew. The Hebrew language had become a defining characteristic of Jewish scriptures.

Rabbinic literature from the following centuries debated the scriptural status of Torah in translation. The rabbis labeled Hebrew "the sacred language" (*leshon haqodesh*, maybe meaning "the temple language") and wrote down their own traditions in Hebrew and Aramaic, but never in Greek. The rabbis also accepted as scripture two books, Daniel and Ezra, that contain chapters written in Aramaic, but no part of the Tanak contains texts originally written in Greek. Some of the ancient rabbis treated translations as if they were sacred texts, while others did not. For example, the Mishnah maintains at one point that worn-out scrolls of translated scriptures must be stored in *genizas*, just like Hebrew scrolls of scriptures (*m. Shab.* 16.1), while at another point saying that translated scrolls are not sacred like Hebrew scriptures (*m. Yad.* 4.5). This debate reflects the conflict between the desire to see scriptures used in their original Hebrew language and the reality that many synagogue members did not understand that language. It probably also reflects the ancient rabbis' efforts to distinguish and insulate Jewish identity from the growing numbers of Greek-speaking Christians.[81]

The earlier rabbinic texts seem more open to reading Torah in Greek if no one in the congregation can read Hebrew. Later texts from the third through fifth centuries restrict the practice. This debate was waged through the Middle Ages and continues in modernity. The use or avoidance of vernacular languages in worship became a distinguishing feature of some Jewish denominations as they evolved in the nineteenth and twentieth centuries. It continues to be debated in congregations today.[82]

In traditional Jewish synagogues, Torah reading and recitation was reserved for men. Women listened and observed, but did not read the Torah and usually were not taught Hebrew. At home, however, Jewish women played an active role in reading scripture and teaching it to their children. While Jewish men may have studied Torah and Talmud at home with their sons, women traditionally read biblical texts in translation together with explanatory stories (*midrash*). Penny Shine Gold observed:

> The irony is that in many homes, the mother, reading the text in the (low prestige) current vernacular and with commentary pitched to an unlearned audience, would have a greater chance of understanding what was being read than the father and son, reading the text in Hebrew and Aramaic.[83]

Literacy in Hebrew, the language of the Torah, marked status at home as well as in the synagogue.

The Languages of Christian Oral Readings

The early Christians adopted the Septuagint Greek translation of the Torah and other biblical books to serve as their scriptures. Many Christian worship services almost from the beginning featured scripture readings in Greek. In the first generations of the movement, Christian missionaries received a more positive response from Greek-speaking Jews than from those who spoke Aramaic. Christianity soon established itself as a Hellenistic religion.

The dominance of Greek in early Christianity finds its clearest expression in the books of the New Testament. The apostle Paul regarded himself as a Jew who followed the teachings of the Jewish messiah, Jesus (Phil. 3:3–7; Gal. 1:13–2:21). He spoke Aramaic and his Pharisaic education trained him in Hebrew. But because he spoke Greek to his Hellenistic congregations, his letters – which are the earliest New Testament books – were written in Greek. So were all the other New Testament books, including the four Gospels that convey the words and deeds of Jesus Christ. Though Jesus spoke Aramaic (Mark 7:11, 34; 15:34), the Gospels record his words already translated into Greek. As a result, Christianity has not preserved the words of its founder in the language in which he spoke them.

The New Testament book of Acts provides a rationale for this development by relating a translation miracle as a model for Christian preaching. At the festival of Pentecost, 50 days after Jesus's crucifixion, his disciples

> *were filled with the Holy Spirit and began to speak in other languages, as the Spirit gave them ability. Now there were devout Jews from every nation under heaven living in Jerusalem. And at this sound the crowd gathered and was bewildered, because each one heard them speaking in the native language of each.* (Acts 2:4–6 NRSV)

This story depicts translation as an act of divine inspiration. The sermon that follows interprets the miracle as an act of prophecy (Acts 2:14–21). The Christian Bible thus models translation both with its Greek Old Testament and with this miraculous origin story for Christian translation activities. The book of Genesis accounts for linguistic diversity with the story of the Tower of Babel (Gen. 11:1–9), in which God causes mutually incomprehensible languages to frustrate human unity. So, as many preachers have pointed out, the Christian Bible depicts languages as a barrier to mutual understanding, and translation as a divinely sanctioned means for overcoming that barrier.

With such precedents for vernacular translation, Greek could not last long as the sole language of Christian scripture. It was soon rivaled by translations into Latin, Syriac, Coptic, and Armenian. Schisms then divided medieval Christianity along linguistic lines. This crystallization of religious identity around biblical translations continues among traditionalists today, especially in the churches of eastern Christianity. Greek Orthodox churches, for example, read the New Testament in its original *koine* Greek, though they often attempt to overcome linguistic barriers by reading it in other languages as well.[84]

In Western Europe, the Renaissance revival of ancient culture and languages breathed new life into the impulse to translate the scriptures. Protestant reformers championed vernacular translations in the sixteenth century. Catholic and Protestant missionaries translated the Bible into hundreds of new languages – thousands by the end of the twentieth century. Not coincidentally, Protestants have also become the most schismatic branch of Christianity, dividing into many independent denominations and churches. Today it is often the case that different denominations using the same language nevertheless endorse different translations of the Bible.

Why did Christian attitudes towards the language of scripture tilt so decisively in favor of translations? Christianity emerged in a pluralistic cultural and linguistic environment in which Jewish communities already read their scriptures in multiple languages. Other reasons included the missionary desire to communicate widely and the possibility that Jesus himself may have taught in more than one language.

Another factor may have been cultural biases for and against certain languages and the people who spoke them. The dominant Hellenistic culture celebrated Greek as the language of philosophy and literature. Conversely, Aramaic may have been regarded in the Roman Empire as provincial. The Christians quickly developed anti-Jewish prejudices and wished to establish a distinct identity for themselves. Embracing Greek and then other languages facilitated their separate group formation. John Sawyer summarized the results.

> The effect of translating Hebrew scripture into Greek was to construct a radically different text, one which, in the history of Christianity, virtually took the place of the Hebrew original as the Church's sacred text, and which the Jewish authorities soon rejected as alien.

Christian translations of scripture have often unified a group of people around a vernacular language. Ancient translations consolidated the

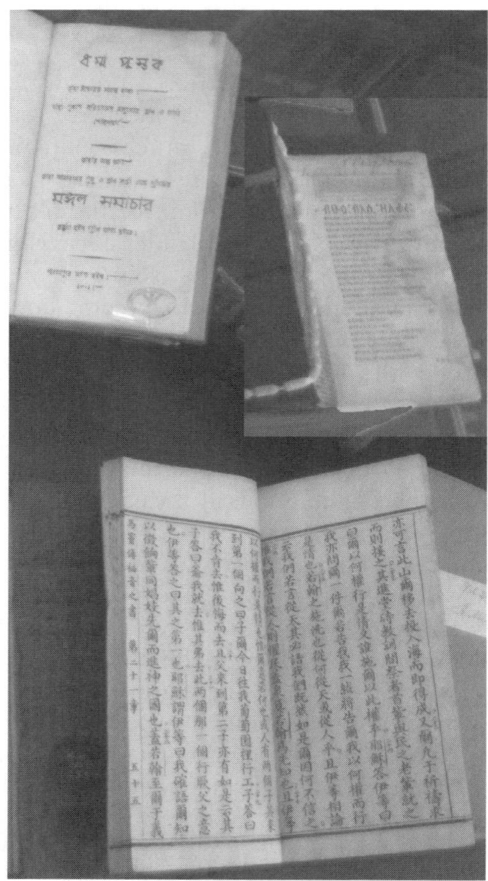

Figure 4.3 Bible translations in Bengali, Coptic, and Chinese.

religious identities of Armenians, Copts, and Syriac Christians. The Roman Church used the language of the Latin Bible and liturgy to create a single Catholic identity across the political divisions of medieval Europe. Two Protestant vernacular translations, the King James Version and the Luther Bible, encouraged nationalism in England and Germany by standardizing "the King's English" and "High German." European colonial empires, both Catholic and Protestant, wielded Bible translation as a tool to dominate people in the Americas, Africa, and Asia. But translation into non-Western languages also inspired the rise of new ethnic churches, especially in Africa and Asia.

Bible translations have an iconic, as well as performative, aspect, since they often bring new scripts to languages. Efforts to convert eastern

Europeans to orthodoxy transcribed their languages into the Greek alphabet or modified it to produce Cyrillic. Colonial translations by Catholics and Protestants brought the Latin alphabet to indigenous languages in the Americas, whether they already had a writing system or not. These alphabets conformed many different languages to European culture by their visual script, even while reproducing the Bible orally in another language. The new bibles sounded native while looking European.[85]

Bible translations, then, have played a major role in distinguishing Christians from Jews and in dividing Christians along national and denominational lines. Worship services establish the religious and ethnic identities of congregations by the sound of the language of their scripture.

Recitation, Cantillation, and Song

Since antiquity, the Torah and other scriptures have been chanted to specific tonal patterns. Synagogue readers now follow rules of cantillation developed in the Middle Ages. The words must be chanted to a melody prescribed by a system of accents. The accents, however, do not appear in Torah scrolls.

The ancient rabbis wrote the rules for reading Torah aloud that many synagogues still follow today. The Torah should not be recited from memory during a synagogue service. It must be read aloud from an undecorated and unpointed Torah scroll. "Unpointed" refers to the

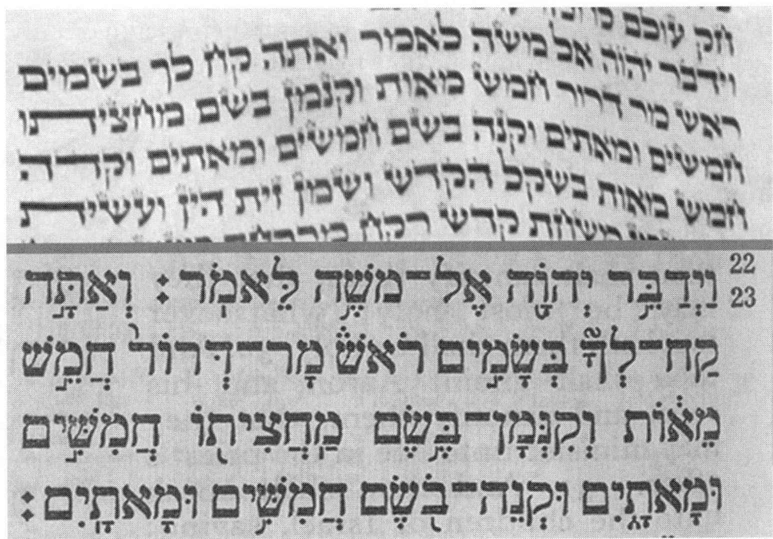

Figure 4.4 Exodus 30:22–23 in a manuscript scroll and a printed *chumash*.

absence of small marks above and below the Hebrew letters that indicate how to pronounce the vowels and how to accent and chant the sentences. Medieval Jewish scholars developed a system of "points" to record how the scriptures should be pronounced. These signs do not appear in the scrolls used for synagogue worship, but are recorded in codices of the Pentateuch (a *chumash*) and of the whole Jewish Bible (a *tanak*). Readers study the proper vocalization and cantillation of the text from a *chumash* or *tanak* before they read scripture aloud from an unpointed scroll in public. Many synagogues employ a trained cantor who both reads to the congregation and trains others to read scripture aloud, as well as leading the congregation in prayers and psalms. Penny Shine Gold observed:

> The special production of and reverence toward the Torah scroll and the repetition, blessing, and chanting of the text when read – all this marks out the text not as studied but as performed, not learned but experienced, not understood but absorbed. In this way the Torah, the embodiment of Judaism, is passed from one generation to the next, a quasi-procreative act, insuring the ongoing life of the Jewish community.[86]

Ancient Christians also chanted their scriptures. The New Testament mentions Jesus and his disciples singing psalms (Matt. 26:30) and Paul recommends the practice (Eph. 5:19). With that precedent, early Christians sang psalms and soon chanted the reading of other scriptures just as Jews did. Some ancient Christian churches employed Jewish cantors to teach the "proper" chanting of scripture. The sound of those ancient chants has been lost over time. However, surviving manuscripts from the tenth century and later contain notations to indicate how to chant scripture readings.[87]

Why do Jews, Christians, and Muslims chant scripture?

Alan Gampel observed: "The practice of cantillation has historically served to guide and remind the reader of this accurate pronunciation and of the hierarchy of word importance within sentences. Clerical leaders have generally viewed the musical element of cantillation to be ancillary to the grammatical and syntactical contributions that help to accurately transmit the word of God. This insistence on the primacy of the text and on a clear understanding of each word led to the imposition of restrictive musical guidelines, which in turn resulted in limited melodic freedom in the traditional cantillation of all three religions."[88]

Chanting scripture according to prescribed melodies distinguishes reading aloud within synagogue and church rituals from reading scripture aloud in group and personal study. This difference encourages a tendency to distinguish liturgical from didactic reading. In practice, however, recitation for study frequently becomes almost as ritualized as the liturgies of synagogues and churches.

Hymns and other kinds of religious songs often quote scripture. Songs allow composers and performers much greater melodic and musical creativity than liturgical scripture readings. Scripture texts feature in many of the most famous musical compositions in Western culture, ranging from medieval Gregorian chants through the hymns of Martin Luther, Isaac Watts, and Charles Wesley, to performance pieces such as George Frideric Händel's *Messiah* and Leonard Bernstein's *Chichester Psalms*. The Christian tendency to focus on New Testament texts, the Psalms, and the Prophets, rather than on the Pentateuch, shapes this musical tradition. Some early Calvinist congregations sang the Ten Commandments. Some classical compositions, such as Franz Joseph Haydn's *Creation*, feature the beginning of Genesis. Christian music for the most part, however, alludes to Pentateuchal stories but does not quote many Pentateuchal texts.

A wide variety of people participate in oral and dramatic performances of scriptures. This situation is very different from the scholarly expertise that dominates scriptural interpretation. It also contrasts with the Bible's own hierarchical depictions of Torah readings in Deuteronomy, Joshua, Kings, and Ezra. Performance leadership in congregations tends to be open to non-specialists and often to people otherwise excluded from religious leadership. Jews consider it a privilege to be "called to the Torah," and this experience plays the central role in a child's *bar* or *bat mitzvah*. Many Christian churches routinely ask lay people to read scripture aloud, including women in traditions that exclude them from being priests. Even more people get involved in singing biblical texts as soloists, in choirs, and as members of congregations. Oral performance practices in Muslim and Sikh communities are similarly inclusive though they take different forms. So, religious communities regularly use oral performance as a way to expand the ranks of worship leaders, even as hierarchies often cling to authoritative interpretation. This expansion of religious leadership through readings, recitations, and dramatizations, together with their inspiring effects, explains much of the social power exerted by the Bible in a wide variety of cultures.

Art, Illustrations, and Maps

The visual arts have been more inclusive of Pentateuchal themes than music has. Artists have found ample material in the Pentateuch's narratives. The stories of creation, Adam and Eve, the tower of Babel, Abraham's near sacrifice of Isaac, the plagues on the Egyptians, the crossing of the Reed Sea, Moses receiving the tablets of commandments, and the Israelites worshipping the golden calf have repeatedly been depicted in art throughout Jewish and Christian history.

Many ancient Jewish synagogues were covered in art. Surviving floor mosaics typically depict a Torah ark flanked by lamp stands (*menorahs*), synagogue furniture that was inspired by Pentateuchal prototypes. The floors often depict the story of Abraham and Isaac from Genesis 22 as well. Their wall art has not survived except in one place: the synagogue of Dura Europos in Syria preserved frescos from the third century CE showing scenes from Genesis, Exodus, Leviticus, Numbers, Samuel, Kings, Ezekiel, and Esther.

Stories from many of these books also appear frequently in Christian art. Icons and sculptures regularly depict portraits of some Pentateuchal characters. Abraham is usually shown with the boy Isaac. Aaron is dressed in priestly vestments and holds a censor. Moses appears very often in church art holding the tablets of the commandments. The tablets, in Moses's hands or by themselves, became a common symbol for Judaism. Christian art regularly uses them to contrast the "old covenant" with the new, which is depicted by codex and chalice. Jews have embraced the

Figure 4.5 Floor mosaic (sixth century CE) of Abraham sacrificing Isaac (Gen. 22:1–11) in the ruins of the Bet Alpha synagogue, Israel.

Figure 4.6 Moses receiving the Ten Commandments. Woodcut from an early sixteenth-century design by Hans Holbein. *Source*: Public domain image from *Icones Veteris Testamenti: Illustrations of the Old Testment, Engraved on Wood, From Designs by Hans Holbein*. London: William Pickering, 1830 (first published 1538).

tablets to visually represent the Torah. They commonly appear on synagogue buildings and on Torah arks (see Chapter 3).

Christian artists have frequently illustrated Pentateuchal stories that theologians have interpreted as foreshadowing Jesus Christ. Such "typologies" focused especially on Adam's sin which brought about human death (for which Christ died) and Abraham's near sacrifice of his innocent son, Isaac (foreshadowing the death of the innocent son of God, Jesus). Typology led to some obscure stories becoming familiar through their artistic reproduction. For example, the parallel with viewing Jesus on the cross led many artists to the story of Moses putting a bronze snake on a pole at whose sight the Israelites were saved from poisonous snake bites (Num. 21:4–9).

Art has sometimes amplified minor interpretations of the biblical text into widespread beliefs. An infamous example appears in most Christian art depicting Moses. Exodus 34:35 describes Moses's face "shining" after his encounter with God, but the Latin Vulgate translated the word as a noun, "horns." The translator, Jerome, used the word to depict Moses positively as strong and powerful, but medieval Christian imagination associated his horns with the devil. Artistic portrayals of the horned Moses

Figure 4.7 Horned Moses, ca. 1894, on Alexander Hall, Princeton University.

came to typify all Jews, leading to the anti-Semitic slur that Jews have horns like the devil. Both the image and the belief continue to circulate in many Christians' imaginations.[89]

Modern photography and mass media have made some biblical art famous worldwide. For example, mention of the biblical creation story often brings to mind Michelangelo's sixteenth-century fresco on the ceiling of the Vatican's Sistine Chapel or William Blake's nineteenth-century painted etchings as much as the text of Genesis 1–2. Mass tourism to view artistic masterpieces can draw attention to obscure Pentateuchal texts. Thus the stained glass windows that Mark Chagall made in 1962 for Hadassah Hospital in Jerusalem draw more attention than do the texts that they illustrate from Genesis 49 and Deuteronomy 33, which are poems blessing each Israelite tribe.

It is more difficult to distinguish the semantic, performative, and iconic dimensions of bibles containing illustrations than of any other aspect of scripture ritualization. Decorated and illustrated bibles clearly ritualize scripture's iconic dimension by enhancing its value and beauty. (See "Publishing Torahs and Bibles" in Chapter 3.) They also interpret the semantic meaning of the text. However, their use to fascinate the religious imagination and inspire their viewers justifies discussing them together with other biblically inspired art as examples of ritualizing the performative dimension of scriptures.

The earliest manuscripts of the Hebrew and Greek Pentateuch are not illustrated or decorated. After official recognition of Christianity in the fourth century CE, Christians began to produce prestige copies of their scriptures in expensive materials and decorations. By the early middle ages, monasteries from Egypt to Ireland competed with each other to produce the most magnificent manuscripts possible. Their "illuminations" used bright colors, frequently including gold leaf, for elaborate calligraphy, decorations, and illustrations of biblical scenes.[90]

Manuscript illustrations usually feature the same biblical stories as Jewish and Christian art generally, often in almost exactly the same way. The codex format, however, permitted longer sequences of images which occasionally led to picture-book bibles. In Paris in the twelfth century, scribes created expensive abridgements of the Old Testament called *Bible Moralisée*. Each page consists of eight pictures that interpret stories typologically by matching Old Testament scenes with their New Testament parallels. Fourteenth-century "pauper's bibles" featured much cruder art that could be reproduced inexpensively by block printing. Picture-book bibles have more recently been marketed primarily to children. In the decades around the turn of the twenty-first century, however, abridged bibles are again taking pictorial form as graphic novels, manga bibles, and art bibles.

Illustrations in bibles usually focus on stories, but not always. The Bible's descriptions of the Tabernacle (Exod. 25–40) and of Solomon's temple (1 Kgs. 6) have stimulated interest in visualizing them. The architecture and furnishings of the Tabernacle dominate late-medieval Jewish illuminations of the Torah's instructions. Some Jewish codices, such as the Perpignan Bible of 1299 and the Farhi Bible of 1366–1383, devote several pages to illustrating the furnishings described in Exodus. The Kennicott Bible of 1476 and some others interleave full-page illustrations of the Tabernacle furnishings with abstract carpet pages that separate the Torah from the Prophets. With the development of printing, illustrated bibles included detailed renderings of the Tabernacle, its contents, and its priests. These scenes sometimes contain a burning altar, but they focus on objects, not ritual practices.

Figure 4.8 Moses receiving the law and giving it to the Israelites. An illuminated page from the Moutier-Grandval Bible created in Tours, France in 835 CE.
Source: Public domain image via Wikimedia Commons.

Maps of the biblical "holy land" have also been used since antiquity to imagine the travels of biblical characters, and to reenact them through pilgrimages. Eusebius and Jerome in the fourth century CE may have included schematic maps to illustrate their lists of biblical place names. In the sixth century, the Church of Saint George in Madaba, Jordan, commissioned a large floor mosaic map of the holy land which can still be

Figure 4.9 Illustration of Tabernacle Furniture and High Priest (Exodus 25, 28). *Source*: Public domain image from Henry Davenport Northrop, *Treasures of the Bible*, Philadelphia: International Publishing, 1894.

seen today. In his eleventh-century commentary, Rabbi Shlomo Yitzchaki, better known by the acronym Rashi, drew schematic maps of the Israelites' route from Egypt to Canaan (Exodus, Numbers) and the territories of the Israelite tribes in the land (Joshua). His influence led to such maps appearing prominently in Protestant bibles in the sixteenth century, where they were usually joined by maps of Palestine in the time of Jesus and of Paul's journeys. These four subjects appeared regularly in Christian bibles of the following centuries, often supplemented by maps of the location of Eden (Gen. 2), the peoples of the world (Gen. 10), the kingdoms of Israel and Judah (1 Kings), and the city of Jerusalem in various periods of biblical history.

Bible maps tend to illustrate texts from the Pentateuch and Old Testament to a much greater degree than other Christian art. That is because maps provide a visual means of reducing complicated and apparently contradictory literature – such as the Pentateuch's confusing itinerary of Israel's wandering in the wilderness – to a single, clear image. Maps summarize itineraries or boundaries detailed in complicated lists, often scattered across multiple chapters or books of the Bible. Nicolas Barbier, the sixteenth-century publisher of the popular English Geneva Bible, explained in the Bible's preface that maps are useful aides for reading. "Their purpose … is to present clearly to the reader's eye what is otherwise difficult to grasp from the text alone." But bible maps do more than that. By illustrating trips and political boundaries directed by God's commandments, they fix a geographic ideal in readers' visual imagination. Like the illustrations of Tabernacle furniture, the maps enable readers to imaginatively accompany the Israelites on their wanderings in the wilderness. They help readers visualize the prototypical journeys that inspire Jewish and Christian pilgrimages: Israel's travels to Sinai, to "the promised land," and to Jerusalem.

Early Protestant publishers were especially likely to include maps in their bibles. Elizabeth M. Ingram explained the interpretive principles at work in bible maps.

> The map functions not only as an aide for clarifying a specific text, but also as silent witness to a basic principle of Calvin's hermeneutics: that scripture is everywhere comprehensible and internally consistent. Consequently, its geographical dimensions must remain equally knowable, externally consistent, and therefore capable of being mapped.

Catherine Delano Smith argued that the early Protestants also wanted to direct how their readers understood the Old Testament.

> Reading, whether voiced or silent, bestows power on the reader. The reader is free to interpret the meaning of the message on the page as he or she likes (or is able). ... Maps, as art and not just like art, became a mechanism for appropriating the (sacred) world by categorizing it in the manner approved by the religious authorities.

Even when Puritans increasingly banned pictures from their bibles (the 1611 Authorized "Kings James" Version was published without any illustrations in its text), maps and chronological charts could be bought separately and added as front- or back-matter. That is where they still appear in many bibles published today.[91]

Biblical maps and social imagination

Minnie Bruce Pratt, in an essay titled "The Maps in My Bible," described her childhood fascination with bible maps. She recalled how they obscured one kind of geography and social reality while strengthening another.

> Looking at these maps, I felt secure yet adventurous. Their details proved what I was learning in my religion, that there was a place whose terrain, cities, buildings corresponded to the words of a Bible that was to be

> believed literally and absolutely. ... I wished I could travel to this Land I felt so connected to, unaware that my maps were a hundred years out-of-date, unaware of my enmeshment in a history that had drawn and re-drawn them. ... There was no map to show me that I was living in a place and a time, Alabama in the deep South of the 1950's and 60's, marked by the convergence of racial and anti-Semitic theories developed in Europe and a specific racism practiced by white people in the United States against African-Americans. Buttressed by the Christian myth of Ham's eternal servitude, the white folks around me admitted no possibility of purification of the Black people living among us, almost all of them raised Christian. ... All of us caught on a map marked off by race, by color, by blood.[92]

Artistic illustrations in bibles, and even more their maps, help readers interpret the biblical text. They therefore help ritualize the Bible's semantic dimension. The physical sight and intricacy of illustrations and maps also makes the bibles that contain them more attractive, thus ritualizing their iconic dimension. I have discussed them in this chapter, however, because biblical maps and illustrations inspire the visual imagination. They make the biblical stories seem more real to readers. In fact, Christian readers are far more likely to study Israel's journey through the wilderness on a map and the details of the Tabernacle's design in an illustration than they are to read the details in Exodus and Numbers. The illustrations and maps, along with other biblically inspired art, music, and films, have become performances of the biblical text that shape many people's religious imagination more than reading or hearing the text itself.

Art extends the oral performance of biblical texts into visual media. It is too simplistic to think that old religious art aimed primarily at illiterate audiences. Its persistence in modern society shows a much more dynamic interaction between written story, oral retellings, and artistic representation. Usually, though not always, you must already know a story in order to recognize that art refers to it. Art, on the other hand, often emphasizes different things than semantic interpretation and leads you to notice different elements. Artists must interpret the text to depict it. We have seen how artists frequently follow the dominant interpretations in their culture, such as typological readings of Isaac as representing Christ. But artists frequently deviate from the standardized views of clergy and scholars. That is because their work does not usually aim to support or challenge the authority of semantic interpretation, but rather to inspire viewers. The art of churches and synagogues therefore extends the ritualization of the Bible's performative dimension which aims to inspire. Much biblical art, from the most common icons to the most famous masterpieces, has clearly inspired millions of viewers.

Theater and Film

Religious street theater developed in Europe during the Middle Ages and brought with it theatrical reenactments of biblical stories. One variety, called "mystery plays," presented narratives from the Christian Bible in vernacular poetry. Pentateuchal stories were featured in plays about "the Creation and Fall of Man," Cain and Abel, Noah's flood, Abraham and Isaac, and Moses. Many towns would sponsor performances of cycles of morality plays during annual festivals.[93]

The advent of the Protestant Reformation led to religious plays becoming instruments of intra-Christian polemic. Though Protestants criticized Catholic art, sometimes to the point of destroying it, they embraced religious theater as a means of spreading their message. For example, an English Reformer, John Bale, wrote and directed 24 plays with a traveling troupe of actors in the 1530s. In his repertoire was *Three Laws*, which dramatized biblical history in three parts as "the law of nature" from Adam to the exodus, the "law of Moses" for the rest of the Old Testament, and the New Testament as "the law of Christ." This play is unusual for emphasizing the Pentateuchal theme of law, even while subordinating it to the New Testament's Christ. After the last decades of the sixteenth century, however, biblical plots disappeared from English plays. This was probably due to the popularity of the secular plays of William Shakespeare and Christopher Marlowe and also to the Puritans' disapproval of all theater. Antagonism between theater and church remained a feature of English Christianity to the end of the nineteenth century.[94]

Biblically inspired tableaus were more acceptable to conservative religious sensibilities. Bible illustrations of the Tabernacle and its furnishings as described in Exodus 25–40 fueled popular interest in scale models of the Tabernacle. In seventeenth-century Holland, Rabbi Jacob Judah Leon became known as "Templo" for displaying scale models of the Jerusalem Temple and Tabernacle. In the same city 200 years later, Rev. Leendert Schouten also attracted visitors with a model of the Tabernacle. In late nineteenth-century America, you could visit a full-size model of the Tabernacle in Chautauqua, New York. Replicas of the Tabernacle appear today at Holy Land Experience in Orlando, Florida, at the Mennonite Information Center in Lancaster, Pennsylvania, at New Holy Land in Eureka Springs, Arkansas, and at Timna Park near Eilat, Israel. Several manufacturers sell kits for constructing scale models of the Tabernacle, which appear on display in the educational rooms of many congregations. Other Pentateuchal scenes have also been the basis for public tableaus. For example, the Saint Louis World's Fair of 1904 featured a walk-through exhibit of the six days of creation. In 2016, creationists in Kentucky unveiled a 510-foot replica of Noah's ark.

Figure 4.10 Full-size reconstruction of the Tabernacle (Exodus 25–40) in Timna Park, Israel.

Modern fascination with the details of the sanctuary, furnishings, and vestments in Exodus does not extend to reenacting the Pentateuch's ritual instructions. They are usually left to verbal explanation or artistic depiction, though Holy Land Experience does stage reenactments of the Day of Atonement ritual (Lev. 16) with a live actor but stuffed animals. Scale models, even those populated by a costumed cast, allow visitors to experience what it was like to be in ancient towns and temples. Christian reenactments usually reproduce traditional typologies of the Tabernacle and Temple rituals as foreshadowing and being superseded by Christ's atoning sacrifice. That is not always the case, however. Some African churches show greater interest in performing purity and offering rituals, to the point that the Musama Disco Christo Church of West Africa has an Ark of the Covenant inside a Holy of Holies which a high priest accesses once a year (Lev. 16). Jewish reconstructions, by contrast, recall the destruction of the ancient temples and, for some, anticipate their reconstruction. The Temple Institute in Jerusalem takes this expectation one step further: it is currently building furniture and making vestments in the expressed hope that they will be used in a rebuilt Jerusalem Temple.[95]

Religious antagonism to professional theater waned in the twentieth century. Churches and professional companies increasingly staged biblical plays. Though Pentateuchal stories have rarely reached the stages of Broadway or London (one exception is *Joseph's Amazing Technicolor Dreamcoat* by Tim Rice and Andrew Lloyd Webber), stories about Moses, Abraham, and the Creation feature prominently in the theatrical productions of religious organizations. For example, Sight and Sound Theaters operates theaters in Lancaster, Pennsylvania, and Branson, Missouri, that stage only biblically based plays.

Biblical stories appear more prominently in films and television shows. Religious producers in many countries have produced devotional films. They distribute them through denominational networks of churches as well as through secular media outlets. The Bible has also provided material for commercial Hollywood producers. The dominance of Christian culture in America guaranteed that Jesus movies based on the Gospels would be most prominent. But the story of Moses in the book of Exodus has provided the themes of several Hollywood blockbusters: Cecil B. DeMille's *The Ten Commandments* (1956), Jeffrey Katzenberg's animated *Prince of Egypt* (1998), and Ridley Scott's *Exodus: Gods and Kings* (2014). As a result, these films today dominate people's imagination of the Pentateuch more than any other artistic medium, and often more than the written text itself.

The visual medium and the conventions of mass-market films lead to significant modifications of the biblical account. As is typical of Christian performances, laws and instructions get little attention. Films of the exodus story focus more on Moses than on God or the Israelites in order to tell a story that conforms to modern heroic expectations. Brian Britt summarized the overall effect.

> Moses films eclipse biblical tradition more emphatically than any other medium. … The biblical Moses is a figure of writing rather than a figure of speech and action. Nevertheless, … each of the films brings writing into the story – not the writing of Moses, but the writing of Egypt … and in the case of *The Ten Commandments*, the fiery writing of God on the tablets of the law…. Forced by the medium and conventions of film to show Moses in heroic action, the movies nevertheless gesture … to a more biblical Moses, a Moses of tradition and writing.[96]

The interest of artists, actors, and film directors in biblical stories has reinforced the Christian tendency to ignore the Pentateuch's laws and instructions. Western cultural influence has spread that tendency around the world.

Biblical Art, Film, and Music beyond Scripture

Bible films reach large and varied audiences, but that is true of biblically inspired art and music too. Of all the ritualized dimensions of scriptures, the performative dimension crosses religious boundaries most easily.

Music and art have the power to move anyone's emotions. People who do not regard themselves as Jews or Christians often find oral and visual performances of scriptures inspiring. The Bible's performative dimension often gets ritualized outside of religious communities in concert halls and museums as well as cinemas. Classical choral masterpieces such as Händel's oratorio, *The Messiah,* and Mozart's *Requiem Mass* perform words drawn mostly or entirely from the Christian Bible to concert hall audiences. Though much of their material comes from prophetic and New Testament books, they also draw on the Pentateuch. Some, such as Haydn's *Creation,* focus there.

In the same way, many paintings and sculptures of biblical scenes appear in museum art collections. Some famous works draw sightseers from around the world and across religions and cultures. The crowds that view Michelangelo's ceiling of the Sistine Chapel, for example, do not need to know the biblical storyline before traveling to Rome to see it. But they are nevertheless treated to a visual summary of the Christian Bible from creation to apocalypse, that is, from Genesis to Revelation. Some pictorial motifs, such as Eve posed naked with the snake, have become cultural clichés readily recognized by many people who have never read Genesis 3.[97]

Synagogues and churches use music and art to draw people's attention and interest. But it is also the case that much biblically inspired music and art escapes ecclesiastical control. In state museums, cinemas, and concert halls, biblical texts are viewed and performed apart from the ritual contexts of Jewish and Christian worship. Here the Bible's performative dimension gets ritualized without the accompanying ritualization of its iconic and semantic dimensions. In these secular contexts, the Bible continues to inspire, but no longer as a scripture.

The Pentateuch's Performative Dimension Before Ezra

Oral performances are by their nature ephemeral, and no art depicting biblical stories has survived from ancient Israel and Judah. Ritualization of the Pentateuch's performative dimension before Ezra appears only in references to oral readings in the Bible itself. The artistic and literary remains of other ancient Middle Eastern cultures, however, show how the peoples around Israel ritualized the performative dimension of their texts. This cultural context allows us to better understand the traditions and innovations reflected in the Pentateuch.

Performing Texts in Ancient Cultures

Ancient texts were written with the expectation that they would be read aloud. Sometimes they specified when they should be read and what effects reading them would bring about. *Enuma Elish*, the Babylonian creation epic from the later second millennium BCE, concludes with a list of the 50 names of the god Marduk. It then admonishes that the names

> *must be grasped: the first one should reveal them, the wise and knowledgeable should ponder them together, the master should repeat, and make the pupil understand. The shepherd, the herdsman should pay attention.*[98]

Ancient treaties explicitly required regular readings of the treaty documents.

There is evidence from cultures across the ancient Middle East and eastern Mediterranean that ritual texts were particularly likely to mandate that their stipulations be followed exactly as written. It is also clear that many priests and kings did so to the point that reading and manipulating ritual texts became part of the ritual itself.

A number of Egyptian texts require verbatim repetition of their contents. For example, the stele in Pahery's tomb from the fourteenth century BCE asks readers to make offerings and recite the prayer for the deceased that is also recorded on the stele.

> *Say, "An offering, given by the king," in the form in which it is written, "An invocation offering," as said by the fathers, and as it comes from the mouth of god.*

Other Egyptian texts link exact repetition of spells and prayers with detailed ritual instructions. For example, an Osiris ritual from the last three centuries BCE records an elaborate liturgy and then ritual instructions that begin:

> *Now when this is recited the place is to be completely secluded, not seen and not heard by anyone except the chief lector-priest and the setem-priest.*[99]

The Egyptian ritual for vivifying the dead, called "Opening the Mouth," shows how ritual texts could be used. One of the priests at this rite was the lector priest, literally "the one who holds the ritual," that is, who holds the papyrus scroll on which the words of the ritual are written. Many tomb paintings, models, and papyri illustrate this official presiding over the ceremony, open scroll in hand (see Figure 3.23 on p. 119).[100]

Such priests were, of course, literate, which means they were also scribes. Reading aloud the ritual texts demonstrated their scribal skills.

Figure 4.11 Statue of a scribe with a baboon representing the scribal god, Thoth, sitting on or fused to his head. Egyptian, ca. 1275–1085 BCE, in the Metropolitan Museum of Art, New York.

Their responsibilities included preserving the ancient scrolls, which required recopying them when they wore out. Egyptian scribes thus embodied their texts: their hands copied the scrolls and their voices read the scrolls aloud. In so far as the ritual texts were believed to have been dictated by gods, the scribes embodied a divine tradition. Portraits portraying Egyptians posing as scribes marked them as both learned and pious. Over the 3,000 years of ancient Egyptian culture, the scribal god, Thoth, was increasingly credited as the author of ritual texts. Sometimes, statues of scribes show them in the company of baboons, one of Thoth's representative animals. In one case, the baboon seems fused to the back of the scribe's head in a striking visual claim to divine inspiration.

Around the time of Ezra, old books were being read aloud in other cultures to revive customs and festivals in much the same way as described in Nehemiah 8. The first-century Roman historian Livy described a Samnite ritual that was performed around 300 BCE. Livy emphasized the antiquity of the ceremony that was revived for this occasion. A priest read an old linen scroll aloud to ensure that the correct words were recited and to show that he was performing the ritual accurately. The rite required an oath of service in the Samnite army. Refusal meant execution as an offering to Jupiter, a threat actually carried out, according to Livy. So the ritual was performed in the face of considerable conflict, and reading the old book aloud helped the priest and his supporters keep the upper hand.[101]

A Samnite reading ritual

A space, about 200 feet square, almost in the centre of their camp, was boarded off and covered all over with linen cloth. In this enclosure a sacrificial service was conducted, the words being read from an old linen book by an aged priest, Ovius Paccius, who announced that he was taking that form of service from the old ritual of the Samnite religion. It was the form which their ancestors used when they formed their secret design of wresting Capua from the Etruscans. (Livy, *History of Rome* 10.38)

Israel's textual culture was, of course, not the same as that of its neighbors. For example, archeologists have found no royal inscriptions by Israelite or Judean kings, though such inscriptions are common in surrounding territories. Nor is there any reason to think that Israelite scribes ever illustrated their manuscripts, though Egyptian scribes produced elaborately illustrated scrolls to accompany the dead into the afterlife. However, the Hebrew Bible preserves direct evidence of oral performance, both in its descriptions of public readings and in the way in which its text is written. Israelite scribes therefore utilized and developed practices of oral performance that were common in other ancient Middle Eastern and Mediterranean cultures.

The Pentateuch's Instructions for Ritual Readings

The Pentateuch explicitly requires its own publication through oral performance. In Deuteronomy, Moses commands the priests to read written Torah aloud at *Sukkot* (Booths) to the entire people of Israel.

> *Moses wrote down this Torah and gave it to the levitical priests who carry the chest of the covenant and to all the Israelite elders. He commanded them: "Every seventh year … during the festival of Sukkot, … you must read this Torah in the hearing of all Israel. Gather the people – men, women, children and immigrants who live in your cities – so that they will hear it and learn it and revere YHWH your God and do all the words of this Torah obediently, so their descendants who do not know it will hear it and learn it and revere YHWH your God."* (Deut. 31:9–13)

He also requires every Israelite to recite the Torah's commandments at home.

> *Repeat them to your children and talk about them when you sit at home and when you walk down the road, when you lie down and when you get up.* (Deut. 6:7)

When they were first written, these texts probably referred to the book of Deuteronomy or just to the lists of laws in Deuteronomy. When Deuteronomy became attached to Exodus and Leviticus, however, the meaning of "this Torah" expanded to include all the laws of the Pentateuch, and eventually the Pentateuch as a whole. As a result, the Pentateuch concludes with instructions for its reading and recitation, just like many other ancient ritual texts.

Public reading served to instruct and inspire listeners, but it also aimed for other effects. Throughout the ancient world, people believed that public reading *activated* the power of texts. Public reading and inscription put new laws into effect. Reading and ritual manipulation activated blessings and curses. Blessings were recited by priests over worshippers (Num. 6:22–27). Curses were recited and then written in order to break the texts or for their ink to be washed into drinking water to make them take effect (Num. 5:23–28).

The Hebrew Bible contains several stories of ritualizing texts this way. Deuteronomy requires that the Torah be activated inside Canaan by being written on a monument on Mount Ebal. Then the Levites must proclaim the book's threats against disobedience over all the people of Israel while facing each other on two mountains, and the people must acknowledge the threatened punishments by answering, "Amen" (Deut. 27–28). Joshua 8 tells us that Joshua led the people in following these instructions. Similarly, near the end of the book of Jeremiah, the prophet orders the performative and iconic actualization of his threats against Babylon.

> *Jeremiah wrote on one scroll all the disasters coming against Babylon .... Jeremiah said to Seraiah, "When you come to Babylon, make sure you read all these words. Then you must say, 'YHWH, you yourself pronounced the destruction and elimination of this place, so that neither humans nor animals will ever live here again.' When you finish reading this scroll, tie a rock to it and throw it into the Euphrates river and say, 'Thus will Babylon sink and rise no more because of the disasters I am bringing against her'."* (Jer. 51:60–64)

Biblical Stories of Torah Readings

Moses sets the example with public Torah readings early in the story of Israel at Mount Sinai. After meeting God on the mountain, he reports to the Israelites what YHWH said to him (Exod. 24:3, referring to Exod. 20–23).

After they agree to the covenant with YHWH, Moses writes down what he has already reported. Again, the Israelites hear the provisions of the covenant, this time read aloud by Moses from the newly written "covenant book." Again, they agree, and Moses ritually seals the covenant by splashing them with the blood of offerings.

Moses reads the covenant book

Moses came and reported to the people all the words of YHWH and all the commandments. All the people responded with one voice: "We will do everything that YHWH said." Then Moses wrote down all the words of YHWH. The next morning, he built an altar below the mountain and set up twelve standing stones to represent the twelve tribes of Israel. He sent young Israelites to raise rising offerings and to slaughter amity slaughter offerings of oxen to YHWH. Moses put half the blood in basins and splashed the other half against the altar. Then he took the book of the covenant and read it in the people's hearing. They said, "We will do and observe everything YHWH said." Then Moses took the blood and splashed it on the people, saying "This is the blood of the covenant that YHWH made with you through all these words." (Exod. 24:3–8)

More than anywhere else in the Hebrew Bible, this story places Torah reading in the middle of a ritual performance, complete with burned offerings and a short unison liturgy of commitment. All three ritual elements together – the offerings, the unison commitment, and the reading of the covenant book – serve to ratify the covenant between Israel and YHWH. Public reading of Torah plays a central role in sealing the relationship between Israel and God.

The Hebrew Bible tells us that Deuteronomy's instructions were followed later by a few of Israel's leaders. Moses's successor, Joshua, did so after Israel's initial victories in Canaan. Joshua built an altar on Mount Ebal and wrote the "law of Moses" on it.

> *Afterwards, he read all the words of the Torah, the blessings and the curses, according to everything written in the book of the Torah. There was not one word that Moses commanded that Joshua did not read to the whole congregation of Israel and the women and the children and the immigrants among them.* (Josh. 8:34–35)

Joshua 8 combines the ceremony of blessings and curses from Deuteronomy 27 with the reading ritual of Deuteronomy 31.

After this point in the story, however, the written Torah disappears from much of the history of Israel and Judah. The books of Judges,

Samuel, and Kings rarely mention the Torah, and the books of Chronicles only slightly more often. This silence draws special attention to those scenes in which the Torah is read aloud.

Around 600 years after Joshua, near the end of the history of the kingdom of Judah, King Josiah again read the Torah aloud to the people of Jerusalem, according to 2 Kings 22–23 and 2 Chronicles 34. This story accounts for the Torah's absence from the preceding history by saying that a Torah scroll was found in the Temple during renovations. It implies that the "book of the Torah" had been forgotten until then. When Josiah heard the book read aloud, he asked for confirmation of its authenticity from the prophet Huldah. She warned that YHWH would carry out the book's threats (2 Kgs. 22:14–20). Then Josiah assembled

> *all the people of Judah and all the inhabitants of Jerusalem, the priests, the prophets and all the people small and large. He read aloud to them all the words of the book of the covenant that had been found in the temple of YHWH.* (2 Kgs. 23:2)

According to 2 Kings, reading the Torah led Josiah to renew the covenant, purify Jerusalem's Temple of illegitimate objects, destroy religious sites in the other towns of Judah, and depose their priests. According to 2 Chronicles, these reforms preceded the discovery of the book. Both agree that, after finding the book, Josiah ordered the people to observe Passover. 2 Kings emphasizes that they should do

> *as is written in this book of the covenant. For no Passover had been observed like this since the days of the Judges.* (2 Kgs. 23:21–22)

The biblical histories also narrate, however, that after Josiah died, his successors reversed his religious policies. There is no record of any other public readings of Torah until the time of Ezra, some 200 years later.

The story of the written Torah that emerges from the whole Hebrew Bible starts with Moses, who wrote it down and read it aloud and commanded Israel to read it regularly. His successor, Joshua, did so, but no one did it again for 600 years until Josiah. Then another two centuries passed until Ezra read the Torah aloud in Jerusalem.[102]

Modern biblical scholars wonder whether these stories of law readings are really historical. They also wonder about the contents of the books of Torah described in these stories. In Chapter 3, we discussed the historical plausibility of Josiah's law book. There we concluded that the writer of 2 Kings must have known of such a book. This writer uses Deuteronomic themes and vocabulary, so his idea of the Torah probably corresponded more or less with the book of Deuteronomy that we have today. We therefore know that Judeans in the time of the Babylonian Exile knew the tradition that the Torah commands its own oral performance and believed that such a performance had taken place at least once in the last years of the kingdom of Judah.

Did the writers of Deuteronomy invent the tradition of public Torah reading? The stories and instructions for public readings in Exodus, Deuteronomy, Joshua, and 2 Kings bear a family resemblance that suggests a common literary model. They all emphasize that the whole book, "all the words of the Torah," was read to all the people. They also focus on the physical Torah by describing it being written, rewritten, or discovered. The instructions in Deuteronomy and Josiah's fulfillment of them in 2 Kings may therefore have been written at nearly the same time. If that was the case, the stories in Joshua and Exodus project a practice of later times back onto Israel's early history.

The story of Ezra's reading in Nehemiah 8 presupposes this same literary tradition, but also emphasizes translation and interpretation of the Torah and the length of time devoted to the reading over several days. It seems to be a later development of the literary theme of public law readings. It presupposes a larger Torah containing much, if not all, of the Pentateuch.

Many commentators on Exodus suspect that the Covenant Code (Exod. 21–23) was originally an independent document that may have concluded with the covenant reading ceremony in 24:3–8.[103] If that is the case, Exodus preserves a story about reading the law that could be older than Deuteronomy's requirements to do so. It may be the model from which the Deuteronomic tradition of law reading developed. Nevertheless, the language of the Pentateuch is the Hebrew that was spoken by Judeans in the eighth to the fifth centuries BCE. There is no evidence of Hebrew literature older than this, though some poetry may have been passed down orally from earlier times. Written stories of reading Torah scrolls aloud therefore all come from these centuries of Israel's history, long after the events narrated in the Pentateuch.

So the writers of the Pentateuch not only expected their work to be read aloud, like all other ancient literature, they also expected it to be read aloud in imitation of Moses's readings and his instructions for readings. We should therefore expect that they shaped the Pentateuch for this purpose. That means it was composed for two very different groups of people: for the mostly illiterate audiences that listened to the readings and also for the literate scribes who performed the readings. We will see that the Pentateuch does contain indications that it was composed to be read aloud by scribes to mixed audiences of listeners.

Composing Torah for a Listening Audience

The stories of public Torah readings describe the listening audience as the whole people of Israel or of Jerusalem – men, women, and children usually explicitly included (Exod. 24:3, 7; Deut. 31:12–13; Josh. 8:33–35; 2 Kgs. 23:2; Neh. 8:1–3).[104] People in such an audience might hear the Torah read aloud every seven years. Perhaps they heard it recited on other occasions, too. Such a listening audience could not be expected to notice many textual details. The Pentateuch instead draws their attention by using various literary and rhetorical devices.

The different kinds of literature contained in the Pentateuch – stories, laws and instructions, hymns and poems, promises and threats – engage a listening audience in different ways. The stories use suspense and surprise to hold listeners' attention and a curt style that makes them memorable. Laws and instructions raise listeners' concerns by regulating how they form their families and spend their wealth. Sanctions heighten their concerns by promising rewards for obeying the laws and threatening dire punishments if listeners do not. And the Pentateuch encourages listeners to join in orally performing the text in songs just like it also requires them to perform the text's teachings in their daily lives.

Passages from all the Pentateuch's component traditions – Deuteronomy, Priestly (P), and not-priestly material outside Deuteronomy – have been shaped for oral performance to a listening audience. This fact shows that P, which never mentions books or reading, shared the same expectations for how its text should be used as the other Pentateuchal sources. These writers all lived in a culture in which reading Torah aloud was not only the most practical means for publishing it but was also a religious ideal.

Stories for a listening audience

Stories use suspense and surprise to keep their audience's attention. The Pentateuch creates suspense with stories of huge catastrophes such as Noah's flood (Gen. 6–8) and the plagues on the Egyptians (Exod. 7–12). It can also use stories of conflicts between people to maintain suspense, such as in the stories of Jacob (Gen. 25–35) and Joseph (Gen. 36–50), and the stories about challenges to Moses's and Aaron's leadership (Num. 11–14, 16, 21). And, of course, the Pentateuch tells of suspenseful encounters with God, such as the night-time experiences of Abraham and Jacob (Gen. 15, 28, 32), the daytime revelations to Moses in the burning bush (Exod. 3), and, most dramatically, the Israelites' encounter with YHWH at Mount Sinai (Exod. 19–20, 24, 40). The Pentateuch can even create suspense when narrating rituals, such as when Aaron inaugurates the Tabernacle service and YHWH burns up the altar offerings (Lev. 9). Stories about conflicts between Israel and YHWH (Exod. 16–18, 32–34; Num. 11–25) create suspense over whether their covenant relationship will last or not. The cycles of rebellions and punishments sustain this suspense over the entire story of Israel's wandering in the wilderness.

As the Tabernacle's inauguration shows, Pentateuchal stories can use plot twists to surprise their audiences. Other surprises include Adam and Eve's punishment by being kicked out of the Garden of Eden (Gen. 3), YHWH's command to Abraham to sacrifice his son (Gen. 22), Jacob's night-time fight with YHWH (Gen. 32), and the sudden deaths of Aaron's sons, Nadab and Abihu, by divine fire (Lev. 10:1). Exodus provides a surprising ending on a larger scale. The Israelites escape Egypt after the tenth plague kills the firstborn sons of the Egyptians (Exod. 12). But then the Egyptian king sends his army in pursuit. The chase ends when the Israelites miraculously cross the Reed Sea while the Egyptian army drowns in the rising water (Exod. 13–15). This double climax reengages the audience's attention when they might think the story is over, and draws out the suspense until providing an even more dramatic conclusion.

Many of the same devices that capture the attention of silent readers of stories work on listeners as well. Biblical stories are composed in prose, much like ancient Egyptian tales but very unlike the epic poetry that dominated the narrative literatures of Mesopotamia, Ugarit, and early Greece. Poetry is naturally performative. Epic poems typically introduce their narrators as singers regaling an audience. Prose stories do not usually invoke a group audience in this way. Yet that has not prevented them from being read aloud. In the fifth century BCE, Herodotus read his prose history to audiences across Greece. In the nineteenth-century CE, families often read novels aloud together.[105]

Many biblical prose stories differ from later novels and histories by their spare and curt style. They are short and leave much to the audience's imagination. For example, the narrator of Genesis uses only 19 verses to tell the story of Abraham's attempt to kill Isaac as a burned offering to God (Gen. 22:1–19). The audience must imagine what Abraham and Isaac were thinking during this experience, as well as the reaction of Sarah, who is not mentioned in the story at all. But brevity also makes the story memorable and easily repeatable. The curt style of many Pentateuchal stories makes them very suitable for listening audiences who are supposed to remember what they hear.

Lists for a listening audience

Unlike stories, you might expect lists to strike a listening audience as boring and uninteresting. Laws and instruction, however, have their own ways of holding an audience's attention. They can address the audience directly. They can use repeated refrains to emphasize how the material is organized. They can change subjects suddenly to recapture the audience's wandering attention. Most of all, laws and instructions can deal with subjects that are of immediate and pressing concern to their audience. The Pentateuch employs all of these rhetorical techniques to capture and hold its audience's attention to its laws and instructions.

The Pentateuch addresses the laws and instructions, "this torah," directly to the people of Israel. In a few passages, most famously the Ten Commandments, God personally addresses them.

> *Remember (or observe) the sabbath day and keep it holy.* (Exod. 20:8; Deut. 5:12)
> *You must not murder.* (Exod. 20:13; Deut. 5:17)

More often in Exodus, Leviticus, and Numbers, God speaks to Moses and asks him to repeat the laws to all the Israelites (Exod. 20:22; Lev. 1:1–2). The provisions in these speeches are usually phrased in third-person, "casuistic" style.

> *Whoever hits and kills a person must be executed.* (Exod. 21:12)
> *If their present is a rising offering from the herd, they must present a perfect male.* (Lev. 1:3)

But even in the context of God's speeches to Moses, provisions frequently address the Israelites directly in the second-person singular or plural.

> *When one of you presents a present of a quadruped to YHWH, you must present your present from the herd or the flock.* (Lev. 1:2)

Direct address to the Israelites frames many of the collections of laws and instructions in the Pentateuch. Second-person address surrounds the third-person casuistic instructions of the Covenant Code (Exod. 20:23–26; 22:21–23:19). The instructions for building the Tabernacle in Exodus 25–31 conclude with a command addressed in the second person to all the people to observe the Sabbath (31:12–17). The instructions for offerings in Leviticus 1–7 also switch near their end to the second person to prohibit eating fat and blood (Lev. 7:22–26).

Some ritual instructions that are particularly important to lay people get voiced consistently in the second person, such as the bread offerings that people must prepare correctly at home (Lev. 2) and the rules for distinguishing clean from unclean animals (Lev. 11). The Holiness Code of mostly third-person casuistic rules (Lev. 17–27) intersperses among them occasional second-person exhortations.

> *You must keep my commandments and do them!* (Lev. 18:5; 19:37; etc.)

It emphasizes the importance of its teachings by requiring Israel to imitate God's holiness.

> *You must be holy because I, YHWH your God, am holy.* (Lev. 11:44; 19:2; etc.)

Deuteronomy insists instead that it was God who made Israel holy (Deut. 7:6; 14:2; etc.).

Deuteronomy, unlike the three books that precede it, is cast almost entirely as Moses's speech to the people of Israel in Moab (Deut. 1:1; 4:1; 5:1). The book therefore uses second-person address throughout. It also punctuates its rehearsal of Israel's history with many exhortations to "hear," "observe," and "remember" the laws and instructions that God has given through Moses. The most famous of these is the *Shema* (Deut. 6:4–9) that has echoed in Jewish liturgy from antiquity to today.

The *Shema*

Listen, Israel, YHWH our God, YHWH is one! You must love YHWH your God with your whole heart and with your whole being and with all your strength. Keep these words that I am commanding you today in your heart. Repeat them to your children and talk about them when you come home and when you walk down the road, when you lie down and when you get up. (Deut. 6:4–7)

Many readers find the laws and instructions hard to read. They seem tediously detailed about issues of no concern to people today. But an ancient Israelite audience would have found them full of details affecting their everyday lives. The laws address issues involving their audience's wealth (offerings and tithes), families (marriage, sex, inheritance), business dealings (theft, fraud, deposits, debt), and bodies (impurity, food, slaves). Just like modern tax laws, these issues affect people's lives and make them interested in the details of the regulations.

The laws and instructions are also repetitious, which modern readers find boring. In the setting of an ancient public reading, however, repetition would have had a different effect. Public speeches use repetition to emphasize points and make the speech memorable. Repetitive refrains make the structure of the speech obvious to listening audiences and give it a predictable rhythm. Interrupting a series of refrains can create surprise and draw attention to key points.

For example, Leviticus 1–7 and 11–16 consists of instructions for making offerings and for cleansing impurity. These chapters are therefore the longest and most detailed ritual instructions in the Bible. Yet they make use of all of these devices of repetitive rhetoric to engage a listening audience. Leviticus marks the conclusions of sets of instructions with repetitive refrains.

> *A rising offering, a fire offering, a soothing scent to YHWH.* (Lev. 1:9, 13, 17)
> *The priest mitigates (atones) for them and they are forgiven (or: they are clean).* (Lev. 4:20, 26, etc.; 14:20, 31, etc.)

The refrains rarely repeat each other exactly. Nevertheless, the refrains build a repetitive rhythm that teaches listeners what to expect next. By fulfilling these expectations, the lists give a vivid impression of systematic instructions that enhances their authority.[106]

The writers occasionally upset these expectations by breaking the pattern to create surprise and draw renewed attention. So Leviticus sometimes interrupts its refrains with urgent statements for emphasis.

> *A food offering, a fire offering for soothing scent – all fat for YHWH!* (Lev. 3:16)
> *It is a guilt offering, a guilt offering, a guilt offering for YHWH!* (Lev. 5:19)

The most shocking reversal of an expected refrain appears in the stories of the inauguration of the Tabernacle rituals. Leviticus 8–10 tells how Moses installed Aaron and his sons as priests, and then how the priests began making offerings in the newly built Tabernacle. But two of Aaron's sons, Nadab and Abihu, offer incense the wrong way and get killed as a result (10:1–3).

The key to understanding this sudden turn of events lies in the refrains that span all three chapters, and which are more obvious to the listening ear than to the reading eye. Chapters 8–9 assure their audience 12 times that the rituals were performed exactly "as YHWH commanded" (Lev. 8:4, 5, 9, 13, 17, 21, 29, 34, 36; 9:6, 7, 10) and four times more "as Moses commanded" (8:31, 35; 9:5, 21). Suddenly, Nadab and Abihu do "what YHWH did not command" (10:1). As a result, the divine fire bolt that burned up the offerings (9:24) burns up the priests too (10:2) just two verses later. The rest of Leviticus 10 reestablishes compliance with YHWH's and Moses's instructions by repeating the refrain of compliance six more times (10:5, 7, 11, 13, 15, 18). The repetition of refrains broken once by the refrain's reversal makes the story's point very clear: the priests and people must follow the instructions given by God through Moses or suffer mortal consequences. Since it is the Pentateuch that contains these instructions, the story emphasizes that lives are at stake in obeying the laws of Torah.

Sanctions for a listening audience

Promises and threats appear among the Pentateuch's laws and instructions. They remind listeners that individual and group obedience is urgently necessary. Such sanctions are familiar from other ancient literature. Many texts promise rewards to those who preserve and reproduce them orally and in writing, while cursing those who alter or destroy them. Inscriptions of laws from ancient Babylon and Greece often end with divine curses on those who ignore their provisions. Ancient treaties are particularly notable for concluding with lists of threats from every god imaginable against those who might break their treaty obligations.

Promises and warnings are scattered irregularly throughout the Pentateuch's lists of laws and instructions. They describe the consequences to individuals of obeying or disobeying the Torah. Sanctions make the Pentateuch's persuasive intent very obvious: its goal is to get listeners to behave in accord with the teachings of Torah and not contrary to them. Long lists of promises and threats for Israel conclude all three collections of laws in the Pentateuch. (See "The Rhetoric of Promise and Threat" in Chapter 2.)

Pentateuchal promises

I/YHWH will bless you (Exod. 20:24; Deut. 15:4, 10, 18)
So that you may live long in the land (Exod. 20:12; Deut. 11:9; 16:20)
The priest mitigates for them and they are forgiven (Lev. 4:20, 26, etc.)

Pentateuchal threats

They must be put to death (Exod. 21:12; Lev. 24:16–17; Deut. 13:5)
They will be cut off (Lev. 7:20; Num. 15:30–31)
They bear liability (Lev. 5:1, 17; cf. Deut. 18:19)
Lest you/he die (Lev. 10:9; 16:2)

Promises and warnings forecast the listening audience's future. The lists of laws and sanctions strike many modern readers as oppressive and punishing. But by giving people the responsibility to obey, the Pentateuch also gives them the choice to disobey. It places control over the future in the audience's hands. Unlike later apocalypses such as Daniel 7–12 and the New Testament's book of Revelation that portray a divine plan for all of history, the Pentateuch does not show God deciding its audience's future in advance. The future depends instead on people's responses to the Torah's demands. They are asked to decide their own fate, and the Pentateuch shows them doing so. Its stories regularly depict Israel choosing to disobey YHWH and suffering divine punishment as a result. These stories thereby turn Israel into a major character in the Pentateuch's plot. The people play the antagonist to the divine protagonist. God does not decide the plot in advance but instead responds to human behavior. The lesson for listeners is clearly stated by the Pentateuch's sanctions: your future depends on how you decide to behave, as Moses warns explicitly in Deuteronomy.

> *Today I call on heaven and earth to testify against you that I have set before you life and death, blessing and curse. Choose life, so that you and your descendants may live, loving YHWH your God, listening to God's voice, and holding tight to God, because it means your life, your long life, on the land that YHWH your God promised to give to your ancestors, Abraham, Isaac and Jacob.* (Deut. 30:19–20)

Responses for a listening audience

The Pentateuch sometimes provides listeners the opportunity to respond and even to join in performing its text. In the *Shema* and other passages, Deuteronomy requires Israelites to learn and repeat its rules, and teach them to their children. Deuteronomy also requires its listeners, when they bring their first fruits offerings and tithes to the sanctuary, to say

> *I declare today to YHWH my God that I have entered the land that YHWH swore to give our ancestors.* (Deut. 26:3)

They must publicly identify themselves with Abraham and with the Israelites who escaped Egypt, and then swear that they have properly distributed the tithes from the land given them by their God (Deut. 26:5–15).

Biblical texts are often chanted or sung, which may have been inspired by including hymns and songs in the Hebrew Bible. They appear not only in the book of Psalms but also in the stories of the Pentateuch and the Prophets.[107] The hymns that climax the story of Israel's escape from Egypt in Exodus 15 and conclude the entire Pentateuch in Deuteronomy 32–33 encourage the listening audience to join in singing them. The Song of the Sea is sung by "Moses and the Israelites" (Exod. 15:1) while Miriam and "all the women" sing a response or sing the entire song again (15:20–21).

Many Greek manuscripts of the Psalms testify to ancient liturgical use of this song by including it at the end of the Psalter. So it is plausible that ancient Judeans would have been familiar with the song's words and tune, and may well have joined in singing it when the reading reached this chapter. Deuteronomy portrays Moses teaching the words of his song to the Israelites at God's command (Deut. 31:19, 22). It seems even more likely that the listening audience would remember and join in singing this warning (Deut. 32) to themselves to observe the Torah. So the inset songs were probably sung from the start. Their performative influence may have spread to the surrounding narratives, resulting in the *liturgizing* of scriptures in song or chant.

The Pentateuch turns listeners into performers by requiring them to repeat the law at home and to repeat the offering liturgies, and by encouraging them to join in singing the hymns. These rhetorical devices break down the distinction between readers and hearers. They incorporate everyone who obeys the Torah into the people of Israel who are bound by covenant to YHWH their God. In this way, the Pentateuch becomes more than literature. Harry Nasuti observed that whereas narrative "might imply (or invite) a reader, biblical law specifies a reader." With direct address and exhortations, the Pentateuch specifies its audience as Israel. It invites listeners to affirm their identity as Israel by joining in the performance, that is, by repeating the laws, by reciting the offering liturgies, and by singing the songs.[108]

Of course, these textual performances reinforce the Pentateuch's explicit exhortations to perform Torah in the ways that matter most: by doing what the laws and instructions command. The Pentateuch's rhetoric aims entirely towards this result. Listening to it read aloud at large festivals, repeating it at home, reciting its liturgies, and singing its songs all function to motivate its enactment in practice. Oral performances encourage the belief that Israel should perform the Torah by living according to its teachings.

Composing Torah for Scribal Readers

The scribes who read Torah aloud had a different experience. Modern printed books make it much easier for readers to scan quickly than did ancient manuscripts. The handwriting, the ink, the parchment, and the scroll form itself all impeded quick reading. In addition, Hebrew was written largely without vowels, which readers would have to decide how to supply. It was standard practice in ancient Middle Eastern and Mediterranean cultures for scribes to study closely the texts that they read aloud or interpreted to others. They often memorized them. The writers of the Pentateuch expected nothing less from their scribal readers. So they wrote literary structures that would be noticed only by someone who studies the Pentateuch's text very closely.

The systematic instructions in Leviticus 1–16 provide many examples of this kind of textual marker. Their opening and closing refrains make the text's structure clear to listening audiences. Nevertheless, they rarely repeat exactly the same words in the same order. Small variations lengthen or abbreviate them, and rearrange their word order. Sometimes these variations simply keep the refrain interesting or build to a climax. For example, in Leviticus 4–5, the formula "their sin that they sinned … as a sin offering" appears exactly that way seven times. Then 5:7 changes the formula to "their guilt that they sinned" while 5:11 contains the strange phrase, "their present that they sinned." In the same chapters, refrains that conclude each section describe how the priests mitigate (or atone) for people so that they are forgiven. But some verses add that they mitigate "their sin" (4:26; 5:6) or "the sin that they sinned" (5:10), "their sin that they sinned against one of these" (5:13), "their mistake that they did by mistake though they did not know (what it was)" (5:18), and then climax the conclusion to the last section with "one of any of the things that one does that brings about guilt" (6:7).

These kinds of changes in refrains could well be noticed by listeners paying close attention to a public reading. In other cases, the variations in refrains might be noticed by listeners, but only scribes studying the text closely would see a pattern in the variations. For example, Leviticus 1–3 has obviously been organized by type of offering: rising offerings in chapter 1, commodity offerings in chapter 2, and amity slaughter offerings in chapter 3. But the structure of the introductory formulas varies by the kinds of offering material being presented: herd animals (1:3; 3:1), flock animals including birds (1:10, 14; 3:6, 7, 12), and vegetable offerings (2:5, 7, 14). These three variations of the introductory formulas call the scribe's attention to an alternative way of categorizing the offerings by offering material.

An elaborate example of using variations in the formulas to construct subtle cross-references appears in the first verse of Leviticus, "He called to Moses and YHWH spoke to him from the meeting tent." It is strange that the subject, "YHWH," is named in the second phrase rather than the first. That oddity might prompt a scribe memorizing the text to remember where these phrases have appeared before. The phrase, "YHWH spoke to Moses/him," is the standard way of introducing divine speeches in Exodus 25–40 and Leviticus. But the phrase, "He/God/YHWH called to Moses from …," has appeared only three times previously, each time to introduce revelations from new locations: from the bush (Exod. 3:4), from the mountain (Exod. 19:3), and from the cloud (Exod. 24:16). Its reappearance in Lev. 1:1 marks what follows as a new phase of divine revelations during the month that the Tabernacle was pitched at the base of Mount Sinai. The verse weaves two introductory formulas together to categorize Leviticus 1–7 as a continuation of Exodus 25–31 and, simultaneously, as a new phase marked by a new location. Similarly, "This is what YHWH commanded to do" in Lev. 8:5 repeats the wording of Exod. 35:1 to mark the fact that Leviticus 8–10 continues the stories of how Moses and the Israelites fulfilled all the ritual instructions given by God at Mount Sinai after the interruption of seven chapters of offering instructions (Lev. 1–7).

It is easy to over-interpret variations in repeated formulas. Patterns may be illusions produced by memory variants. Because scribes memorized the texts they reproduced, they often introduced small changes due to remembering the text slightly differently than how it was written. Such memory variants tend to substitute one homonym for another, to add or omit optional particles or phrases, and to harmonize slight differences. Most variations in the formulas in legal and instructional material fall into these categories. Nevertheless, it is notable how much the formulas that structure legal materials in Leviticus vary among themselves and seem to have resisted harmonization by later copyists. In judging whether they perform a marking function or not, modern interpreters, just like ancient scribes, must consider in each case whether the variation was produced by the process of scribal transmission or is a significant part of the text.

Variations also appear in the repetition of the Ten Commandments. Deuteronomy 5 matches Exodus 20 very closely, though the rest of Deuteronomy formulates the laws of Torah quite differently than do the preceding books. Nevertheless, sometimes the two versions of the Ten Commandments use different homonyms and sometimes Deuteronomy has additional words. Small changes in sentence structure may reflect efforts to distinguish 10 different commandments (though the count of "ten words" does not appear in either chapter but only in Exod. 34:28 and Deut. 10:4). The largest difference between the decalogues is that Exodus cites God's creation of the world to motivate obeying the Sabbath commandment, while Deuteronomy cites Israel's experience of oppression in Egypt.[109] The Decalogue may have been recited regularly already in the early Second Temple period. The Ten Commandments also appear in ancient manuscripts that served as amulets, such as the Nash Papyrus. The variations between the biblical versions of the Ten Commandments therefore likely reflects memory variants produced by its use in liturgy as well as by scribes who frequently copied amulet texts from memory.[110]

The Pentateuch therefore shows evidence of being written both for listening audiences and for scribal readers. Memory variants in the repeated passages and among manuscripts show that it was, in fact, memorized by ancient scribes. The cues called the attention of expert scribes to intellectual issues of literary structure and offering catalogs that are of minor concern to the overall text, while repetitive refrains and surprising juxtapositions make the Pentateuch's more important points obvious to all. The most important religious messages get emphasized and repeated for all to hear and obey.

Evolving Torah through Oral Performance

The evidence for oral performance in the Pentateuch's text and in its reception history should be kept in mind when investigating its literary themes and religious messages. Some features of the Pentateuch that are discernible to textual scholars would lose significance if they were not recognized by listeners or, at least, by scribes during its public or private performances. When we examine our written texts of the Pentateuch, we should always ask if a listening audience or a scribe memorizing the text would have noticed the literary patterns that we think we have discovered. If not, there is every reason to suspect that we may be over-analyzing the text. On the other hand, with oral performance in mind, refrains and repetitive patterns should be given greater attention than they have usually received in Pentateuchal studies.

Deuteronomy's mandates for performance and the evidence for performance practices in antiquity confirm that Israel's scriptures aimed for a broad popular audience. However, Deuteronomy's mandates for public readings of the entire Torah have not in fact been standard liturgical practice in synagogues and churches for the past two millennia. This fact warns us against assuming that people actually followed the Pentateuch's reading instructions. Correctly identifying the performance intended by the writers will help us understand why they wrote the text in this way, but it does not necessarily describe the performances it has received. The synagogue's subdivision of the Pentateuch into 52 weekly portions does not correspond to its literary structure. Even less does the juxtaposition of the Torah portions with weekly *haftorah* readings from the prophets reflect the intentions of their authors. Christian reading practices take us even further afield: they usually read a Gospel, not Torah, sequentially through at least part of the liturgical year, accompanied by only selected short portions from the Old Testament. Christian lectionaries omit most of the Pentateuch altogether.

Commentators have long assumed that this failure to follow the instructions of Deuteronomy 31 was driven by practical necessity. The Pentateuch, much less the whole Tanak or Christian Bible, grew too large to be read at one time. Though this sounds like common sense, it defies the experience of many ancient and modern religious communities. The audiences at the Dionysia festival in ancient Athens viewed between 12 and 16 five-act plays during a period of one week. Modern Muslims, Sikhs, and Hindus frequently perform large scriptures (the Qur'an, the Guru Granth, the Ramayana) in their entirety, frequently from memory. Occasionally the Bible too is performed orally in its entirety. For example, a group in the USA has been reading the whole Protestant Bible aloud every year since 1990 as a prelude to the National Day of Prayer. These examples show that there are no practical barriers to reading the whole Torah, Tanak, or Christian Bible in public. Jews and Christians have simply felt no particular compunction to do so, despite Deuteronomy 31.

Performance instructions and information about normal textual performance patterns at the time of composition can give us insights into why the writers shaped their texts in particular ways. But neither the text's instructions nor its form tell us anything about how it was actually performed and the nature of its reception. For information about that, we must depend on accounts of the performances themselves, whenever we can find them.

Attention to performance can be helpful to biblical studies in an entirely different way. The ritual performance of texts plays a major role in elevating their status to the level of scripture. Readings, recitations, chants, and singing of scriptural texts provide a very important medium through which scriptures are experienced in religions around the world, even in our text-centered age. By engaging the ritual performance of texts, we make an important step towards understanding how they function as scripture.

Attention to ritualizing the Pentateuch's performative dimension thus provides two significant benefits for biblical scholars. First, noticing that writers of Deuteronomy, Joshua, Kings, and Ezra pay explicit attention to oral performance confirms their intention to write for such situations. The practice of reading aloud should therefore provide a check on our ingenuity for discovering literary patterns by asking: Would an audience hearing the text read, or a scribe memorizing the text, have likely recognized the patterns we discover? Second, the performative dimension provides access to the social transactions conducted around scriptures in communities past and present. Biblical scholars have long recognized the readings by Josiah and Ezra as key events in the developing authority of scripture. Ritualizing the performative dimension remains an important factor in the inspirational influence of the Torah and the Bible today. By mandating its own performance, the Pentateuch mandated the conditions, if not the exact means, by which its influence would grow and spread throughout the centuries and across the globe.

5

TEXTUAL INTERPRETATION

RITUALIZING THE PENTATEUCH'S SEMANTIC DIMENSION

To read a text, any written text, you must first recognize it as a text. That is its iconic dimension. Then you must turn its visual signs into spoken or mental language. That is its performative dimension. But one more step is required: you must understand the meaning of the text's language. That is its semantic dimension. Literate people normally take all three steps without thinking about them. We pay attention to the performative and semantic dimensions only when we do not understand what we read – maybe because the text is in a language we do not know or because its contents confuse us. The Pentateuch gets interpreted for both reasons. Its original language, biblical Hebrew, is foreign to most readers and listeners. Even when they understand its language, they find its contents confusing.

All readers and listeners interpret the Pentateuch's semantic meanings. Composers, artists, and scriptwriters must interpret it to ritualize its performative dimension. But the business of biblical interpretation is dominated by religious congregations and scholars. For more than two millennia, Jewish and Christian scholars have spent vast amounts of time, effort, ink, parchment, and paper to interpret and explain the meaning of the Pentateuch. Pentateuchal research shows no signs of slowing in the twenty-first century. Seventy-five books with the Pentateuch or the Torah in their titles were published in English and Hebrew between 2001 and 2015.

Understanding the Pentateuch as a Scripture, First Edition. James W. Watts.

That does not count the hundreds of books about Genesis, Exodus, Leviticus, Numbers, or Deuteronomy individually or about the Bible as a whole, nor does it count books in other languages. And, of course, books represent only a tiny fraction of all the Pentateuchal interpretation taking place around the world at any given time in the form of sermons and group bible studies.

This book can only provide a brief glimpse of the Pentateuch's interpretation since the time of Ezra and what it says about the origins of the Pentateuch before Ezra. Each half of the chapter begins with how semantic interpretation becomes persuasive through the rhetoric of scholarly expertise. The rest is organized under headings used in Chapter 2, in reverse order: the rhetoric of identity, the rhetoric of promise and threat, and the rhetoric of law. Each half of the chapter concludes with the subject that has drawn the most modern attention to the Pentateuch, its rhetoric of origins.

The Semantic Dimension of Scriptures

Intensive study and interpretation ritualize a scripture's semantic dimension. As a result, study and interpretation become acts of religious devotion. Congregations encourage people to study the scriptures. They honor teachers and scholars who excel at interpreting the scriptures for the community. In many traditions that revere written scriptures, scholars get elevated to positions of religious leadership. The most influential Muslim imams, Buddhist monks, Jewish rabbis, and Christian preachers are famous for their ability to interpret sacred texts. Written commentaries extend the influence of scriptures and, by their large number and widespread use, emphasize the importance of the scriptures. The authors of the most widely read commentaries can influence the teachings of a religion for centuries or even millennia.

Thus ritualizing the semantic dimension of scriptures conveys religious authority. Religious communities sponsor training in interpretation not only for personal devotion but also to help the group make decisions. They interpret scriptures in order to direct community behavior and to resolve conflicts. Because religious communities understand the text to be divine communication, its interpretation becomes a form of divination. It is usually the preferred and sometimes the only legitimate means for determining God's will. Religious leadership in these communities therefore depends to some degree, frequently to a great degree, on interpretive mastery of the semantic meaning of scripture.

The Pentateuch's Semantic Dimension After Ezra

The semantic dimension of the Pentateuch always receives most of the attention of scholars, for the very good reason that the Jewish and Christian traditions place great emphasis on scholarly expertise in scriptural interpretation. A concern for interpreting the Pentateuch appears already in the Hebrew Bible itself. The stories of Josiah's and Ezra's Torah readings (2 Kgs. 22–23; Neh. 8) end with the listeners interpreting the laws to know how to perform their rituals or conduct their marriages or celebrate festivals like Passover and *Sukkot*. Historians have used evidence of the Pentateuch's interpretation to trace its growing scriptural status in the Second Temple period.

The Rhetoric of Scholarly Expertise After Ezra

The books of Ezra and Nehemiah celebrate the scribal skills of Ezra and his Levite assistants. Their emphasis on expert interpretation has echoed throughout later Jewish and Christian traditions.

Ezra as expert scribe

The book of Ezra introduces Ezra as a priest and a scribe, but his priestly standing is hereditary and the story never depicts him officiating at the temple. The book instead celebrates his achievements as a scribe, as a scholar of Torah. That does not contradict his priestly identity, since the priests' job included interpreting and teaching Torah (Lev. 10:11). Nevertheless, this depiction of Ezra is unusual in emphasizing his textual scholarship. It describes Ezra's "skill" and devotion to Torah study, his commitment to observing the Torah's commands, and his dedication to teaching Torah (Ezra 7:6, 10). The book of Ezra, for the first time in Jewish literature, celebrates scholarly commitment and textual expertise in the Torah as a religious ideal.

Interpretive expertise in Ezra-Nehemiah

Ezra ... was a scribe skilled in the Torah of Moses given by YHWH the God of Israel. ... For Ezra had committed himself to study the Torah of YHWH and to do it and to teach its mandates and regulations in Israel. (Ezra 7:6, 10)

The Levites helped the people understand the Torah ... They read the Torah with interpretation to provide insight, so the people would understand the reading. (Neh. 8:7–8)

On the second day, the clan leaders of all the people came with the priests and Levites to the scribe Ezra to gain insight into the words of the Torah. (Neh. 8:13)

The book of Nehemiah continues the story of Ezra and its emphasis on interpreting the Torah's semantic dimension. Its story of Ezra reading the Torah aloud in Jerusalem describes Levites interpreting Ezra's reading (Neh. 8:7–8). Their activity may have consisted, at least in part, in translating the Hebrew Torah into Aramaic, the colloquial language of the time (see Chapter 4). The story emphasizes that it was important for the people to understand what they were hearing. Thirteen Levites mixed with the crowd to make sure they did, and the story celebrates the Levites' interpretive skill and dedication by listing their names. Though public readings of Torah appear prominently in several earlier episodes in Israel's history (Exod. 24:3–8; Deut. 31:9–13; Josh. 8:34–35; 2 Kgs. 23:2–3), only this story of Ezra's reading describes such interpretation.

Nehemiah 8's emphasis on interpretation continues in its account of the following days, when the leaders of the people gathered with Ezra, the other priests, and the Levites for that purpose. They discovered the instructions for celebrating *Sukkot*, the festival of Booths, recorded in Lev. 23:39–43 and Num. 29:12–38. All the people then celebrated *Sukkot* "as it is written" and "according to the regulation" (Neh. 8:15, 18). Later in the same month, the people gathered to confess their sins and recommit themselves to YHWH. On this occasion, the Levites recited a prayer that summarized the biblical storyline. They emphasized God's deliverance of Israel from Egypt and the people's repeated failures to keep the covenant (Neh. 9). Their knowledge and interpretation of Torah and of Israel's history shaped the people's religious experience and behavior.

Later communities have frequently used the figure of Ezra to mirror their own disputes over scripture and religious identity. One legend about Ezra has been particularly useful for this purpose.

Shortly after the Romans' destruction of the Second Temple in 70 CE, a Jewish writer wrote a book usually called *4 Ezra* or the *Ezra Apocalypse*. Here Ezra complains how hard it is to avoid God's judgment and punishment in this life. He then sees visions of judgment in the afterlife and reward for those who observe Torah faithfully. Ezra is inspired to rewrite the 24 books of the Tanak that *4 Ezra* claims were lost in the Babylonian Exile, and 70 secret books as well, probably including *4 Ezra* itself. Because of Ezra's scribal efforts, people will again have the chance to observe God's Torah and find reward in the afterlife.

This story of Ezra rewriting scripture echoed through the apologetics and polemics of different religious communities in the first millennium CE. Jewish rabbis celebrated Ezra as a second Moses whose inspired and faithful rewriting saved the Torah. But Christian, Samaritan, and Muslim critics claimed that Ezra falsified the scriptures. They reasoned that God's true revelation to Moses must have mentioned Jesus Christ, or the temple on Mount Gerizim, or the Prophet Mohammed. These omissions must therefore be due to Ezra's negligence or malfeasance. This late and fictional story of Ezra rewriting scripture has shaped the reputation of Ezra in all these traditions, as well as the reputation of their scriptures in each other's eyes.[111]

My book also highlights Ezra to mark a crucial turning point in the history of scripture. I have used the story of Ezra reading Torah (Neh. 8) as a marker for when the Pentateuch began to be ritualized as scripture. I have organized our surveys of its ritualization in each textual dimension by how it was ritualized "after Ezra" and what we can reconstruct about how it developed and was ritualized "before Ezra" (Chapters 3, 4, and 5). It may be that the time of Ezra also marked a crucial stage in completing the literary contents and shape of the Pentateuch (see below, "The Pentateuch's Semantic Dimension Before Ezra"). However, unlike the religious traditions that use the figure of Ezra to mark the preservation or corruption of scripture's contents, this book argues that the crucial change brought about in Ezra's time was one of scripturalization. The story of Ezra shows that it was then, in the early Second Temple period, specifically the middle or late Persian period, that the Pentateuch began to be ritualized in all three dimensions as a scripture.

Expert interpreters

The books of Ezra and Nehemiah apply the Pentateuch's rhetoric about community identity, about promise and threat, and about law to the situation of Judeans in the fifth and fourth centuries BCE. These themes continue to shape Pentateuchal interpretation up to the present day, so the rest of this chapter follows this topical outline. But first, we need to review the heritage of the Pentateuch's celebration of scribal expertise.

The writers of Ezra-Nehemiah and other biblical books from the fourth, third, and second centuries BCE increasingly conformed to Ezra's model of scribal expertise themselves. They not only wrote about the Torah, they also began to cite specific Pentateuchal laws and instructions. It is not always clear exactly which text they had in mind or even whether their Pentateuch had exactly the same contents as ours, but the growing trend of citing written Torah is clear enough (see Box, "Citations of the Pentateuch in later books of the Hebrew Bible" on p. 180).

The books of 1 and 2 Chronicles were probably written several decades after Ezra and Nehemiah. They share these books' belief in the importance of Torah interpretation and instruction. Chronicles repeats much of the history of Israel and Judah from the books of Samuel and Kings, but the writers also added new material not found in those sources. One of these additional stories tells of King Jehoshaphat's efforts to bring Torah instruction to the villages of Judah. He appointed a committee composed of royal officials, Levites, and priests to teach the people from the Torah scroll which they carried with them (2 Chr. 17:7–9). Chronicles does not specify the contents of the teaching.

Citations of the Pentateuch in later books of the Hebrew Bible

Ezra 3:2 ← Lev. 1–7
Ezra 9:10–12 ← Deut. 7:1–4; cf. 23:2–8
Neh. 8:15 ← Lev. 23:39–43
Neh. 8:18 ← Num. 29:12–38
Neh. 13:1–2 ← Deut. 23:3–6
2 Chr. 23:18 ← Lev. 1–7
2 Chr. 25:4/2 Kgs 14:6 ← Deut. 24:16
2 Chr. 30:16 ← Lev. 1:5; 3:2
Mal. 1:8, 13–14 ← Lev. 1:3, 10
Mal. 3:10 ← Lev. 27:30–33; Num. 18:21
Dan 9:13 ← Lev. 26; Deut. 27–28

A somewhat similar story of traveling Torah experts appears in the *Letter of Aristeas*, a second-century BCE account of the translation of the Pentateuch into Greek in the third century. The very existence this early of a scholarly Greek translation of the Pentateuch shows how important the interpretation of written Torah had become to Jews living in Egypt. *Aristeas* claims that the translation project was motivated by the goal of adding Jewish books to the comprehensive collection of the Alexandria library. He quotes the head librarian's letter to the king.

> *These (books) also must be in your library in an accurate version, because this legislation, as could be expected from its divine nature, is very philosophical and genuine. Writers therefore and poets and the whole army of historians have been reluctant to refer to the aforementioned books, and to the men past (and present) who featured largely in them, because the consideration of them is sacred and hallowed.* (*Aris.* 31)

The king then requested translators from Eleazar, the Jewish high priest in Jerusalem, who sent 72 scholars to Egypt. This translation is therefore called the *Septuagint*, from the Latin word for "seventy." *Aristeas* documents how the Egyptian Jews ritualized the Torah's iconic and performative dimensions, but the letter lavishes the most attention on the semantic dimension.

It presents a long speech by Eleazar praising the noble contents of the Torah (139–69), and devotes most of its space to celebrating the scholarship, piety, and wisdom of the 70 translators (121–27, 187–294, 305–306).

> *Eleazar selected men of the highest merit and of excellent education due to the distinction of their parentage; they had not only mastered the Jewish literature, but had made a serious study of that of the Greeks as well. They were therefore well qualified for the embassy, and brought it to fruition as occasion demanded; they had a tremendous natural facility for the negotiations and questions arising from the Law, with the middle way as their commendable ideal; they forsook any uncouth and uncultured attitude of mind; in the same way, they rose above conceit and contempt of other people, and instead engaged in discourse and listening to and answering each and every one, as is meet and right.* (*Aris.* 121–122)[112]

The accuracy of their translation was affirmed by the Jewish community in Alexandria and guaranteed by reciting curses on anyone who might tamper with its text (310–11). The king, for his part, "marveled profoundly at the genius of the lawgiver" (311). The reputations of the Septuagint translators grew over the centuries. Philo of Alexandria, writing in the first century CE, claimed that the Septuagint's translators were divinely inspired and that their individual translations were miraculously identical (see Box, "Philo of Alexandria on the Septuagint as a miracle of translation"). Christians quickly adopted the Septuagint as their Old Testament, and used Philo's story to validate the divine inspiration of their Greek scriptures.

Philo of Alexandria on the Septuagint as a miracle of translation

The translators of the Septuagint,

> *like men inspired, prophesied, not one saying one thing and another another, but every one of them employed the self-same nouns and verbs, as if some unseen prompter had suggested all their language to them. … in every case, exactly corresponding Greek words were employed to translate literally the appropriate Chaldaic words, being adapted with exceeding propriety to the matters which were to be explained. … considering these translators not mere interpreters but hierophants and prophets to whom it had been granted their honest and guileless minds to go along with the most pure spirit of Moses. On which account, even to this very day, there is every year a solemn assembly held and a festival celebrated in the island of Pharos, to which not only the Jews but a great number of persons of other nations sail across, reverencing the place in which the first light of interpretation shone forth, and thanking God for that ancient piece of beneficence which was always young and fresh.* (Philo, *Vita Moses* 2.37–41).[113]

The growing authority of the Pentateuch in the later Second Temple period led to its interpretation being projected into the early history of Israel. Even the patriarchs of Genesis were depicted as Torah scholars. The books of *Jubilees* and *1 Enoch* claim that, before Moses, the heavenly Torah was revealed to Enoch, Abraham, Jacob, and Levi. The *Testament of Levi* shows Levi being instructed in the priesthood by his grandfather, Isaac.[114]

The discovery of the Dead Sea Scrolls in the middle decades of the twentieth century gave us a new window onto the culture of Torah interpretation in late Second Temple Judaism. Several of these works discovered near Qumran are devoted to that subject. The *Community Rule* (*1QS*) and related texts interpret and extend Pentateuchal laws to regulate the conduct of members of the Qumran community. The *Temple Scroll* (*11QT*) rewrites Deuteronomy 12–23 in God's voice, rather than that of Moses. It adds ritual regulations from Exodus, Leviticus, and Numbers to present the community's views on how the temple rituals should be run. That the Qumran scribes did not approve of the conduct of the temple priests is abundantly clear from another text, an open letter to the temple authorities called *Miqṣat Maʿaśe ha-Torah* "Some Precepts of the Torah" (*4QMMT*). This letter cites regulations from Leviticus and Deuteronomy to argue that rituals should be carried out differently than was current practice in the Jerusalem temple.

Citing and debating Torah in *4QMMT*

Multiple manuscripts of the letter *4QMMT* were found among the Dead Sea Scrolls. They are fragmentary, so brackets [] mark gaps and reconstructed letters.

> *These are some of our regulations*:
>
> (On Num. 19:2–10) *And also in what pertains to the purity of the red heifer in the sin-offering that whoever slaughters it and whoever burns it and whoever collects the ash and whoever sprinkles the [water of] purification, all these ought to be pure at sunset, so that whoever is pure sprinkles the impure. …*
>
> (On Lev. 4:12) *And concerning what is written […] outside the camp, "a bull, or a [she]ep or a she-goat" … And we think that the temple […Je]rusalem is the camp, and outside the camp is [outside Jerusalem;] it is the camp of their cities. …*
>
> (On Lev. 19:19 and Deut. 22:9, and citing Jer. 2:3, Lev. 19:2, and Lev. 21:7) *And concerning the practice of illegal marriage that exists among the people, despite their being sons of holy [seed], as is written, Israel is holy. And concerning his (Israel's) [clean] animal it is written that one must not let it mate*

with another species, and concerning his clothes [it is written that they should not] be of mixed stuff; and he must not sow his field and vineyard with mixed species. Because they (Israel) are holy, and the sons of Aaron are [most holy]. But you know that some of the priests and [the laity mingle with each other.] [And they] unite with each other and pollute the holy seed as well as their own [seed] with women whom they are forbidden to marry. ...

(On scripture) *To you we have wr[itten] that you must understand the book of Moses [and the books of the pro]phets and of David. ...*

(On Deut. 27–30) *And we are aware that part of the blessings and curses have occurred that are written in the b[ook of Mo]ses and this is the end of days, when they go back to Israel for[ever]. ...*

(On Torah) *We have written to you some of the precepts of the torah which we think are good for you and for your people. ...*[115]

Early Christian texts reproduce the Jewish emphasis on authority from scripture interpretation. The Gospel of Luke depicts Jesus as an insightful interpreter of scripture from his childhood (Luke 2:46–47) through his adult ministry (4:16–30) to after his resurrection (24:27). The Gospel of Matthew portrays Jesus citing and intensifying the demands of Torah (Matt. 5:17–48). According to Matthew, his teachings impressed listeners as exceeding the authority of the scribes (7:29). The book of Acts shows the Christian apostles summarizing the history of Israel from Torah and Prophets before announcing Jesus as the Messiah (Acts 7:2–53; 8:35; 13:16–41). The apostle Paul emphasizes his education in the Torah (Gal. 1:14; Phil. 3:5; Acts 22:3) and his letters demonstrate it by discussing Pentateuchal stories and laws (e.g. Gal. 3; Rom. 7, 9–11). The New Testament's most detailed exposition of the Pentateuch appears in the Letter to the Hebrews. This anonymous writer cites scriptures throughout. He analyzes the Pentateuch's laws for rituals and priests to argue that Jesus is the new high priest whose self-sacrifice atones for human sins (Heb. 5–11). So the early Christians used interpretation of scripture to advance their movement. They also celebrated the interpretive abilities of Jesus and his apostles as models of Christian preaching and piety.

By the end of the Second Temple period, ritualization of the semantic dimension of Torah had become characteristic of all Jewish religious movements. After the failed Jewish revolts against Rome in the first and second centuries CE, semantic ritualization of Torah and scripture became even more pervasive and determinative of religious authority.

Rabbinic Judaism traced its authority through a line of Torah experts stretching from Moses and Joshua to the rabbis Hillel and Shammai in the first century and to Judah *ha-Nasi* and his colleagues at the beginning of the third (*m. ʾAvot* 1–2). These rabbis claimed that an oral tradition of Torah interpretation accompanied revelation of the written Torah and was passed down along with it. The Pharisees of the late Second Temple period taught this "Oral Torah" and the rabbis of Late Antiquity wrote it down in the Mishnah (around 200 CE) and in the two Talmuds (around 450 and 550 CE). The Talmuds and other rabbinic literature established an interpretive framework around the Torah that has remained influential, and frequently authoritative, for Jews ever since.

The contents of the Mishnah do not follow the Pentateuch's literary sequence, but are organized around major themes, such as agriculture, family laws, and rituals. Other rabbinic literature takes up the task of harmonizing Mishnaic regulations with the written Torah in the form of legal commentaries (e.g. *Sifra* on Leviticus and *Sifre* on Numbers and Deuteronomy), and in collections of *midrash* that embellish biblical stories with rabbinic interpretation. The Jerusalem Talmud and the Babylonian Talmud synthesize much of this discussion.

A distinctive feature of rabbinic literature is that it usually quotes the rabbis arguing over points of interpretation and law. It shows interpretation taking place through discussion and debate. It cites the rabbis by name, who often cast their arguments as representing the views of their teachers. Sometimes the majority decides an issue, but at other times the literature allows different views to remain unreconciled.

Rabbinic interpretation through discussion and debate

Genesis Rabbah is a collection of rabbinic interpretations arranged as a sequential commentary on the book of Genesis. It was completed around 400 CE. The following excerpts interpret the end of the first creation story in Gen. 1:31–2:1.

> *"And God saw everything that He had made and, behold, it was very good"* (Gen. 1:31). *R. Johanan and R. Simeon b. Lakish each commented thereon. R. Johanan said: When a mortal king builds a palace, he can only take in the upper stories with one look and the lower stories with another, but the Holy One, blessed be He, casts but a single look at the upper and the lower portions simultaneously. R. Simeon b. Lakish said: "Behold, it was very good" implies this world; and "behold" implies the next world: The Holy One, blessed be He, cast but one look at this world and at the future world [together].* (*Genesis Rabbah* ix.3, ix.12)
>
> *All our Rabbis said the following in R. Flanina's name, while R. Phinehas and R. Hilkiah said it in R. Simon's name:* Meʾod *is identical with* ʾadam *(man), for the letters of both are identical. Thus it is written, "And God saw everything that He had made, and, behold, it was very (*meʾod*) good," i.e., and behold,* ʾadam *(man) was good.* (*Genesis Rabbah* ix.12)

> *"And the heaven and the earth were finished," etc.* (Gen. 2:1) *How did the Holy One, blessed be He, create His world? Said R. Johanan: The Lord took two balls, one of fire and the other of snow, and worked them into each other, and from these the world was created. R. Hanina said: [He took] four [balls], for the four corners [of the universe]. R. Hama said: Six: four for the four corners and one for above and one for below.* (*Genesis Rabbah* x.3)[116]

By this discourse of perpetual debate, rabbinic literature displays the ancient rabbis' knowledge of the Torah, both written and oral, and their interpretive and reasoning skills. It celebrates their scholarship and makes them models of Jewish piety. Rabbinic literature also establishes the ancient rabbis as the pre-eminent authorities for determining the meaning of Torah. Their debates model the directions in which interpretive reasoning may be pursued, but they also set the boundaries within which such reasoning should be limited. For example, they exclude the views of heretics and Christians as unworthy of consideration.

Rabbinic literature presents the rabbis as having the power to direct Jewish religious and legal life since the destruction of the Temple in 70 CE. Actually, it seems to have taken many centuries for rabbinic teachings to become normative in the synagogues of Late Antiquity. Nevertheless, in the end the rabbis and their literature became authoritative for determining the ideas and practices of Judaism. The hereditary priests who led Jews during the Second Temple period were replaced in Late Antiquity by the religious leadership of scholarly rabbis. This "Rabbinic Judaism" privileged Torah study as the highest form of piety and Torah expertise as the most important qualification for leadership to create what some historians have called an "aristocracy of learning."[117]

In the Middle Ages, many Jewish interpreters found new interest in the "plain meaning" (*pshat*) of biblical texts. This development reflected the influence of the Aristotelian philosophy of Maimonides. It was also motivated by challenges from a Jewish sect, the Kairites, who rejected Talmudic interpretation, and by inter-religious criticisms of Jewish scripture by Muslims and Christians. The result was a flowering of biblical interpretation by scholars who are still read widely today, including Abraham Ibn Ezra, David Kimchi, and, most famous of all, Shlomo Yitzchaki, better known by the acronym Rashi. Their focus on plain meaning led them to take literary context into account in interpretation. It also drew their attention to the ambiguities and contradictions in the Pentateuch's text that raise questions about some traditional beliefs. Ibn Ezra, for example, gently questioned how Moses could possibly have written the account of his own death in Deuteronomy 34.[118]

Expert translators

Christians also valued expertise in scripture interpretation. In Late Antiquity, churches increasingly granted leadership to bishops ordained by other bishops in a line that could be traced back to Christ's apostles, arguing that they are best placed to interpret scripture (see Chapter 6). Christians also depend on translations for at least their Old Testament in the Greek Orthodox churches, or for their entire Bible in all other churches. There was a tendency among early Christians to legitimize their translations through miracle stories, such as the Pentecost story (Acts 2) and Philo's description of the miracle of the Septuagint translators (see above). Slowly, however, linguistic expertise rather than miraculous inspiration established itself as the benchmark of Christian biblical scholarship.

In the third century, Origen edited an Old Testament that presented different versions side by side. It was called the *Hexapla* for its six columns consisting of the Hebrew text, the Hebrew transliterated in Greek letters, and four different Greek translations. Origen's work was not widely reproduced, however, because he chose a losing side in the religious politics of his day.

The prototypical Christian biblical scholar is Jerome, the fourth-century hermit who produced the Latin "Vulgate" translation that became the official Bible of the Roman Catholic Church. Instead of working from the Septuagint Greek as many other church leaders preferred, he learned Hebrew and translated the Latin Old Testament directly from Jewish manuscripts. He also used Origen's *Hexapla*. His asceticism and orthodoxy made Jerome influential, and the superiority of his translation secured his reputation as a saint and "doctor" of the Western Church.[119]

Jerome established two precedents for most subsequent Christian translations of scripture. The first is that Bible translators should, whenever possible, produce vernacular translations directly from the original Hebrew and Greek languages. The second is the authority of philological expertise in the ancient languages for establishing the wording of Christian bibles.

Jerome's use of Hebrew as the basis for translating the Christian Old Testament undermined appeals to Greek as Christianity's "original" language by establishing a bilingual original scripture. This also reinforced the tendency to use vernacular scripture readings in the liturgy. Hebrew and, outside the Greek Orthodox churches, Greek were left to experts who gained authority and prestige from their expertise in these languages. This effect was not widely felt in the Middle Ages when knowledge of Hebrew was rare even among Christian theologians. Since the Renaissance,

Figure 5.1 Jerome at his desk. Detail of stained glass window, ca. 1490. In the Stadtschloss Museum in Weimar, Germany.

however, expertise in the languages of scripture has become a hallmark of the Christian scholar.

Western Europe's rediscovery of classical and ancient languages in the fifteenth and sixteenth centuries led to widespread Christian study of the Bible's original languages. The invention of the printing press made it easier to produce and distribute multilingual publications in multiple fonts, such as the Complutensian Polyglot. Printing also increased concern for standardizing biblical texts that varied from one manuscript to another. The humanist scholar Desiderius Erasmus published a composite text of the Greek New Testament in 1516. He compared seven different manuscripts to determine where they diverged from each other, and then printed the readings he thought most likely original. This text became the basis for most vernacular translations of the New Testament until the nineteenth century.

The Protestant Reformation of the sixteenth century fueled efforts to translate the Christian Bible into vernacular languages. The Protestants considered it important to follow the example of Jerome, so they learned Hebrew as well as Greek. The German translation by Martin Luther and all the Reformation-Era English bibles (Tyndale's, Geneva, Bishop's, King James, and also the Roman Catholic Douay–Rheims version) translated the Old Testament from Hebrew and the New Testament from Greek, which remains the standard practice today.[120]

Thus, despite the Pentecost story, Christian Bible translations have increasingly emphasized human linguistic expertise together with piety, rather than claiming divine inspiration for the translators. Inspired translation closes the gap between translation and original, giving the translation equal or even greater status than the scripture in the original language. That has happened several times in Christian history, but the more prominent accounts of Christian scripture translation have emphasized human expertise and piety. The *Letter of Aristeas* in the second century BCE lavished attention on the Septuagint translators' scholarship and devotion. Jerome in the fourth century CE presented himself as both an ascetic and a philologist. Similarly, accounts of the sixteenth- and seventeenth-century translation work of Martin Luther and of the scholars that produced the King James Version emphasize their expertise in Hebrew and Greek as well as their religious piety.

Translation has been less important to Jewish tradition because of the dominance of the Hebrew language in ritual and in traditional Jewish education. Jewish scholars therefore tend to use Hebrew terms rather than worry about their translation even when writing in vernacular languages. The political emancipation of European Jews in the nineteenth century and the emergence of the Reform movement led Jewish publishers to produce German and English translations of the Tanak that were fairly traditional in content. In the twentieth century, several prominent scholars created more distinctively Jewish translations. The philosophers Franz Rosenzweig and Martin Buber tried to reproduce the aesthetic and literary qualities of Hebrew in their German translation of 1925–1936. The reputation of the translators and their innovative methods immediately made their translation famous and controversial. Everett Fox reproduced their methods in English translation in 1995, while the well-known literary critic Robert Alter wrote a more idiomatic English translation in 2004. In the twentieth and twenty-first centuries, then, bible translation has become important in Jewish scholarship as well.[121]

Celebration of translators' expertise calls attention to the ritualization of scripture's semantic dimension through scholarship. It uses the iconic legitimacy of the original text to authorize reading in the translated language. Celebration of scholarly translation thus allows the translated text to assume the original's semantic authority while simultaneously preserving the iconic memory, if not knowledge, of the original language behind the translation. Celebration of particular translators can buttress veneration of one translation against others, as has sometimes been the case for the Latin Vulgate and the English King James Version. Nevertheless, vesting the translation's accuracy in human expertise leaves the door open for new translations based on greater expertise.

The Rhetoric of Communal Identity and Priesthood After Ezra

The Pentateuch's laws and stories have defined Jewish and Samaritan identity ever since the Torah first began to function as a scripture. Demarcating Jewish identity is a major concern of the books of Ezra and Nehemiah. They show the scribe, Ezra, and the governor, Nehemiah, discriminating by ancestry between those who are members of the covenant community and those who are not. They require those whose families belong in the community to swear fidelity to the Torah (Neh. 10), and they require everyone else to leave (Ezra 10:6–44; Neh. 13:1–9, 23–30).

In the following centuries and millennia, Jewish identity has not usually been policed so harshly as it was by Ezra and Nehemiah. But the Torah's role as a key component of Jewish identity became ever stronger. Jewish prayers in the Second Temple period frequently referred to the stories of the Pentateuch, and sometimes also to stories in Joshua, Judges, Samuel, and Kings (the Deuteronomistic History). Ezra led the people of Jerusalem to confess their ancestors' sins against YHWH before committing themselves to do better (Ezra 9; Neh. 9; compare Ps. 106). Psalms recounted God's rescue of Israel in the past to plead for divine intervention in the present (Pss. 77, 78, 99, 105, 114). These prayers reproduce the Pentateuch's rhetoric by calling on worshippers to identify themselves as Israel and learn from their predecessors' mistakes.

This use of the Torah and history books to provide positive and negative role models continues in the rhetoric of Chronicles (1 Chr. 16:8–36; 2 Chr. 20:5–12) and of Jesus ben Sira (Sir. 44–49), and became common in later literature. By at least the second century BCE, Jews consciously distinguished themselves from Hellenistic culture by living according to the Pentateuch's regulations, especially by worshipping only the God of Israel, resting on the Sabbath, circumcising their sons, and following the Pentateuch's diet laws. For example, the stories of Judith and of Daniel and his friends among the Babylonians show their piety by their dedication to eating pure food (Judt. 12:1–4; Dan. 1:8–17) and refusal to worship Babylonian gods (Dan. 3:4–12; 6:6–11). We are told that the Maccabees used Torah scrolls for divination in the same way that "the Gentiles consult images of their gods" (1 Macc. 3:48). The book of 1 Maccabees reports that the Jews who collaborated with the Seleucid Greeks "removed the mark of circumcision and abandoned the sacred covenant" (1 Macc. 1:15).

The growing identification of Jews with the Torah's rules raised concern for how to apply them in changing circumstances. Some Jewish rebels against the Seleucid Empire were defeated because they rested on the Sabbath, a policy that the more successful Maccabees ignored (1 Macc. 2:29–41). The Maccabees also had to decide what to do with the Temple's altar that the Seleucids had defiled. Lacking any clear instructions for this situation in the Pentateuch, they put the altar stones in storage "until a prophet should come to tell them what to do with them" (1 Macc. 4:44–47).

The Torah's validation of Aaronide priests as the only hierarchy in Israel had political consequences in the Hellenistic period. The high priest Jaddua successfully negotiated with Alexander when his armies swept by Judea (Josephus, *Ant.* 11.317–345). With the permission of the Hellenistic empires, high priests of the Oniad family ruled Judea until the second century. When Hasmonean war lords led Judea to independence, they buttressed their authority with their Aaronide ancestry that allowed them to claim the high priesthood for themselves. At the end of the first century CE, Josephus wrote that Jews distinguished themselves by being a nation led by priests rather than kings. He invented the term "theocracy" for their system of government (*Ap.* 2:16).

Jewish priestly groups opposed to the Hasmoneans also invested time and effort into the reading and interpretation of the Pentateuch and the Prophets. The Dead Sea Scrolls found near Qumran contain the library of a community led by priests who had split from the hierarchy in Jerusalem. Their library of over 800 manuscripts contained more than a dozen copies of every book of the Pentateuch, as well as of Isaiah and collections of Psalms (see Box, "Books with more than ten 10 copies found among the Dead Sea Scrolls"). Other Qumran scrolls provide evidence of systematic interpretation of Torah and prophetic texts by strings of citations (in *4QMMT*) and by commentary (in the *Habakkuk Pesher*). Russell Hobson pointed out that the texts of books that deal with rituals, that is, the Pentateuch, were standardized at Qumran more than other books that appear there in multiple copies.[122] The Qumran community's interest in ritual interpretation, as demonstrated by *4QMMT*, raised their concern for the accuracy of ritual texts.

The investment of Jewish identity in Torah and in its interpretation became even greater in Late Antiquity when the temple disappeared and its priests lost their positions as religious authorities. Without their land or temple, Jews could not follow many of the Pentateuch's laws as written. The ancient rabbis provided alternative ways to fulfill Torah. They taught that prayer and good deeds can take the place of animal offerings in the Temple (*b. Berak.* 26a; *Avot d'Rabbi Natan* 4:21). They maintained that study of the Pentateuch's rules for offerings would earn the same merit as making those offerings (*b. Menaḥ.* 110a; *b. San.* 43b). In this way, the Torah's commandments could be fulfilled in the very different circumstances in which Jews found themselves after 70 CE. Torah study became a ritual practice as well as an intellectual pursuit. So the Torah continued to define what it means to be Jewish. Indeed, the story of the exodus and wilderness wandering took on new poignancy for Jews living outside the traditional land of Israel. The annual celebration of Passover in obedience to the Torah's directives (Exod. 12–13) became a commemoration of the land's loss and of hopes for its eventual recovery, encapsulated in the concluding refrain, "Next year in Jerusalem!"

Books with more than 10 copies found among the Dead Sea Scrolls (counts are approximate)

Psalms	36
Deuteronomy	30
Isaiah	21
Genesis	19
Leviticus	17
Exodus	15
Jubilees	14
Community Rule	12

The meaning of the Pentateuch was contextualized in Late Antiquity by the rabbis' Oral Torah. Eventually written down in the Mishnah and Talmuds and other rabbinic collections, it interpreted the Pentateuch by the categories and concerns animating the rabbis' rulings. The Torah that defines what it means to be Jewish became the Torah as presented by the Talmuds. They shaped Jewish life and identity throughout the Middle Ages and modernity. Even later Jewish groups who modified or rejected Talmudic teachings, such as the Karaites, the Reform movement, and the Zionists, defined themselves by their relationship to rabbinic literature.

By making Torah study an important form of piety, the rabbis made literacy a religious virtue. Though illiterate people were not excluded from the synagogue, learning to read Hebrew and Aramaic became increasingly important for living according to the Torah. Jewish communities therefore invested much effort in educating boys in Torah and Talmud. This led to different religious lives for Jewish women, who were not expected to study Torah. Even when many women became literate, Talmud study was reserved for men. Ironically, this situation led to women becoming more familiar with the Bible in vernacular languages than some of their husbands (see Box, "The gendering of Talmud and Tanak" on p. 192, and also p. 137 above).

Despite mass literacy today, women's access to Torah and Talmud remains a divisive issue between Jewish denominations. While Reformed and Conservative congregations encourage girls to study Torah for their *bat mitzvahs* along with the boys, many Orthodox congregations continue to segregate the genders in worship and study.

The gendering of Talmud and Tanak

Penny Shine Gold observed: "While the Bible had been a focus of sustained adult male interpretive attention in the ancient and medieval periods – hence the development of midrash and commentary – it was the Talmud, the nonbiblical part of Torah, that became the focal point of Jewish education and learning in the medieval period and later. Midrash and commentary were still referred to and passed on, particularly through incorporation into sermons centered on the weekly Torah portion, but serious learning, beginning with the entry of male teenagers into the yeshivah and continuing with adult study, was centered on the Talmud. ... The Bible – as an object of study rather than as a ritual object engaged in liturgy – was a text for children and women."[123]

The themes of exodus and travel to the promised land played a large roll in Zionism, the Jewish movement of the late nineteenth and early twentieth century that led to founding the modern State of Israel in 1948. The leading theorist of early Zionism, Theodor Herzl, depicted his plan as an "exodus to the Promised Land." Jewish settlers in Palestine celebrated the land's agricultural potential with art depicting the spies exploring the land (Num. 13). They often showed the Tabernacle set up in the land to represent Israel's return. But because many Zionists explicitly rejected traditional rabbinic religion, they drew on nationalistic themes from the books of Maccabees more than on the exodus and wilderness themes that had characterized Jewish diaspora experience for millennia. Nevertheless, the renaming of a blockade-running immigrant ship as *The Exodus* in 1947 was immortalized as a symbol of the nation's founding by news media, as well as by Leon Uris's novel of the same name and its film adaptation starring Paul Newman. Jewish experience in the nineteenth and twentieth centuries – from emancipation to *Shoah*/Holocaust to the founding of the state of Israel – has resonated for many with the story of Israel in the Pentateuch and in Joshua.[124]

Among Christians, the Pentateuch's rhetoric of identification with exodus Israel has received a more complicated response. Paul argued that

Figure 5.2 Poster for 1960 film *Exodus*. Artist: Paul Bass. *Source*: In the public domain.

non-Jews (Gentiles) can become Christian without adopting Jewish practices and identity (Rom. 9–11). Because of this New Testament argument, Christians have felt free to distinguish themselves from Jews and to ignore many of the Pentateuch's laws. Paul insisted that God's support for Israel remains unchanged (Rom. 11), but on the basis of other New Testament texts, Christians have claimed for themselves God's promises to Israel in the Pentateuch. They have declared themselves to be "the new Israel" that replaced the Jews in God's plan for humanity (Matt. 21:33–44; Gal. 3:28–29; Heb. 8:13). This supersessionist logic leaves no room for Israel outside the Church, and has led many Christians to persecute Jews over the centuries. As a result, Christians' message of love for all people has often been contradicted by their anti-Semitism.

The universalism of the Christian message has not prevented particular groups of Christians from claiming the Pentateuch's description of Israel for themselves. As we saw in Chapter 2, the Pentateuch's rhetoric works to get hearers and readers to identify with the Israelites of the exodus. Many different Christian groups as well as Jews have accepted that rhetoric and applied the exodus story to their own experiences. Some have revived Israelite practices and institutions that most Jews and Christians do not replicate.

Samaritans plausibly trace their ancestry to the northern kingdom of Israel around whose capital, Samaria (now Nablus), they have lived since antiquity. Their traditions of Torah observance may well be as old as those preserved in Jewish tradition. They claim the Pentateuch's promises as Israelites and continue to live on part of the land promised to Abraham. The politics of two millennia, however, have not been kind to the Samaritans, who now number less than 1,000 people.

Others groups also remember ancestral links to ancient Israel. Ethiopia's kings claimed descent from King Solomon through the son of the Queen of Sheba (1 Kgs. 10). Many Ethiopians believe that he brought the Ark of the Covenant to Ethiopia. They claim to still keep it in a church in Aksum, where it is hidden from view. Most Ethiopians gradually converted from Judaism to Christianity after the fourth century CE. They remember their Jewish heritage by following the Pentateuch's diet laws and by circumcising infant boys. The last ruler of their Solomonic dynasty, the Emperor Haile Selassie, was deposed and died in 1975.

Identifying with exodus Israel

Eric Kling described two typical ways in which groups have appropriated the identity of exodus Israel as their own: "Time after time in myriad creative ways, Jews and Christians (even Muslims) envisioned themselves as the Israelites of old, subjected to oppressive conditions but delivered by God's power and rewarded a Promised Land (figuratively or literally) for maintaining their faith. … Historically, exodus movements have been generally expressed in two ways. Some movements, such as those of the New England Puritans, the Mormons, the Afrikaners of South Africa, and the Jews of America, were actual physical migrations, viewed as a kind of exodus to the Promised Land. … Other exodus movements, such as those identified with black liberation theology in North America and liberation theology in Latin America, appropriated the exodus motif theologically, in the sense of liberating one's outlook, raising one's consciousness, and demanding justice on behalf of the poor and oppressed."[125]

The exodus story has played an especially important role in the development of American identity. In 1630, on board the ship Mayflower on its way to Massachusetts Bay, the Puritan leader, John Winthrop, preached a sermon comparing the passengers to exodus Israel. He paraphrased Deuteronomy 30 to suggest that God was giving the Puritans a new land on condition that they keep God's commandments and covenant, or else they would lose the land again. The theme of America as a promised land and of its immigrant people as a new Israel was prominent in religious and political rhetoric through the seventeenth and eighteenth centuries. It climaxed in celebrations of the founding of the United States after 1776.[126]

However, the exodus story also held a very prominent place in the imagination of another group of Americans who had no reason to celebrate: Africans brought to America as slaves. After adopting Christianity in the evangelical revivals of the eighteenth century, they found the story of Israel's exodus from Egypt particularly poignant. Albert Raboteau observed:

> No single symbol captures more clearly the distinctiveness of Afro-American Christianity than the symbol of Exodus. From the earliest days of colonization, white Christians had represented their journey across the Atlantic to America as the exodus of a New Israel from the bondage of Egypt into the Promised Land of milk and honey. For black Christians, the imagery was reversed: the Middle Passage had brought them to Egypt land, where they suffered bondage under a new Pharaoh. White Christians saw themselves as the New Israel; slaves identified themselves as the Old.

Identification with Israel in the exodus became a prominent theme in African American preaching and music. Black spirituals voiced the pain of bondage and echoed the command of Moses to "Let my people go!" (see Box, "Go Down, Moses"). The songs and sermons actualized the biblical story to become the lens through which African Americans interpreted their experience of slavery. Raboteau continued:

> In the ecstasy of worship, time and distance collapsed, and the slaves literally became the children of Israel. ... Identification with Israel, then, gave the slaves a communal identity as a special, divinely favored people. This identity stood in stark contrast with racist propaganda, which depicted them as inferior to whites, as destined by nature and providence to the status of slaves. Exodus, the Promised Land, and Canaan were inextricably linked in the slaves' minds with the idea of freedom. Canaan referred not only to the condition of freedom but also to the territory of freedom – the North or Canada.[127]

After the Civil War, initial celebrations of being emancipated faded as African Americans experienced continuing discrimination, disenfranchisement, and violent oppression. So they still identified with Israel in Egypt and in the wilderness through the Civil Rights Movement of the 1950s and 1960s. In the most poignant use of the Pentateuch in American rhetoric, Martin Luther King, Jr evoked Moses's experience from Deuteronomy 34 in his last sermon on April 3, 1968, the day before he was assassinated.

> I've been to the mountaintop. And I don't mind. Like anybody, I would like to live a long life. Longevity has its place. But I'm not concerned about that now. I just want to do God's will. And He's allowed me to go up to the mountain. And I've looked over. And I've seen the promised land. I may not get there with you. But I want you to know tonight that we, as a people, will get to the promised land.[128]

American history, then, shows that the evocative power of the exodus story continues to influence politics and religion. It also shows that it can fuel both the self-righteous pride of ruling classes and a spirit of resistance among oppressed people.

Other groups have also used the exodus story to resist colonialism and the cultural imperialism that brought the Bible to them in the first

Go Down, Moses

African American spiritual, from ca. 1850s Virginia

When Israel was in Egypt's land,
let my people go;
oppressed so hard they could not stand,
let my people go.

Refrain:
Go down, (go down) Moses, (Moses)
way down in Egypt's land;
tell old Pharaoh
to let my people go!

"Thus saith the Lord," bold Moses said,
let my people go;
"if not, I'll smite your first-born dead,"
let my people go. (*Refrain*)

No more shall they in bondage toil,
let my people go;
let them come out with Egypt's spoil,
let my people go. (*Refrain*)

We need not always weep and mourn,
let my people go;
and wear those slavery chains forlorn,
let my people go. (*Refrain*)

Come, Moses, you will not get lost,
let my people go;
stretch out your rod and come across,
let my people go. (*Refrain*)

As Israel stood by the water's side,
let my people go;
at God's command it did divide,
let my people go. (*Refrain*)

When they had reached the other shore,
let my people go;
they sang a song of triumph o'er,
let my people go. (*Refrain*)

O Moses, the cloud shall cleave the way,
let my people go;
a fire by night, a shade by day,
let my people go. (*Refrain*)

Your foes shall not before you stand,
let my people go;
and you'll possess fair Canaan's land,
let my people go. (*Refrain*)

This world's a wilderness of woe,
let my people go;
O let us on to Canaan go,
let my people go. (*Refrain*)

O let us all from bondage flee,
let my people go;
and let us all in Christ be free,
let my people go. (*Refrain*)

place. The Christian tendency to ignore purity and offering instructions presents an opportunity to claim ritual practices that are truer to the meaning of the Pentateuch's text. In twentieth-century Jamaica, Rastas identified with exodus Israel by modeling their purity practices on those of the Nazarites in Numbers 6. Rastafarian preaching also proclaimed Ethiopian emperor Haile Selassie, who claimed descent from Solomon, as the Messiah. In nineteenth-century south India, the Hindu Christian Church observed Jewish festivals and Pentateuchal purity rules to cleanse Christianity of its Western decadence. African Zionist churches also advocate observance of the Pentateuch's purity regulations. In these communities, acceptance of the Pentateuch's rhetoric of identification with exodus Israel means observing its laws. Doing so allows them to criticize Western Christianity on the basis of the Bible and claim for themselves a more authentic Christian identity as the new Israel.[129]

Some victims of Western colonialism have instead rejected the biblical story of Israel's exodus and settlement in Canaan as a mythic justification for settler colonialism. They have identified with the story's Canaanites, the peoples subjected by conquest, rather than with Israel. At least, that is how scholars such as Robert Warrior depict the choice for Native Americans and how Edward Said described it for Palestinians.[130] Its religious expression often takes the form of rejecting the exodus story and the Bible altogether in favor of an alternative scripture or an indigenous tradition. Many people, such as Christian Palestinians and Christian Native Americans, find themselves identifying with both sides of the story simultaneously. In Israel and Palestine, conflicts over land have brought attention to the political consequences of historical and archeological research on ancient Israel.

The Pentateuch's rhetoric of identification with exodus Israel has proven to be very effective at shaping Jewish and Christian identities. It has preserved Jewish communities and traditions while fueling Christian persecution of Jews. It has legitimized colonial conquests and inspired resistance to them. Interpreting the Pentateuch's semantic dimensions is therefore deeply implicated in religious and political struggles of both the past and the present.

The Rhetoric of Promise and Threat After Ezra

As we have seen, the rhetoric of sanctions in the Pentateuch and prophetic books was internalized by the post-exilic community depicted in Ezra, Nehemiah, and Chronicles. They accepted the defeat of the kingdoms of Israel and Judah as God's punishment for abandoning the covenant, thus fulfilling the threats of Lev. 26:27–39 and Deut. 28:25–68 as well as of the prophets. They committed themselves to keeping the covenant in hopes of receiving the promises offered by the Pentateuch and prophets. The books of the Hebrew Bible portray human decisions as shaping the future for individuals and for the community.

However, the history of the Second Temple period did not bear out the Pentateuch's promises of rewards for observing Torah. Though Jews became progressively more Torah-observant, foreign empires continued to rule them. The Jews' reputation for Torah-observance led to outright religious persecution in the early second century BCE. According to 1 Maccabees 1, the Seleucid king Antiochus Epiphanes tried to replace worship of YHWH with the worship of Zeus in the Jerusalem temple and in Jewish villages. Relief from persecution came through 80 years of independence under the Jewish priest-kings of the Hasmonean dynasty, but their achievement was blemished by internal conflicts between Jewish sects. Independence ended with the Roman conquest of Judea in 63 BCE. Attempts to regain it led to frequent conflicts and then two catastrophic wars, in 66–73 CE and in 132–135 CE. These wars left the Temple in ruins and Judea inhabited mostly by non-Jewish people.

Religious persecution increasingly shaped Jewish world views in the later Second Temple period, as well as those of Christians and Jews in Late Antiquity. Contrary to the Torah's promises that fidelity to the covenant would bring protection and reward individually and as a community (Lev. 26:3–13; Deut. 28:1–14), they discovered that righteous living often led to being singled out for persecution. While they believed that the kingdoms of Israel and Judah had been punished for their lack of faith in God, they found that they themselves were punished for their faithfulness. Evil seemed to rule the world instead of God.

This experience of persecution expressed itself religiously in apocalyptic literature. Apocalyptic thinking provided a powerful sense of hope to many Jews and Christians who felt as if they had no control over their circumstances. Apocalyptic depicts the future as set by God in advance. God allows evil, often personified as Satan or the devil, to control the world and persecute the people of God for a set period of time. Then God's armies will defeat evil in battle and bring an end to history or, in some versions, destroy the whole world. Both the living and the dead will then be judged for their deeds and rewarded or punished accordingly in the afterlife.

Apocalyptic depicts the course of history as predestined. Human decisions can at most determine our individual fates, and mostly in the next life rather than in this one. Apocalyptic reflects the experience of communal persecution under the rule of foreign empires. It describes a divine plan for all of history that allows evil to rule the world temporarily. But it promises that in the end, righteousness will be rewarded and evil will be punished.

Apocalyptic literature became very popular in the later part of the Second Temple period. A large number of Jewish apocalypses survive to this day, ranging from Daniel 7–12, *1 Enoch*, and *Jubilees* in the third and second centuries to the Qumran *War Scroll* and *4 Baruch* in the first century BCE. The Christian New Testament is full of apocalyptic ideas, and ends with the Apocalypse of John, better known as the Book of Revelation. Because of books like these, apocalyptic thinking changed Jewish and Christian eschatology, that is, their ideas about the future.

Apocalyptic eschatology

At that time Michael, the great prince, the one who stands by your people, will stand up. It will be a time of anguish, such as has never occurred since nations first came into existence. But at that time your people will be delivered, everyone who is found written in the book. Many of those who sleep in the dust of the earth will awake, some to eternal life, and some to shame and eternal contempt. … "How long will it be until these wonders end?" … It will be for a time, two times, and half a time, and when the shattering of the power of the holy people comes to an end, all these things will happen. (Daniel 12:1–2, 6–7)

Apocalyptic thinking provided persecuted people hope and inspired resistance to foreign empires. Its message of powerlessness in this life and consequences in the next also fueled fanaticism. Martyrdom for God's sake became an ideal. At the end of the Second Temple period, the apocalyptic expectation that angels would fight to defend Jerusalem, according to the *War Scroll*, probably encouraged the uncompromising rebellion that led to the Temple's destruction. Sixty years later, another Jewish rebellion gained strength on the belief that its leader, Shimon Bar Kochba, was the Messiah sent by God to save the Jews.

In the catastrophic aftermath of these revolts, Rabbinic Judaism rid itself of the political consequences of apocalyptic fanaticism. The rabbis privatized apocalyptic expectations to focus once again on the influence of personal piety. In rabbinic literature, world history and imperial politics do not determine the future. Instead, the coming of the Messiah and the restoration of Israel depend only on the prayers, good works, and Torah-observance of the Jewish people.

The story of Jesus's crucifixion by Roman soldiers established the martyr ideal at the center of Christian theology. Apocalyptic thinking provided a powerful explanation for the persecution of Christians in the second and third centuries CE. When the Roman Empire became Christian in the fourth century, however, history took a turn that no prophet or apocalypse had predicted. Now a religion that had defined itself by suffering persecution was wielding political power. Eastern churches of the Byzantine Empire often identified the rule of God with that of the Christian empire. Roman Catholic churches in the west tended to distinguish the "city of God" from "the city of the world," in Augustine's words. Both approaches drove apocalyptic to the fringes of Christian politics. The Jewish and Christian mainstreams preserved apocalyptic ideas such as reward and punishment in the afterlife but downplayed its political implications. Yet apocalyptic expectations continue to flourish whenever political discontent creates real or imagined feelings of persecution.

The Christian Bible's presentation of both Pentateuchal and apocalyptic rhetoric about the future still echoes in modern politics. For example, twenty-first-century debates about environmental climate change have, in the USA, pitted environmentalists' warnings and proposals for change against fatalistic defenses of the status quo by, especially, Evangelical Christians. The scientists promise benefits from reducing carbon emissions while warning that current human behavior will produce worldwide catastrophe. Like Moses, their threats are longer and more detailed than their promises. Their opponents argue that climate change is not real or is the product of natural processes because they believe in the inevitability of the future. Like Daniel, they believe that our actions influence only our individual afterlives while world history follows a predetermined plan. The Bible's two different visions of the future continue to shape many people's ideas of what is possible and what is not.

The Rhetoric of Law After Ezra

There is no ancient evidence that written laws directed legal practice until the third or second century BCE. That is surprising, given how much the Pentateuch and other ancient texts talk about law. However, close examination shows that their rhetoric does not apply written law to legal practice. For example, the fourth-century Chronicler claims that King Jehoshaphat appointed a court of appeal in Jerusalem and instructed all judges to decide cases "for YHWH, who is with you in matters of justice" (2 Chr. 19:6; the story in 19:4–11 does not appear in the older book of 2 Kings). Since Chronicles also tells of Jehoshaphat's officers teaching Torah in the villages (2 Chr. 17:7–9), the two stories together could imply that Torah should guide the administration of justice in Judah's law courts. However, the Chronicler does not connect written Torah to legal practice explicitly.

Instead, it was the Pentateuch's ritual rules that first became normative for ritual practices, especially in the temples in Jerusalem and Samaria. Like other ancient cultures, Judean concern for following written instructions first focused on performing rituals by the book.[131] So Ezra's Torah reading leads listeners to wonder how to celebrate *Sukkot* properly (Neh. 8:13–18). It also leads the people to recommit themselves to

> *following God's Torah which was given through God's servant Moses, and to observe and do all the commandments and regulations and mandates of our Lord YHWH.* (Neh. 10:29)

The following verses tell us that "all" the Torah's obligations consist of giving tithes and other offerings to the temple, resting on the Sabbath, observing sabbatical years, and keeping separate from neighboring peoples, especially by avoiding intermarriage (Neh. 10:30–39). The offerings and Sabbath observances are obviously ritual concerns, but so is the commitment not to intermarry with other peoples. Ezra and Nehemiah are most concerned with the priests' marriages (Ezra 10:18–23; Neh. 13:1–9, 28–30). Priests must maintain their purity so that they can minister in the temple. Leviticus therefore restricts whom they can marry (Lev. 21:7–15), though it limits only the high priest to marrying "among his people" (21:14). The books of Ezra and Nehemiah think the community's holiness requires extending these rules to everyone. The people's ritual concern to preserve the purity of the community should motivate them to obey written Torah when marrying.

In the following centuries, the authority of written laws in Judea continued to direct purity practices and offerings, but began to be extended to legal procedures as well. Stories that mention marriage contracts and charges of illicit sex evoke the regulations and punishments written in the Pentateuch (Tob. 1:8; 7:12–13; Sus. 62; John 8:5). The histories of second-century Judea depict the Maccabees following written Torah to purify the temple and make offerings (1 Macc. 2:19–22, 27, 48; 4:47, 53), and also when recruiting soldiers (1 Macc. 3:56). This Jewish development paralleled the increasing tendency to invoke written law in Hellenistic cultures at this time.

The Pentateuch's spreading authority beyond the temple did not change its primary application to ritual. Instead, it had the effect of ritualizing more and more aspects of daily life. Like Ezra and Nehemiah, the Dead Sea Scrolls redefined the temple community to cover the whole city of Jerusalem and bring all its inhabitants under the rules of the temple. Their *Temple Scroll* (*11QT*) is primarily concerned with temple offerings, purity requirements, and festivals. Their interest in civil law seems limited to repeating the Pentateuch's provisions with little amplification, except when it comes to regulating the internal life of the Qumran community itself. Then the *Community Rule* (*1QS*) and the *Damascus Document* (*CD*) add many rules of behavior and discipline to extend the Torah's application to their own community. This line of interpretation seems to be based on the idea that the Torah, as the law book of the Temple, applies to whoever is in the temple community.

As interest spread in obeying the provisions of written Torah, concern to explain its rules also grew, especially around the diet rules that served as markers of Jewish identity. Already in the second century BCE, the *Letter of Aristeas* explained the distinction between clean and unclean animals (Lev. 11; Deut. 14) as a moral object lesson: herbivores are classified as clean and predators as unclean to teach people to avoid violence (see Box, "The *Letter of Aristeas* on food laws"). Two centuries later, Philo of Alexandria described observing the biblical diet rules as an ascetic exercise aimed at teaching moderation (*Spec.* 4.100–118). Moral interpretations of the diet rules were elaborated in subsequent Jewish and Christian interpretation, and continue to find scholarly support today.[132]

The *Letter of Aristeas* on food laws

Do not take the contemptible view that Moses enacted this legislation because of an excessive preoccupation with mice and weasels or suchlike creatures. The fact is that everything has been solemnly set in order for unblemished investigation and amendment of life for the sake of righteousness. The birds which we use are all domesticated and of exceptional cleanliness, their food consisting of wheat and pulse – such birds as pigeons, turtledoves, locusts, partridges, and, in addition, geese and others of the same kind. As for the birds which are forbidden, you will find wild and carnivorous kinds, and the rest which dominate by their own strength, and who find their food at the expense of the aforementioned domesticated birds – which is an injustice; and not only that, they also seize lambs and kids and outrage human beings dead or alive. By calling them impure, he has thereby indicated that it is the solemn binding duty of those for whom the legislation has been established to practice righteousness and not to lord it over anyone in reliance upon their own strength, nor to deprive him of anything but to govern their lives righteously, in the manner of the gentle creatures among the aforementioned birds which feed on those plants which grow on the ground and do not exercise a domination leading to the destruction of their fellow creatures. (*Aris.* 142–148)[133]

The ancient rabbis frequently interpreted Pentateuchal laws more flexibly than the strict interpretations in the Dead Sea Scrolls. The rabbis were therefore able to adjust for the catastrophic loss of temple and land at the end of the first century CE by focusing Jewish religious practice on prayer, good works, and Torah study. For example, they taught that you can gain the same merit by studying the laws of offerings as by making those offerings. Such rulings make it possible to keep the covenant and to obey the Torah even when it is impossible to perform many commandments literally.

The rabbis on offerings and Torah study

Resh Lakish said, What is the significance of the verse, "This is the law for the burnt offering, for the meal offering, for the sin offering, and for the guilt offering"? (Lev. 7:37) *It teaches that whosoever occupies himself with the study of the Torah is as though he were offering a burnt offering, a meal offering, a sin offering, and a guilt offering, Raba asked, Why then does the verse say. "For the burnt offering, for the meal offering"? It should have said, "a burnt offering, a meal offering"! Rather, said Raba, it means that whosoever occupies himself with the study of the Torah needs neither burnt offering, nor meal offering, nor sin offering, nor guilt offering.*

R. Isaac said, What is the significance of the verses, "This is the law of the sin offering" (Lev. 6:25); *and "This is the law of the guilt offering"?* (Lev. 7:1) *They teach that whosoever occupies himself with the study of the laws of the sin offering is as though he were offering a sin offering, and whosoever occupies himself with the study of the laws of the guilt offering is as though he were offering a guilt offering.* (*b. Menaḥ.* 110a)[134]

In fact, the rabbis tried to make Torah observance more important to Jewish everyday life than it had ever been before. They elaborated the Pentateuch's laws in order to "build a fence around the Torah" (*m. ʾAvot* 1.1). That is, they established additional rules around the Pentateuch's regulations to ensure that the Torah's laws would not be broken. This led to greater attention to ritual purity in Jewish homes. For example, where Exod. 23:19 prohibits "boiling a kid in its mother's milk," the rabbis prohibited ever mixing meat with dairy foods (*b. Ḥul.* 108a–b). It also led to more scrupulous adherence to procedural safeguards when rabbinic courts heard legal cases. For example, Deut. 17:6 requires the evidence of at least two witnesses to impose the death penalty. The rabbis required witnesses to also warn the accused in advance about the death penalty for doing this act. The accused must also verbally acknowledge this fact before doing the deed in order for the death penalty to apply (*m. Mak.* 1:10; *y. Sanh.* 22c). So, though the rabbis acknowledged that the Pentateuch mandates death as the punishment for many crimes, rabbinic procedures made the death penalty very difficult to carry out. In these and many other ways, Rabbinic Judaism made it possible to fulfill all 613 separate laws that the rabbis found in the Pentateuch (*b. Mak.* 23b) in whatever circumstances Jews might find themselves.

While the ancient rabbis were emphasizing obedience to all the laws of Torah, most early Christians substituted faith in Christ for Torah observance. This new emphasis appeared first in the letters of the apostle Paul. Paul realized that some Jewish practices, especially circumcision and diet restrictions, limited Christianity's appeal among Gentiles (non-Jews). He therefore argued that Gentiles should be allowed to become Christians without observing these Pentateuchal laws (Acts 15). To justify these exceptions, Paul developed a far-reaching argument that contrasts obeying the law, that is, the Torah, with faith in Christ (Rom. 7). The law became a temporary custodian that convicts people of their sins under the Sinai covenant, but faith in Christ liberates people from the law's control (Gal. 3). Paul believed that Christians must still behave morally because they have been changed into moral people by Christ's salvation, not because of the Torah's rules.

The Apostle Paul on the law

Christ is the goal of the Law, which leads to righteousness for all who have faith in God. (Rom. 10:4 CEB)

All those who rely on the works of the Law are under a curse, because it is written, "Everyone is cursed who does not keep on doing all the things that have been written in the Law scroll." But since no one is made righteous by the Law as far as God is concerned, it is clear that "the righteous one will live on the basis of faith." (Gal. 3:10–11 CEB, quoting Deut. 27:26 and Hab. 2:4)

Before faith came, we were guarded under the Law, locked up until faith that was coming would be revealed, so that the Law became our custodian until Christ so that we might be made righteous by faith. But now that faith has come, we are no longer under a custodian. (Gal. 3:23–25 CEB)

Christ canceled the detailed rules of the Law so that he could create one new person out of the two groups, making peace. (Eph. 2:15 CEB)

The Gospels depict Jesus voicing paradoxical views of Pentateuchal law. Some texts quote his support for the Ten Commandments (Matt. 19:18–19) and the rest of scripture.

> *Do not think that I have come to abolish the law or the prophets; I have come not to abolish but to fulfil. ... Therefore, whoever breaks one of the least of these commandments, and teaches others to do the same, will be called least in the kingdom of heaven; but whoever does them and teaches them will be called great in the kingdom of heaven.* (Matt. 5:17–19 NRSV)

In some cases, he interprets Pentateuchal laws strictly and even makes them harsher.

> *You have heard that it was said, "You shall not commit adultery." But I say to you that everyone who looks at a woman with lust has already committed adultery with her in his heart.* (Matt. 5:27–28 NRSV quoting Exod. 20:14)

On the other hand, the Gospels show Jesus ignoring purity rules that would restrict whom he can meet or touch (Mark 5:25–34; Matt. 9:11) and he seems to moralize food laws away.

> *There is nothing outside a person that by going in can defile, but the things that come out are what defile.* (Mark 7:15 NRSV)

Jesus advocates interpreting the law based on underlying principles, such as the so-called "golden rule."

> *Do to others as you would have them do to you; for this is the law and the prophets.* (Matt. 7:12 NRSV)

The Gospels denounce other traditions of legal interpretation, especially those of the Pharisees (Mark 7:1–13; Matt. 23). They depict Jesus teaching with great personal authority instead of quoting older traditions (Matt. 7:28–29). The Gospels, then, which were written in the late first century CE, already distinguished between early rabbinic traditions of Oral Torah and Christian teachings based on Jesus's prophetic and messianic authority.

So the New Testament portrays Jesus making ambiguous statements about Mosaic law and Paul deploying a systematic argument for its replacement. However, it quotes some Pentateuchal laws repeatedly and approvingly, especially the commands to love God (Deut. 6:5) and your neighbor and the immigrant (Lev. 19:18, 34). These verses are notable for the number of times the New Testament repeats them.

> *"Teacher, which commandment in the law is the greatest?" He said to him, "'You shall love the Lord your God with all your heart, and with all your soul, and with all your mind.' This is the greatest and first commandment. And a second is like it: 'You shall love your neighbor as yourself.' On these two commandments hang all the law and the prophets."* (Matt. 22:36–40 NRSV; see also Matt. 5:43–48; 19:19; Mark 12:28–34; Luke 10:25–37; Rom. 13:9; Gal. 5:14; Jam. 2:8)

As a result, Christians have read the New Testament as urging them to observe some Pentateuchal laws, but not others. Their problem has been to figure out which are which.

Paul seems to have wanted a two-track Christianity in which Jews would observe circumcision and diet laws while Gentiles would not, while both groups would be saved by Christ (Rom. 11). Instead, over the course of several centuries, Jews and Christians evolved into two separate religions, distinguished especially by their contrasting attitudes towards the laws of the Pentateuch. Already by 110 CE, some bishops threatened to excommunicate Christians who continued to observe Passover, as mandated in Exodus 12–13. They argued that the Christian celebration of the Lord's Supper, also called Communion or the Eucharist (Luke 22:7–23; 1 Cor. 11:17–27), completely replaces the Passover meal. Later Christian churches frequently persecuted people who performed Jewish rituals, labeling them heretics.

Nevertheless, the continuing presence of rules for offerings and purity in the Christian Old Testament has proven attractive to dissident Christians throughout history. In various times and places during the Middle Ages, popular lay movements were reputed to practice Jewish rituals. It is hard to evaluate the accuracy of these claims, because anti-Semitic prejudices and charges of "Judaizing" were very common in Christian polemics.

The attraction to some Pentateuchal rituals among modern Christian groups is better documented. Christians have been especially drawn to Pentateuchal Sabbath laws. Many reject the Christian tradition of worshipping on Sundays, the day of Jesus's resurrection (Mark 16:2). They instead observe the seventh day, Saturday, as a day of rest and worship following Pentateuchal law (Exod. 20:8–11; Deut. 5:12–15). Today, the Seventh-Day Adventists are the most familiar Christian "Sabbatarian" movement.

In the nineteenth and twentieth centuries, anti-colonial Christian movements in India, Africa, and Jamaica criticized Western Christianity for failing to follow the laws in its own Bible (see above). In North America, some Evangelicals created communities of Jewish-Christians who observe Torah and also follow Christ. These "Messianic Jews" imitate the first Christian movement, which the New Testament depicts as consisting of Jewish followers of Jesus (Acts 6:1–7). Jewish organizations do not recognize them as Jewish.

Christians generally believe that Jesus's crucifixion constitutes the ultimate and final sacrifice (Heb. 3–10). They therefore have almost never tried to make animal offerings to God. They accept the Ten Commandments and laws regarding love of God and neighbors because Jesus himself quoted them approvingly. However, interpreters have labored to determine which other Pentateuchal laws apply to Christians and which do not. Christian arguments about Pentateuchal laws have mostly revolved around its rules about the Sabbath, food, false religion, idolatry, slavery, and sex.

The books of the New Testament do not foresee Christians becoming politically powerful. They offer no advice about how to rule nations. Christian rulers have therefore frequently looked to their Old Testament for models of how to be "godly" rulers and for how to draft laws. The Christian emperors of Rome and of later European kingdoms inherited traditional legal procedures ("common law"), so in no case did they use only the Bible to draft their law codes. However, the Pentateuch provided a model of an authoritative written law in a single collection. That probably explains why it was Christian emperors, Theodosius and Justinian, who collected and edited Roman laws for the first time in the fifth and sixth centuries CE. Other early medieval kings followed suit. Thus in the ninth century, the Anglo-Saxon laws of Alfred began with Exod. 20:1–23:13 and validated them for Christians by quoting Matt. 5:17, 7:12 and Acts 15:23–29 to justify creating further Christian laws which were collected by Alfred. For medieval Christian rulers, biblical law served as example and precedent for their own legislation.

In the twelfth century, the theologian Thomas Aquinas divided biblical laws into three categories: moral, judicial, and ritual. He argued that moral rules like the Ten Commandments apply to all Christians, while judicial rules may or may not apply depending on local circumstances. But Christians must not follow the Pentateuch's ritual laws. Aquinas's three categories of biblical law shape Catholic and Protestant thinking about biblical law up to the present day. Debates continue, however, over which laws belong in the mandatory moral category.

The codification of the Roman Catholic Church's rules as canon law in the twelfth century influenced the subsequent development of national law throughout Europe. However, the Protestant Reformation in the sixteenth century disposed of canon law in the parts of northern Europe under Lutheran and Calvinist control. Political thinkers then discussed the proper sources of law and of legitimate government and increasingly cited the Pentateuch's example. Its description of Israel governed by written law but no king, or at least no royal legislation, led many to think of it as the "Mosaic constitution" of a "Hebrew Republic." Some based their calls to redistribute land on the biblical model of dividing land among the Israelite tribes and families. They also seized on the fact that God agrees to a written covenant with Israel to argue that kings should be subject to national constitutions. After all, if even God agrees to be constrained by written covenant, how can human kings claim the freedom of absolute sovereignty?[135]

In the eighteenth century, Enlightenment rationalism led political philosophers to dismiss religious precedents and argue for laws based on reason and experience alone. Their influence created the secular legal systems of the US Constitution (1789) and the French Code of Napoleon (1804). These laws guaranteed freedom of religion and prohibited government support for specific churches. Many other nations have followed their examples.

Nevertheless, some of the Pentateuch's regulations continued to exert considerable influence over later laws. Its prohibitions on magic (Exod. 22:18; Lev. 20:6; Deut. 18:9–12) were frequently used to justify witch hunts in Christian communities. The Pentateuch's slave laws (Exod. 21:1–6; Lev. 25:39–55; Deut. 15:12–18) were cited to defend the African slave trade and its perpetuation in America. Their more humane provisions were also cited by abolitionists trying to end slavery. The lists of prohibited sex acts (Lev. 18, 20) informed legal definitions of incest and are now commonly cited in arguments over sexual behavior and identity. All these debates have brought the old problem of distinguishing which Pentateuchal laws still apply into current political conflicts. Arguments on both sides of these debates often invoke the medieval distinction between binding moral law and superseded ritual law, but disagree over which is which.

To summarize: the law codes of the Pentateuch have rarely functioned with legal authority by themselves. Rabbinic literature molded and amplified Torah to direct the actions of rabbinic courts as well as other aspects of Jewish religion and life. The New Testament set aside many aspects of Pentateuchal law while validating others. The Pentateuch's law codes have, however, been imitated by many later legal developments: as a model of a collected written law for Roman Emperors, as a model of written religious law for the codifiers of medieval canon law, and as a model of constitutional law, even of republican values, for early modern political theorists. In the same way, many of its specific regulations still function as precedents. The Pentateuch's rhetoric of law thus remains part of modern legal rhetoric, even though the Bible itself is rarely recognized anymore as having legal authority.

The heritage of Pentateuchal law has often been expressed by attention to the figure of Moses. Already in late Second Temple literature and the New Testament, the Pentateuch and especially its laws were called simply "Moses," as in the phrase, "Moses and the Prophets" (*1QS* 1.2–3; *4QMMT* C 17; Luke 16:29; 24:27). Just as Moses embodies the law in Western art (see Chapter 3), the story of Moses has personified the idea of law in intellectual traditions. Moses has repeatedly been cast as a great lawgiver and compared to the lawgivers of other cultures, such as Hammurabi, Solon, and Mohammed. In antiquity, Philo and Josephus also depicted him as a solitary hero who rescued his people. Nineteenth-century historians, even while casting doubts on the accuracy of the Pentateuchal story, nevertheless celebrated this depiction of Moses, as Brian Britt noted.

> As the pivotal figure between Genesis and the history books, Moses combines myth and history to epitomize the German idealist hero. Moses is the lynchpin of biblical tradition, a liminal figure *par excellence*. For biblical scholars, Moses embodies legend itself. Whatever their status *vis-à-vis* history, legends of Moses present him as the central figure in a specific, heroic narrative.[136]

For many modern thinkers, Moses's uniqueness involves especially monotheism, the belief in the existence of only one God, and in laws that enforce this belief in religious practice. Sigmund Freud and Jan Assmann, for example, cast Moses as a precedent and figurehead for monotheism and religious intolerance in Judaism, Christianity, and Islam.[137]

The Pentateuch's rhetoric of law, then, has influenced cultures by shaping some specific laws. More often it has shaped their ideas about broader topics, such as the nature and function of law, of government, and of religion itself.

The Rhetoric of Origins After Ezra

The Pentateuch's rhetoric of origins explains where Israel and its religious institutions came from by telling stories about ancestors, about Israel's exodus from Egypt, and about the covenant with God at Mount Sinai. It also reaches further back in time to tell of the origins of the nations, of civilization, and of the whole world. Through most of history, Jews and Christians believed these stories to be true accounts of past events. They were, in fact, the oldest accounts of human and world origins available to them. Intellectual advances over the last 500 years have systematically challenged that belief. Developments in astronomy, biology, political theory, history, and archeology have undermined the Pentateuch's account of the past. History and archeology have also revealed older cultures and literatures in the ancient Middle East from which the Pentateuch drew many of its ideas about origins. As a result, the Pentateuch is no longer regarded as the oldest literature in the world. Its stories of origins compete with those of other cultures and are evaluated against the reconstructions of scientists, philosophers, and historians.

The Pentateuch and science

In Genesis, the stories of world creation and world flood reflect the same conception of the universe, or "cosmology."

> *When God started to create the heavens and the earth, the earth was formless and void. Darkness covered the deep, and God's spirit moved over the water.* (Gen. 1:1–2)

God creates the world by separating a cosmic ocean. The created world is a bubble floating in water: water surrounds the land while the dome of the sky holds back the water above (1:6–10). The sun, moon, and stars move underneath the sky's dome (1:14–18). The story of God destroying the world in Genesis 6–8 uses the same cosmology. The bubble begins to burst and the water floods in from below and above.

> *The fountains of the deep split and the windows of heaven opened.* (Gen. 7:11)

So Genesis depicts the universe as a bubble of air and dry land in a cosmic ocean – a world view similar to maps drawn in ancient Egypt and Mesopotamia. It makes sense of what we see around us: an apparently flat earth and a blue sky that frequently leaks water.

Ancient Greek philosophers suggested that the earth is not flat but a sphere. They proposed a model of the universe in which the sun, moon, planets, and stars revolve around a spherical earth. This model is usually called the "Ptolemaic" universe after the mathematician who perfected it in the second century CE. Most Christian theologians in Late Antiquity and the Middle Ages accepted the Ptolemaic model, despite the fact that it contradicted Genesis's picture of a flat earth. To them, what mattered was not the shape of the earth but that it was at the center of the universe, which put humans at the center of God's creation.[138]

The Ptolemaic model was disproven in the sixteenth century by the mathematical calculations of Nicolaus Copernicus and the observations of Galileo Galilei, who used the newly invented telescope. They demonstrated that the earth orbits the sun. Some Roman Catholic bishops rejected this conclusion and forced Galileo to recant his observations. He became famous as a scientific martyr of religious persecution. This did not stop most European scientists from quickly accepting the Copernican model of the universe. The credibility of religious beliefs as providing accurate insights into the nature of the physical universe suffered a severe blow.

However, early modern interaction between science and the stories of Genesis was not just conflictual. Peter Harrison has shown that, in the seventeenth century, a common interpretation of the story of Adam and Eve's "fall" in Genesis 3 encouraged experimental science. Many people had long believed that, before being ejected from Eden, humans reasoned clearly and had access to all knowledge. Human sin led to confused reasoning and losing that knowledge. But some philosophers concluded from this story that through rigorous effort humans can reason more clearly and improve their knowledge. The idea that accurate knowledge requires trial and error and painstaking effort motivated the work of early empirical scientists, such as Francis Bacon, and the empiricist philosophy of John Locke.

Adam's sin, reason, and empirical science

Peter Harrison concluded: "During the seventeenth century, … the bible came to occupy a position of unparalleled authority, informing discussions about the nature of the state, the rights of the individual, private property, education, international sovereignty, the status of indigenous peoples, work and leisure, agriculture and gardening, anthropology and moral psychology. In each of these spheres, the story of Adam had a significant place. … Advocates of 'rationalism' and 'empiricism' largely fall out along lines related to an underlying theological anthropology. Descartes' confident assertion that the 'natural light' of reason could provide the basis of a complete and certain science presupposed the persistence of the natural light and the divine image even in fallen human beings. This was strongly contested by those who believed that the Fall had effaced the divine image and all but extinguished the natural light. On this latter view, if knowledge were possible at all, it would be painstakingly accumulated through much labour, through trials and the testing of nature, and would rise to a modest knowledge that did not penetrate to the essences of things and was at best probable rather than certain. Such mitigated skepticism characterized the experimental approach commonly associated with such figures as Francis Bacon and Robert Boyle."[139]

The popular perception that scientific discoveries were falsifying the Bible increased in the nineteenth century. Jews and Christians had traditionally thought the world was less than 6,000 years old based on biblical genealogies. Observations of sedimentary rock layers led geologists to estimate the earth's age at nearly four billion years. Fossils in sedimentary rocks, together with observations of diverse living species, led Charles Darwin to conclude that life on earth evolved from simple to complex creatures over more than one billion years. This process of evolution was driven by competition between species ("survival of the fittest"), rather than by a divine design.

Biologists quickly accepted and extended Darwin's conclusions. Many other people, however, think biological evolution undermines not just details of the biblical account of creation, but its fundamental premise: that God created the world and everything in it by an intentional plan. Though many theologians found ways to accommodate biological evolution with their religious beliefs, popular movements opposing the teaching of evolution have gained strength over the past century. In the early twentieth century, Christian fundamentalism began opposing the conclusions of historians (see below) and also rejected biological evolution. Fundamentalists influenced some US states to ban the teaching of evolution in their schools. This led to the highly publicized "monkey trial" of school teacher John Scopes in Tennessee in 1925. Attempts to counter evolution marshaled various kinds of evidence into theories of theistic "creationism" or "intelligent design," which could be taught to school children instead of, or at least in addition to, evolution. Advocacy of creationism has increased with the worldwide growth of Evangelical Christianity since the 1950s. Creationism has also found a receptive audience among some Orthodox Jews and, increasingly, among conservative Muslims.[140]

These conflicts over the relationship between Genesis and science have become sharper in modern centuries. That is not just because of new scientific discoveries. It is also because modern people tend to read the Bible differently than their predecessors in ancient and medieval times. When biblical texts were commonly interpreted by *midrash* and allegory, that is, as symbolic expressions of religious truth, conflicts between the Bible and cosmological beliefs could easily be explained away. Modern reading practices, however, have increasingly focused on the plain meaning of the text, often called its "literal" meaning. This change was inspired by medieval Jewish philosophy and early modern Protestant theology, and led to modern historians reading the Bible "like any other book" (see below). But its practice also caused many defenders of traditional religion to abandon symbolic interpretation and stake their cause on what they consider the literal meaning of Genesis 1–3. Modern conflicts between religion and science, then, are due to changes in Bible reading practices as well as to scientific discoveries.

The Pentateuch and human nature

Genesis does not just tell about the origins of the physical world and the origins of Israel's ancestors. It also narrates the origins of differences between human beings, especially between men and women and between nations and races. These texts have frequently been used in Jewish and Christian history to justify discrimination against women and prejudice against particular races, even to the point of violence. The same texts have also been interpreted to counteract sexism and racism.

The first story of creation describes women and men as created equally in the image of God (Gen. 1:27). However, the Garden of Eden story says the man was created first, then God created a woman out of his rib to be his "helper" (2:20). The snake convinced the woman to eat the forbidden fruit first and she then gave it to the man (3:1–6). God punished the woman for this sin by saying that the man "will rule over you" (3:16).

Traditional interpreters therefore blamed the first woman and, by extension, women generally for human sin and its consequences, which they understood to include death (3:19). Already in the second century BCE, ben Sira concluded,

> *From a woman sin had its beginning, and because of her we all die.* (Sir. 25:24)

The New Testament repeats this interpretation (2 Cor. 11:3) and concludes from it that women should "not teach or have authority over a man" (1 Tim. 2:11–15).[141]

Women in significant numbers entered the ranks of professional biblical scholars only in the decades following 1970. Many of them introduced feminist perspectives that revolutionized the interpretation of some biblical texts. For example, Phyllis Trible pointed out that Genesis 3:16 describes patriarchy negatively. The first woman is not created subordinate to the man but punished for disobeying God by being subjected to the man's rule. She noted that the word *'ezer* "helper" used to describe Eve in Gen. 2:20 appears most commonly in the Hebrew Bible to describe God (e.g. Ps. 115:9–11). So it also implies no subordination to the man. Trible's observations simply read the story as written, but it required a woman interpreter to expose the male biases in the story's usual interpretation.

Phyllis Trible on Genesis 3:16

We misread if we assume that these judgments are mandates. They describe; they do not prescribe. They protest; they do not condone. Of special concern are the words telling the woman that her husband shall rule over her (3:16). This statement is not license for male supremacy, but rather it is condemnation of that very pattern. Subjugation and supremacy are perversions of creation. Through disobedience the woman has become slave. Her initiative and her freedom vanish. The man is corrupted also, for he has become master, ruling over the one who is his God-given equal. The subordination of female to male signifies their shared sin.[142]

Feminist theories also highlighted the pervasive patriarchalism of Pentateuchal stories about male heroes and of Pentateuchal laws that privilege the legal rights of free, male Israelites. Feminists uncovered the neglected stories of matriarchs such as Sarah, Hagar, and Rebekah, and the crucial roles of professional women such as the Hebrew midwives in Exodus 1 and the prophet Miriam. Today, their analysis has expanded to embrace a wider range of gender identities.[143] The work of feminists and gender critics has added fuel to debates about how the Pentateuch can remain authoritative for contemporary people who embrace different cultural values, such as gender equality, as well as modern scientific, political, and historical perspectives.

Slave owners used the Bible to justify owning people as property. Though they quoted Pentateuchal laws allowing slavery (Exod. 21:1–6; Lev. 25:39–55; Deut. 15:12–18), no biblical text has been cited more often to justify enslaving Africans than the so-called "curse of Ham." Genesis 9 tells the story of Noah getting drunk and falling asleep, when

> *Ham the father of Canaan, saw the nakedness of his father (Noah) and told his brothers.* (Gen. 9:22)

After waking up, Noah said,

> *Cursed be Canaan: he will be a servile slave to his brothers.* (Gen. 9:25)

The list of nations descending from Noah's sons then records Ham's descendants (Gen. 10:6) as Canaan and the African nations of Egypt, Cush (Ethiopia), and Put (Libya). Later generations include Babylonia and Assyria in Mesopotamia as well (10:10–11). The Psalms also locate Egypt "in the land of Ham" (Pss. 78:51; 105:27; 106:22). The story, then, seems to blame the ancestor of African peoples for some kind of sexual offense against Noah, though Noah's curse falls on his grandson, Canaan.

Why Noah curses Canaan instead of Ham is not clear. An ancient line of interpretation held that Noah actually cursed Ham. Some rabbinic texts speculated that Ham's skin was blackened because he had sex with his wife inside the ark, which was not allowed. The "curse of Ham" was used to justify the African slave trade when it spread into the Middle East in the seventh century CE and into Europe and the Americas in the sixteenth. It became routine to regard Africans as "blackened" by Ham's sin and cursed to slavery. Few Jews, Christians, or Muslims noticed that Genesis 9 says no such thing. Their interpretations obscured the biblical text and condemned generations of African descent, often Christians and Muslims themselves, to violent enslavement.[144]

From at least the nineteenth century on, many African and African American preachers, scholars, and writers tried to counter the effects of this tradition by pointing out that Noah cursed Canaan, not Ham. They claimed Ham's identity with Africans and celebrated the cultural achievements of Ham's descendants in Egypt, Ethiopia, and Babylon. Descent from Ham became a point of pride. Zora Neale Hurston, for example, retold the Genesis 9 story in her 1922 play, *The First One*, which ends with Ham and his wife leaving the family for "where the sun shines forever, to the end of the Earth." Ham tells his father and brothers: "Oh, remain with your flocks and fields and vineyards, to covet, to sweat, to die and know no peace. I go to the sun."[145]

The Pentateuch and history

As we have seen, for many centuries Jewish and Christian interpretation of the Pentateuch took the form mostly of *midrash*, typology, and allegory. Interpreters assumed that its stories were true accounts of past events, but they were less interested in past history than in the text's religious meaning for themselves in the present.

Modern readers of the Bible, whether religious or secular, tend to read it "like any other book" even when they regard it as the most important book. Like any other book, their interpretations of particular passages attend first to the immediate literary context. This change in reading practices has religious roots. Jewish medieval interpreters focused on the "plain meaning" (*pschat*) of the biblical text and Protestant Reformers believed that the Bible's message would be plainly evident to every reader. It also has roots in philosophical efforts in the seventeenth and eighteenth century to analyze the Bible critically like any other ancient book. These tendencies joined, in the nineteenth century, with new methods of historical analysis to create "historical criticism" of the Bible. Historical research on the Pentateuch has proven to be one of the most interesting and controversial parts of biblical studies ever since.

Already in 1670, the Jewish philosopher Baruch Spinoza argued that Moses could not have written the Pentateuch, which is "faulty, mutilated, tampered with, and inconsistent." The French philosopher Voltaire mocked the Pentateuch and historical books of the Bible as violent, superstitious, and full of unbelievable stories. Such attacks prompted ardent defenses of biblical truth from Jews and Christians, who condemned Spinoza and Voltaire as heretics. They also led some scholars to try to reconcile religious faith with human reason by investigating biblical books more systematically using historical methods of research.[146]

Such approaches found a home especially in nineteenth-century German universities. Protestant German scholars developed a "higher criticism" that went beyond the lower criticism of philology and manuscript criticism. They investigated ancient religious history and the history of the biblical books themselves. Their methods and results began to be employed by British and American scholars in the later nineteenth century, and historical criticism dominated biblical studies in the twentieth century. Its results transformed modern understandings of the origins and development of the Pentateuch.[147]

Doubts that Moses wrote the Pentateuch led historians to search for its origins in other periods of Israel's history. The most influential proposal came from Wilhelm De Wette in 1805. He pointed out that the religious reforms of King Josiah, who destroyed divine images and shrines to other gods and centralized the worship of YHWH in one temple (2 Kgs. 22–23), reflect the themes of the book of Deuteronomy. De Wette argued that Deuteronomy was probably written in the time of Josiah in the seventh century BCE to motivate and justify these reforms. Later scholars have found this dating convincing because Josiah's reforms seem to reflect some of Deuteronomy's themes. Deuteronomy's Hebrew language is also very similar to that of 2 Kings and the book of Jeremiah, both of which narrate events down to the sixth century BCE. Dating Deuteronomy to the seventh century became the basis for dating other parts of the Pentateuch before or after this book.

Historical critics also tried to explain the strange literary form of the Pentateuch. Many readers notice that the Pentateuch does not read very smoothly. Its books contain contradictions in their plots and in their laws, they tell two or three versions of the same story, and they are inconsistent in how they characterize God and even how they name God. Eighteenth- and nineteenth-century historians concluded that several different sources were combined to create the Pentateuch. They distinguished one source by its vocabulary and concern for rituals such as offerings, festivals, and calendars, so they called it the "priestly" source (P). They regarded Leviticus as completely from P. The P source appears in Genesis, Exodus, and Numbers mixed with other material. The not-P material in Genesis divides between texts that refer to the deity by the personal name, *YHWH*, and others that use only *Elohim* "God." Historians therefore labeled them the "Yahwist" (J) and the "Elohist" (E) sources. They thought they had been combined together with P and then with Deuteronomy (D) by one or more editors, also called redactors (R).

Jean Astruc in 1753 first distinguished the Yahwist and Elohist sources in Genesis. Johann Gottfried Eichhorn in 1780–83 extended this distinction to Exodus. Both regarded Moses as the redactor who edited the sources together, though Eichhorn abandoned this view by the end of his life. They thought the Elohist was the oldest source, and in 1853 Hermann Hupfeld divided it into two, later called E and P. Around the same time, Karl Heinrich Graf and Abraham Kuenen argued that P was the youngest source. They dated it after Deuteronomy to the sixth century. This division into four sources in the chronological sequence JEDP became known as "the Documentary Hypothesis." It was popularized by Julius Wellhausen in 1876 and became one of the most famous accomplishments of historical criticism of the Bible. For the next century, most critical historians presupposed the Documentary Hypothesis. Many still defend it today.

According to the Documentary Hypothesis, J and P, and maybe E, originally told the entire Pentateuchal story from creation through Israel's wilderness wandering, reaching perhaps as far as the conquest of the land in Joshua. The Pentateuch often preserves each source's account, sometimes separately and sometimes woven together. So the P creation story (Gen. 1) precedes JE's story of the Garden of Eden (Gen. 2–3), but P's account of the covenant with Abraham (Gen. 17) follows J's (Gen. 15). The flood story in Genesis 6–8 weaves all three sources together, as indicated by the different counts of the animals – one pair of each species (Gen. 6:19–20; 7:8–9, 15) or seven pairs of clean species (7:2–3) – and the different calculations for the duration of the flood (7:4, 11–12, 17, 24; 8:3–6, 12–13). Exodus usually mixes different versions of the same story together, such as the plagues story (Exod. 7–12), but preserves two separate accounts of God revealing the divine name to Moses (J's in 3:13–15; P's in 6:2–8).

However, underneath this broad consensus around the division and dating of four Pentateuchal sources there was much disagreement about the nature of these sources. Wellhausen thought the J and E writers incorporated older oral traditions. In 1922, Hermann Gunkel inaugurated a twentieth-century trend of reconstructing the oral stories used by J and E. He regarded these stories as relatively short and self-contained and thought that J and E did not alter them much. By contrast, Gerhard von Rad in 1938 described J as a theologian in the court of King Solomon who molded older traditions into a national history from creation through the conquest of the land. Ten years later, Martin Noth built on Gunkel's and von Rad's work to argue that the stories were clustered into separate oral traditions around the themes of Abraham, Jacob, the exodus from Egypt, and the Torah at Mount Sinai. J and E simply arranged them in chronological sequence. These scholars all agreed that, unlike J and E, the priestly writers (P) thoroughly rewrote their sources in their own style and theology.

The Documentary Hypothesis dated all the sources hundreds of years after Moses. It undermined the traditional belief that Moses wrote the whole Pentateuch and the text's explicit claim that Moses wrote down the laws (Exod. 24:3–4; Deut. 31:9, 24). Conservative Protestant, Catholic, and Jewish scholars disputed the arguments of historical critics and have remained influential. For example, the nineteenth-century commentaries on the Old Testament by Carl Friedrich Keil and Franz Delitzsch continue to be read by conservatives today.

The ramifications of historical criticism, however, reached far beyond the circles of biblical scholars. Religious groups reacted with alarm when historical critics denied that God revealed the Torah to Moses at Mount Sinai. Pope Leo III in 1893 declared that the Bible is completely inspired and contains no mistakes, a belief commonly called "inerrancy." The Vatican prohibited Roman Catholic scholars from participating in higher criticism of the Bible until the middle of the twentieth century. Among Protestants, opposition to critical scholarship on the Bible coalesced in the early-twentieth-century Fundamentalist movement, named for a series of 90 essays published from 1910 to 1915 titled *The Fundamentals*. Many Protestant denominations in America divided between conservatives and liberals who adapted their beliefs to the findings of historical research. Fundamentalists, on the other hand, made belief in the inerrancy and infallibility of the Bible crucial to Christian faith.

Jews of all denominations rejected higher criticism as a "higher anti-Semitism," in the words of Solomon Schechter. They remained nearly united in opposing it until the middle of the twentieth century, when Reform and Conservative movements adapted themselves to some of its ideas. Then their seminaries and the new Israeli universities began to support critical study of the Pentateuch. Many Jewish Orthodox movements continue to emphasize the divine origins of the Torah in every detail. Historical criticism of the Pentateuch has therefore shaped the denominational history of many traditions.

Nineteenth-century historical research also challenged traditional ideas about the Bible in a completely different way. Europeans exploring ancient ruins in the Middle East brought home written texts in forgotten languages. After Egyptian hieroglyphics and Akkadian cuneiform were deciphered in the early nineteenth century, scholars translated and published many of these texts. The discoveries included Egyptian and Sumerian texts dating from the third millennium BCE and Akkadian texts from the early second millennium – not only older than biblical texts, but even older than characters such as Abraham and Moses featured in biblical texts. The Hebrew Bible was no longer the oldest literature in the world.

Furthermore, some of these ancient texts contained stories that resembled parts of the Hebrew Bible in one way or another. Perhaps most shocking were the flood stories written in Akkadian cuneiform, which George Smith published in English translation in 1871. These accounts of a prehistoric world flood resemble Genesis 6–8 in their plot and details as well as overall theme. Yet the oldest of these stories is older than any possible date for the Hebrew story of Noah's flood. The Akkadian texts also tell the flood story using the polytheistic theology of ancient Babylon. Their publication made it clear that the biblical writers used an older, non-Israelite story and adapted it to their own theological perspective.

Modern publication of significant ancient Middle Eastern texts

Language & contents	Text & century BCE	Scholar	Date of translation
Egyptian hieroglyphics deciphered	Rosetta Stone (2nd c.)	Jean-François Champollion	1822
Akkadian cuneiform deciphered	Behistun Inscription (5th c.)	Henry Rawlinson	1846–1851
Akkadian flood stories	*Gilgamesh* (7th c.) and *Atrahasis* (17th c. copy from older original)	George Smith	1871
Akkadian creation myth	*Enuma Elish* (7th c. copy from 18th–12th c. original)	George Smith	1871
Egyptian tomb inscriptions	Pyramid Texts (24th c.)	Kurt Sethe	1908
Ugaritic myths	*Baal Cycle* (14th c.)	Charles Virollaud	1931–1935
Hebrew Dead Sea Scrolls	*Temple Scroll* (2nd c.)	Yigael Yadin	1977–1983

Many other ancient texts were published in the course of the nineteenth and twentieth centuries that deepened our understanding of the historical, literary, and religious contexts in which Israel's theology and literature developed. The Babylonian creation epic, *Enuma Elish,* provides a vivid example of a violent cosmogony against which Genesis 1 describes creation as deliberate and uncontested. Egyptian tomb inscriptions show that belief in an afterlife judgment was common in Egyptian culture, which contrasts with the Hebrew Bible's almost total avoidance of afterlife ideas. The Ugaritic myths provide a glimpse into the religious thought of Baal devotees, whom the books of Kings attack as idol worshippers. Finally, the Dead Sea Scrolls, though written later than the books of the Hebrew Bible, show how quickly the Hebrew Bible's ideas developed and changed in the last few centuries BCE.

By the middle of the twentieth century, then, the realization had sunk in that the Pentateuch is no longer the oldest literature in Western civilization, just as it is no longer a model for national laws, nor a credible account of world or human origins. It is nevertheless still part of Jewish and Christian scripture, and therefore still vital to the religious identities of many Jews and Christians. Denominations and individual scholars engaged this new understanding of the Pentateuch in a variety of ways.

Jewish settlement in Palestine and the founding of the state of Israel in 1948 created strong support for archeological excavations to discover Israel's biblical past. Jewish scholars also began to engage in historical criticism of the Pentateuch. Yehezkel Kaufmann brought a modified form of the Documentary Hypothesis to the attention of Israeli students. He reversed Wellhausen's disparagement of priestly ritual and argued that P was older than D, so its ritual rules formed an original part of Israel's religion. Kaufmann influenced a generation of prominent Jewish biblical scholars. They argued for dating P earlier on the basis of linguistics and comparisons with other ritual texts from antiquity as well as on source-critical grounds.[148]

In the 1950s and 1960s, the Roman Catholic Church stopped opposing scientific and historical research. The Vatican allowed Catholics to engage in historical criticism, and Catholic biblical scholars have played prominent roles in Pentateuchal studies ever since. Research on the Pentateuch has therefore become an ecumenical and inter-religious enterprise. The largest academic association of biblical scholars, the Society of Biblical Literature, counts adherents to a wide variety of religious denominations as well as to none among its more than 8,000 members. At its meetings, it is usually impossible to determine the speakers' religious affiliations from the contents of their papers alone.

The spread of Christianity around the world has generated increasing research on the Pentateuch by Asian, African, and South American scholars, though Europeans, Israelis, and North Americans still dominate the field. Non-Western scholars have brought new energy to investigating historical issues as well as post-colonial perspectives on the Bible and on ancient religious history (see "The Rhetoric of Communal Identity and Priesthood After Ezra," above).

The last 50 years have also witnessed several profound challenges to the dominance of historical criticism within the academic study of the Bible. The first of these applied literary methods of analyzing modern stories and poetry to biblical literature. Literary criticism in biblical studies emphasized interpretation of the final, received form of the text instead of reconstructing earlier sources and stages of editing. It is therefore frequently called "synchronic" analysis in contrast to "diachronic" historical study. Its focus on plot, characterization, themes, and structural devices frequently explained difficulties that historical critics take as evidence of editing as intentional literary effects instead. For 20 years starting in the 1970s, literary analysis threatened to displace historical criticism as the dominant method for studying biblical texts.

Literary scholars criticized historical critics for the speculative nature of their reconstructed sources and editions, as demonstrated by lack of agreement between different scholars. The literary focus on the existing text seemed to offer a firmer basis for interpretation. The allusions, word plays, and elaborate structures uncovered by literary analysis, however, also turned out to be very speculative. Different scholars produced different literary interpretations just as often as they did different historical reconstructions. When these observations led scholars of modern literature to take a "post-modern" turn that focused on how texts deconstruct their own interpretation, biblical scholars followed suit by showing the indeterminacy of many biblical texts. However, because ancient biblical texts have always been ambiguous and difficult to interpret, deconstruction proved less novel in biblical studies than it did for modern literature.

The Pentateuch provides much material for literary analysis in Genesis and Exodus. Its lists of instructions, laws, genealogies, and sanctions in Leviticus, Numbers, and Deuteronomy are less amenable to interpretive methods developed for modern novels and poetry. The appearance of this material within a narrative framework requires analytical methods less dependent on narrative models than either literary or historical criticism. This book therefore uses a rhetorical analysis of persuasion to summarize the effects of their combination (Chapter 2 above). Unlike literary criticism, rhetoric requires attention to the speaker and audience as well as to the speech. So this book has described the various audiences of the Pentateuch's rhetoric throughout history and tried to understand how they felt themselves addressed by its rhetoric. Literary critics are probably right that the intentions of authors can never really be reconstructed. Nevertheless, the process of hearing or reading a text always requires the audience to think about who is addressing them so they know how to respond. The implied author therefore remains an essential part of the reading process, though its identity can change whenever the audience changes.

For this and other reasons, research on the cultural history of the Bible has become a prominent part of the field of biblical studies. Many books are published every year on the Bible's interpretation in one or another culture or time period, and many more focus on its influence on art, literature, and film. Major collections of essays bring together and summarize this research, such as the four volumes of the *New Cambridge History of the Bible* and of *Hebrew Bible/Old Testament: The History of its Interpretation*, and the 12 volumes (so far) of the *Encyclopedia of the Bible and its Reception*. This book summarizes some of this research in the "… After Ezra" sections of Chapters 3, 4, and 5.

Despite these shifts in research on the Pentateuch over the last 50 years, historical criticism remains a central part of the enterprise. But research on the Pentateuch's compositional history has also undergone radical revision during this period. In the early 1970s, Rolf Rendtorff challenged the assumptions of the Documentary Hypothesis by arguing that Israel's stories of origin – about Abraham, Jacob, Joseph, about the exodus from Egypt, about giving the law at Mount Sinai, and about wandering in the wilderness – developed independently of each other. The stories about ancestors were stitched together by a series of editors, but it was only the priestly editor (P) working in the sixth century BCE who put them all together for the first time. Earlier literary sources (J, E) combining these stories never existed. Rendtorff therefore called for reorienting Pentateuchal studies away from source criticism to focus on the history of independent traditions and their editorial combination.

Rendtorff was not the first to make these observations and his ideas were not immediately influential. Over the following decades, however, increasing numbers of European scholars published models of Pentateuchal composition describing the growth of traditions rather than parallel sources telling the same story. Much of their effort has focused on discerning the editorial links created by redactors to stitch the traditions together. Scholars in Europe and North America argue, often independently of Rendtorff and each other, that P was the editor who brought all the independent traditions together while adding a great deal of his own material as well. Many others continue to maintain P's independent existence and think another editor combined it with non-P material. All of them think material continued to be added to the Pentateuch long after the basic storyline was set. These additions may have included most if not all of the book of Numbers.

These studies have not coalesced into a common model, much less a new consensus about the composition of the Pentateuch. They do show a tendency to think that the Pentateuch, though containing older independent traditions, was brought together only around the time of the exile or in the early Persian period, and continued to be amplified until the Hellenistic period. So while the Documentary Hypothesis dated the Pentateuch's composition between the tenth and sixth centuries BCE, these models tend to date it later, between the seventh and third centuries. Where previously only P was dated to the Exile or later, now the Pentateuch and most of its component traditions seem to be products of the Babylonian Exile and the Second Temple period.[149]

Many scholars reject these conclusions. Some continue to defend the outline of the Documentary Hypothesis, even if modifying some of its details. Others challenge the late dating of Pentateuchal materials and argue that they were written, if not combined, in the Judean monarchy before the Babylonian Exile. And, of course, many religious conservatives continue to defend Moses's authorship of the whole Pentateuch.

The Pentateuch's own rhetoric of origins leads listeners and readers to think that what is most important is how it began, in God's revelation of the Torah to Moses at Mount Sinai in the middle of the second millennium BCE. Historians' efforts to establish the Pentateuch's real origins contradict the historical setting of this story, but their theories reproduce the story's emphasis on the importance of scripture's origins.

The actual history of the Pentateuch's influence suggests otherwise. Every theory of the composition of the Pentateuch locates its origins in the fragmented literature of a small group of people within or on the edges of large ancient empires. Archeological discoveries have provided us with a lot of literature like that, as well as many texts from those empires themselves. Judean literature fits this ancient context more than it stands out from it.

Israel's origin traditions only became important when the Pentateuch began to be ritualized in the iconic, performative, and semantic dimension by Jewish and Samaritan priests in the Second Temple period. Rabbinic literature increased its importance for Jews by codifying its place in ritual practice and interpretation. Its incorporation into Christian scripture, even if secondary to the importance of the Gospels, guaranteed the Pentateuch's influence in Christian thought and Western culture. With modern revolutions in printing technology, the Pentateuch's place at the beginning of Christian bibles led to its reproduction worldwide in more copies and languages than any other literature. It is as Jewish and Christian scripture that the Pentateuch became religiously and culturally important, and never for more people than in the twenty-first century CE.

The Pentateuch's Semantic Dimension Before Ezra

Despite thousands of years of intensive interpretation, the Pentateuch itself does not explicitly recommend ritualizing its semantic dimension. In contrast to its commands to ritualize its iconic and performative dimensions (see Chapters 3 and 4), nowhere does it emphasize the need to interpret its instructions carefully and diligently, much less its stories. Nevertheless, its detailed legal contents and urgent pleas to obey them imply that interpretation is necessary to comply properly. Furthermore, contradictions between key commands require sophisticated ritual and legal interpretation, as do contradictions within and between some of its stories. The need to interpret the Pentateuch, then, arises not just from its scriptural role in religious communities, but also from the nature of its contents.

Scribal Expertise in the Ancient Middle East and in the Pentateuch

Reading and, especially, writing require training. The invention of writing around 5,000 years ago was therefore also the beginning of literacy education. Throughout ancient history, literacy skills were taught to only a small percentage of people, mostly boys who were being trained for careers as scribes. Scribes served as secretaries, accountants, and tax collectors. The best scribal jobs were in temple bureaucracies and royal courts.[150]

Though professional scribes wrote almost all ancient texts, they wrote some texts particularly for themselves and their students. This "wisdom literature" emphasizes the importance of diligent study for learning scribal skills. The same studious work ethic is needed to comprehend how the world works. Wisdom literature depicts the wise scribe as understanding nature, human behavior, and even the gods. It encourages belief in meritocracy: the smartest and most diligent scribes rise to the positions of greatest power and prestige in royal courts.

The Hebrew Bible contains several wisdom books (Proverbs, Ecclesiastes, and Job), and some wisdom psalms (e.g. Pss. 1, 37, 49). It also features stories about four wise sages who epitomize this scribal ideal: Joseph in Genesis, Mordechai in Esther, Daniel and Ezra in the books that bear their names. Within the Pentateuch, Joseph exemplifies the wise sage. He is a foreigner who rises from slavery and imprisonment to the top of the Egyptian bureaucracy because of his wise advice to the king. He then uses that position to save his Israelite relatives from famine (Gen. 36–50). Like Mordechai, Daniel, and Ezra, Joseph is so smart that he can serve the king of Egypt, his own people, and God all faithfully.

The other books of the Pentateuch, however, present a different scribal ideal. The Pentateuch does not say who can copy its text or read its contents. It does, however, specify its official interpreters. A divine oracle to Aaron grants his family the authority to teach Torah to the Israelites and to decide on correct ritual procedures (Lev. 10:10–11). The Pentateuch, then, designates its authoritative interpreters as a hereditary class, the Aaronide priests, rather than a scribal meritocracy. Unlike the stories about Joseph, Mordechai, Daniel, and even the priest-scribe Ezra, the Pentateuch presupposes scribal activity within a temple hierarchy rather than a royal court.

The Pentateuch's ideal scribe is Moses. It portrays Moses writing down the Torah at God's instruction (Exod. 24:4; Deut. 31:9) and repeating it to the Israelites (Exod. 24:7, and all of Deuteronomy).

Figure 5.3 A scribe standing before Barrakib, the king of Samal. Relief from Samal/Zincirli, ca. 730 BCE. In the Vorderasiatisches Museum, Berlin.

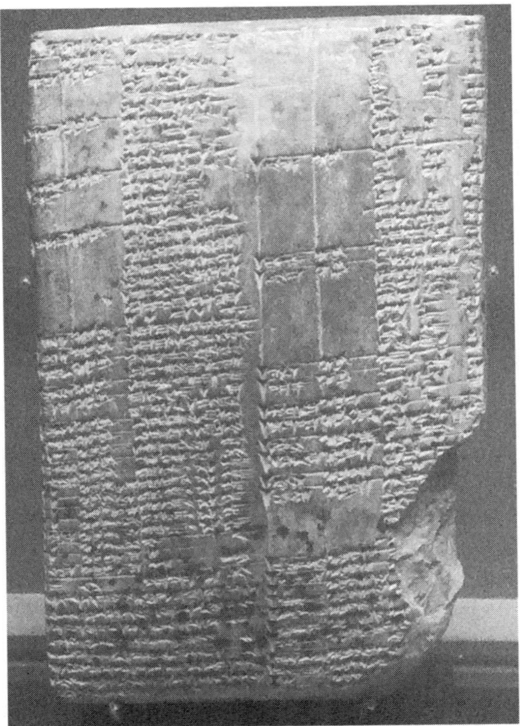

Figure 5.4 Cuneiform tablet cataloguing 68 works of Sumerian literature, probably the collection of a temple library. From Nippur, ca. 2,000 BCE. In the Louvre, Paris.

Moses also acts as a priest, making offerings (Exod. 24:4–6), directing the construction of the Tabernacle (Exod. 35–40), and inaugurating Aaron and his sons as priests (Lev. 8).

Interpreters often claim that the Pentateuch depicts the prophet Moses as superior to priests by doing their job as well as instructing them how to do it. This dichotomy between priests and prophets ignores the fact that priests, prophets, and scribes are often interchangeable in the Hebrew Bible. Both Jeremiah and Ezekiel, for example, were priests and prophets (Jer. 1:1; Ezek. 1:3), and Isaiah seems to have worked in the Jerusalem temple (Isa. 6:1). It is Aaron, not Moses, whom YHWH calls a prophet in the confrontation with Pharaoh (Exod. 7:1). The special privileges and responsibilities of Aaron's family include all these roles: the Pentateuch casts Moses as Aaron's younger brother (Exod. 4:14) and the prophet Miriam as their sister (Exod. 15:20). In the Pentateuch, legitimate religious leadership of all kinds is a family affair (Num. 12).

The Pentateuch's model scribe is therefore not Joseph, but Moses. Moses does not serve any human king: unlike Joseph, he humiliates and defeats the Egyptian Pharaoh. Unlike the Bible's other ideal scribes and wisdom literature generally, Moses is very concerned with the ritual practices of the sanctuary. Moses's speech in the book of Deuteronomy does employ wisdom rhetoric about learning and obedience (Deut. 4:1, 9; 5:1; 6:6–9). Near its end, it portrays Moses most fully as a scribe who writes down the Torah, ensures its preservation and publication, and teaches a song to the Israelites to warn them to obey it (Deut. 31:9–13, 22, 24–29).[151]

Exodus and Deuteronomy cast Moses as the model for all later readers, copyists, and interpreters of scripture. In the Hebrew Bible, nobody follows this model more than Ezra, who is presented as an expert scribe, "skilled in the Torah of Moses" (Ezra 7:6). This description links the two scribes through the text they both control, the Torah written by Moses and read by Ezra. And it casts Moses and Ezra as models to be emulated by future scribes, teachers, and scholars.

The influence of wisdom literature on Deuteronomy has led interpreters to contrast the Deuteronomic scribes with the priests of the P source. The styles and interests of these two parts of the Pentateuch do diverge by emphasizing wisdom and ritual concerns respectively. But it is wrong to distinguish their writers as scribes and priests, and to describe these two groups as pursuing contrary agendas. All ancient literature was produced by scribes. They composed some of it and wrote other texts from dictation, but they produced all of it. Competent scribes wrote and copied many different genres. Wisdom literature for scribal schools and ritual texts for temples were just two of the many kinds of texts that they produced. The distinction between wisdom and ritual texts points to the different settings for which they were intended rather than who wrote them.

Nevertheless, the differences between P and Deuteronomy do indicate that they were produced by two different groups of scribes. The evidence for this is that other biblical books resemble the style and ideas of one or the other Pentateuchal source. 2 Kings and Jeremiah match Deuteronomy very closely, while Ezekiel resembles P. Chronicles, Ezra, and Nehemiah show the influence of both P and Deuteronomy. It is therefore very likely that two different groups of scribes produced much of the literature of the Pentateuch and the Prophets in the sixth or fifth centuries BCE. We can date their work by the fact that 2 Kings, Jeremiah, and Ezekiel all relate historical events down to the middle of the sixth century (2 Kgs. 25:22–30; Jer. 40–44; Ezek. 1:1; 40:1). Scribes in the later fifth and fourth centuries, when Ezra-Nehemiah is set, were using both collections. So it was likely in the sixth or fifth century that scribes wrote P and Deuteronomy and then juxtaposed them to create the Pentateuch.

Linguistics confirms this dating. The language of the Pentateuch is the same Hebrew used by the writers of these other books. Languages change over time. Vocabulary and grammar provide clues for dating texts to the time periods when their language was spoken and written. Many scholars currently distinguish classical biblical Hebrew from late biblical Hebrew. They disagree with each other over whether this distinction can be used to date P or not.[152] Be that as it may, biblical literature provides overwhelming evidence that biblical Hebrew, classical and late, was spoken and written in Judea between the eighth and fifth centuries BCE. Scribes in the fourth and third centuries could still compose in the older idiom. But the scribes who wrote the Dead Sea Scrolls after the third century could not. The Hebrew language of the Pentateuch therefore provides solid evidence that it and any written sources and traditions it uses were written between the eighth and third centuries BCE.

Scribal activities in other ancient cultures show that it is plausible that the Pentateuch was composed from multiple sources that were extensively edited. The different manuscripts of the Babylonian *Gilgamesh Epic* display its revisions and supplementations over more than 1,000 years. The different editions of the book of Jeremiah preserved in Hebrew and Greek manuscripts show these processes at work in biblical books. The Dead Sea Scrolls demonstrate the variety of approaches taken by ancient scribes, from faithful reproduction of scriptural books to extensive rewriting of biblical traditions, including the Pentateuch in works like *Jubilees* and the *Temple Scroll*. Though there is no direct manuscript evidence like this for the editing of the Pentateuch, the manuscripts of these other books provide empirical support for the methods and presuppositions of historical criticism.[153]

The word "scribe" emphasizes writing, but there is strong evidence that written and oral traditions interacted throughout the composition and early stages of the transmission of texts. Ancient scribes often produced copies of texts by memorizing them and then writing them from memory, rather than by copying visually from an original manuscript. This process produced "memory variants" every time a text was reproduced. Variants produced by recalling a memorized text make good sense, unlike graphic and aural mistakes that disrupt a text with accidental omissions or repetitions or with misunderstood signs or sounds. Memory variants instead tend to substitute one homonym for another, add or omit optional particles, and harmonize slight differences. Memory variants appear throughout the biblical manuscript tradition, though late Second Temple texts begin to show signs of standardization, especially of ritual texts.

Memory variants and historical criticism

David Carr observed that the prevalence of memory variants in earlier stages of a tradition will inevitably frustrate attempts to reconstruct which stage came first, because new ones tend to appear every time a text is copied. In Pentateuchal manuscripts, memory variants produced meaningful differences in repeated phrases and sentences both in different Hebrew manuscripts and between the Hebrew and the ancient translations. Memory variants therefore undermine text-critical efforts to reconstruct an "original" text or even to group manuscripts into various families. They also undermine efforts to assign a few words or phrases to different sources.[154]

Comparative study of scribal practices therefore supports the inductive conclusions of historical critics that the Pentateuch was frequently revised in antiquity. It warns, however, that the nature and extent of those changes become harder to determine as units of analysis become smaller. So, on the one hand, the empirical evidence for ancient scribal practices shows that source- and redaction-critical models of the composition of the Pentateuch are plausible. On the other hand, the lack of manuscript evidence and the pervasiveness of memory variants make it implausible to distinguish sources and editorial layers at the scale of phrases and individual verses, and perhaps even of paragraphs.

The Rhetoric of Communal Identity and Priesthood Before Ezra

To write the history of the composition of the Pentateuch, or of any other text, we must be able to connect its contents to the historical period – the people and institutions – that generated it. Texts function as a means of communication between people. To read a text we must always make assumptions about who wrote it and for whom they intended it. Without such connections to human relationships, texts become capable of any and almost all meanings. So even if we know nothing about the authors and their readers, we must guess their motives and intentions. Otherwise, we can play with texts but we cannot read them.

Biblical scholars therefore try to place ancient texts within their original historical contexts. Modern critical scholarship began by recognizing that many biblical texts, and especially the five books of the Pentateuch, do not come from the time periods that they narrate, but from much later in Israel's history. Once the stories are separated from the periods they describe, however, the problem becomes how to find a way to date them at all.

De Wette established a link between literature and history by identifying the law book of Josiah's reform (2 Kgs. 22–23) with the book of Deuteronomy. On the basis of this identification, scholars looked for evidence to date other biblical texts relative to Deuteronomy. The historical value of this identification has made it a staple of biblical scholarship ever since. Deuteronomy, however, does not actually fit the story in 2 Kings very well. Though Josiah destroyed local sanctuaries and centralized temple worship in Jerusalem, which Deuteronomy supports, other aspects of Deuteronomy's teaching are not reflected in Josiah's actions. Furthermore, the king's active role as religious innovator and reformer, while typical of ancient Middle Eastern kings in many cultures, finds no support from Deuteronomy. Many interpreters now think that 2 Kings 22–23 reflects only some precursor to Deuteronomy. The book as we have it was finished later, perhaps in the sixth or fifth century BCE. As a result, the dating of other biblical literature relative to Deuteronomy has become more difficult.

Before that happened, Julius Wellhausen linked the history of the four hypothetical sources of the Pentateuch to the development of Israel's worship practices. By placing the literary sources within distinct periods of religious history, he reconstructed the history of Israel in sequential stages. Wellhausen's religious history of Israel, however, has not survived scathing criticism from twentieth-century historians. They pointed out that nineteenth-century theories of global religious development shaped his account more than did the likely course of ancient religious history. For example, P's ritual concern to mitigate sin and guilt, which Wellhausen identified as a late corruption of Israel's religion, turns out to be common in ritual texts from throughout ancient history. As a result of such criticisms, the four sources of his Documentary Hypothesis have become disconnected from any social and religious contexts.

De Wette and Wellhausen were right to look first for a way to place Pentateuchal literature within the ancient history of Israel. Their desire to write the history of Israel's religion on the basis of the history of the Pentateuch's composition has, however, become methodologically untenable. The history of Israel, or even just of Israel's religion, cannot depend on the very unsure results of Pentateuchal criticism. Pentateuchal research must instead base its work on what we know of Israel's history from other sources.

According to the books of Ezra and Nehemiah, Judean exiles returned and rebuilt Jerusalem in the sixth and fifth centuries BCE. They were initially led by a Davidic prince, Zerubbabel, as well as an Aaronide priest, Joshua ben Jozadak (Ezra 3:1–2). The monarchy of David's dynasty, however, was not reestablished. The Persian Empire appointed governors instead, while Joshua's family ran the temples of YHWH in Judea and, maybe, in Samaria from the sixth century on.

The Pentateuch, of course, is set 1,000 years earlier during Israel's exodus from Egypt, but its description of Israel's social institutions fits the Persian period very well. It provides no governing role for an Israelite king, requiring him only to study Torah under the direction of priests (Deut. 17:14–20). The Pentateuch's laws make no provision for other forms of government either, but simply presuppose groups of village elders and tribal leaders. They establish only one hierarchy in Israel, that of the Aaronide priests. The stories of rebellion against Moses and Aaron in Numbers 11–17 buttress Aaronide institutions of the early Second Temple period, such as the authority of Mosaic law over the teaching of priests and prophets (Num. 12), Levite pre-eminence over other tribes (Num. 17), and Aaronide pre-eminence over other Levites and lay leaders (Num. 16, 18). They establish ritual reminders of these lessons in tassels to be worn on everyone's clothes (Num. 15:37–41). They also show that priests are effective intercessors for the people when Aaron stops a plague with his incense offering (Num. 16:46–48). The Pentateuch's depiction of Israel's social institutions matches literary and linguistic evidence for dating the Pentateuch to the Persian period of the sixth and fifth centuries.

Many of these stories are usually classified as not-P material, and therefore earlier than P according to the Documentary Hypothesis. Some recent reconstructions of the Pentateuch's editorial history date this material, along with much of the rest of Numbers, later than P. The space between Leviticus and Deuteronomy may have been a convenient place to continue adding stories and instructions up to the third century BCE. There is too little evidence to reconstruct how these additions were made. What is clear is that the pro-Aaronide stories of Numbers fit the rhetoric of priestly dynasties during the Persian and Hellenistic periods (as in Zech. 3, 6).[155]

While the Pentateuch's pro-Aaronide rhetoric is most obvious in Exodus, Leviticus, and Numbers, the first and last books of the Pentateuch do not contradict it. Deuteronomy advocates that priests oversee the work of kings and elders (Deut. 17:8–20), and argues fiercely for constraining prophets to agree with what is written in the Torah (Deut. 13). By contrast, Jeremiah's and Ezekiel's sarcastic comments about some priestly laws show that tension over the authority of written Torah was already acute in the sixth century (see Box, "Prophets versus Deuteronomy about written Torah" on p. 232). Other prophetic and psalmic voices questioned the effectiveness of ritual offerings for mitigating Israel's sins (Amos 5:21–27; Isa. 1:11–17; 66:2–4; Ps. 51:16–17). Though the history and details of these debates cannot be reconstructed, this evidence makes it clear that the Pentateuch championed the Aaronides' religious pre-eminence against considerable opposition in the first half of the Second Temple period. The growing power of the Aaronide dynasties at the same time as the Torah's increasing scripturalization shows that their mutual support buttressed the authority of both.

Prophets versus Deuteronomy about written Torah

How can you say, "We are wise because YHWH's Torah is with us," when the lying pen of the scribes has turned it into lies? (Jer. 8:8)

I gave them mandates that are not good and regulations by which they cannot live. I polluted them with their gifts in offering every firstborn to horrify them so they will know that I am YHWH. (Ezek. 20:25–26)

If a prophet or dream interpreter arises among you and gives a sign or prediction that comes true, and then says to you, "Let's worship other gods that you have not known before and serve them," you must not listen to this prophet or dream interpreter. For YHWH your God is testing you to see if you love YHWH your God with all your heart and soul. You must worship YHWH your God and fear God. You must observe God's commandments and listen to God's voice. You must serve and stick to God. (Deut. 13:1–4)

It is more difficult to place Genesis within these debates. Its not-P stories show the patriarchs building altars themselves (Gen. 12:7; 22:13; 35:7, 14), while P describes no offerings until Moses. The latter accords with the Aaronide monopoly over offerings, but it is hard to say if the not-P stories present an alternative view or simply record a previous religious stage before Mosaic Torah and the Tabernacle cult. That is, at least, how they function in the Pentateuch that combines these materials together.

None of this – neither the Pentateuch's endorsement of Aaronide pre-eminence nor the more skeptical voices of prophets and psalmists nor even the household religion of the ancestors – resonates with descriptions of the kingdoms of Israel and Judah in the books of Samuel and Kings. In these books, prophets and priests are on the royal payroll. The books focus on prophets who champion YHWH worship against less faithful kings. The heroes of this history are prophets like Samuel, Nathan, Micaiah, Elijah, Elishah, and Isaiah. Its writers occasionally tell stories of priests who tutor young kings in fidelity to YHWH (e.g. 2 Kgs. 12:2; also 2 Kgs. 11; cf. Deut. 17:14–20). Overall, however, the books of Samuel and Kings cast prophets as the kings' antagonists, while priests are minor characters. These books show the promise and pitfalls of having human monarchs rule a people belonging to the divine king, YHWH, just as the prophet Samuel predicted (1 Sam. 8). The Pentateuch, on the other hand, ignores this theme completely.

Historians have nevertheless tried to read the Pentateuch's emphasis on hereditary priesthood into every mention of priests and Levites in the Deuteronomistic History. Their reconstructions try to trace the rise and fall of different priestly families. Judges 17–18 identifies the priests serving the sanctuary at Dan until the exile of Israel as Levites from Benjamin and descendants of Moses (Judg. 17:7; 18:30). But 1 Kgs. 12:28–32 asserts that King Jeroboam of Israel appointed non-levitical priests at the royal temples in Dan and Bethel, among other places. The most explicit story about a priestly family appears in 1 Sam. 2–4. The priest Eli and his sons served in the Tabernacle while it was at Shiloh. But his sons were corrupt, so they were killed in war as divine punishment. Their descendants were later slaughtered by King Saul at Nob (1 Sam. 22). The only survivor of the family, Abiathar, became one of King David's chief priests (1 Sam 23:6). David's other chief priest was Zadok, whose name leads many historians to identify him as a Jerusalem native (2 Sam. 8:17). King Solomon then banished Abiathar (1 Kgs. 2:26–27), leaving Zadok to take charge of Jerusalem's temple (cf. Ezek. 44:10–15).

The genealogies of the book of 1 Chronicles place Zadok among the descendants of Aaron, so its history conforms to the Pentateuch's claim that Aaronides are the only legitimate priests (1 Chr. 6:1–14, 48–52). But the Deuteronomistic History mentions Aaron's family only once, early on when Aaron's grandson Phineas was priest in Bethel (Judg. 20:27–28). Historians have therefore found in its stories allusions to many different priestly families associated with various shrines in Israel during the settlement and monarchic periods: Elides at Shiloh and Nob, Mushites (descendants of Moses) at Dan, Aaronides at Bethel, and Zadokites in Jerusalem. The term "Levite" seems to reflect a professional role more than a genealogical claim in many of these stories (e.g. Judg. 17:7). Historians' theories of how the Aaronides emerged supreme in the Second Temple period differ starkly from one another.[156]

The Deuteronomistic History, however, does not show much interest in priestly genealogies. It is much more interested in the families of kings. The priests are royal or tribal appointees and their families prosper to the degree that they please human rulers, or YHWH in 1 Sam. 2–4. The stories therefore provide very little evidence for reconstructing the family history of pre-exilic priests. Their dependence on rulers is very different from the independence of Joshua ben Jozadak's dynasty in the Second Temple period, an independence supported by the prophet Zechariah

(Zech. 3, 6) and guaranteed by the Pentateuch's divine grant. If the Deuteronomistic History accurately reflects pre-exilic conditions, then it is clear that the Pentateuch's priestly rhetoric belongs to the time of the Aaronide dynasties in and after the sixth century, and not to the time of the earlier tribes and monarchies.

There is only one prominent institution of Israel's long history in the land that receives explicit and unmistakable support from the Pentateuch. That is the Aaronide priesthood and its dynasties of high priests. Leviticus 8 depicts Moses inaugurating Aaron and his sons as priests, robing them in the special vestments of the priests and high priest (described in detail in Exod. 28), and granting them the exclusive right to preside over the offerings of Israel (Lev. 1–16). Leviticus 9 shows them fulfilling their duties in the Tabernacle in exact obedience to the divine instructions they received from Moses. And Lev. 10:8–11, in a divine revelation to Aaron himself, grants to the high priest the ultimate authority to interpret how the ritual instructions should be put into practice.[157]

It is strange that the Pentateuch does not specifically anticipate the Jerusalem temple, despite the fact that it served as its law book and legitimating authority. Instead, the Pentateuch gives a lot of space to describing the structure and furnishings of a tent sanctuary, the Tabernacle, which did not exist during most of the history of Israel in the land, and may never have existed. We have no dependable evidence that anyone ever tried to build a Tabernacle according to the Pentateuch`s design in the monarchic, exilic, or post-exilic periods (though modern reconstructions have been more plentiful; see Chapter 4).

Unlike the Pentateuch's stories about the Tabernacle and wilderness camp of Israel which read like nostalgia for a lost age, its depiction of the Aaronide priests involves a powerful dynasty in Israel's later history. Though the history of Israel's priesthood is not clear to modern scholars, texts from the Second Temple period claim that the priests who then controlled the Jerusalem temple were descended from Aaron (1 Chr. 6:1–14, 48–52; 9:10–12; Ezra 2:36–39, 61–63). This dynasty, descended from Joshua ben Jozadak and now usually called "the Oniads," probably controlled the high priesthood in Jerusalem for more than 300 years. During that time, the high priests in Jerusalem accumulated secular power as well as religious authority until, in the Hellenistic period, they were the acknowledged political and religious leaders of Judea and the Jews. The same family seems to have held the Samaritan high priesthood as well. When this family lost control of the Jerusalem temple in the turmoil after Seleucid intervention in Judah's religious affairs, it was replaced by another Aaronide priestly family, the Hasmoneans. They gained power by military means and eventually added the title "king" to that of "high priest."[158]

The Pentateuch, most obviously in its ritual instructions and stories in Leviticus 1–16 and Numbers 1–18, legitimized the Aaronide dynasties that governed Jewish and Samaritan temples in the Second Temple period. It was in this same period that the Pentateuch gained scriptural authority, so much so that observing the laws of the written Torah became characteristic of both Samaritan and Jewish religions in later Second Temple times. We have clear evidence then that the Torah functioned as a powerful persuasive agent in this period, but it does not seem to have done so previously. The story of King Josiah's law book is the only hint of written Torah's influence in the entire Deuteronomistic History of the monarchy. Since the Torah explicitly legitimizes the Aaronide priests who wielded increasing power from the sixth century on, the historical context for the composition of the Pentateuch should be sought in this period of Aaronide pre-eminence. So, where Wellhausen began with the altar laws to reconstruct the history of Israel's religion, we should instead begin with the rhetoric of a priestly dynasty seeking to justify its monopoly over Jewish and Samaritan temples to find the historical setting of the Pentateuch.

The Rhetoric of Promise and Threat Before Ezra

The Pentateuch predicts a good or bad future for Israel depending on whether people obey its teachings. Its threats and promises reflect the political rhetoric of the ancient Middle East. Royal inscriptions concluded with promises of divine blessing on those who followed their instructions and threats of divine punishment on those who did not. See, for example, Kurigalzu's inscription quoted in Chapter 2, on p. 26. The rhetoric of sanctions became very violent in suzerainty treaties that powerful kings dictated to their vassals. Their threats often parallel the details of the Pentateuch's threats against disobedient Israelites.

Some scholars have used the resemblance between the Pentateuch's sanctions and the Hittite treaties to date the Pentateuch's composition in the second millennium BCE, that is, to the time of Moses. But other features of the Pentateuch's sanctions, especially their long and detailed threats and their address to the whole people, more closely resemble the first-millennium Neo-Assyrian treaties. For example, King Esarhaddon bound his subjects to teach their children about the treaty.

> *You shall speak to your sons and grandsons, your seed and your seed's seed which shall be born in the future, and give them orders as follows …*

Sanctions in ancient suzerainty treaties

The Pentateuch's sanctions lists (Lev. 26; Deut. 27–30) are similar to the sanctions in treaties from the Hittite Empire (14th–13th centuries BCE) and the Neo-Assyrian Empire (8th–7th centuries BCE). The Pentateuch makes promises as well as threats, like the Hittite treaties, but its threats are long and detailed, like the Neo-Assyrian treaties. For example, King Esarhaddon required his subjects to swear a loyalty oath (*adê*) to his son, Assurbanipal. The copy of this succession treaty found at Tell Tayinat in 2009 included the entire local community.

> *The adê of Esarhaddon, king of Assyria, son of Sennacherib, king of Assyria, with the governor of Kunalia, with the deputy, the majordomo, the scribes, the chariot drivers, the third men, the village managers, the information officers, the prefects, the cohort commanders, the charioteers, the cavalrymen, the exempt, the outriders, the specialists, the shi[eld bearers (?)], the craftsmen, (and) with [all] the men [of his hands], great and small, as many as there are – [wi]th them and with the men who are born after the adê in the [f]uture, from the east [...] to the west, all those over whom Esarhaddon, king of Assyria, exercises kingship and lordship, concerning Assurbanipal, the great crown prince designate, the son of Esarhaddon, king of Assyria.*

The treaty concludes with divine threats against anyone who breaks this loyalty oath.

> *May Aramiš, lord of the city and land of Qarnê (and) lord of the city and land of Aza'i, fill you with green water.*
>
> *May Adad (and) Šāla of Kurba'il create piercing pain and ill health everywhere in your land.*
>
> *May Šarrat-Ekron make a worm fall from your insides.*
>
> *May they strike down you, your sons, and your daughters like a spring lamb or kid.*[159]

Though good examples have survived only from the Hittite and Neo-Assyrian periods, it is likely that treaties like these were widely used in ancient politics. In that case, the Pentateuch's use of treaty rhetoric cannot help date its composition.

The Pentateuch's story-list-sanction rhetoric and especially its detailed lists of sanctions do show how imperial ideology shaped Israel's ideas about its covenant with God. The relationship is imperial, because YHWH demonstrates complete mastery of the world and its nations, most obviously by rescuing Israel from Egypt. Like a conquering king, God demands loyalty from vassals.[160]

These relationships were usually with individual vassal rulers, but some Neo-Assyrian treaties demanded the loyalty of a city's inhabitants or of entire tribes (see Box, "Sanctions in ancient suzerainty treaties" on p. 236). In the same way, God's covenant with the Israelites at Mount Sinai was not with Moses, their leader, but with the people as a whole. (This contrasts with the covenants that God made individually with Abraham and David, which nevertheless had consequences for the people of Israel; see Gen. 15 and 2 Sam. 7.) YHWH's laws and instructions from Mount Sinai addressed all the people (Exod. 19:3–6; 24:3; Deut. 31:11–13) and expected their obedience, both individually and as a group.

The Pentateuch, then, depicts God in the role of Assyrian and Persian rulers who claimed to rule the world and demanded loyalty from their subjects. It describes YHWH as the world's creator and ruler who chose Israel for a special relationship defined by treaty/covenant.

> *If you listen to my voice and keep my covenant, you will be my treasured possession out of all the peoples. The whole world is mine, but you will be a kingdom of priests for me and a holy nation.* (Exod. 19:5–6)

This relationship depends on Israel's obedience, as the lists of sanctions in Leviticus 26 and Deuteronomy 27–30 make explicitly clear.

Many other books of the Hebrew Bible share the view that God rewards and punishes Israel according to how well it keeps the covenant. The books of Hosea, Micah, and Isaiah, in oracles they date to the eighth century BCE, predict the destruction of the kingdoms of Israel and Judah because of the people's infidelity to YHWH. After the Babylonians' conquest of Judah in 597 BCE, the books of Jeremiah and Ezekiel show these prophets warning Judeans that the punishment is not yet over. They predict another, more destructive conquest and the exile of many more people, which in fact occurred in 587 BCE. The books of Kings narrate the kingdoms' history up to and including their utter destruction by the Assyrians and Babylonians to show that the threats of the prophets came true. The Psalter contains hymns that confess this history and ask for God's mercy (e.g. Ps. 106). Much of the Hebrew Bible explains the catastrophic history of the kingdoms of Israel and Judah as God's punishment of Israel because they broke the covenant by worshipping other gods and by oppressing their own people.

Sanctions in the Hebrew Bible outside the Pentateuch

The rhetoric of divine sanctions is prominent in the prophets, in history books, and in the psalms. For example:

Hear the word of YHWH, people of Israel;
for YHWH indicts those living in the land.
There is no faithfulness or loving kindness
or knowledge of God in the land. ...
My people are destroyed for lack of knowledge.
Because you have rejected knowledge,
I reject you as my priest.
Because you have forgotten your God's Torah,
I will forget your children, I will! (Hos. 4:1, 6)

YHWH sent bands of the Chaldeans, Arameans, Moabites, and Ammonites against Judah to destroy it, according to YHWH's word spoken through his servants, the prophets. It was certainly by YHWH's command that this happened to Judah to take them away, because of the sins of Manasseh and everything he did, for the innocent blood that he shed ..., which YHWH was not willing to forgive. (2 Kgs. 24:2–4)

They polluted themselves by their actions,
and prostituted themselves by their deeds.
Then YHWH's anger burned against his people,
and he abhorred his inheritance;
YHWH handed them over to the nations,
so that their enemies ruled over them. (Ps. 106:39–41)

Other ancient Middle Eastern texts share the Hebrew Bible's tendency to explain historical events as reward or punishment from the gods. They depict the successes or failures of kings as due to their piety or impiety, usually as measured by their gifts to temples. For example, the sixth-century Weidner Chronicle explains the fortunes of a long list of Babylonian kings by their treatment of the temple of Marduk and concludes:

Whosoever offends the gods of this city, his star will not stand in the sky.[161]

Within the biblical storyline, the Pentateuch provides the first warnings that Israel's history as YHWH's "treasured possession" may not turn out well. Both Leviticus and Deuteronomy explicitly threaten expulsion from the land God has given Israel (Lev. 26:32–39; Deut. 28:64–68). The warnings of the prophets then become repetitions of threats already voiced by

Moses. The Deuteronomistic History's narration of the kingdoms' destruction demonstrates that these predictions came true. All this literature shows how, in the middle of the first millennium BCE, some Judeans accepted and internalized responsibility for their catastrophic history. They were already committing themselves to observe the covenant with God better than their ancestors (Neh. 9–10) when they began to ritualize the Pentateuch as scripture in the time of Ezra (Neh. 8).

The Rhetoric of Law Before Ezra

In the rhetoric of ancient Wisdom literature, the ideal life was living according to eternal principles. Egyptian culture combined truth and justice in one idea, *ma'at*, which should direct the behavior of people, kings, and gods. Similarly, in the Hebrew Bible, Proverbs recommends *torah* as the guide to a good and righteous life.

> *The torah of the wise is a fountain of life to avoid the traps of death.* (Prov. 13:14)
> *My son, listen to your father's instruction; do not reject your mother's torah.* (Prov. 1:8)

The word *torah* here does not mean the Pentateuch or any written text. The word instead describes a way of life in accord with wisdom and divine will. This sense of *torah* as the ideal way of life colors all more specific uses of the term.

Ancient royal rhetoric used law as a political ideal to cast kings as legitimate and just rulers. The Babylonian usurper, Hammurabi, collected and published laws, *dinu* in Akkadian, to show that his rule was just and legitimate. Persian emperors boasted that they had established justice, *da'at* in Aramaic, throughout the world. But as we have seen, written law did not govern legal practice prior to the last few centuries BCE.

Instead, ancient people's concern to follow written rules focused on ritual instructions. Old written texts assured people that rituals were being conducted in the traditional way, as required by the gods. See the examples quoted on pp. 116–118. This same theme of an old text guiding the revival of rituals plays a central role in the story of Josiah's reforms (2 Kgs. 22–23). Recent scholarship has cast doubt on identifying Josiah's law book with Deuteronomy. Nevertheless, the story plausibly credits the growing influence of written law in Israel to concerns for ritual accuracy. That matches the concerns expressed in many other ancient cultures, as well as the ritual use to which Torah was put in the early Second Temple period. Ritual concern obviously guided the composers and editors of the Pentateuch who placed ritual rules at its center in Exodus, Leviticus, and Numbers.

The traditions of Mesopotamian law also influenced the contents of the Pentateuch. Legal collections from Sumerian, Babylonian, Assyrian, and Hittite cultures reflect a common legal tradition starting already in the third millennium BCE. Their connections appear in their similar way of drafting laws and the similar cases that appear in each collection. These collections of laws did not direct the proceedings of law courts, which decided cases based on custom rather than written law. They instead reflect an academic tradition of thinking about law by compiling lists of legal decisions. The same tradition of legal reflection and many of the same cases appear also in the Pentateuch.[162]

Interaction with Mesopotamian legal tradition is especially evident in the Covenant Code (Exod. 21–23). The Documentary Hypothesis maintained that the Covenant Code was the oldest of the Pentateuch's three legal collections. Its laws were revised and expanded by Deuteronomy 12–26, whose laws were in turn modified in the Holiness Code (Lev. 17–27). Despite the collapse of support for the Documentary Hypothesis and some challenges to this sequence of legal collections, this remains the most plausible reconstruction of the history of biblical law. The Covenant Code reflects a rural society and a barter economy. It is closest to the old Mesopotamian legal tradition, even though collections such as Hammurabi's reflect a more urban society. Deuteronomy revises rules from Exodus to fit a later, more stratified culture. The Holiness Code revises Deuteronomy's provisions. It also describes an explicit problem of legal interpretation, about applying ritual rules to non-Israelites (Lev. 24:10–23). Stories like this about legal interpretation appear only in priestly texts and contexts of the Pentateuch (Lev. 10:16–20; Num. 9:6–14; 27:1–11; 36:1–12). The Pentateuch's three legal collections then show clear evidence of developing over time towards greater social complexity and legal sophistication.[163]

Were the laws of Deuteronomy and of the Holiness Code written to replace their predecessors or to supplement them? Contemporary scholars give opposite answers to this question. There is less debate about the fact that the editing of the law collections into the Pentateuch as a whole did very little to smooth out the differences between them. Just as the Pentateuch includes two or three different versions of some stories, it includes three different legal collections. They clearly come from different sources, but that fact alone does not explain the editors' tolerance for their contradictions. The Pentateuch stands out from ancient Mesopotamian collections and from subsequent Jewish and Christian law in its tolerance for contradictory legal rules.

It seems likely, therefore, that some external circumstance must have led the editors of the Pentateuch to combine contradictory stories and laws without harmonizing them. We do not have any information about those circumstances. Peter Frei suggested that the Persian Empire required communities to submit one local law code for imperial authorization. In that case, Judeans may have placed their rival law codes together in the Pentateuch as a compromise document to meet this imperial demand. However, there is no evidence that the Persians required imperial authorization of local laws, though they do seem to have provided it at the request of particular communities.[164] Nor does this theory explain the presence of so many stories in the Pentateuch, including multiple versions of the same story. Nevertheless, the Pentateuch seems to be a compromise document cobbled together from the narrative and legal traditions of different groups. These groups clearly included priests on the one hand (P) and lay leaders on the other (Deuteronomy), and Judeans and Samaritans, and perhaps other divisions within these Persian period communities. The resulting Pentateuch contains three distinct legal collections as well as three narrative traditions and does not remove their repetitions and contradictions.

The three legal collections do not exhaust all of the Pentateuch's lists of instructions. It also includes three versions of the Ten Commandments in Exodus 20, 34, and Deuteronomy 5, the Passover instructions in Exodus 12–13, and laws scattered through the stories of Genesis and Numbers. P's instructions for building and furnishing the Tabernacle (Exod. 25–31), for making offerings (Lev. 1–7), and for maintaining purity (Lev. 11–16) are the longest sets of rules in the Pentateuch, especially when combined with stories that narrate their fulfillment (Exod. 35–40; Lev. 8–10). P's ritual instructions do not duplicate the regulations of the three law codes, though laws in Numbers supplement and modify some of P's legislation.

Perhaps the dominance of P's unrivaled ritual legislation in Exodus and Leviticus hints at the circumstances behind the Pentateuch's contradictory contents. Both the Middle Eastern cultural context and the history of Second Temple Judaism indicate that only written rules for rituals were regarded as normative prior to the third or second centuries BCE. People were concerned to do what written texts required only when they involved rituals. The scribes who assembled the Pentateuch expected P's ritual rules to be normative, but not its other legal collections and certainly not its stories. This expectation may have provided the room to incorporate traditions from different groups without harmonizing them in order to get those groups to agree to follow P's ritual instructions. It is clear that construction and maintenance of the temple and its rituals were of major concern to the priests, prophets, and lay leaders of Judea and

Samaria in the early Second Temple period, as the books of Haggai, Zechariah, Ezra, and Nehemiah attest.

This explanation does not account for the fact that the three legal collections also contain ritual rules that contradict each other, such as the altar laws of Exod. 20:21–23, 27:1–8, Lev. 17:2–9, and Deut. 12:13–27. So do the stories: compare the rules for eating the Passover meal at home in Exodus 12 with the requirement to eat it at the sanctuary in Deut. 16:1–8. Nevertheless, P's ritual instructions dominate the center of the Pentateuch without much contradiction. The book of Numbers presents some different instructions, but many of these are described explicitly as extensions or modifications of previous rules. For example, YHWH provides an alternative date for celebrating Passover to people who cannot participate at the usual time because they are unclean (Num. 9:1–14).

It is likely, therefore, that the effort to agree to a single written law to govern the rituals of the YHWH temples in Judea and Samaria led to including repetitive and contradictory legal codes and narratives in the Pentateuch. Perhaps this compromise aimed to gain Persian imperial authorization of this temple law, or maybe it was needed just to ensure economic support of the temples from different local communities. At any rate, the editors were not concerned by the legal and narrative contradictions because only written ritual rules were regarded as normative. Any lingering problems due to contradictions could be resolved later. P's laws grant the Aaronide priests the authority to settle ritual problems (Lev. 10:9–11) and the stories of Numbers provide examples of how to do so (Num. 9, 27, 36). These stories may be later additions that begin to deal with how to reconcile the Pentateuch's contradictions. That problem has preoccupied interpreters from the later Second Temple period until today.

The focus on ritual offerings at the center of the Pentateuch does not mean that we know exactly how these rituals developed and functioned. P's instructions do not include all the steps necessary to conduct the rituals. For example, they do not say how to kill the oxen, sheep, and goats being presented as offerings. Contrary to modern ideas about the word "sacrifice," the biblical rules do not emphasize killing. P's instructions focus instead on the kinds and amounts of offerings, the kinds of occasions that require offerings, and the distribution of offering food between the altar, the priests and lay worshippers.[165]

Older theories of sacrifice that place Israel's offerings within an evolution of human religion and society have been disproven by comparative evidence from other ancient cultures. It is now clear that Israel's offering rituals were similar to those that preceded them, such as the rituals in Ugaritic texts from the late second millennium BCE, and to those that followed them in time, such as the civic rituals of the Greeks and Romans. Israel's temples, like those in Greece, did participate in a religious trend to grill meat and grain offerings on open-air altars. This trend began in Anatolia and Syria in the early second millennium and gradually spread to Canaan/Israel/Palestine and to Greece and Rome, as confirmed by archeology and art as well as literary references. Altars for grilling meat eventually became popular even in the urban centers of Mesopotamia and Egypt, whose older rites offered tables full of food to the gods but did not cook it in their presence. We do not know what changes in theological ideas, if any, accompanied this ritual trend.[166]

The Pentateuch's stories and instructions also match other ancient cultures by highlighting the gender of priests and of offering animals. More strictly than most other cultures, the Pentateuch requires that Israel's priests must be men and from a particular patriarchal lineage, that of Aaron. The most prestigious offerings are male animals (Gen. 22:13; Lev. 1:3, 10). Women can make offerings and, in fact, must do so after they give birth (Lev. 12), though the Pentateuch's offering instructions generally exclude mothers. Nicole Ruane has demonstrated that Israel's rituals specifically exclude new mothers and potential mothers on their menstrual periods (Lev. 12, 15), as well as mother animals together with their newborns (Lev. 22:27–28). The Pentateuch's offering rules do not include food products from mother animals, such as milk and eggs.[167]

Because customs such as burning altars and the exclusion of mothers echo in other ancient cultures, we know these themes characterized Israel's religion prior to and apart from the writing of P's ritual instructions. The rhetorical agendas behind biblical legislation and stories, however, interfere with reconstructing ancient Israel's ritual practices in much more detail, because they tell us what *should* happen rather than what *did* happen. Interpretation is limited instead to trying to understand why the Pentateuch emphasizes rituals and how its ritual instructions have influenced its listeners and readers.[168]

The Rhetoric of Origins Before Ezra

The Pentateuch began to be ritualized as scripture in the fifth or fourth centuries BCE. Its largest component parts, P and Deuteronomy, seem to reflect conditions in the Babylonian Exile or early Second Temple period, that is, the sixth and fifth centuries BCE. However, their stories in Exodus, Leviticus, Numbers, and Deuteronomy tell of events almost 1,000 years earlier. The stories of Genesis go back even further. One historical challenge in interpreting the Pentateuch, then, is whether we can reconstruct the development of its stories during that long period of time between the events and the documents that record them.

The stories of the Pentateuch show many signs of different sources and extensive editing. It is clear that older material has been incorporated in multiple stages to create the Pentateuch as we have it. The major blocks of material, P, not-P, and Deuteronomy, can be separated reliably by their literary styles and typical themes over the large scale of the five books. The more one focuses on details in individual paragraphs or verses, however, the more subjective these distinctions become. On this smaller scale, it has proven impossible to find criteria by which different interpreters can consistently reconstruct the chronological development of sources and editions.

The search for external evidence to support the Pentateuch's stories has also not been very successful. Archeologists have looked in vain for any signs of Israel's presence in Egypt. Asiatic people from the north-east show up frequently in Egyptian art, which distinguishes them from Egyptians and Africans by the style of their hair, beards, and clothes. Egyptian texts also document the presence of many Asiatics in Egypt in the second and first millennia. There was much travel and trade between Egypt and the eastern Mediterranean coast throughout this time, just as biblical stories indicate (e.g. Gen. 12:10; 47:27). However, only one second-millennium Egyptian text explicitly mentions Israel. The Merneptah Stele from 1208 BCE lists Israel among the people Pharaoh Merneptah defeated.

> *Canaan is plundered, Ashkelon is carried off, and Gezer is captured. Yenoam is made into non-existence; Israel is wasted, its seed is not; and Hurru has become a widow because of Egypt.*[169]

Though historians dismiss Merneptah's claims as propaganda and some doubt that the name is really "Israel," this inscription provides the most plausible piece of evidence for the existence of a people calling themselves Israel in the late second millennium.[170]

Biblical interpreters have used details in the story of the exodus from Egypt to try to corroborate the Pentateuch's account. The name of the Egyptian city, "Raʿamses," in Exod. 1:11 echoes the throne names of 11 Egyptian kings from the thirteenth through the eleventh centuries. The names of Moses, Aaron, and Phineas are all Egyptian in origin, rather than Hebrew. These details indicate that Israel's traditions transmitted a genuine memory of Egyptian geography and culture. However, Egyptian trade, politics, and culture remained influential in Israel and Judah throughout the first millennium, too. The Pentateuch's familiarity with the land of Egypt and the Egyptian language does not help date its composition.

The stories of ancestors in Genesis portray a time and place very different from Israel's later history. Nevertheless, they sometimes project first-millennium conditions into stories that are supposed to have taken place in the preceding second millennium, such as the presence of Chaldeans in lower Mesopotamia (Gen. 11:31) and Philistines in Canaan (21:34; 26:1). It is difficult to decide if such anachronisms were produced by later editors of older stories or if the stories themselves come from the time reflected by these references.

One archeological discovery provided spectacular confirmation about one Pentateuchal character. Balaam son of Beor appears in Numbers 22–24 as a non-Israelite prophet living in trans-Jordan. He is hired to curse Israel, but YHWH forces him to bless Israel instead. In 1967, archeologists discovered at Tell Deir Alla in Jordan an inscription on plaster from the eighth century BCE. It begins with the lines:

> *The misfortunes of the Book of Balaam, son of Beor. A divine seer was he. The gods came to him at night, And he beheld a vision in accordance with El's utterance. They said to Balaam, son of Beor: "So will it be done, with naught surviving, No one has seen [the likes of] what you have heard!" ...*[171]

Though not the same oracles as recorded in Numbers 23–24, the Deir Alla inscription shows that Balaam was a well-known prophet in trans-Jordan in the early first millennium.

Other books of the Hebrew Bible give mixed evidence that Pentateuchal traditions were known in the kingdoms of Israel and Judah before the Babylonian Exile. Hosea 12 refers to many episodes in Jacob's life and alludes to the festival of *Sukkot*/Booths (Hos. 12:9). It also alludes to the exodus from Egypt and to Moses, though without naming him.

> *I am YHWH your God from the land of Egypt. ...*
> *By a prophet YHWH brought Israel from Egypt,*
> *and by a prophet he was guarded.* (Hos. 12:9, 13; also 11:1)

The books of Samuel and Micah name Moses and Aaron, and once Miriam, as the leaders of Israel's exodus from Egypt (1 Sam. 12:6, 8; Mic. 6:4). Micah also refers to Abraham (Mic. 7:20), the only reference to this ancestor in the pre-exilic prophets. Just as in the Pentateuch, dating the composition of these verses in Hosea, Micah, and Samuel is difficult and controversial. Nevertheless, they hint that the story of Jacob and of the exodus was known to Israelites and Judeans prior to the Babylonian Exile. The exilic prophets, Jeremiah, Ezekiel, and Deutero-Isaiah, as well as the Deuteronomistic History, use themes from the exodus and ancestral stories much more often. So these stories apparently increased in circulation in the sixth century.

The major Pentateuchal theme of God giving the Torah to Israel on Mount Sinai, however, is missing from prophetic literature earlier than the fifth century. Some poetic texts depict YHWH as "from Sinai" (Judg. 5:4–5; Ps. 68:9, 18; Deut. 33:2). But the revelation of Torah there or in any other location appears only in texts that reflect the influence of Deuteronomy or P. The story of Moses receiving the Torah at Mount Sinai does not seem to have been widely known before the Babylonian Exile, if at all.

These observations support the conclusions of recent redaction critics that the Pentateuch was composed by editing together independent blocks of tradition, rather than the source-critical claim that several authors composed parallel accounts stretching from the stories of Genesis to Joshua. Some of these independent traditions were probably known in Israel's monarchic period, such as the stories about Jacob and about Israel's exodus from Egypt. Others do not appear in older texts and were not widely known before the Exile. They may have been composed when the blocks of traditions began to be combined in the sixth and fifth centuries BCE. This later material includes the giving of Torah at Sinai, as well as Genesis's stories of world origins.

This account of the Pentateuch's composition explains why Moses and Aaron do not appear prominently in other biblical books. Prophetic books mention Moses by name only four times and Aaron only once. It is especially surprising that neither name appears in Ezekiel, a book that has much in common with P. The Psalms contain more references to both of them, and they are frequently mentioned in Chronicles, Ezra, and Nehemiah, all books that postdate the Pentateuch and reflect its influence. Characters from stories in Genesis 1–11 appear only in literature from the sixth century and later. Deutero-Isaiah and Ezekiel mention Noah. But characters that have generated so much interest in post-biblical Judaism and Christianity – such as Adam, Eve, Cain, and Abel – get mentioned only in the Pentateuch and in literature from the Second Temple period.

Influence from other Middle Eastern literary traditions provides another hint of the historical setting of the Pentateuch's writers. Neo-Assyrian treaties shaped the portrayal of the Sinai covenant and its contents (Exod. 19–24; Deuteronomy). The story of Noah's flood (Gen. 6–8) follows the plot of the Mesopotamian flood story closely but modifies it to match Israel's theology, as we can see by comparing it with *Atrahasis* and *Gilgamesh*. The story of the tower of Babel (Gen. 11) comments sarcastically on the characteristic architecture of Mesopotamian cities. P's story of world creation (Gen. 1) also seems to react against widespread stories of creation through reproduction and warfare, such as the Babylonian creation epic, *Enuma Elish*. So the portions of the Pentateuchal story that are unparalleled in earlier biblical literature are more likely than others to reflect knowledge of foreign literature.

The beginning of Exodus also uses Mesopotamian literary traditions. The story of the baby Moses being cast adrift on a river and adopted by an Egyptian princess sounds similar to the birth legend of King Sargon of Akkad. Sargon ruled in the third millennium BCE. He was the first Akkadian king to conquer and unite the cities of Mesopotamia, so he was remembered as a model king in later Akkadian literature. An eighth-century Assyrian king even took the name, Sargon, as his own throne name. He sponsored the reproduction of the birth legend of the earlier Sargon in first-millennium Akkadian texts (see Box, "The birth legend of King Sargon"). By adopting this storyline for Moses, the writers of Exod. 2:1–10 depict him as destined to defeat powerful enemies. They foreshadow his conflict with Egypt's king, Pharaoh.

The birth legend of King Sargon

My mother, the high priestess, conceived me, she bore me in secret.
She placed me in a reed basket, she sealed my hatch with pitch.
She left me to the river, whence I could not come up.
The river carried me off, it brought me to Aqqi, drawer of water.
Aqqi, drawer of water, brought me up as he dipped his bucket.
Aqqi, drawer of water, raised me as his adopted son.
Aqqi, drawer of water, set (me) to his orchard work.
During my orchard work, Ishtar loved me, ...[172]

Historians have frequently cited such parallels to date the composition of these Pentateuchal stories to the sixth-century Babylonian Exile. In exile, Judean scribes would have been exposed to Mesopotamian culture and literature. It should be kept in mind, however, that exile lasted longer than the 70 years remembered by biblical tradition. Northern Israelites were exiled already by the Assyrians in 701 BCE. For the next four centuries, Judah existed in dependence on Mesopotamian empires and, briefly, on Egypt. There were probably many opportunities for Judean scribes to learn about these traditions, not least by being employed in imperial bureaucracies. Biblical books depict Daniel, Mordechai, Ezra, and Nehemiah as serving Babylonian and Persian rulers. Nevertheless, the Pentateuch's knowledge of other cultures and literatures is more noticeable in the creation and Sinai stories that are not reflected in older biblical literature. This observation reinforces the impression that they date from the sixth and fifth centuries BCE when Judea was ruled by the Babylonians and Persians.

The way in which editors assembled the Pentateuch is evident from themes that structure the five books. One way that editors organized the Pentateuch, and especially Genesis, was with genealogies. Even world creation gets a genealogical summary.

> *These are the generations of the heavens and the earth when they were created.* (Gen. 2:4)

Each of the following cycles of stories begins with genealogies, called *toledot* in Hebrew (see p. 32). As we have seen, the contents of these stories are diverse in style and theme. The genealogies therefore stand out as an editorial framework around material from diverse sources. The genealogies themselves probably come from different written and oral sources. Editors have used them to unite stories about ancestral and world origins into the book of Genesis. But genealogy does not seem to have originally connected Israel's stories of the past. The genealogical framework was constructed by P and maybe other editors to unite these stories into a single timeline.[173]

Exodus begins by evoking this genealogical history (Exod. 1:1–6). Numbers carries it further by listing the generation of Israelite men who followed Moses out of Egypt (Num. 1, 3–4) and, later, the next generation born in the wilderness (Num. 26).[174] The Pentateuch's story of Israel's origin is thus arranged across four generations of ancestors in Genesis and two wilderness generations in Exodus, Leviticus, Numbers, and Deuteronomy.

Editors also used God's promises to the ancestors to unite the stories of Genesis with the rest of the Pentateuch. God swore to give the land to the descendants of Abraham, Isaac, and Jacob according to Gen. 50:24, Exod. 32:13; 33:1, Num. 32:11, and Deut. 34:4. The promise of land and descendants gets repeated to the patriarchs individually many times. Though this promise plays a major role in the structure of some chapters (e.g. Gen. 15, 17), in many other places it looks like an editorial addition that links materials together (e.g. Gen. 12:1–3; 26:2–5; 35:11–12). The promise to the ancestors then gets cited as motivation for God's rescue of Israel from Egypt, thus linking stories about ancestors and exodus together (Exod. 2:24; 6:8; 32:13).

God's promises are in some places described as oaths and in other places as covenants. So their editorial use to tie the stories of Genesis together and to the rest of the Pentateuch probably took place in several stages. It is possible that P was the first editor to use genealogies and the promise theme to unite the ancestral stories with the exodus and Sinai stories. Later editors added more links when they juxtaposed P and Deuteronomy.[175] Or maybe it was P who used them to bring not-P stories and Deuteronomy together with his own priestly material to create the first version of the Pentateuch. It is very difficult to be conclusive about such reconstructions based only on inductive arguments from the literature as we have it.

What is much clearer is that the combined Pentateuch emphasizes the origins of Torah in ancient tablets given by God to Moses and deposited in Israel's Ark of the Covenant. It also claims that Moses wrote a Torah scroll that Israel also kept beside the Ark. These claims are made by all three blocks of Pentateuchal materials: P, not-P, and D. So though the story of Torah at Sinai is not found in other biblical books older than Deuteronomy and P, it forms a common foundation between the three blocks of Pentateuchal traditions. Deuteronomy also requires the iconic and performative ritualization of Torah explicitly, and the semantic dimension implicitly, in ways that later became characteristic of religious scriptures. As a result, the Pentateuch proclaims the supernatural origins of Torah by both modeling and requiring its iconic, performative, and semantic ritualization.

Ritualizing Decalogue and Torah in Pentateuchal traditions

From P: Exod. 25, 31, 37
From not-P: Exod. 24, 32, 34
From D: Deut. 6, 10, 31

Among the Pentateuch's blocks of material, not-P and Deuteronomy especially emphasize the performative dimension (Exod. 24; Deut. 6, 31). Ritualizing the semantic dimension of interpretation is implicit throughout the Pentateuch's rhetoric of obeying its laws and instructions. However, it is the Torah's iconic form as Decalogue tablets in the Ark of the Covenant that all three blocks of Sinai material ritualize most explicitly. All three blocks of tradition also label their laws as spoken by God at Sinai to identify Torah scrolls with the tablets and the ark. Deuteronomy makes this identification explicit by having the Torah scroll placed next to the ark in the Tabernacle (Deut. 31:26). These literary examples of ritualizing the Torah's iconic dimension legitimize the Pentateuch's origins as well as the people and institutions associated with it.

So, in an important sense, scripture did begin with the story of Moses receiving the Torah on Mount Sinai. Though we cannot trace the events it narrates back to the time of Moses, we can trace the ritual practices it so vividly describes to the time of Ezra. By showing Moses enshrining Torah in the ark and reading it to the Israelites, receiving their unanimous agreement to its commandments, and demanding that they obey them, the story of Moses and Israel at Mount Sinai inscribed how to ritualize scripture into Jewish and Christian imaginations. This story has functioned ever since Ezra's time to ground their scriptural practices in ritual behavior that Deuteronomy also explicitly commands. In this story and these commandments lie the origins of Western scriptures.

6

SCRIPTURES
FROM TORAH TO BIBLE

This book has used the time of Ezra as a pivot between the history of the Torah as scripture and the Pentateuch's pre-scriptural history. Nehemiah 8's story of reading the Torah scroll aloud shows Ezra ritualizing all three textual dimensions. We have seen that the Pentateuch was increasingly ritualized in these three ways after Ezra's time. The iconic and performative dimensions may have been ritualized by Josiah 200 years earlier and the book of Deuteronomy requires their ritualization. But regular three-dimensional ritualization of the Torah begins with Ezra's story. Ritualization in the iconic, performative, and semantic dimensions is a distinguishing characteristic of scriptures in later religious communities. So it appears that scripturalizing Torah began in the time of Ezra.

Scripturalization and Canonization

Biblical scholars usually describe the development of scripture as a process of "canonization." The word "canon" has been used since the fourth century CE to refer to the list of books in Christian scripture. Discussions

Understanding the Pentateuch as a Scripture, First Edition. James W. Watts.

of canonization focus on the contents of scripture and the criteria by which books were selected or rejected. Current studies also discuss the evolution of concepts about scripture and canons.[176] Ancient lists of canonical books are, however, after-the-fact rationalizations for using some books and not others. They reflect the fact that some books have already been scripturalized rather than how it began.

This book had instead sifted the evidence for the origins and growth of Jewish and Christian scriptures by focusing on how religious communities ritualize texts. As we have seen, the Pentateuch commands and models its own ritualization. To the best of our knowledge, the story of Ezra's reading first imitated that model in all three textual dimensions, and began a scripturalizing trend that has continued ever since.

It is hard to say whether Ezra himself brought about this development. Our information about the Persian period in Judea is very limited. There are also many questions about the composition of the books of Ezra and Nehemiah. So we cannot say whether Ezra scripturalized the Torah or whether his story simply reflects prevailing practices at the time.

What is clear is that Ezra's actions exemplify what the Pentateuch itself commands and models in Moses's behavior. After Nehemiah 8's portrayal of Ezra in the fifth or fourth centuries BCE, ritualization of the Torah's three dimensions gradually grew in Second Temple Judaism. Then Ezra's story became a model of how to embody Moses's ideal for religious leaders of later millennia.

Jewish and Christian scripturalization, however, changed direction at least three other times in antiquity. Each time is associated with the actions of a particular individual. Like Ezra, we cannot know whether these people actually caused the changes or just exemplify developments around them. Associating stages of scripturalization with these individuals highlights how human choices have shaped the history of scripture. Scripturalization was not just a gradual development. Scripturalizing choices could have been made differently and, in fact, were decided differently by other groups of people.

Biblical scripturalizing changed direction four times at three different points in ancient history. Besides the time of Ezra in the fifth century BCE, it changed in the time of Judah Maccabee in the second century BCE and in the time of Judah *ha-Nasi* and Bishop Irenaeus at the end of the second century CE. Each change in the scriptures was accompanied by changes in religious leadership. A New Testament writer already observed this connection.

> *When there is a change in the priesthood, there is necessarily a change in the law as well* (Heb. 7:12 NRSV).

When Jewish and Christian scriptures changed

Torah/Pentateuch	Ezra	ca. 400 BCE
Prophets, histories, psalms	Judah Maccabee	ca. 150 BCE
Mishnah	Judah *ha-Nasi*	ca. 200 CE
Gospels	Irenaeus	ca. 200 CE

In the Time of Judah Maccabee

In the second century BCE, King Antiochus IV Epiphanes tried to unify the Seleucid Empire by forcing Hellenistic (Greek) cultural institutions onto Judea. According to the books of 1 and 2 Maccabees, many Judeans embraced Greek sports and educational institutions. But the Seleucids also suppressed traditional Jewish religious practices and required offerings to Greek gods in Judean villages and on the altar of the Jerusalem temple (1 Macc. 1). That provoked violent resistance from a country priest and his sons, who were nicknamed the *Maccabees* "hammers." From 167 to 164 BCE, they led an armed revolt against the Seleucid Empire (1 Macc. 2–4).

As a result of the Maccabean Revolt, Judea became semi-autonomous and, eventually, independent. War continued for two more decades, during which the Maccabean brothers Judah, Jonathan, and Simon established themselves as dynastic rulers of Judea. This family is usually called "the Hasmoneans" after one of their ancestors. Starting with Jonathan, the Hasmoneans took the title and functions of high priest for themselves. Simon's grandsons also took the title "king." For the first time in almost 500 years, Jewish kings ruled an independent Judea. The Hasmonean kingdom lasted for a century until Rome conquered it in 63 BCE.

The sources do not give us much information about the Hasmoneans' influence over Judean literature. One brief story tells of Judah Maccabee collecting books in Jerusalem that had been scattered in the war (2 Macc. 2:13–15). The Hasmonean period seems to coincide with the growing influence of many of the books classified as "prophets" and "writings" in the Tanak. ("Tanak," a common term for Jewish scriptures, is an acronym from the names of its three sections: *Torah* "law," *Nevi'im* "prophets," and *Ketuvim* "writings.") As Aaronide priests, the Hasmoneans benefitted from the Pentateuch's rhetoric authorizing their priesthood and control of the Jerusalem temple. David Carr has argued that as kings of a wider territory around Jerusalem, they also needed to counter the influence of Hellenistic literature among upper-class lay people. To that end, they seem to have authorized a larger and more diverse collection of Hebrew texts to define classical Jewish culture and education over against the Hellenistic model.[177]

The Libraries of Nehemiah and Judah Maccabee

Reported in the records and in the memoirs of Nehemiah … that he founded a library and collected the books about the kings and prophets, and the writings of David, and letters of kings about votive offerings. In the same way Judah also collected all the books that had been lost on account of the war that had come upon us, and they are in our possession. So if you have need of them, send people to get them for you. (2 Macc. 2:13–15 NRSV)

The reference in 2 Maccabees refers to books about kings and prophets, which describes rather well the histories and oracular collections in the second division of the Tanak. "The writings of David" refers to Psalms. The contents of the Tanak show that the Hasmoneans also distinguished these books by language and age. Only books apparently written before the fourth century and mostly in Hebrew were counted as among "the Prophets." (The division into "Prophets and Writings" probably developed later.) Hebrew was no longer the vernacular language of Judea, so it now became a distinguishing mark of "classical" Jewish literature. The books' antiquity associated them with the age of prophecy, which was believed to have ended several centuries before the Maccabean Revolt.

The Hasmoneans fought wars to defend Judea's independence and tried to extend their territory into the lands of the old northern kingdom of Israel. This political context gave new importance to the books of Joshua, Samuel, and Kings. These histories demonstrated the antiquity of Judean territorial claims and political independence. Prophetic books showed Jewish oracular authority, poetic books demonstrated literary genius, and wisdom literature paraded learned Jewish scholarship. The books now divided between the Prophets and the Writings thus provided examples of classical Jewish learning to compete with Hellenistic literature.

Starting in the Hasmonean period in the second and first centuries BCE, mastery of Torah and Prophets became the Jewish educational ideal for priests and lay people alike. Though only elite families had the resources to master these texts, this ideal itself became a hallmark of Jewish identity and of resistance to Hellenistic culture. Jews now had a national literature to demonstrate the antiquity and legitimacy of their religious and political claims.

The Samaritans frequently found themselves at odds with the Jerusalem community during the Second Temple period, according to Jewish books recounting this history (Ezra, Nehemiah, 1 Maccabees, and Josephus's *Antiquities of the Jews*). Their conflicts became violent during the second century BCE. The Hasmonean high priest John Hyrcanus conquered the

Samaritan cities of Samaria and Shechem and demolished the Samaritans' temple on Mount Gerizim. It is therefore no surprise that Samaritan scriptures never included the books of the Deuteronomistic History and the prophets that advanced Judean policies. To this day, the Samaritan scripture consists only of the Pentateuch. The scripturalizing choices of the Hasmoneans are highlighted by the different choices of the Samaritans.

Understanding the Tanak as a Scripture

So far as we know, the books of the Tanak apart from the Pentateuch were not ritualized as scripture prior to the second century BCE. But several centuries later, by at least the end of the Second Temple period, prophetic books were being read aloud in synagogue services (Luke 4:16–17) and psalms were being sung outside the Temple as well as inside (Matt. 26:30).

The books of the Prophets and Writings have been inconsistently ritualized in later Jewish practice. Historical and prophetic books have frequently been ritualized in the semantic dimension to interpret Israel's past and future. They get read aloud in the performative dimension, but piecemeal to accompany particular Torah readings. Use of the Psalms emphasizes their performance, as is natural for hymns designed to be sung aloud. The five scrolls associated with Jewish festivals, Ruth, Esther, Song of Songs, Ecclesiastes, and Lamentations, also receive regular oral performances. Esther scrolls frequently get decorated and illustrated to function as iconic symbols of Jewish identity. Their illustrations also distinguish them from the more sacred but undecorated Torah scrolls.

So despite the expansion of Jewish scriptures starting around the time of Judah Maccabee, the books of the Prophets and Writings have not been regularly ritualized in all three dimensions. Some books of the Tanak, such as Chronicles, Ezra, and Nehemiah, have hardly been ritualized at all. Because they contain the name of God, the ancient rabbis insisted that they all must be treated as holy objects. But only the Torah has been regularly ritualized in its iconic, performative, and semantic dimensions, which has maintained its pre-eminent status among Jewish scriptures.

Nevertheless, the Hasmonean expansion of scripture changed how Jews and Christians interpret the Pentateuch as well as these other books. James Kugel observed that, because it is scripture, people read biblical literature as relevant, cryptic, perfect, and divinely inspired. By relevant, Kugel meant that readers think what scripture says must be relevant to

Figure 6.1 A *Megillah* (Esther scroll) from Italy, ca. 1616. In the National Library of Israel.

themselves in their present circumstances. Readers also think scripture is cryptic: its significance is not limited to the normal meaning of its words, but reflects other, deeper messages. They also expect scripture to be perfectly harmonious: everything about it is significant and any part of scripture may inform the meaning of any other part. Readers assume that scriptures are relevant, cryptic, and perfect because they think scriptures come from God. Therefore, scriptures must contain divinely inspired messages. But Kugel cautioned that claims for divine inspiration do not appear as often or as early as the other three assumptions. This sequence suggests that belief in divine inspiration could have been a product of reading scriptures as relevant, cryptic, and perfect, rather than a precondition for doing so. All four assumptions likely grew together.[178]

Kugel found these assumptions about scriptural books in Jewish and Christian literature starting from around 200 BCE, shortly before the Maccabean Revolt. His survey included literature from periods in which Jewish and Christian scriptures began to be ritualized as scripture for the first time or in decisively new ways. Kugel started after the time of Ezra around 400 BCE, but the scripturalization of the Torah in Ezra's time may have participated in this trend, or even caused it. Kugel's observations concisely described the changes to the semantic meaning of biblical literature that came about through its ritualization as scripture in all three dimensions. The Bible has for the most part been interpreted like this by Jews and Christians ever since.

The expansion of Jewish scriptures starting in the Hasmonean period may have encouraged these interpretive trends. Scripturalizing the genres of the Prophets, the Psalms, and Wisdom books led to applying the reading conventions of each genre to other books of scripture. We have already seen how including lists of ritual rules in the Pentateuch led to its stories becoming normative (see Box, The Rhetoric of Lists, on pp. 48–49). Other examples of this kind of transformation came from including prophetic books and the Psalter in scripture.

Scripturalizing Prophecy

Prophetic oracles seem, for the most part, to have been spoken in response to very particular situations. They were addressed to specific people at certain times. For example, Isaiah predicted that a young woman would conceive and bear a son as a way of promising King Ahaz rescue from military attack within a few years (Isa. 7). However, collecting prophetic oracles together and editing them into written books implies that they continue to be relevant beyond that original situation. In written form, they can be read again at any time and interpreted to apply to situations faced by readers and their communities. Written prophecies therefore invite ongoing interpretation and reapplication. So the Gospel of Matthew takes Isaiah 7 as predicting Jesus's birth hundreds of years later (Matt. 1:22–23) and the Gospel of Luke depicts Jesus reading Isaiah 61 and applying it to himself (Luke 4:16–21). Similarly, the book of Daniel quotes Jeremiah's prediction of a 70-year exile as meaning "seventy weeks of years," that is, 490 years, which applies it to the writer's own time in the second century (compare Dan. 9:2, 24 with Jer. 29:10).

Once prophetic books began to be ritualized as scripture, this way of reading and reapplying oracles to one's own time and situation spread to other parts of scripture. The "relevant" and "cryptic" reading tendencies identified by Kugel can be recognized as extending oracular interpretation to non-oracular texts. This trend was accelerated by the popularity of apocalyptic thinking in the late Second Temple period. Apocalyptic increased readers' inclination to find scripture cryptic and relevant to their near future. It led them to search every scriptural text for clues to future events, which also strengthened scripture's reputation for perfect harmony and universal significance. Now psalms were read as oracles predicting Jewish revolts against Rome or the coming of the Christian messiah. Instructions for the Tabernacle were read as oracular visions of heavenly worship. Even stories about the past could be read as forecasting coming events. For example, because of Abraham's attempt to sacrifice him (Gen. 22), Isaac became a prophetic model or "type" that shaped how Jews and Christians think typologically about innocent victims. Prophetic books introduced an oracular way of reading that was then applied to the rest of the scriptures.

Prophetic books also brought into scripture an oracular emphasis on the identities of the prophets. They name the prophets and date their experiences of revelation to validate the legitimacy of their messages (Jer. 1:1–3; cf. Isa. 1:1; Ezek. 1:1–3; Amos 1:1; etc.). Because they need to validate the prophet's authority, prophetic books give much more attention to their composers and settings than do other genres of biblical literature.

Ritualizing prophetic books as part of scripture and reading the rest of scripture like prophetic oracles raised readers' interest in validating the prophetic authors of other books as well. Now the anonymous writers of stories, psalms, and wisdom collections began to be identified with known heroes of the biblical tradition. The assumption that all scripture must be divinely inspired, which Kugel identified as appearing in later Second Temple literature, can be recognized as extending oracular interpretation to non-oracular texts. The logic soon seemed irrefutable that all scripture must have been written by people whom scripture describes as divinely inspired or motivated. Each book should therefore be credited to known, legitimate prophets or other biblical heroes.

Since the Pentateuch tells of Moses writing down the laws, it was easy to credit him with all five books. Samuel was proclaimed the author of Joshua and Judges, Jeremiah the historian of the books of Samuel and Kings, David of all the Psalms, and Solomon of most of the wisdom literature. The oracular concern for validating authorship takes new forms in modern historical criticism's reconstructions of the Pentateuch's composition. Historians who cannot agree with the traditional identifications of biblical authors still labor to identify the writers. So the presuppositions of oracular reading continue to shape how the Bible is read and interpreted by preachers, lay people, and scholars alike.

Scripturalizing Psalms

Like hymns in many religious communities, Psalms provide scripts for congregational and individual singing. They are sung in Jewish synagogue services, festivals, and wedding ceremonies. They are sung in Christian churches, monasteries, and prayer meetings. The Psalms have exerted an overwhelming influence on Western music. They have inspired new hymnic compositions and collections since at least the first century BCE, when Qumran's library included several collections. They continue to feature in the ever-expanding corpus of modern religious music for both lay singers and expert performers.

By scripturalizing song in the form of the Psalter, psalms function as a model for singing or chanting the rest of scripture as well. We do not know how early the tradition of singing scripture began, but it is attested by the fourth century CE in both Jewish and Christian sources (see Chapter 4). Because religious and literary texts were designed to be read aloud, ancient public readings tended to use tone and rhythm to project the voice and make the reading more memorable. Though we cannot be sure that scripturalizing the Psalter began the trend of singing other scriptures, at the very least, the Psalms encouraged it to develop into the traditions of chant and hymnody that mark Jewish and Christian worship throughout history.

Scripturalizing the Psalter also influenced Jewish and Christian traditions of individual devotion and piety. The Psalms were composed so people could appropriate their words to express their own appeals and praise to God. Their language is frequently ambiguous in order to make it easier for different people to use them. Recent interpreters have also pointed out that the Psalter, as a collection, has been shaped for use in private devotion apart from public worship. For example, it begins by celebrating the pious student of Torah (Ps. 1) and ends with five songs of praise to YHWH (Pss. 146–150), which suggests that it was arranged to be sung through in sequence.[179]

Scriptural texts were modified to model devotional use of psalms. Psalms were inserted into the narratives of biblical heroes to make them models of piety and to provide a theological interpretation of their stories. Thus Psalm 18 has been inserted in 2 Samuel 22 to provide a theological conclusion to David's story. Hannah's song similarly announces God's plan for a king in 2 Samuel 2. Such inset psalms deliberately shape biblical stories to be used as devotional scripture. Other examples include the Song of the Sea in Exodus 15, the psalms and poems concluding the Pentateuch in Deuteronomy 32–33, and Hezekiah's prayer in Isaiah 38 inserted into narratives taken from 2 Kings. Superscriptions to some of the Psalms suggest more such applications to specific stories (e.g. Pss. 3, 7, 34, etc.).[180]

Psalms, then, model a way of reading and listening that encourages applying their words to my own circumstances and concerns. Ritualizing the Psalter as part of scripture led to reading the rest of scripture in the same way. The assumption of "relevance" that Kugel identified as characteristic of scriptural interpretation can be recognized as extending hymnic interpretation and singing practices to non-hymnic texts. Just as psalms can give voice to my hopes and fears, so can scripture's prophetic, narrative, and legal texts.

Scripturalizing Wisdom

Including books of wisdom like Proverbs in scripture strengthened the tendency to read scripture as relevant to my personal circumstances. The ancient Middle Eastern wisdom genre featured moral and practical advice. Wisdom texts explicitly tell readers how to behave for their own good. Of course, the Pentateuch's commandments also call on readers and listeners to follow their instructions, and Deuteronomy incorporates wisdom themes to make this appeal. Scripturalizing wisdom books then strengthened the tendency to read all scriptures as good advice for daily life.

Wisdom was transformed during and after Hasmonean rule. Unlike the Hebrew Bible's wisdom books (Proverbs, Ecclesiastes, Job), literature from the late Second Temple period amalgamates wisdom with Israel's history and its religious institutions (Wis. 10–11). It identifies wisdom with the Torah of Moses (Sir. 24:23; Bar. 4:1). It praises the Jerusalem Temple and its priests (Sir. 45, 50). And it incorporates apocalyptic themes: eternal life as reward for the righteous (Wis. 5:15), the devil as cause of death (Wis. 2:24), Israel's salvation from foreign empires (Bar. 5), the glorious restoration of Jerusalem (Tob. 13), and wisdom in the form of divine light as a messiah figure (Wis. 7:24–8:1; John 1). It combines wisdom with law, prophecy, and apocalyptic to make scripture give advice for this life and the next. These Jewish and Christian texts of the Hellenistic and Roman periods make wisdom more "biblical" than do the wisdom books of the Hebrew Bible itself.

In the Time of Judah *Ha-Nasi*

By the end of the second century CE, rabbis were trying to rebuild Jewish life after two catastrophic wars against Rome. The failure of the Jewish revolts of 66–73 and 132–135 CE had left the temple in ruins and Jerusalem populated mostly by non-Jews. Aaronide priests lost their power base in the temple and its income. The wars also disrupted many of the Jewish sects that competed for religious influence in previous centuries. However, the Pharisees' Oral Torah survived in schools of rabbis. They developed it further to build religious institutions for the new circumstances faced by Jewish communities.

Judah ben Simeon ben Gamaliel II (135–220 CE) was born into a family descended from the famous first-century rabbi Hillel. Judah succeeded his father as leader of the rabbinic assembly (*bet din*) with authority over Galilee and Judea. Hence his title *ha-Nasi* "the prince" or "the patriarch," though it could also reflect his family's supposed descent from King David. Judah's decisive leadership and diplomacy smoothed relations with Roman rulers. Renowned for his deep scholarship, humility, wealth, and generosity, he was the leading Jewish figure of his day.

Judah's fame in subsequent Judaism, however, stems from the fact that he edited the Mishnah. Over many generations, the Pharisees had developed traditions of law and interpretation called the "Oral Torah" to accompany the written Torah of the Pentateuch. After the wars against Rome, the Oral Torah began to be written down and edited into various collections, and Judah gathered them together. His edition emphasized the teachings of four generations of students of Rabbi Akiva (d. 135 CE), especially the last generation.

Judah's dominant influence established the Mishnah as the authoritative basis for Jewish law and religious practice. All subsequent rabbinic literature shows its normative influence. The Mishnah's paragraphs formed the central text of later Talmuds that surrounded them with commentary. For his role in editing the Mishnah, Judah earned a remarkable honor. Of all the hundreds of rabbis cited in rabbinic literature, the simple title "rabbi," without any name or further qualification, refers specifically to him.[181]

The Mishnah is not a commentary on biblical laws, but takes up legal issues by topic. Yet it also gives a great deal of space to issues, such as temple rituals, that were no longer of practical importance after the Jerusalem Temple was destroyed in 70 CE. So the Mishnah is not just a code of practice. It discusses both practical and theoretical issues that the rabbis thought should be of major concern to Jews.

The sections of the Mishnah

Zeraim "Seeds" about agriculture and prayer
Mo'ed "Festival" about Sabbaths and other holidays
Nashim "Women" dealing with marriage and divorce
Nezikin "Damages" about civil and criminal laws
Qodashim "Holy Things" about temple rituals and diet
Tohorot "Purities" about impurities and purification

Even more importantly, it establishes how one should think about issues that arise when trying to observe Torah. Judah's answer to that question was: through a life-long dedication to the study of Torah. That requires not just study of the written Pentateuch but also the entire tradition of rabbinic interpretation. The Mishnah therefore reports the rabbis' decisions and it reports their debates and disagreements as well. Its goal is not simply to teach students the answers to particular questions, but how to think through issues with legal precedents and reasoning. In this way, Judah established a rabbinic "aristocracy of learning" that privileged scholars as both spiritual and political leaders.

As a result, in much of subsequent Judaism, the meaning of the written Torah and the rest of the Tanak became what the Mishnah, and the rabbis who interpreted the Mishnah, said it means. The Torah scroll remained the central icon of Jewish devotion, and the Torah scroll and prayer book together exemplified scripture's performative dimension. But from the time of Judah *ha-Nasi* on, the Mishnah and, later, the Talmuds dominated the semantic dimension of legal interpretation and textual commentary on the Pentateuch.

In the Time of Irenaeus

At the same time that rabbis were reorganizing Judaism under their Oral Torah, Christians were forming their communities around traditions about Jesus and his apostles. In the late first century, these traditions took literary form as narratives about Jesus's life and teachings called "gospels" and as letters from first-generation apostles such as Peter, Paul, James, and John. In the second century, Christian communities divided over which gospels and apostles to follow.

Irenaeus (ca. 140–201 CE) was the bishop of Lyon. His community of Christians included followers of Marcion, who advocated only Luke's Gospel and Paul's letters as the true teachings about Christ. Others followed Valentinus, who preached that Jesus taught mystical knowledge available only to those with spiritual insight. His ideas were popularized in second- and third-century gospels, such as the recently rediscovered Gospel of Thomas. (In 1945, codices containing more than 50 mystical texts were discovered in Nag Hammadi, Egypt. These Coptic texts from the fourth century included translations of older Greek gospels about Jesus that were previously unknown to modern scholars.)

Irenaeus insisted on the importance of "apostolic succession" for deciding on Christian scripture as well as on church leaders. He argued that only gospels written by apostles (the 11 disciples of Jesus plus Paul) or associates of apostles are trustworthy. On this criterion, Irenaeus identified four and only four legitimate gospels. Though none of these texts identify their authors, he thought that two were written by the apostles Matthew and John, and that two others were written by Mark on the basis of Peter's recollections and Luke who reflected Paul's teachings.

Irenaeus insisted that God intended Christians to use only these four gospels and that all four were equally inspired. He found scriptural support for this idea in Ezekiel's vision of four supernatural winged sphinxes, called *cherubim* in Hebrew, that surround God's throne (Ezek. 1). Irenaeus's application of Ezekiel's vision to the four gospels replaced the Jewish myth of a heavenly Torah with a myth of heavenly gospels. Ever since, artists have usually portrayed the writers of the four New Testament gospels together with one of the four cherubim who dictate the gospels to their human writers.[182]

Irenaeus on the necessity of four Gospels

The Gospels could not possibly be either more or less in number than they are. Since there are four zones of the world in which we live, and four principal winds, while the Church is spread over all the earth, and the pillar and foundation of the Church is the gospel, and the Spirit of life, it fittingly has four pillars, everywhere breathing out incorruption and revivifying men. From this it is clear that the Word, the artificer of all things, being manifested to men gave us the gospel, fourfold in form but held together by one Spirit. As David said, when asking for his coming, "O sitter upon the cherubim, show yourself" [Ps 80:1]. For the cherubim have four faces, and their faces are images of the activity of the Son of God. For the first living creature, it says [Ezek 1:5, 10; Rev 4:7–8], was like a lion, signifying his active and princely and royal character; the second was like an ox, showing his sacrificial and priestly order; the third had the face of a man, indicating very clearly his coming in human guise; and the fourth was like a flying eagle, making plain the giving of the Spirit who broods over the Church. Now the Gospels, in which Christ is enthroned, are like these. … As is the activity of the Son of God, such is the form of the living creatures; and as is the form of the living creatures, such is also the character of the Gospel. For the living creatures were quadriform, and the gospel and the activity of the Lord is fourfold. Therefore four general covenants were given to mankind: one was that of Noah's deluge, by the [rain] bow; the second was Abraham's, by the sign of circumcision; the third was the giving of the Law by Moses; and the fourth is that of the Gospel, through our Lord Jesus Christ. (*Adversus Haereses*, 3.11.8)[183]

Figure 6.2 (a) The four Gospels represented by a human-faced angel for Matthew, a lion for Mark, (b) an ox for Luke, and an eagle for John. Details of mosaics in Santa Prassede basilica, Rome, 817–824 CE.

Irenaeus defended the Old Testament as Christian scripture because New Testament books cite it as authoritative. However, following the lead of Luke 24:26–27, 44–47, he maintained that Jewish scriptures must be interpreted only through the Christian belief that Jesus is the Christ.

> *If anyone, therefore, reads the Scriptures with attention, he will find in them an account of Christ, ... When at this present time the law is read to the Jews, it is like a fable; for they do not possess the explanation of all things pertaining to the advent of the Son of God, which took place in human nature; but when it is read by the Christians, it is a treasure, hid indeed in a field, but brought to light by the cross of Christ* (*Adversus Haereses*, 4.26.1).

Therefore, the Gospels and Paul's letters – eventually, the New Testament as a whole – replaced the Pentateuch as the interpretive key to Christian scripture.

The Gospels and Paul's letters were already being collected and bound together in books (codices) to be read aloud in churches. Soon the Gospels were being paraded in processions in church rituals. Wealthy people were buying expensive copies in elaborate bindings. The arguments of Irenaeus provided a theological rationale for ritualizing the Gospels in place of the Torah. Christians ritualize the Gospels' semantic, performative, and iconic dimensions more than other parts of their New Testament. The role of the Pentateuch and other Old Testament books in Christian liturgy and interpretation is to support the New Testament, like the Prophets and Writings support the Torah in Jewish liturgy and interpretation.

Irenaeus built his argument for the legitimacy of the four New Testament Gospels onto his rationale for selecting church leaders. He thought that authority to interpret the Gospels and other scriptures rested only with legitimate successors to the apostles. That is, only bishops ordained by other bishops in a line of succession stretching back to the apostles ("apostolic succession") can settle the meaning of scripture. So Irenaeus used arguments for the authority of the four New Testament Gospels to unify Christians organizationally around the bishops and to standardize Christian beliefs on the basis of a limited number of books.

The four Gospels established the claims of "orthodox" Catholic Christianity, which gathered influence and power over the centuries, especially after the Emperor Constantine converted in 318 CE. Controversies over the exact list of books that comprise the Christian Bible continued, as they did over other matters of Christian belief. In fact, the nature of "true" Christianity remains contested today, as the diversity of twenty-first-century Christianities shows. But Irenaeus played a crucial part in setting the four Gospels and Paul's letters at the center of Christian worship and doctrine, where they have continued to be ritualized as scripture ever since.

Understanding the Bible as a Scripture

The Bible known to us today changed several more times in subsequent history. It was shaped especially by the religious reformations and counter-reformations of the sixteenth century and by revolutions in printing technology in the fifteenth and nineteenth centuries. But the four ancient turning points in the times of Ezra, Judah Maccabee, Judah *ha-Nasi,* and Irenaeus established many of the enduring forms of Jewish and Christian scriptures and the practices that sustain them. For example, Christians ritualized Gospels more than other New Testament books, just as Jews ritualize Torah more than the other books of the Tanak, until the printing revolution made pandect Bibles the most common physical form of scripture. Then Christians increasingly focused iconic, performative, and semantic ritualization on the whole scripture, which they reproduce and visualize now as one book.

The choices about scripture made in the times of Ezra, Judah Maccabee, Judah *ha-Nasi*, and Irenaeus could have been decided differently. We know this because other groups of people did make different choices. Most other religious groups in the Middle East and around the Mediterranean did not ritualize written texts in three dimensions as scripture. Those who did so distinguished themselves in antiquity for resembling Jews and Christians. The prophet Mani in the second century CE scripturalized his Manichean texts during his own lifetime. In the seventh century, the followers of the prophet Mohammed quickly ritualized the Qur'an as Muslim scripture.

Within the traditions of Israel, the Samaritans did not expand their scripture beyond the Torah like the Hasmoneans did. They also maintained the religious authority of Aaronide priests, unlike Rabbinic Judaism and Christianity. Jews and Christians displaced the Aaronides with different lineages of leadership. The rabbis claimed an unbroken line of scholarly succession from teacher to student all the way back to Moses, while Christian bishops claimed an unbroken priestly succession through ordination back to Jesus. Comparing the traditions shows clearly the connection between scripturalization and religious leadership, a connection first established by the Pentateuch's endorsement of Aaron's priesthood. All three religions retain the Pentateuch as scripture, but they use it differently.[184]

As we have seen, Jewish, Samaritan, and Christian traditions ritualize each dimension of their scriptures distinctively. In the iconic dimension, Christians ritualize the Gospel codex or the entire Bible like Jews and Samaritans ritualize the Torah scroll: they display and process it prominently and they decorate or cover it distinctively so as to distinguish it from other books. Rabbinic rules for handling all scriptures demarcate other books of the Tanak that are not ritualized as much as the Torah. Now the unification of Jewish and Christian scriptures in a single codex, a Tanak or a Bible, demarcates all of its contents as sacred text. Nevertheless, the Jewish ritualization of Torah scrolls leads to different objects representing their respective religions in religious art and popular culture: a scroll or Decalogue tablets symbolize Judaism while a codex stands for Christianity.

In the performative dimension, Jews and Christians ritualize more of their scriptures but the Torah and the Gospels still get the most attention. They are read aloud more often and more sequentially than other scriptures. Congregational responses such as standing and blessings distinguish them from other readings. And their contents appear more often in religious art.

It is, however, in ritualizing the semantic dimension of scriptures that the three religions differ the most. Judah *ha-Nasi* and his rabbinic colleagues made the Mishnah and Talmuds authoritative for interpreting the Torah in most subsequent Jewish communities. The learned rabbi became the indispensable medium of scriptural tradition. Irenaeus and his colleagues established the New Testament as authoritative for Christian interpretation of the Pentateuch. The ordained bishop became the guarantor of correct doctrine and practice. Aaronide high priests remain the religious leaders of Samaritan communities. Conflicts over religious leadership have marked the history of all three religions and challenged the primacy of priests, rabbis, and bishops. Now Jewish and Christian biblical scholars interact with each other and often present alternative interpretations to rabbinic and church teachings. But these developments have not undermined the Torah's priority in Judaism and the New Testament's precedence in Christianity.

Jewish Torah and Christian Gospels or New Testament overshadow the rest of their respective scriptures, though in ritualizing the semantic dimension of Jewish scripture, Mishnah and Talmud have traditionally overshadowed even the Torah. So despite the fact that the semantic contents of the Protestant Old Testament are the same as the Jewish Tanak, they function very differently. The Pentateuch in particular has different roles in Jewish, Samaritan, and Christian traditions. We may well wonder if the Jewish or Samaritan Torah is the same *thing* as the Christian Pentateuch after all.

CITED WORKS AND FURTHER READING

Preface

1. On comparative scripture studies, see Wilfred Cantwell Smith, "The Study of Religion and the Study of the Bible," *Journal of the American Academy of Religion* 39 (1971), 131–40; reprinted in *Rethinking Scripture: Essays from a Comparative Perspective*, ed. Miriam Levering, Albany, NY: SUNY Press, 1989, 18–28; Wilfred Cantwell Smith, "Scripture as Form and Concept: Their Emergence for the Western World," in *Rethinking Scripture*, 29–57; and William A. Graham, *Beyond the Written Word: Oral Aspects of Scripture in the History of Religion*. Cambridge: Cambridge University Press, 1987.
2. On the canonical approach, see Brevard S. Childs, *Introduction to the Old Testament as Scripture*, Minneapolis: Fortress, 1979; and Brevard S. Childs, *The New Testament as Canon: An Introduction*, Minneapolis: Fortress, 1984.
3. On the Iconic Books Project, see James W. Watts, ed., *Iconic Books and Texts*. London: Equinox, 2013, and http://iconicbooks.net. For SCRIPT, see www.script-site.net.

Chapter 1

4. On Torah, see H. Kleinknecht, "νόμος," *TDNT* 4 (1967), 1024–35; and James W. Watts, "Torah," in *The New Interpreter's Dictionary of the Bible* (Nashville: Abingdon, 2009), 5:629–30.

Understanding the Pentateuch as a Scripture, First Edition. James W. Watts.

5. On scriptures, see William A. Graham, "Scripture," in *The Encyclopedia of Religion*, Volume 12 (2nd ed.; ed. L. Jones, M. Eliade, and C. J. Adams; Detroit: Macmillan Reference USA, 2005), 8194–8205; F. E. Peters, *The Voice, the Word, the Books: The Sacred Scripture of the Jews, Christians, and Muslims*, Princeton: Princeton University Press, 2007; Gerald T. Sheppard, "Canon," in *The Encyclopedia of Religion*, Volume 3 (ed. M. Eliade; New York: Macmillan, 1987), 62–69; and Robert E. Van Voorst, ed., *Anthology of World Scriptures*, Belmont: Wadsworth, 1997.
6. On ritual, see Jonathan Z. Smith, *To Take Place: Toward Theory in Ritual* (Chicago: University of Chicago Press, 1987), 90; Catherine Bell, *Ritual Theory, Ritual Practice* (Oxford: Oxford University Press, 1992), 109; Roy Rappaport, *Ritual and Religion in the Making of Humanity* (Cambridge: Cambridge University Press, 1999), 119; and Philippe Buc, *The Dangers of Ritual: Between Early Medieval Texts and Social Scientific Theory*, Princeton: Princeton University Press, 2001.
7. Aristotle, *Rhetoric* II.1.1–3. in John Henry Freese, *Aristotle with an English Translation: The Art of Rhetoric*, Loeb Classical Library, New York: Putnam, 1921.
8. On ritualized texts, see James W. Watts, "The Three Dimensions of Scriptures," *Postscripts* 2/2 (2006), 135–59 reprinted in *Iconic Books and Texts* (ed. J. W. Watts; London: Equinox, 2013), 9–32; James W. Watts, "Ritual Legitimacy and Scriptural Authority," *Journal of Biblical Literature* 124/3 (2005): 401–417.
9. On Ezra, Persia, and the books of Ezra, Nehemiah, and 1 Esdras, see Lisbeth S. Fried, *Ezra and the Law in History and Tradition*, Columbia, SC: University of South Carolina Press, 2014; Konrad Schmid, "The Persian Imperial Authorization as an Historical Problem and as a Biblical Construct: A Plea for Distinctions in the Current Debate," in *The Pentateuch as Torah: New Models for Understanding Its Promulgation and Acceptance* (ed. G. N. Knoppers and B.M. Levinson; Winona Lake: Eisenbrauns, 2007), 22–38; James W. Watts, ed., *Persia and Torah: The Theory of Imperial Authorization of the Pentateuch*, Atlanta: Society of Biblical Literature, 2001; and Jacob L. Wright, "Writing the Restoration: Compositional Agenda and the Role of Ezra in Nehemiah 8," *Journal of Hebrew Scriptures* 7 (2007), online at http://www.jhsonline.org/Articles/article_71.pdf.

Chapter 2

10. On the Pentateuch as literature, see David J. A. Clines, *The Theme of the Pentateuch*, JSOTSup 10, Sheffield: JSOT, 1978; Robert Alter, *The Art of Biblical Narrative*, New York: Basic, 1981; Thomas W. Mann, *The Book of the Torah: The Narrative Integrity of the Pentateuch*, Atlanta: John Knox, 1988, 2nd ed., Cascade Books, 2013; and Walter Houston, *The Pentateuch*, London: SCM Press, 2013.
11. On the Pentateuch as rhetoric, see Dale Patrick and Allen Scult, *Rhetoric and Biblical Interpretation*, JSOTSup 82, Sheffield: Almond, 1990; and James W. Watts, *Reading Law: The Rhetorical Shaping of the Pentateuch*, Biblical Seminar 59, Sheffield: Sheffield Academic Press, 1999.

12. On comparative ancient rhetoric, see George A. Kennedy, *Comparative Rhetoric: An Historical and Cross-Cultural Introduction*, New York: Oxford, 1998; Carol S. Lipson and Roberta A. Binkley, eds., *Rhetoric Before and Beyond the Greeks*, Albany: SUNY Press, 2004; Carol S. Lipson and Roberta A. Binkley, eds., *Ancient Non-Greek Rhetorics*, West Lafayette, IN: Parlor, 2009.
13. For ancient Middle Eastern examples of the story-list-sanction rhetoric, see James W. Watts, "Ritual Rhetoric in Ancient Near Eastern Texts," in *Ancient Non-Greek Rhetorics* (ed. C. S. Lipson and R. A. Binkley; West Lafayette, IN: Parlor Press, 2009), 39–66.
14. For the Azatiwata inscription, see the translation by tr. J. D. Hawkins in the *Context of Scripture* (ed. W. W. Hallo and K. L. Younger, Jr; 3 vols.; Leiden: Brill, 1997, 2000, 2002), 2.21.
15. The Kurigalzu inscription is translated by Benjamin R. Foster, *Before the Muses: An Anthology of Akkadian Literature* (3rd ed.; Bethesda: CDL, 2005), 365–66.
16. On inset genres in narrative, see James W. Watts, *Psalm and Story: Inset Hymns in Hebrew Narrative*, JSOTSup 139; Sheffield: Sheffield Academic Press, 1992; James W. Watts, "Biblical Psalms Outside the Psalter," in *The Book of Psalms: Composition and Reception* (ed. P. W. Flint and P. D. Miller; Leiden: Brill, 2004), 87–101.
17. Robert M. Cover, "Foreword: *Nomos* and Narrative," *Harvard Law Review* 97/1 (1983), 4–68, quotation from pp. 4–5.
18. On the ancestors' origins in Genesis 12–50, see R. W. L. Moberly, *The Old Testament of the Old Testament: Patriarchal Narratives and Mosaic Yahwism*, Minneapolis: Fortress Press, 1992.
19. On Exodus 1–18, see David M. Gunn, "The 'Hardening of Pharaoh's Heart'? Plot, Character and Theology in Exodus 1–14," in *Art and Meaning: Rhetoric in Biblical Literature* (ed. A. J. Hauser, D. J. A. Clines, and D. M. Gunn; Sheffield: JSOT Press, 1982), 72–96; and William H. Propp, *Exodus 1–18*, Anchor Bible, New Haven: Yale University Press, 1999.
20. See further in James W. Watts, "YHWH is King: The Unstated Premise of the Pentateuch's Enthymeme," forthcoming.
21. On the Torah's origins in Exodus 19–24 and 32–34, see Dale Patrick, *The Rhetoric of Revelation in the Hebrew Bible*, Overtures to Biblical Theology, Minneapolis: Fortress, 1999; and James W. Watts, "Aaron and the Golden Calf in the Rhetoric of the Pentateuch." *Journal of Biblical Literature* 130 (2011), 417–30.
22. On the sanctuary's origins, see Michael B. Hundley, *Keeping Heaven on Earth: Safeguarding the Divine Presence in the Priestly Tabernacle*, FAT 2/50, Tübingen: Mohr Siebeck, 2011; William H. Propp, *Exodus 19–40*, Anchor Bible, New Haven: Yale University Press, 2006; and Mark S. Smith, *The Pilgrimage Pattern in Exodus*, JSOTSup 239, Sheffield: Sheffield Academic Press, 1997.
23. On religious hierarchy in Leviticus 8–10 and Numbers 11–18, see James W. Watts, *Ritual and Rhetoric in Leviticus: From Sacrifice to Scripture* (Cambridge: Cambridge University Press, 2007), 97–129; James W. Watts, *Leviticus 1–10*, Historical Commentary on the Old Testament (Leuven: Peeters, 2013),

429–552; and Adriane Leveen, *Memory and Tradition in Numbers*, Cambridge: Cambridge University Press, 2007.

24. On the rhetoric of lists, see J. D. O'Banion, *Reorienting Rhetoric: The Dialectic of List and Story* (University Park, PA: Pennsylvania State University Press, 1992), quotation from p. 12; Cornelia Vismann, *Files: Law and Media Technology* (tr. G. Winthrop-Young; Stanford: Stanford University Press, 2008; German 2000), quotation from p. 6; Jonathan Z. Smith, "Sacred Persistence: Toward a Redescription of Canon," in *Imagining Religion: From Babylon to Jonestown* (Chicago: U. of Chicago Press, 1982), 36–52, quotation from p. 44; and Jack Goody, *The Logic of Writing and the Organization of Society* (Cambridge: Cambridge University Press, 1986), 42–121.
25. On the search for relevance in interpreting scripture, see James L. Kugel, *The Bible as It Was* (Cambridge, MA: Harvard University Press, 1997), 15–17.
26. On the rhetoric of biblical law, see R. Sonsino, *Motive Clauses in Hebrew Law: Biblical Forms and Near Eastern Parallels*, Chico, CA: Scholars Press, 1980; and James W. Watts, *Reading Law: the Rhetorical Shaping of the Pentateuch*, Sheffield: Sheffield Academic Press, 1999.
27. On the rhetoric of promise and threat, see Timothy G. Crawford, *Blessing and Curse in Syro-Palestinian Inscriptions of the Iron Age*, New York: Peter Lang, 1992; John G. Gager, ed., *Curse Tablets and Binding Spells from the Ancient World*, New York: Oxford University Press, 1992; and Timothy A. Lenchak, *Choose Life!: A Rhetorical-Critical Investigation of Deuteronomy 28,69–30,20*, Rome: Pontifical Biblical Institute, 1993.
28. On God's character in the Pentateuch, see Jack Miles, *God: A Biography*, New York: Knopf, 1995; and James W. Watts, "The Legal Characterization of God in the Pentateuch," *Hebrew Union College Annual* 67 (1996), 1–14.
29. On Moses's character in the Pentateuch, see John Van Seters, *The Life of Moses: The Yahwist as Historian in Exodus-Numbers*, Leuven: Peeters, 1994; and James W. Watts, "The Legal Characterization of Moses in the Rhetoric of the Pentateuch," *Journal of Biblical Literature* 117 (1998), 415–26.

Chapter 3

30. On iconic books, see the essays in *Iconic Books and Texts* (ed. J. W. Watts; London: Equinox, 2013), especially Dorina Miller Parmenter, "The Iconic Book: The Image of the Bible in Early Christian Rituals," pp. 63–92.
31. Quotation of the *Letter of Aristeas* is from the translation by R. J. H. Schutt in *The Old Testament Pseudepigrapha* (ed. J. H. Charlesworth; Garden City, NY: Doubleday, 1985), 2:24.
32. On Pentateuch manuscripts among the Dead Sea Scrolls, see Emanuel Tov, "The Scribal and Textual Transmission of the Torah Analyzed in Light of its Sanctity," in *Pentateuchal Traditions in the Late Second Temple Period* (ed. A. Moriya and G. Hata; Leiden: Brill, 2012), 57–72 [64–65].
33. Translation of *m. Yoma* 7:1 and *m. Sotah* 7:7 by Lawrence H. Schiffman, "The Early History of Public Reading of the Torah," *Jews, Christians, and Polytheists in the Ancient Synagogue: Cultural Interaction during the Greco-Roman Period* (ed. S. Fine; New York: Routledge, 1999), 48.

34. Ruth Langer, "From Study of Scripture to a Reenactment of Sinai: The Emergence of the Synagogue Torah Service," *Worship* 72:1 (1998): 43–67.
35. On mezuzahs and tefillin, see Yehudah B. Cohn, *Tangled Up in Text: Tefillin and the Ancient World* (BJS 351; Providence: Brown University, 2008), and Robert T. Anderson and Terry Giles, *Tradition Kept: The Literature of the Samaritans* (Peabody, MA: Hendrickson, 2005), 408–9.
36. On divine names in Jewish and Christian texts, see John Barton, *Holy Writings, Sacred Text: The Canon in Early Christianity* (Louiville: Westminster John Knox, 1997), 106–130; and Patricia Cox Miller, "In Praise of Nonsense," in *Classical Mediterranean Spirituality* (ed. A. H. Armstrong; New York: Crossroad, 1986), 481–505; reprinted in P. C. Miller, *The Poetry of Thought in Late Antiquity* (Burlington: Ashgate, 2001), 221–245, who provides (1986, p. 224) the translated quotation from *The Discourse on the Eighth and the Ninth*, Nag Hammadi Codex VI, 6, p. 296.
37. On Torah arks in ancient synagogues, see Eric M. Meyers, "The Torah Shrine in the Ancient Synagogue," in *Jews, Christians, and Polytheists in the Ancient Synagogue: Cultural Interaction during the Greco-Roman Period* (ed. S. Fine; New York: Routledge, 1999), 201–223, who provides on pp. 206–7 the translation of John Chrysostom's polemic in *Adversus Judaeos*, 6:7; PG 48, col. 913. See also Rachel Hachlili, *Ancient Jewish Art and Archaeology in the Land of Israel* (Leiden: Brill, 1988), 273–80.
38. Ruth Langer, "From Study of Scripture to a Reenactment of Sinai: The Emergence of the Synagogue Torah Service," *Worship* 72:1 (1998): 43–67; see also Katrin Kogman-Appel, *A Mahzor from Worms: Art and Religion in a Medieval Jewish Community*, Cambridge, MA: Harvard University Press, 2011.
39. On synagogue scrolls as sacred objects, see William Scott Green, "Scripture in Classical Judaism," in *The Encyclopedia of Judaism* (ed. J. Neusner, S. Peck, and W. S. Green; New York: Continuum/Leiden: Brill, 1999), 1302–1309, quotation from 1305; Marianne Schleicher, "Artifactual and Hermeneutical Use of Scripture in Jewish Tradition," in *Jewish and Christian Scripture as Artifact and Canon* (ed. C. A. Evans and H. D. Zacharias; London: T. & T. Clark, 2009), 48–65; Marianne Schleicher, "Accounts of a Dying Scroll: On Jewish Handling of Sacred Texts in Need of Restoration or Disposal," in *The Death of Sacred Texts* (ed. K. Myrvold; London: Ashgate, 2010), 11–30; and Shalom Sabar, "Torah and Magic: The Torah Scroll and its Appurtenances as Magical Objects in Traditional Jewish Culture," *European Journal of Jewish Studies* 3 (2009), 135–70, who on p. 154 supplies the translation of the dedicatory plaque from Ioannina.
40. Daniel Sarefield, "The Symbolics of Book Burning: The Establishment of a Christian Ritual of Persecution," in *The Early Christian Book* (ed. W. E. Klingshirn and L. Safran; Washington, DC: Catholic University of America, 2007), 159–73, quotation from p. 159.
41. Quotation from *Samaritan Joshua* 47, a thirteenth-to-fifteenth-century Arabic manuscript translated by Oliver Crane in Robert T. Anderson and Terry Giles, *Tradition Kept: The Literature of the Samaritans* (Peabody, MA: Hendrickson, 2005), 137–38.

42. For Josephus's account of a desecrated Torah, see Louis H. Feldman, *Josephus: Jewish Antiquities, Book XX* (Loeb Classics; Cambridge, MA: Harvard University Press, 1965), quotation from pp. 61–63.
43. Matti Friedman, *The Aleppo Codex: In Pursuit of One of the World's Most Coveted, Sacred, and Mysterious Books*, Chapel Hill: Algonquin Books, 2013.
44. On relic torahs, see Shalom Sabar, "Torah and Magic: The Torah Scroll and its Appurtenances as Magical Objects in Traditional Jewish Culture," *European Journal of Jewish Studies* 3 (2009), 167, 169; and James W. Watts, "Relic Texts," *The Iconic Books Blog* (June 8, 2012), online at http://iconicbooks.blogspot.de/2012/06/relic-texts.html.
45. On heavenly tablets in Jubilees, see Hindy Najman, "Interpretation as Primordial Writing: Jubilees and its Authority Conferring Strategies," *Journal for the Study of Judaism* 30 (1999), 379–410; and Florentino García Martínez, "The Heavenly Tablets in the Book of Jubilees," in *Studies in the Book of Jubilees* (ed. M. Albani, J. Frey, and A. Lange; Tübingen: Mohr Siebeck, 1997), 243–60.
46. On myths of heavenly books, see Stephanie Dalley, *The Legacy of Mesopotamia* (Oxford: Oxford University Press, 1998), quotations from p. 166; John F. A. Sawyer, *Sacred Languages and Sacred Texts* (London: Routledge, 1999), quotation from p. 105, and Dorina Miller Parmenter, "The Bible as Icon: Myths of the Divine Origins of Scripture," in *Jewish and Christian Scripture as Artifact and Canon* (ed. C. A. Evans and H. D. Zacharias; London: T. & T. Clark, 2009), 298–310.
47. On ancient Christian rituals with Gospel books, see the essays in William E. Klingshirn and Linda Safran, eds., *The Early Christian Book*, Washington, DC: Catholic University of America Press, 2007, especially John Lowden, "The Word Made Visible: The Exterior of the Early Christian Book as Visual Argument," 13–47, and Caroline Humfress, "Judging by the Book: Christian Codices and Late Antique Legal Culture," 141–58; also Dorina Miller Parmenter, "The Iconic Book: The Image of the Bible in Early Christian Rituals," in *Iconic Books and Texts* (ed. J. W. Watts; London: Equinox, 2013), 63–92, and Jason Larson, "The Gospels as Imperialized Sites of Memory in Late Ancient Christianity," in *Iconic Books and Texts*, 373–388.
48. On the iconic Bible in modern Protestantism, see Martin Marty, "America's Iconic Book," in *Humanizing America's Iconic Book: Society of Biblical Literature Centennial Addresses 1980* (ed. G. M. Tucker and D. A. Knight; Chico, CA: Scholars Press. 1982), 1–23; and Dorina Miller Parmenter, "A Fitting Ceremony: Christian Concerns for Bible Disposal," in *The Death of Sacred Texts: Ritual Disposal and Renovation of Texts in World Religions* (ed. K. Myrvold; London: Ashgate, 2010), 55–70.
49. On the Bible in Masonic rituals, see Cheryl Townsend Gilkes, "The Virtues of Brotherhood and Sisterhood: African American Fraternal Organizations and Their Bibles," in *African Americans and the Bible: Sacred Texts and Social Textures* (ed. V. L. Wimbush; New York: Continuum, 2003), 389–403.
50. The quotation of John Chrysostom's *Homily on John* 32.3 can be found in *NPNF*, ser. 1, vol. 14, 114 and in Parmenter, "Iconic Book," 80.

51. On the history of Bible production and publishing, see *The New Cambridge History of the Bible*, 4 vols., Cambridge: Cambridge University Press, 2012–2016; also David M. Stern, "The Hebrew Bible in Europe in the Middle Ages: A Preliminary Typology," *Jewish Studies, an Internet Journal* 11 (2012), 76–77; Michelle Brown, "Images to be Read and Words to be Seen: The Iconic Role of the Early Medieval Book," in *Iconic Books and Texts* (ed. J. W. Watts; London: Equinox, 2013), 93–118; Paul C. Gutjahr, *An American Bible: A History of the Good Book in the United States, 1777–1880*, Stanford: Stanford University Press, 1999; Jeremy Stolow, *Orthodox by Design: Judaism, Print Politics, and the ArtScroll Revolution*, Berkeley: University of California Press, 2010; and Timothy K. Beal, *The Rise and Fall of the Bible: The Unexpected History of an Accidental Book*, Boston: Houghton Mifflin Harcourt, 2011.
52. On the evolution of scripts and publishing fonts, see the summary in S. Brent Plate, "Looking at Words," in *Iconic Books and Texts* (ed. J. W. Watts; London: Equinox, 2013), 119–33.
53. On Decalogue monuments, see James W. Watts, "Ten Commandments Monuments and the Rivalry of Iconic Texts," *Journal of Religion & Society* 6 (2004) online at http://moses.creighton.edu/jrs/2004/2004-13.pdf.
54. On the Ark of the Covenant, see C. L. Seow, "Ark of the Covenant," *Anchor Bible Dictionary* (New York: Doubleday, 1992), 1:386–93; and John Day, "Whatever Happened to the Ark of the Covenant?" in *Temple and Worship in Biblical Israel* (ed. J. Day; London: T&T Clark, 2007), 250–270.
55. On Egyptian Anubis chests, see Harco Willems, *The Coffin of Heqata: (Cairo JdE 36418): A Case Study of Egyptian Funerary Culture of the Early Middle Kingdom* (OLA 70; Peeters Publishers, 1996), 142–145.
56. On comparing the ritual use of Torah scrolls and of statues of gods, see Martin Goodman, "Sacred Scripture and 'Defiling the Hands'," *Journal of Theological Studies* 41 (1990), 99–107; and Karel van der Toorn, "The Iconic Book: Analogies Between the Babylonian Cult of Images and the Veneration of the Torah," in *The Image and the Book: Iconic Cults, Aniconism and the Rise of Book Religion in Israel and the Ancient Near East* (ed. K. van der Toorn; Louven: Peeters, 1997), 229–248.
57. On the Ketef Hinnom amulets and the priestly blessing, see Brian B. Schmidt, "The Social Matrix of Early Judean Magic and Divination: From 'Top Down' or 'Bottom Up'?" in *Beyond Hatti: A Tribute to Gary Beckman* (ed. B. J. Collins and P. Michalowski; Atlanta: Lockwood, 2013), 279–294; and Jeremy Daniel Smoak, *The Priestly Blessing in Inscription and Scripture: The Early History of Numbers 6:24–26*, Oxford: Oxford University Press, 2015.
58. On monumental inscriptions and other iconic texts in the ancient Middle East, see James W. Watts, "Ancient Iconic Texts and Scholarly Expertise," in *Iconic Books and Texts* (ed. J. W. Watts; London: Equinox, 2013), 407–418.
59. On lost-and-found ritual texts in antiquity, compare Katherine Stott, "Finding the Lost Book of the Law: Re-reading the Story of 'The Book of the Law' (Deuteronomy–2 Kings) in Light of Classical Literature," *Journal for the Study of the Old Testament* 30 (2005), 153–169, who provides examples from

Greco-Roman literature, with the response by Nadav Na'aman, "The 'Discovered Book' and the Legitimation of Josiah's Reform," *Journal of Biblical Literature* 130 (2011), 47–62, who provides many ancient Middle Eastern examples of the theme.

60. Shulgi's boast is a quotation from lines 270–280 of Shulgi B, translated in *The Electronic Text Corpus of Sumerian Literature* (ETCSL) online project of the Faculty of Oriental Studies, University of Oxford.
61. The Hittite examples are translated by Itamar Singer, *Hittite Prayers* (WAW 11; Atlanta: SBL, 2002), 58–59, 83.
62. The quotation from a Nabonidus inscription is translated by Jean-Jacques Glassner, *Mesopotamian Chronicles* (WAW 19; Atlanta: SBL, 2005), 315.
63. For Pausanius on the Messenian text, see W. H. S. Jones, *Pausanius' Description of Greece* (Loeb edition; London: Heinemann, 1917–1935), 4.20.2–8; 4.26.7–8; 4.27.5; 4.33.5.
64. On Torah scrolls replacing the Ark in the Pentateuch, see James W. Watts, "From Ark of the Covenant to Torah Scroll: Ritualizing Israel's Iconic Texts" in *Ritual Innovation* (ed. N. MacDonald; BZAW 468; Berlin: Walter De Gruyter, 2016), 21–34.

Chapter 4

65. On the oral performance of scriptures in different religions, see William A. Graham, *Beyond the Written Word: Oral Aspects of Scripture in the History of Religion* (Cambridge: Cambridge University Press, 1987), quotation from p. 65.
66. On the role of language and translation in ancient religions, see John F. A. Sawyer, *Sacred Languages and Sacred Texts*, London: Routledge, 1999.
67. On the vernacular language in Ezra's Jerusalem, see Ingo Kottsieper, "'And They Did Not Care to Speak Yehudit': On Linguistic Change in Judah during the Late Persian Period," in *Judah and the Judeans in the Fourth Century B.C.E.* (ed. O. Lipschitz, G.N. Knoppers, and R. Albertz; Winona Lake, IN: Eisenbrauns, 2007), 95–124.
68. On the evidence for reading scriptures in late Second Temple Judaism, see Philo, *On Dreams* 2:127; *Hypothetica* 7:12–13; *Omnus probus* 81–82; Josephus, *Antiquities* 16:43; *Apion* 2:175; Luke 4:16–17; Acts 13:13–15.
69. Translation of the Theodotus Inscription by the Israel Museum in Jerusalem.
70. On enacting blessings and curses at Qumran, see *1QS* 1.16–2.18, and Steven D. Fraade, "Rhetoric and Hermeneutics in *Miqsat Maʿaśe ha-Torah* (*4QMMT*): The Case of Blessings and Curses," *Dead Sea Discoveries* 10/1 (2003), 150–161.
71. On public scripture reading at Qumran, see Lawrence H. Schiffman, "The Early History of Public Reading of the Torah," in *Jews, Christians, and Polytheists in the Ancient Synagogue: Cultural Interaction during the Greco-Roman Period* (ed. S. Fine; New York: Routledge, 1999), 44–56. The two quoted texts are Schiffman's translations (p. 45) from the Rule of the Community, *1QS* 6.7–8, *4Q266 5.ii.1–3* and parallels, and from the Zadokite fragment/Damascus Document, *4Q266* 5 ii.1–3 = *4Q267* 5 iii:3–5 = *4Q273* 2 1.

72. The translation of the parallel passages from *m. Yoma* 7:1 and *m. Sot.* 7:7, 8 are by Schiffman, "Early History of Public Reading of the Torah," 48.
73. Translation by Michael L. Rodkinson, *The Babylonian Talmud* (2nd ed.; Boston: New Talmud Publishing Co., 1918), vol. 4.
74. On reading Torah and other scripture in the synagogue liturgy, see Ruth Langer, "From Study of Scripture to a Reenactment of Sinai: The Emergence of the Synagogue Torah Service," *Worship* 72:1 (1998), 43–67; Elsie R. Stern, "What is Jewish Scripture?" *Biblical Theology Bulletin* 43 (2013), 191–199; Louis Jacobs, "Torah, Reading of," *Encyclopaedia Judaica* (ed. M. Berenbaum and F. Skolnik; 2nd ed.; Detroit: Macmillan Reference USA, 2007), 20:46–50; and Schiffman, "Early History of Public Reading of the Torah." See also Daniella Talmon-Heller, "Reciting the Qur'an and Reading the Torah: Muslim and Jewish Attitudes and Practices in a Comparative Historical Perspective," *Religion Compass* 6/8 (2012), 369–380.
75. For text, transliteration, and translation, see Nosson Sherman, *The Rabbinical Council of America Edition of the Artscroll Siddur* (Brooklyn, NY: Mesorah Publications, 1984), 440, 444.
76. On scripture, especially Gospel, reading in Christian churches, see Adrian Fortescue, "Gospel in the Liturgy," *The Catholic Encyclopedia* (New York: Robert Appleton Company, 1909), vol. 6, online at http://www.newadvent.org/cathen/06659a.htm.
77. On Christian lectionaries, see *The Revised Common Lectionary* by the Consultation On Common Texts (Minneapolis: Augsburg Fortress, 2012), especially p. 4; Horace T. Allen, "Introduction: Preaching in a Christian Context," in *Handbook for the Revised Common Lectionary* (ed. P. C. Bower; Nashville: Abingdon, 1996), 1–24; and Felix Just, "Lectionary Statistics" on the Roman Catholic *Lectionary for Mass* (2009), online at http://catholic-resources.org/Lectionary/Statistics.htm.
78. William Graham, *Beyond the Written Word*, 131.
79. On the Aramaic targums, see Willem F. Smelik, "The Translation as a Bilingual Text: The Curious Case of the Targum," *AJS Perspectives* (Fall, 2015), online at http://perspectives.ajsnet.org/translation-issue/the-translation-as-a-bilingual-text-the-curious-case-of-the-targum/; and Paul V. M. Flesher and Bruce Chilton, *The Targums: A Critical Introduction* (Waco, TX: Baylor University Press, 2011), esp. 71–89.
80. On the Hasmoneans' advocacy of Hebrew literature, see David M. Carr, *Writing on the Tablet of the Heart: Origins of Scripture and Literature* (Oxford: Oxford University Press, 2005), quotation from p. 262.
81. On the ancient rabbis' advocacy of reading Torah in Hebrew, see Seth Schwartz, "Language, Power and Identity in Ancient Palestine," *Past and Present* 148 (1995), 3–47 [33]; Philip Alexander, "The Rabbis, the Greek Bible and Hellenism," in *The Jewish-Greek Tradition in Antiquity and the Byzantine Empire* (ed. J. K. Aitken and J. C. Paget; Cambridge: Cambridge University Press, 2014), 229–46; and Irven M. Resnick, "The Codex in Early Jewish and Christian Communities," *The Journal of Religious History* 17/1 (1992): 1–17 [6].
82. On reading the Torah in Greek, see the *Letter of Aristeas* 308–312, translated by R. J. H. Shutt in *Old Testament Pseudepigrapha* (ed. J. H. Charlesworth; 2 vols.;

New York: Doubleday, 1983), 7–34; Philo, *Vita Mosis* 2. 41–2; in ancient rabbinic literature: *m. Meg.* 2.1, *t. Meg. 3:13*, *y. Meg.* 4.3, 75a; and see Willem F. Smelik, "Code-Switching: The Public Reading of the Bible," in *Was ist ein Text? Alttestamentliche, ägyptologische und altorientalische Perspektiven* (ed. L. Morenz and S. Schorch; BZAW 362; Berlin: de Gruyter, 2007), 123–51 [134–37].

83. Penny Shine Gold, *Making the Bible Modern: Children's Bibles and Jewish Education in Twentieth-Century America* (Ithaca, NY: Cornell University Press, 2004), quotation from p. 13.
84. On ancient Christian translations of scripture, see Sawyer, *Sacred Languages*, 83–89, 94–95, and Willard G. Oxtoby, "'Telling in Their Own Tongues': Old and Modern Bible Translations as Expressions of Ethnic Cultural Identity," in *The Bible As Cultural Heritage* (ed. W. Beuken and S. Freyne; London: SCM, 1995), 24–35 [29–30].
85. On the cultural effects of different scripts, see David Damrosch, "Scriptworlds: Writing Systems and the Formation of World Literature," *Modern Language Quarterly* 68/2 (2007), 195–219.
86. Gold, *Making the Bible Modern*, 12.
87. On chanting scriptures, see Timothy Thibodeau, "Western Christendom," in *The Oxford History of Christian Worship* (ed. G. Wainwright; Oxford: Oxford University Press, 2006), 242–246; and William T. Flynn, "Liturgical Music," in *The Oxford History of Christian Worship*, 769–792.
88. Alan Gampel, "The Origins of Musical Notation in the Abrahamic Religious Traditions," in *Age of Transition: Byzantine Culture in the Islamic World* (ed. H. C. Evans; New York: Metropolitan Museum of Art, 2015), 144–154, quotation from p. 144.
89. See Ruth Mellinkoff, *The Horned Moses in Medieval Art and Thought*, Berkeley: University of California Press, 1970.
90. On illuminated manuscripts, see Michelle P. Brown, *The Lindisfarne Gospels: Society, Spirituality and the Scribe*, London: British Library, 2003.
91. On maps in bibles, see Catherine Delano Smith, "Maps as Art and Science: Maps in Sixteenth Century Bibles," *Imago Mundi* 42 (1990), 65–83; E. Wajntraub and G. Wajntraub, "Medieval Hebrew Manuscript Maps," *Imago Mundi* 44 (1992), 99–105; Elizabeth M. Ingram, "Maps as Readers' Aids: Maps and Plans in Geneva Bibles," *Imago Mundi* 45 (1993), 29–44, quotation from p. 35, and who provides the French quotation from Barbier and translates it on p. 30.
92. Minnie Bruce Pratt, "The Maps in My Bible," *Bridges*, 2/1 (1991), 93–116, quotations from pp. 94, 103, 104.
93. On scripture in medieval mystery plays, see Peter Happe, *English Mystery Plays*, London: Penguin, 1975; and Timothy Thibodeau, "Western Christendom," in *The Oxford History of Christian Worship* (ed. G. Wainwright; Oxford: Oxford University Press, 2006), 246–247.
94. On the Bible in theater, see Paul Whitfield White, "The Bible as Play in Reformation England," in *The Cambridge History of British Theatre, Volume 1: Origins to 1660* (ed. J. Milling and P. Thomson; Cambridge: Cambridge University Press, 2004), 87–115.

95. On modern reconstructions of the Tabernacle and other biblical scenes, see the displays in Amsterdam's Jewish Museum and Bible Museum, and Burke O. Long, *Imagining the Holy Land: Maps, Models, and Fantasy Travels*, Bloomington, IN: Indiana University Press, 2003; and Timothy Beal, *Roadside Religion: In Search of the Sacred, the Strange, and the Substance of Faith*, Boston: Beacon, 2006. On the Musama Disco Christo Church, see Philip Jenkins, *The New Faces of Christianity: Believing the Bible in the Global South* (Oxford: Oxford University Press, 2006), 50. On the Temple Institute in Jerusalem, see its website: http://www.templeinstitute.org.
96. On films about Moses, see Brian Britt, *Rewriting Moses: The Narrative Eclipse of the Text* (London: T. & T. Clark, 2004), 40–58, quotation from p. 58; and Adele Reinhartz, *Bible and Cinema: An Introduction* (London: Routledge, 2013), 17–56.
97. On religious art in secular society, see Sally M. Promey, "Religion, Sensation, and Materiality," in *Sensational Religion: Sensory Cultures in Material Practice* (New Haven: Yale University Press, 2014), 1–21; and Katie Edwards, *Admen and Eve: The Bible in Contemporary Advertising*, Sheffield: Sheffield Phoenix, 2012.
98. Translated by Benjamin Foster, *Before the Muses: An Anthology of Akkadian Literature* (2 vols.; Bethesda, MD: CDL Press, 1993), 400.
99. Both quotations translated by Miriam Lichtheim, *Ancient Egyptian Literature: A Book of Readings* (3 vols.; Berkeley: University of California Press, 1973, 1976, 1980), 2:20; 3:116–21.
100. On Egyptian lector priests, see David Lorton, "The Theology of the Cult Statues in Ancient Egypt," in *Born in Heaven, Made on Earth: The Making of the Cult Image in the Ancient Near East* (ed. M. Dick; Winona Lake, IN: Eisenbrauns, 1999), 149.
101. For the Samnite ritual, see Livy, *History of Rome* (ed. E. Rhys; trans. Rev. Canon Roberts; Everyman's Library; New York: E. P. Dutton, 1912), 10:38.
102. On stories of reading Torah in the Hebrew Bible, see James W. Watts, *Reading Law: the Rhetorical Shaping of the Pentateuch* (Sheffield: Sheffield Academic Press, 1999), 15–31.
103. On Exodus 24:3–8 as the conclusion to the Covenant Code, see Thomas B. Dozeman, *Exodus* (Grand Rapids: Eerdmans, 2009), 562–63.
104. On the listening audience presupposed by the Pentateuch, see Watts, *Reading Law*, 61–88.
105. On the oral performance of biblical stories, see Susan Niditch, *Oral World and Written Word: Ancient Israelite Literature* (Louisville: Westminster John Knox, 1996), 8–38; also Raymond F. Person, Jr, *The Deuteronomic School: History, Social Setting, and Literature* (Atlanta: SBL, 2002), 83–101.
106. On refrains in Leviticus, see James W. Watts, *Leviticus 1–10* (Historical Commentary on the Old Testament; Leuven: Peeters, 2013), 159–65, 301–303, 429–35, 508–17.
107. On the effects of inset poetry in biblical prose, see James W. Watts, *Psalms and Story: Inset Hymns in Hebrew Narrative*, JSOTSup 139; Sheffield: JSOT

Press, 1992; James W. Watts, "Biblical Psalms Outside the Psalter," in *The Book of Psalms: Composition and Reception* (ed. P. W. Flint and P. D. Miller; VTSup 99; Leiden: Brill, 2004), 288–309; and Steven Weitzman, *Song and Story in Biblical Narrative: The History of a Literary Convention in Ancient Israel*, Bloomington, IN: Indiana University Press, 1997.

108. On how the Pentateuch shapes Israel's identity, see Harry Nasuti, "Identity, Identification, and Imitation: The Narrative Hermeneutics of Biblical Law," *Journal of Law and Religion* 4.1 (1986), 9–23, quotation on p. 12; Seth L. Sanders, *The Invention of Hebrew* (Urbana: University of Illinois, 2009), esp. 157–71.
109. On variations among copies of the Ten Commandments, see Yuichi Osumi, "One Decalogue in Different Texts," in *Pentateuchal Traditions in the Late Second Temple Period* (ed. A. Moriya and G. Hata; Leiden: Brill, 2012), 23–38.
110. On memory variants, see David L. Carr, *The Formation of the Hebrew Bible: A New Reconstruction* (Oxford: Oxford University Press, 2011), 25–36.

Chapter 5

111. On the figure of Ezra in history, the Bible, and later traditions, see Lisbeth S. Fried, *Ezra and the Law in History and Tradition*, Columbia, SC: University of South Carolina Press, 2014.
112. The *Letter of Aristeas* was translated by R. J. H. Shutt in *Old Testament Pseudepigrapha* (ed. J. H. Charlesworth; 2 vols.; New York: Doubleday, 1983), 7–34.
113. Translated by C. D. Yonge, *The Works of Philo Judaeus* (London: H. G. Bohn, 1854–1890), 2.37–41.
114. See James Kugel, "Levi's Elevation to the Priesthood in Second Temple Writings," *Harvard Theological Review* 86/1 (1993), 1–64; and Hindy Najman, "Interpretation as Primordial Writing: Jubilees and its Authority Conferring Strategies," *Journal for the Study of Judaism* 30 (1999), 379–410.
115. For the translation of excerpts from *4QMMT*, see Florentino García Martínez, *The Dead Sea Scrolls Translated* (Leiden: Brill, 1994), 77–79; and Elisha Qimron and John Strugnell, *Qumran Cave 4: V, Miqṣat Maʿaśe ha-Torah* (Discoveries in the Judean Desert 10; Oxford: Clarendon, 1994), 45–63.
116. For the translation of Genesis Rabbah, see H. Freedman and Maurice Simon, *Midrash Rabbah Translated into English*, 10 vols., London: Soncino, 1931.
117. On the rabbis in Late Antique synagogues, see Michael D. Swartz, "Sage, Priest, and Poet: Typologies of Religious Leadership in the Ancient Synagogue," in *Jews, Christians, and Polytheists in the Ancient Synagogue* (ed. S. Fine; New York: Routledge, 1999), 101–17.
118. On medieval Jewish interpretation, see Barry D. Walfish, "An Introduction to Medieval Jewish Biblical Interpretation," in *With Reverence for the Word: Medieval Scriptural Exegesis in Judaism, Christianity, and Islam* (ed. J. D. McAuliffe; Oxford: Oxford University Press, 2003), 3–12.

119. On Jerome as translator of the Vulgate, see Megan Hale Williams, *The Monk and the Book: Jerome and the Making of Christian Scholarship*, Chicago: University of Chicago, 2006.
120. On the history of modern Bible translations, see Paul Ellingworth, "From Martin Luther to the English Revised Version," in *A History of Bible Translation* (ed. P. A. Noss; New York: American Bible Society, 2007), 105–139.
121. For modern Jewish translations, see Martin Buber and Franz Rosenzweig, *Scripture and Translation*, tr. L. Rosenwald and E. Fox; Bloomington: Indiana University Press, 1994 (German 1936); Everett, Fox, *The Five Books of Moses*, Schocken Bible: Vol. 1, New York: Schocken, 1995; Robert Alter, *The Five Books of Moses: A Translation with Commentary*, New York: Norton, 2004.
122. On the standardization of ritual texts, see Russell Hobson, *Transforming Literature into Scripture: Texts as Cult Objects at Nineveh and Qumran*, Sheffield: Equinox, 2012.
123. Penny Shine Gold, *Making the Bible Modern: Children's Bibles and Jewish Education in Twentieth-Century America* (Ithaca, NY: Cornell University Press, 2004), quotation from pp. 14–15.
124. On the Exodus story in Zionism, see Ariah Saposnik, "The Desert Comes to Zion: A Narrative Ends its Wandering," in *Exodus in the Jewish Experience: Echoes and Reverberations*, (ed. P. Barmash and W. David Nelson; Lanham, MD: Lexington, 2015), 213–246.
125. David W. Kling, *The Bible in History: How the Texts Have Shaped the Times*, (Oxford: Oxford University Press, 2004), 193–229, quotation from pp. 195–96.
126. On the exodus story for Americans, see Conrad Cherry, *God's New Israel: Religious Interpretations of American Destiny*, Englewood Cliffs, NJ: Prentice Hall, 1971; and John Winthrop, "A Modell of Christian Charity," in *Winthrop Papers* (Boston: Massachusetts Historical Society, 1931), 2:282–84, 292–95.
127. On the exodus story for African Americans, see Albert Raboteau, "African-Americans, Exodus, and the American Israel," in *African-American Christianity* (ed. P. E. Johnson; Berkeley: University of California, 1994), 1–17, quotations from pp. 9 and 13–14; and Herbert Robinson Marbury, *Pillars of Cloud and Fire: The Politics of Exodus in African American Biblical Interpretation*, New York: NYU Press, 2015.
128. For the last speech of Martin Luther King, Jr, see Keith D. Miller, *Martin Luther King's Biblical Epic: His Final, Great Speech* (Jackson, MS: University Press of Mississippi, 2011), Appendix 1.
129. On colonial and post-colonial Christian identification with Israel, see R. S. Sugirtharajah, *The Bible and the Third World: Precolonial, Colonial and Postcolonial Encounters*, Cambridge: Cambridge University Press, 2001; R. S. Sugirtharajah, *The Bible and Empire: Postcolonial Explorations*, Cambridge: Cambridge University Press, 2005; and Philip Jenkins, *The New Faces of Christianity: Believing the Bible in the Global South*, Oxford: Oxford University Press, 2006.
130. On identifying with the Canaanites, see Edward W. Said, "Michael Walzer's *Exodus and Revolution*: A Canaanite Reading," in *Blaming the Victims: Spurious Scholarship and the Palestinian Question* (ed. E. W. Said and C. Hitchens;

New York: Verso, 1988), 151–78; and Robert Warrior, "Canaanites, Cowboys, and Indians: Deliverance, Conquest, and Liberation Theology," *Christianity and Crisis* 29 (1989), 261–65.

131. On normative written ritual rules, see James W. Watts, "Ritual Legitimacy and Scriptural Authority," *Journal of Biblical Literature* 124/3 (2005), 401–417.
132. On Philo's interpretation of diet laws, see Hans Svebakken, *Philo of Alexandria's Exposition of the Tenth Commandment*, Atlanta: SBL, 2012. For contemporary interpretations of diet laws as moral examples, see Jacob Milgrom, "Ethics and Ritual: The Foundations of the Biblical Dietary Laws," in *Religion and Law: Biblical, Jewish, and Islamic Perspectives* (ed. E. B. Firmage; Winona Lake, IN: Eisenbrauns, 1989), 159–91; and Mary Douglas, *Leviticus as Literature* (Oxford: Oxford University Press, 1999), 134–51, 232.
133. For the translation of the *Letter of Aristeas*, see *The Letter of Aristeas*, translated by R. J. H. Shutt in *Old Testament Pseudepigrapha* (ed. J. H. Charlesworth; 2 vols.; New York: Doubleday, 1983), 7–34.
134. For the translation of *b. Menaḥ*. 110a, see Isidore Epstein, ed., *Menachos*, vol. 4, The Soncino Babylonian Talmud, London: Soncino, 1989.
135. On the Pentateuch in early modern political thought, see Daniel Elazar, *The Covenant Tradition in Politics*, 4 vols, New Brunswick, NJ: Transaction Publishers, 1995–98; Eric Nelson, *The Hebrew Republic: Jewish Sources and the Transformation of European Political Thought*, Cambridge, MA: Harvard University Press, 2010; and Graham Hammill, *The Mosaic Constitution: Political Theology and Imagination from Machiavelli to Milton*, Chicago: Chicago University Press, 2012.
136. On Moses as embodying Torah and monotheism, see Brian Britt, *Rewriting Moses: The Narrative Eclipse of the Text* (London: T. & T. Clark, 2004), quotation from p. 80.
137. Sigmund Freud, *Moses and Monotheism*, New York: Vintage, 1939; Jan Assmann, *Moses the Egyptian: The Memory of Egypt in Western Monotheism*, Cambridge, MA: Harvard University Press, 1998.
138. On Genesis and cosmology, see Kyle Greenwood, *Scripture and Cosmology: Reading the Bible Between the Ancient World and Modern Science*, Downers Grove, IL: IVP Academic, 2015.
139. Peter Harrison, *The Fall of Man and the Foundations of Science* (Oxford: Oxford University Press, 2007), quotations from pp. 2–3 and 6.
140. On Genesis, evolution, and creationism, see Ronald L. Numbers, "Scientific Creationism and Intelligent Design," in *The Cambridge Companion to Science and Religion* (ed. P. Harrison; Cambridge: Cambridge University Press, 2010), 127–147.
141. On the interpretation of Eve in Genesis 1–3, see Hermann Spieckermann, Stefan Krauter, Benjamin G. Wright III, Tamar Kadari, Elyse Goldstein, Brian K. Reynolds, Gordon Nickel, Elizabeth J. Harris, Anthony Swindell, Anne Lapidus Lerner, Ori Z. Soltes, Linda Maria Koldau, and Alice Ogden Bellis, "Eve," in the *Encyclopedia of the Bible and its Reception* (ed. D. C. Allison, Jr, et al.; Berlin: De Gruyter, 2015), 8:285–316.

142. Phyllis Trible, "Depatriarchalizing in Biblical Interpretation," *Journal of the American Academy of Religion* 41 (1973), 30–48, quotation from p. 41.
143. On feminist biblical criticism, see Jorunn Økland, "Feminist Readings of the Bible," in *The New Cambridge History of the Bible, Volume 4: From 1750 to the Present* (ed. J. Riches; Cambridge: Cambridge University Press, 2015), 261–272.
144. On racism, slavery, and the "curse of Ham," see David M. Goldenberg, *The Curse of Ham: Race and Slavery in Early Judaism, Christianity, and Islam*, Princeton, NJ: Princeton University Press, 2009; Stephen R. Haynes, *Noah's Curse: The Biblical Justification of American Slavery*, Oxford: Oxford University Press, 2002; and Markus Witte, Michael G. Wechsler, Dennis W. Jowers, Sylvester A. Johnson, Clyde R. Forsberg, Jr, Jaakko Hämeen-Anttila, Lee M. Jefferson, and Anton Karl Kozlovic, "Ham," in the *Encyclopedia of the Bible and its Reception* (ed. D. C. Allison, Jr, et al.; Berlin: De Gruyter, 2015), 11:62–80.
145. Zora Neale Hurston, "The First One: A Play in One Act," in *Ebony and Topaz: A Collectanea* (ed. C. S. Johnson, 1927; reprinted Freeport, NY: Books for Libraries Press, 1971), quoted in Haynes, *Noah's Curse*, pp. 193–94.
146. On the rhetoric of origins in early modern biblical criticism, see Jean-Louis Ska, "The Study of the Book of Genesis: The Beginning of Critical Reading," in *The Book of Genesis: Composition, Reception and Interpretation* (ed. C. A. Evans, J. N. Lohr, and D. L. Peterson; Leiden: Brill, 2012), 3–26.
147. On nineteenth-century historical criticism, see Thomas Römer, "'Higher Criticism: The Historical and Literary-Critical Approach," in *Hebrew Bible/Old Testament: The History of Its Interpretation* 3/1 (ed. M. Saebø; Berlin: Vandenhoeck & Ruprecht, 2013), 393–423.
148. On twentieth-century Jewish scholarship on the Pentateuch, see S. David Sperling, "Major Developments in Jewish Biblical Scholarship," in *Hebrew Bible/Old Testament: The History of Its Interpretation* 3/2 (ed. M. Saebø; Berlin: Vandenhoeck & Ruprecht, 2015), 371–388.
149. On late twentieth-century historical criticism, see David M. Carr, "Changes in Pentateuchal Criticism," in *Hebrew Bible/Old Testament: The History of Its Interpretation* 3/2 (ed. M. Saebø; Berlin: Vandenhoeck & Ruprecht, 2015), 433–466.
150. On scribal expertise in the ancient world, see David M. Carr, *Writing on the Tablet of the Heart: Origins of Scripture and Literature*, Oxford: Oxford University Press, 2005.
151. On wisdom literature's influence on Deuteronomy, see Moshe Weinfeld, *Deuteronomy and the Deuteronomic School*, Winona Lake, IN: Eisenbrauns, 1972.
152. On linguistic dating of biblical books, compare Avi Hurvitz, *A Concise Lexicon of Late Biblical Hebrew*, Leiden: Brill, 2014, with Ian Young, Robert Resetko, and Martin Ehrensvärd, *Linguistic Dating of Biblical Texts*, 2 vols., London: Equinox, 2008.
153. On empirical evidence for historical criticism, see Jeffrey H. Tigay, *Empirical Models for Biblical Criticism*, Philadelphia: University of Pennsylvania, 1985.

154. On memory variants, see David M. Carr, *The Formation of the Hebrew Bible: A New Reconstruction* (New York: Oxford University Press, 2011), 17–33, 98.
155. On the composition of Numbers, see Christian Frevel, "The Book of Numbers – Formation, Composition, and Interpretation of a Late Part of the Torah," in *Torah and the Book of Numbers* (ed. C. Frevel, T. Pola, and A. Schart; Tübingen: Mohr Siebeck, 2013), 1–38.
156. On the history of priests before the Babylonian Exile, see the essays in Mark Leuchter and Jeremy Michael Hutton, *Levites and Priests in Biblical History and Tradition*, Atlanta: Society of Biblical Literature, 2011.
157. On the Second Temple priests and the Pentateuch's ritual instructions, see James W. Watts, *Leviticus 1–10* (HCOT; Leuven: Peeters, 2013), especially 86–133.
158. For a history of the Second Temple high priests, see James C. VanderKam, *From Joshua to Caiaphas: High Priests After the Exile*, Minneapolis: Augsburg Fortress, 2004.
159. For translations of Esarhaddon's Succession Treaty, see Jacob Lauinger, "Esarhaddon's Succession Treaty at Tell Tayinat: Text and Commentary," *Journal of Cuneiform Studies* 64 (2012), 112–13; and Simo Parpola and Kazuko Watanabe, eds., *Neo-Assyrian Treaties and Loyalty Oaths*, State Archives of Assyria, vol. 2 (Helsinki: Helsinki University Press, 1988), text 5, line 1; text 6, lines 1 and 283.
160. On ancient suzerainty treaties and the Pentateuch, see Bernard M. Levinson, "Esarhaddon's Succession Treaty as the Source for the Canon Formula in Deuteronomy 13:1," *Journal of the American Oriental Society* 130 (2010), 337–47.
161. For translation and discussion of the Weidner Chronicle, see Jean-Jacques Glassner, *Mesopotamian Chronicles* (Atlanta: SBL, 2004), 263–69. On ancient Middle Eastern rhetoric of divine punishment of kings, see James W. Watts, "Ritual Rhetoric in Ancient Near Eastern Texts," in *Ancient Non-Greek Rhetorics* (ed. C. Lipson and R. Binckley; West Lafayette, IN: Parlor Press, 2009), 39–66.
162. On Mesopotamian legal tradition in the Pentateuch, see the essays edited by Bernard M. Levinson in *Theory and Method in Biblical and Cuneiform Law: Revision, Interpolation and Development*, Sheffield: Sheffield Academic Press, 1994; and David P. Wright, *Inventing God's Law: How the Covenant Code of the Bible Used and Revised the Laws of Hammurabi*, New York: Oxford University Press, 2009.
163. On revision, supplementation, and replacement between the Pentateuchal legal collections, see Bernard M. Levinson, *Deuteronomy and the Hermeneutics of Legal Innovation*, Oxford: Oxford University Press, 1997; and Jeffrey Stackert, *Rewriting the Torah: Literary Revision in Deuteronomy and the Holiness Legislation*, Tübingen: Mohr Siebeck, 2007.
164. On the theory of Persian authorization of biblical laws, see the essays edited by James W. Watts in *Persia and Torah: The Theory of Imperial Authorization of the Pentateuch*, Atlanta: Society of Biblical Literature, 2001.

165. On offering instructions emphasizing distribution rather than killing, see Kathryn McClymond, *Beyond Sacred Violence: A Comparative Study of Sacrifice*, Baltimore: Johns Hopkins University Press, 2008.
166. On the spread of burned offerings in the second and first millennia, see Watts, *Leviticus 1–10*, 172–73.
167. On women, especially mothers, in Israel's rituals, see Nicole J. Ruane, *Sacrifice and Gender in Biblical Law*, Cambridge: Cambridge University Press, 2013.
168. On textual rhetoric interfering with ritual reconstruction, see James W. Watts, *Ritual and Rhetoric in Leviticus: From Sacrifice to Scripture* (New York: Cambridge University Press, 2007), 27–36.
169. The translation of the Merneptah Stele is by James K. Hoffmeier in *The Context of Scripture* (ed. W. Hallo; Leiden: Brill, 2003), 2.6.
170. On reconstructing the early history of Israel, see the essays in John Day, *In Search of Pre-Exilic Israel*, London: T. & T. Clark, 2004.
171. The translation of the Deir Alla inscription is by Baruch A. Levine in *The Context of Scripture* (ed. W. Hallo; Leiden: Brill, 2003), 2.27.
172. The birth legend of King Sargon was translated by Benjamin R. Foster in *The Context of Scripture* (ed. W. Hallo; Leiden: Brill, 2003), 1.133.
173. On the composition of Genesis and its connection to the Pentateuch, see Konrad Schmid, "Genesis in the Pentateuch," in *The Book of Genesis: Composition, Reception and Interpretation* (ed. C. A. Evans, J. N. Lohr, and D. L. Peterson; Leiden: Brill, 2012), 27–50; or Konrad Schmid, *Genesis and the Moses Story: Israel's Dual Origins in the Hebrew Bible*, Winona Lake, IN: Eisenbrauns, 2010.
174. On the genealogical structure of Numbers, see Dennis Olsen, *The Death of the Old and the Birth of the New: The Framework of the Book of Numbers and the Pentateuch*, Chico, CA: Scholars Press, 1985.
175. On the late composition of Genesis 1–11, see Joseph Blenkinsopp, *The Pentateuch: An Introduction to the First Five Books of the Bible* (New York: Doubleday, 1992), 93–94.

Chapter 6

176. On the canonization of scripture, see Timothy H. Lim, *The Formation of the Jewish Canon*, New Haven: Yale University Press, 2013; and Tomas Bokedal, *The Formation and Significance of the Christian Biblical Canon: A Study in Text, Ritual and Interpretation*, London: Bloomsbury T. & T. Clark, 2014.
177. On the Hasmonean influence on scripturalization, see especially David Carr, *Writing on the Tablet of the Heart: Origins of Scripture and Literature* (Oxford: Oxford University Press, 2005), 253–75.
178. On readers' assumptions when interpreting scriptures, see James L. Kugel, *The Bible As It Was* (Cambridge, MA: Belknap, 1997), 14–23.
179. On the devotional shaping of the Psalter, see J. Clinton McCann, Jr, "The Shape and Shaping of the Psalter: Psalms in Their Literary Context," in *The Oxford Handbook of the Psalms* (ed. W. P. Brown; Oxford: Oxford University Press, 2014), 350–362.

180. On inset psalms shaping narratives for use as scripture, see James W. Watts, *Psalm and Story: Inset Hymns in Hebrew Narrative*, JSOTSup 139, Sheffield: Sheffield Academic Press, 1992.
181. On Judah *ha-Nasi* and the Mishnah, see Stephen G. Wald, "Judah Ha-Nasi," *Encyclopaedia Judaica* (2nd ed. 2007), 11:501–505; and William Scott Green, *Persons and Institutions in Early Rabbinic Judaism*, Atlanta: Scholars Press, 1977.
182. On Irenaeus and the Gospels, see Elaine Pagels, *Beyond Belief: The Secret Gospel of Thomas*, New York: Vintage, 2003.
183. For the translation of Irenaeus's *Adversus Haereses*, see Alexander Roberts and W. H. Rambaut, *The Writings of Irenaeus*, Edinburgh: T. & T. Clark, 1868.
184. On comparing Jewish, Samaritan, and Christian scriptures, see James W. Watts, "The Pentateuch as 'Torah'," in *The Oxford Handbook of the Pentateuch*, ed. C. Nihan and J. Baden; Oxford: Oxford University Press, 2018.

INDEX OF QUOTATIONS AND CITATIONS OF BIBLICAL AND RABBINIC TEXTS

(**bold-face** = quotations)

INDEX OF SUBJECTS AND AUTHORS

(not including Cited Words and Further Reading)
(**bold-face** = quotations and boxes, *italics* = figures)

Understanding the Pentateuch as a Scripture, First Edition. James W. Watts.